"There is a dawning realization that more of the same policies, more patchwork, more tinkering will not bring us out of our present crisis state. All of us, public leaders as well as private citizens, are

coming up against the wall. Can we get over the wall? Can we tunnel through? Can we go around it? Rather than panic, it would be wise to stand back and size up our predicament."

Allan J. MacEachen

COVER CREDITS

left: Bethlehem Steel Corporation
left center: Bethlehem Steel Corporation
right center: Richard L. Baron
right: NASA

profiles of involvement

Our thanks to Bob Barnes

TABLE OF CONTENTS

VOLUME I

Introduction - "Frankly, Profiles of Involvement is a $300,000 Experiment in Communications" I—8

Perspectives - An Editorial Overview I—12

Pragmatics of Involvement
Muffet Russell Shayon I—15

Redeploying Corporate Resources Toward New Priorities: The New "Consumer Demand"
Hazel Henderson I—40

Corporate Commitment: A Matter of Survival
Elmer Young, Jr. I—54

Communities and Business: Expectations and Frustrations
Wayne L. Owens I—65

Society and the Balance Sheet
Robert D. Lilley I—75

The Corporation and Social Change: A New Relationship - A New Dimension to Planning
Ian H. Wilson I—88

How to Make Social Responsibility Profitable
Robert Theobald I—105

Biographical Sketches I—112

Two Personal Reflections I—119
Theresa Abbott I—121
Saul Alinsky I—123

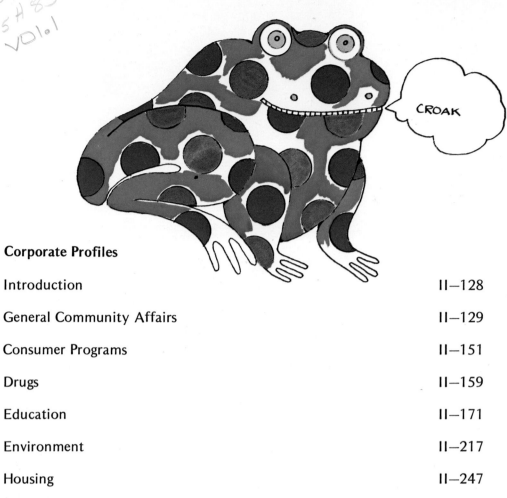

CROAK

Corporate Profiles

Introduction	II—128
General Community Affairs	II—129
Consumer Programs	II—151
Drugs	II—159
Education	II—171
Environment	II—217
Housing	II—247
Employment Opportunities	II—267
Job Training	II—279
Minority Enterprise	II—317
Health	II—347
Urban Development	II—361
Consumer Safety	II—371
Volunteerism	II—381
Youth	II—391
The Arts	II—425
Miscellaneous	II—435
An Unusual Profile International Basic Economy Corporation	II—456

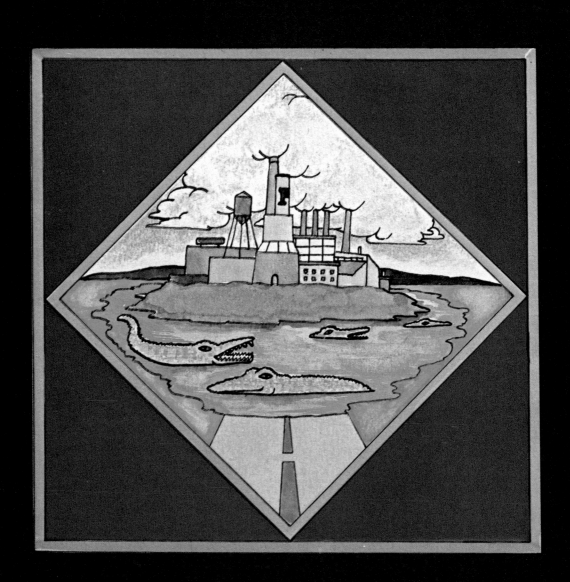

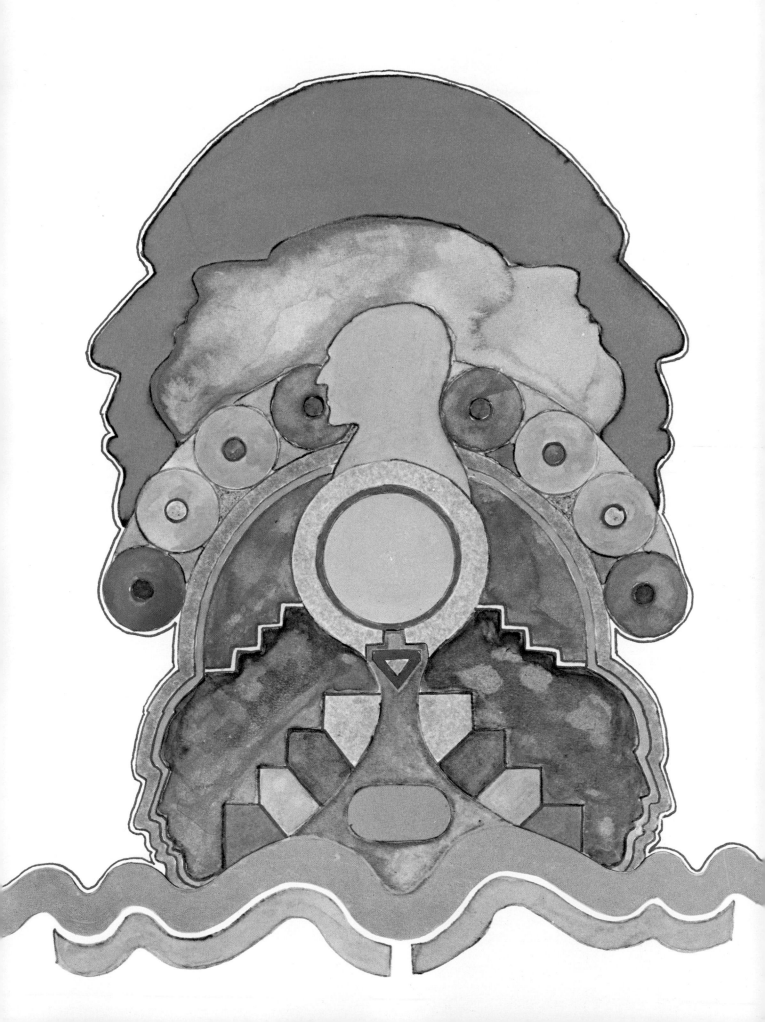

"Frankly, Profiles of Involvement is a $300,000 experiment in communications."

It is becoming a cliche to note that our society lies on the brink of several disasters, both natural and man-made. Like thousands of our fellow citizens, we, too, are growing tired of hearing the oft-quoted statistics prophesying the lack of water, the over-abundance of trash, the absence of breathable air and natural land. But it is very unlikely that either the well-used phrases, or the overly conspicuous problems will disappear or lessen because of our collective and individual dislike for them.

Facing this reality is necessary and demanding.

It is true that our society has never really faced such staggering problems before. This is not to say that generations before us haven't experienced Frankensteins in their lives. But it is to argue that never has so much happened to so many in such a short period of time.

We are learning the lessons of history while trying to cope with an unleashed, and unmanageable technology.

Never before has a national or global society been instantly divided in feelings and loyalty as happens now . . .

Never before has a national or global economy shaken in momentous responsiveness to the remarks of one man . . .

Never before has a nation of 200 million people teetered on the edge of a blackout that would, in the space of minutes, rob us of the life-giving power we are dependent upon . . .

Never before has our world faced instant annihilation at the mercy of the rationality of a few powerful men . . .

We do not advocate complacency by any means, but realistically we must admit that some of our condition lies beyond our control. And in this perspective, we must turn our work and energies to the conditions upon which we can make an impact.

We believe that the key questions confronting our society are: Can we as a nation, recognize that all of us as individuals have an enormous stake in our collective future? That everyone should have the opportunity and the understanding to play a part in determining the course of his life?

Can we as a nation with unparalleled technology and affluence, develop the means to bring democracy and self-determination closer to reality, or will our own hugeness so confuse and demean us all, that we must be content with whatever small shred of dignity and individuality we can scrape together?

A pragmatic examination of our nation's power structure confirms MacLuhan's theory that access to knowledge and understanding of individual and collective environs does yield power. And more significantly, the lack of access, the lack of knowledge and understanding leaves one powerless.

All 200-odd million of us are deeply affected by this, whether we live in ghettos, suburbia, or the White House.

It is in the spirit of recognizing and addressing this condition that we of Human Resources Network decided to undertake "Profiles of Involvement," last August.

There can be no argument that business is the cornerstone of our nation, or that the future actions of the business community will have the greatest impact on our nation or the world, short of nuclear war.

Until this point in time, business involvement in social conditions has been indirect (that is through products or services more than through social programs). But the frequency of corporate expeditions into the social arenas is growing sharply enough to warrant a collective exchange of ideas and experiences about these tangential enterprises in the hope of reducing error and increasing the opportunities for success.

This is our rationale for developing and publishing "Profiles . . . " Frankly, it is a $300,000 experiment in communications. Hopefully it will serve as a contemporary example of the way in which access to knowledge and understanding can be disseminated for all of us to share in.

We present information about corporations, social organizations, and government agencies in the most readable, useful way we have been able to devise.

And, to the extent we can, we will share information and material with you as it becomes available to us.

To help us experiment in access, in communications, and in developing a sense of self-determination, we now call upon you to use this medium called "Profiles of Involvement" in the most inventive, productive ways you can. Search through these 800-odd pages for leads that will help you, and call us when you cannot find what you are looking for.

After all, your stake in America is just as real as ours. It's high time we start acting instead of reacting.

Stephen E. Nowlan
Diana Russell Shayon

perspectives

PRAGMATICS
of involvement

Corporations are under fire from all sides to be socially involved and responsible. The traditional objective of business is to make a profit, but the complexity, power, and scope of corporations today have defined a new relationship between business and society. The economic powers that corporations wield result in daily decisions replete with political and social implications that affect hundreds of thousands of people.

The interlocking directorate of the early 1900s has been infiltrated by knowledgeable consumer activists and articulate social critics. They agree that the business of business is business, but profit maximization today requires an awareness of social inequities and a commitment to their alleviation. Corporate social involvement need not be seen as altruistic but rather as a part of sound management technique.

Human Resources Network is a non-profit educational corporation whose charter purpose is to collect and disseminate important information about pressing social issues. It is an urban clearinghouse of information and a catalyst for communications. The first opportunity to fulfill this charter purpose evolved into a unique communications device—*Profiles of Involvement.*

THE PROFILES

The task of assembling the first national compendium of corporate social involvement began last November when we sent 2,300 letters to American corporations with a sales volume of $60 million or more, and select banks and insurance companies asking them to fill out a profile form which described their social action programs. The letters were personally addressed to the chairman of the board or the president of the company. A second follow-up letter was later sent to public relations directors or directors of communications of the 650 largest corporations who had

Topic: _____

Company Name: _____

Address: _____

Business: _____   Sales Volume: _____

Project Name: _____

Director or Person to Contact: _____   Telephone No. _____

Address: _____

Project Purpose: _____

_____

Who does it help: _____

_____

How many people does it reach? _____ When was it started? _____

Describe functions of the project (100 words) _____

_____

_____

Do you expect to make changes in the format of the project? _____

_____

_____

What measures of success do you have? _____

_____

What is the overall budget of the project: _____

How many people from your company are involved (and to what degree)? _____

_____

Do other companies co-sponsor the project? (If yes, please name)   Yes   No _____

_____

Do you publicize the project as part of your corporate image program?   Yes No   Print_____   Broadcast_____

Paid Space_____   Brochures_____   Leaflets_____

Do you publicize the project so more people will gain help from it?   Yes No

Did you initiate program, or respond to community request? _____

_____

Person completing form   _____

   Title   _____

   Mailing address   _____

   Telephone Number   _____

I certify that the information on this profile form is correct to the best of my knowledge, and authorize publication of the information in "Profiles of Involvement" – A Compendum of Corporate Efforts to Solve Community Problems.

_____

Signature

not answered the original inquiry. A number of
follow-up telephone calls were also made to select companies
and banks who had not responded.

The kind of information we could obtain and the kind of
rapport we could establish with any corporation or bank
depended largely on our luck in making contact with the right
person. Official titles do not insure the best channel
into a company. In some instances the director of communications was the least communicative person we spoke with,
and a chairman of the board or president proved to be
the most informative and congenial.

Some companies sent us the completed profile forms and
nothing else. Others sent us additional materials—brochures,
annual reports, press releases—which explained in greater
detail and with public relations eloquence their social
commitment and programs.

The majority of companies failed to reply to our inquiry.
Those who sent negative replies presented arguments
against participation which became familiar to us: "We
don't want to be barraged by requests for aid." "We feel
that publicity would jeopardize the effectiveness of our
programs." "We let our actions speak for our involvement."
"We get too many requests for this kind of information so
we have established a new policy that we will only respond to those required by law." In some cases these
sentiments were legitimate; in others they were obviously rationalizations for non-involvement or excu-
ses for indifference.

The completed profiles began to filter in slowly, but
our telephones were rarely quiet. People wanted more
information about Human Resources Network and *Profiles of
Involvement.* Some were skeptical—was the book going
to be a whitewash of corporate commitment, a public relations
job, a digest of corporate egos? We emphasized that
Profiles of Involvement would merely print the information that the corporations and banks had sent us. The
material would not be manipulated or edited to conform to
any ulterior design of Human Resources Network. We handled
all such inquiries with careful consideration to the
novelty of our idea and the resultant hesitancy to participate that it seemed to engender.

There was often a lack of consensus within a corporation.
Programs submitted by one corporate representative would
be contradicted or overruled by a higher executive. In some
cases a subsidiary or division of a large company would
agree to participate, send us completed profiles, and we
would promptly receive a call from the "mother" company
politely stating that the programs could not be printed.
The size of corporations requires power hierarchies, but corporate bureaucracies tend to inhibit action.

Eventually we had a positive response from 186 corporations, banks, and insurance companies with a total of 535 social action programs. The completed profile forms provided a wealth of raw information from which we were able to draw some conclusions about the present status of corporate social involvement.

ANALYSIS OF REPLIES

The sponsoring companies initiated about half of the programs. The other half were responses to community requests or a joint initiation between the companies and the communities. Some companies joined together with other companies in both initiated and responsive programs. A small number of programs were started as a result of recent changes in law.

Most of the programs were initiated during the last two years. For the most part they seem to be quick responses to the crises of the Sixties—"band-aid" jobs rather than a root analysis of the problem at hand. The profiles themselves dictated the topic breakdown:

General Community Affairs	29
Consumer Programs	11
Drug Abuse	17
Education	85
Environment	47
Housing	26
Employment Opportunities	18
Job Training	72
Minority Enterprise	53
Health	21
Safety	12
Urban Development	13
Volunteerism	11
Youth	62
The Arts	14
Miscellaneous	37

It is not surprising that the greatest number of programs is in the area of Employment. For the most part, they are designed to train employees, upgrade job skills, and prepare the hard-core unemployed to perform well enough to fit into the system. Some of these programs are directly tied in to the internal operations and sound management of a particular company. Others are more broadly conceived to prepare a skilled labor force for society at large. The recruitment and training of workers is of obvious benefit to any corporation. It is significant, however, that the second largest category is Education.

The education programs underway are largely remedial or compensatory. They are geared to minority peoples; and whether they are teaching straight technical skills, greater proficiency in the English language, or offering high school equivalency courses, they are all making up for wasted years spent in schools throughout the country. Evidently our educational system has not prepared a working force that can cope with today's varied and fast-changing demands, and thus, the responsibility for learning basic skills falls on business rather than on our public schools. If half the money and resources being poured into these compensatory programs were used instead to re-evaluate and redesign our current educational system, such programs would not be needed.

School-industry partnerships are an attempt to attack the problem of lack of basic skills at an early stage. Some corporations work with a number of students from a particular school or schools. The students must attend classes five mornings a week and maintain a pre-established grade average. If they meet these two criteria, in the afternoons of those five days a week they go to the company's nearest plant, and after a training program, they work there and are remunerated for their efforts. This kind of program is clearly beneficial to both parties concerned: the young people are given a tangible motive to stay in school, and the company gets young workers who are eager to perform well.

Stockholders are often hesitant to see their potential dividends diverted to social programs; therefore, programs closely tied into company operations are perhaps the easiest to justify. Many are beneficial: day-care centers for working mothers, the recruitment and training of prospective employees, drug and alcohol counseling to reduce absenteeism. On the other hand, many inwardly geared programs are deceptive and hypocritical: a company boasting of its minority hiring practices when in actuality it is merely conforming to government requirements regarding equal employment; a company boasting of its ecological conscience when it is merely cleaning up the mess it has produced.

In some cases, a straight financial contribution from corporations is nothing more than a "dollar cop-out" or "conscience money"—the easy way out of social involvement. Legitimate kinds of financial involvement do, however, exist. Two examples are illustrated by the programs we have.

A cooperative effort between the federal government and private industry enables a large corporation to set up a subsidiary called a Minority Enterprise Small Business Investment Company (MESBIC) which invests money in minority enterprises. A MESBIC subsidiary researches and evaluates existing minority small business enterprises throughout the country. It then offers selected ventures straight funds in the form of a loan or an investment in the form of a stock purchase. A MESBIC loan qualifies a minority businessman for a subsequent Small Business Administration loan and facilitates additional private bank funding if necessary.

MESBIC money can be used to start a new business or to expand and improve an existing one.

MESBIC programs are, however, open to considerable controversy since management of a particular program is a key factor in their success or failure.

A second alternative is for corporations to independently form profit-making subsidiaries, wholly geared to social involvement such as housing development, minority enterprise investments, or research in the broad area of the human behavioral sciences. If a corporation is not in a position to do this or is not interested, it can invest in socially oriented companies that are already formed.

An overview of the majority of programs indicates that American corporations were confronted with an urgent and complex set of demands in the late Sixties and early Seventies. They had to respond under pressure without the time to make long-range plans or research the problems in depth. Many programs were superficial overtures made in haste.

After close study of the 535 programs, an interesting pattern began to emerge. Certain programs continually stood out as fresh, interesting, or in some way different from the norm. Upon further analysis, three points seemed to crystallize; at least one of these characterized each program.

1. They involved participation on the part of the people being helped.
2. They involved an exchange of perspectives.
3. They were programs that in some way contributed to a strengthening of self-esteem.

The information in the programs themselves evolved this pattern; it was not preconceived.

These programs were, however, by far the exception. The majority were conspicuously similar in their conception and format. We were impressed especially by two things: 1) the tremendous amount of human and material resources that these corporations possess; 2) the overwhelming lack of creativity and imagination evidenced in their programs. If a corporation has made the decision to be socially involved, why is there such an apparent lack of creativity and imagination in the pragmatics of their involvement? Where are the benefits of the resource potentials they harbor?

A first obvious answer is that corporations do not really care, and that their programs are a minimal response to social pressure in order to maintain a positive public image. But, if companies are this sensitive to public pressure, why haven't they used their tremendous resources to create imaginative programs which would benefit their public image even more? Ineffective programs are a detriment to both the monetary and the social balance

sheet. Why then are their programs so limited and unimagi-
native? Why in general is America's response to social
problems so uncreative and inadequate?

ELECTRONIC LITERACY

Our country is gripped by a silent powerlessness. We
have become a nation of spectators reduced to the role of
passive receivers by man's "second best friend"—television.
Our sophisticated technologies have radically expanded
the traditional parameters of communication. Face-to-face
or small group communication has been replaced by electronic
ubiquity.

Using the profiles as a framework, there seems to be a
direct correlation between the characteristics of effective
programs and the negative effects of television.

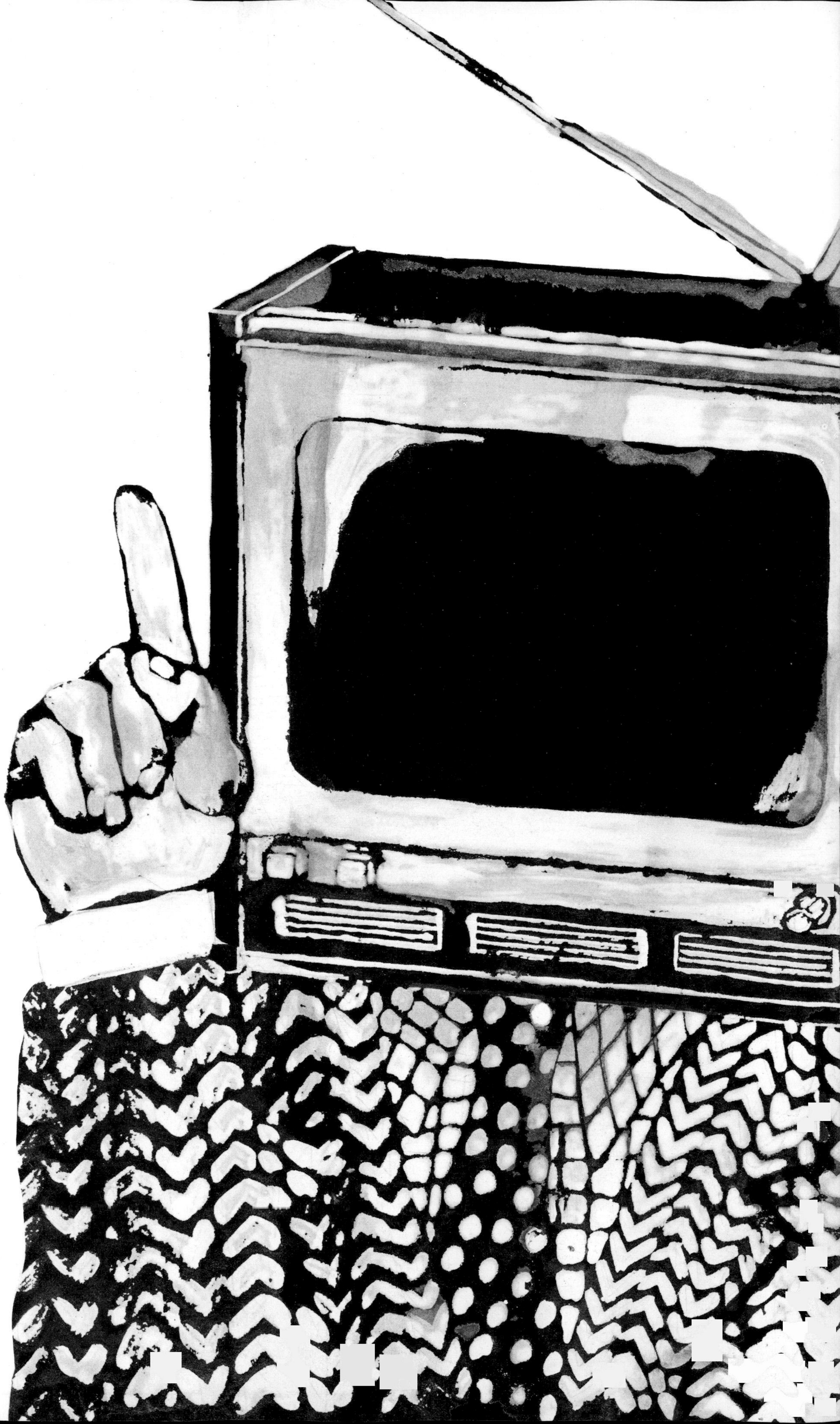

Our country is gripped by a silent powerlessness. We have become a nation of spectators reduced to the role of passive receivers by man's second best friend, "television."

Television has:

1. denied the viewer participation,
2. denied him the opportunity to engage in an on-going dialogue or exchange of perspectives,
3. as a result, weakened his self-esteem and his ability to be creative.

These three "social ills" give rise to a vicious cycle that impedes the alleviation of social inequities; until perspectives are exchanged and participation is allowed (or assumed), self-esteem will remain low and the ability to be creative and imaginative will be limited. However, until self-esteem is strengthened, an exchange of perspectives is precluded and participation is thus denied.

Ignorance about the communications revolution has stymied our ability to create viable solutions to pressing social problems. Most people have no knowledge of what television is or how it works beyond the rudimentary ability to turn the set on and select a channel. They look to television for entertainment, unaware of the implicit messages that it imparts.

What is real is what we see on television, and only what we see on television is of major significance. Television enforces strong identity norms. The viewer is continually confronted with handsome, slick, resourceful television stars, (95 per cent white) who triumph with ease in any confrontation situation. There is an immediate credibility gap between the average white viewer and such a super-human star. To say nothing of the lack of identity that is felt by minority peoples who at best see themselves on the screen as villains, bad-guys, or underdogs.

By the end of the Forties, the vast majority of Americans owned radios; by the end of the Sixties they owned television sets as well. The camera and the microphone are omnipresent, and television, a primary source of information, is our deceptively powerful mentor. Human dialogue has been replaced by electronic monologue.

To be electronically literate one must be aware of the tremendously powerful impact the mass media, television in particular, has had on this nation. When people are unable to send messages—to initiate a communication—they are forced into a receivership role. Their self-image and self-esteem are weakened. Passive, low-esteem individuals have little courage or ability to be imaginative or creative.

Corporations tend, by definition, to be conservative. As societal institutions they must conserve their identity as unique entities. The tragic irony, however, is that identities are often best conserved and strengthened in an interface or confrontation situation.

We are all caught in the same bind. There are no villains or heroes in the world of corporate social responsibility, and the divisions that have been made are erroneous. The real villain is electronic illiteracy and the paralysis it has caused.

Corporate management is faced with an unprecedented challenge. The upheavals of the Sixties gave rise to a new social imperative, replete with ethical and economic demands. In a short period of time, corporations were asked to redeploy their resources toward social problems. There were no guidelines from which corporate managers could glean the best or most effective way to begin. The pervasiveness of television began to take its toll. Few corporate executives were prepared to assume a leadership role, take the initiative, and respond with imaginative solutions.

There were, however, those exceptional programs characterized by at least one of the following:

1. participation on the part of the people being helped,
2. an exchange of perspectives,
3. contributing to a strengthening of self-esteem.

Following are three such case studies.

THREE CASE STUDIES

The Southland Corporation

The Western Stores Division of the Southland Corporation is in the business of Convenience Markets. Their best-known chain is 7-Eleven Food Stores. In April 1970, a Crime Committee was formed by the Southland Corporation to do something about the tremendous crime rate in their 400 franchised 7-Eleven Stores. From 1969-1970, they suffered an 80 per cent increase in robberies and burglaries. The Committee reached a stalemate, and according to Dick Dole, Western Stores Division Manager, "the same old concepts of deterring crime were discussed and few, if any, new ideas were forthcoming." The robberies continued and 7-Eleven Stores were losing money and employees.

And then the Committee received a phone call from Robert McKinney, Director of Project J.O.V.E. (Job, Occupation, Vocation, Education). McKinney, an ex-convict himself, proposed to supply the Committee with eight ex-cons who had spent a combined total of over 100 years in major penitentiaries throughout the country. Three of them had previous records of 7-Eleven hold-ups, and some had committed armed robbery 40 to 50 times.

The Committee accepted McKinney's proposal and a seminar was set up at Southland's La Mesa, California headquarters. The ex-cons (including one man who had served sixteen years in prison and been wounded nine times in shootouts with the law) sat down to a leisurely lunch joined by law enforcement officers, food store operators, and retailers from other fields. The ex-cons talked for three hours and the businessmen listened.

"Some stores make hold-ups so enticing I can hardly believe it," said Frank, an articulate man with eight years of prison behind him. He was referring to magazine racks, display fixtures for sunglasses, high stacks  of canned goods, and window banners . . . "you have a great habit of plastering those signs in the windows," so that the view is blocked from the inside out and vice-versa. Frank used to welcome the jammed windows in 7-Eleven Stores— "I knew I could go in, do my 'business' and not be seen by people passing." He suggested that they make their stores less attractive to hold-up men by putting the clerk and his cash register in the front showcase.

Tony, a quiet young man, came to the seminar intent on presenting an object lesson that would leave an impression. The night before the seminar he had successfully staged four mock hold-ups at four local stores. "Your employees are friendly, accommodating and service-minded. But, they are not robbery-oriented." In each case, Tony was able to talk the clerk into leaving the cash register completely unguarded. In one instance he talked three employees into a walk-in refrigerator while he waited outside for a friend who was ostensibly the butt of a practical joke. The employees laughed all the way in until Tony turned the key.

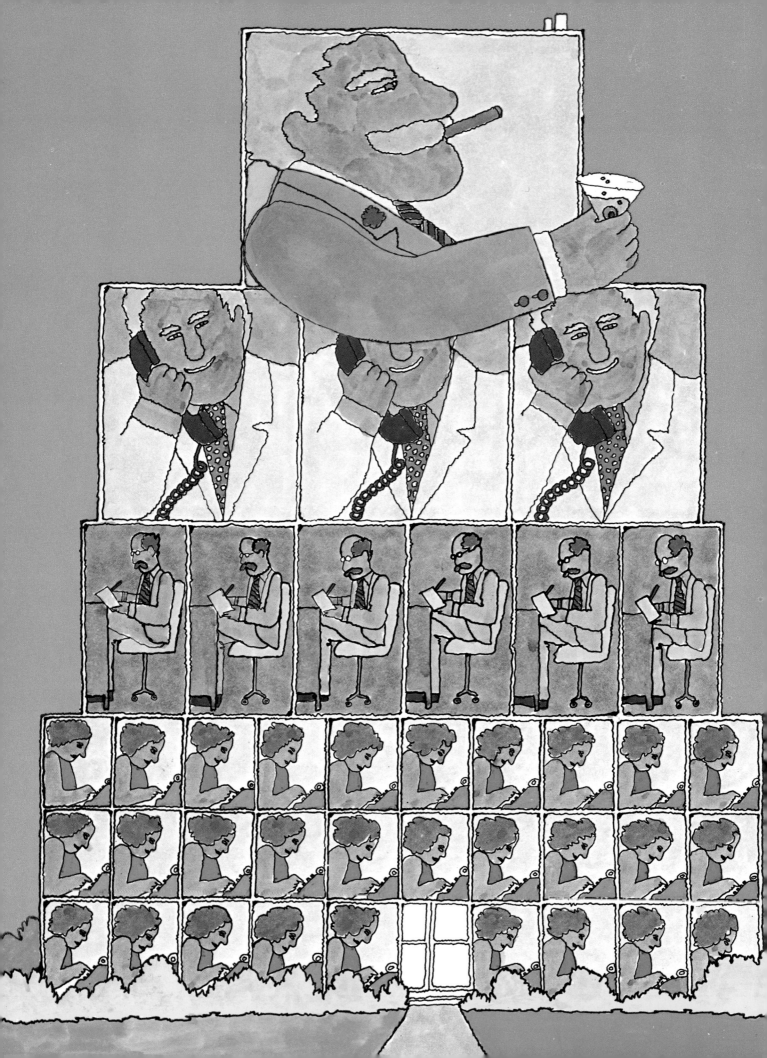

The business professionals of the Southland Corporation
gave the professionals of the robbery business a chance
to speak. Out of the seminar came a widely circulated
handbook of "Do's and Don'ts" for deterring robberies and
burglaries. Corporate officials were so impressed with
the success of the seminar that they sent eight ex-cons,
chosen by McKinney, through their franchise owners'
one-week training program and then placed them in a Southeast San Diego 7-Eleven Store. (Newly franchised owners
pay $1,000 for the training program—the ex-convicts
paid nothing.) The store, previously closed down, was renovated at a cost of approximately $30,000 and its
management was turned over completely to the ex-cons.

Because of 7-Eleven's relationship with J.O.V.E., their
dollar loss is lower than ever before. As one manager
explained, "We've heard that among the criminal
fraternity, word has spread that we're trying to help
ex-convicts. They're saying in effect, 'Lay off the 7-Eleven
Stores. They're O.K.' "

Said John, a 22-year-old ex-convict now working as
a 7-Eleven clerk, "I was real mad at the system when I got
out of prison. I couldn't find an employer to give me
a chance. But look at me now. These people have faith in me.
That sure makes a difference."

Xerox Corporation

In 1964 Rochester, New York was wracked by riots.
Minority migrations to Rochester rose steadily during the
late Fifties and early Sixties. Jobs were scarce
and skills limited. An instant ghetto formed and
spilled over into an explosion.

In 1965 the Council of Churches brought in Saul Alinsky,
a radical organizer and head of the Industrial Areas
Foundation in Chicago. Alinsky worked with Rochester's poor,
and together they formed a militant community organization—
FIGHT: Freedom, Independence, God, Honor, Today. FIGHT
quickly won respect from the black community and also
a grudging respect from white business and civic leaders.
Deleon McEwen, Jr., former president of FIGHT, said,
"I remember that back in '64 there wasn't a man in this
country who could get the blacks who hit the streets
and burned buildings to get together for anything
constructive. Today that's not true. We now have FIGHT to
battle for the rights and for better working and living
conditions for the blacks of Rochester."

In 1969, FIGHT came to Xerox with a proposal to set
up a people's manufacturing enterprise to be called
FIGHTON, Inc. It was to be a black run and operated company
geared toward the disadvantaged, employing inner-city
residents. Xerox gave their backing and FIGHT discussed

the now-viable project with the Rochester Business Opportunities Corporation (RBOC is a non-profit group formed by the managements of Eastman Kodak and other local companies to finance and develop businesses run by inner-city people), the Department of Labor, and the SBA.

The following agreement was drawn up: 1) Xerox pledged to purchase $1 million of FIGHTON products over a two-year period; 2) the Department of Labor made FIGHTON a $445,677 training grant; 3) the SBA gave an 80 per cent loan guarantee to RBOC for the purchase and renovation of a one-time clothing plant to be used for FIGHTON's plant; 4) loans for purchase of equipment were made by a Rochester bank and guaranteed by an SBA loan.

With backing assured, FIGHT's next challenge was to decide on a product to manufacture. Early in 1968 a FIGHT committee got together with Xerox to attack this problem. The product had to be one of low engineering content, but one that lent itself to high employment. Hundreds of potential products were considered and rejected. Finally they came up with two—metal stampings and electrical transformers.

McEwen, a one-time barber with little administrative experience and no metalworking experience, was trained by an expert from Xerox and became President and General Manager of FIGHTON, Inc. Xerox also furnished a staff of specialists to train prospective FIGHTON employees. Eighty per cent of FIGHTON's employees were hard-core unemployed when hired.

Xerox had designed a small vacuum cleaner for use in cleaning Xerox machines but had never taken it beyond the design stage. While employees were being trained for the production of the transformers and stampings, Xerox gave the vacuum cleaner design to FIGHTON as a warm-up assembly job. McEwen said, "This was when we first ran up against Xerox's rigid quality control standards . . . . We not only met them, we completed the job well ahead of schedule. That vacuum cleaner was assembled by absolutely unskilled people without any previous metal-working experience." For the first time in their lives these workers had a stake in their work and pride in its quality. Every employee is a company shareholder.

FIGHTON is a pioneer venture in black capitalism. According to Peter McColough, Chairman of the Board of Xerox Corporation, "We feel this kind of ownership and management participation in corporate America is needed to reverse the trend of hopelessness and despair in the black communities by giving the black man a concrete example to look up to and follow."

McEwen agrees. "We will be giving our people a chance to make it on their own, through their own business, a significant manufacturing business. It will give the black man in Rochester a share and a personal stake in corporate America. This represents an important first. A venture

of this kind has never been done before anywhere in the nation. FIGHT has again proven that true black power is what can be accomplished when a militant community organization gets together with the private sector."

The Coca-Cola Company

The Coca-Cola Foods Division employs agricultural workers in the state of Florida. The plight of seasonal migrant workers is degrading and deplorable. They share the ranks with the poorest, least educated, and most exploited in this country. According to one company employee, "seasonal agricultural workers have far too long been enmeshed in a tragic cycle of poverty, hopelessness and despair." Coca-Cola is taking steps "to block this cycle in its own Florida citrus groves."

In 1970 Coca-Cola implemented a costly and ambitious program of total redevelopment in the area of agri-labor. Their purpose was to assist and improve the lives of agricultural workers employed by the company and to set a model that could be used by other companies.

The program is based on five underlying principles that guide all their activities.

1) *Involvement of People.* Coca-Cola believes that the program will only be effective to the extent that it involves the workers themselves in the solutions of their own problems, and in the shaping of their own futures.

2) *Emphasis on Long-Term Accomplishments rather than Promises.* After years of empty promises, agricultural workers are skeptical. They want immediate and tangible proof that action is being taken to improve their plight.

3) *Assurance of Economic Viability.* The program must be a viable, self-supporting economic venture so that it can operate on a long-range scale and serve as a realistic model to others.

4) *Emphasis on Self-Help.* Coca-Cola clearly understands that "paternalistically applied welfare programs, no matter how well intended, tend to demean the recipient as well as the donor and thus, interfere with the development of that human dignity and self-respect which is so essential to meaningful human progress." Their program is geared toward the potentialities within the individual being helped.

5) *A Sound Integrated Total Systems Approach.* The complexity of the problems the program is directed toward requires systematic, thorough, and integrated research if it is to bring about social change.

There are five main areas of activity in the program: Employment and Income; Housing; Health, Education and Social Services; Organizational Development and Support; Community Relations and Support.

Extensive research was conducted in each of these areas

"I am convinced that whether we like it or not, the distinctions between the private sector and the public sector are becoming increasingly blurred. America stands on the brink of revitalizing its economy through a solid commitment by industry joining with the government to rebuild and reclaim our human resources." Cleo W. Blackburn, President, Board for Fundamental Education

before any action was taken. Coca-Cola officials went to the agricultural workers themselves for an assessment of the situation and the best ways to make changes. The initial research uncovered basic problems that had to be acknowledged and dealt with.

Work patterns were irregular and the norm was to work a day here and there, and four or five-day weekends were not uncommon. Productivity standards were low; it made little difference whether three people picked 100 boxes of fruit or 100 people picked three boxes of fruit.

Foremen often operated on the level of slum-landlords and loan-sharking robber barons. They had the power to fire or dock a worker on the slightest whim. Usually there was no one in the field of higher rank than the foreman so he could operate unobserved.

Basic amenities such as drinking water, toilets, some sort of shade did not exist in the groves.

Housing conditions were far below minimum standards. Sanitation was rare, and drunkenness and violence were frequent in the labor camps. There were no recreation facilities, no transportation to town, and no opportunity for self-governance.

Workers had little hope of developing a career in the company so loyalty and identification did not exist.

Coca-Cola realized that they were dealing with deeply rooted agricultural traditions. "The attitudes and norms of the surrounding culture had become accepted and were even supported by many within the management structure." Coca-Cola's first action was to involve top management executives in every aspect of the agricultural operations. A Vice-President and Project Manager from the Houston office was appointed to assume on-site responsibilities.

The program objective was to evolve new "organization norms" rather than merely carry on "project activities." Communications lines were open between the management of the citrus operations, the workers, and Coca-Cola executives.

Worker-management committees were set up in all areas covered by the project. There were immediate increases in wage and benefit programs for grove workers. The benefits granted were the same as those for any Coca-Cola employee. New, year-round programs were offered to harvesting workers with a guaranteed minimum weekly income.

Basic field amenities were immediately provided for. Foremen of labor crews have been made salaried employees of the company and are aided by assistant foremen.

Adequate housing is being supplied in accordance with workers' desires and needs and income potential for ownership. The company is no longer interested in providing free or any other type of housing. "It was felt that a worker's sense of independence was decreased when the Company controlled not only his working conditions but his living conditions as well." Two sites have been chosen on company-owned land for construction of the new homes.

In the interim, labor camps have been replaced by comfortable dormitory campuses equipped with recreation facilities, and health and education services. Free transportation to town is available on weekends. "The key to successfully operating these facilities has been the development of worker-management committees to communicate with management and provide for self-government."

More than one half of the company's agricultural workers are now year-round full-time employees of Coca-Cola. Eighty-five new homes have been partially built and are occupied. Day-care centers have been established to care for employees' children. Organization development

seminars are held for all grove and harvesting management from the assistant fore- man up, and practices consonant with the Agricultural Labor Projects Objectives have been codified and are enforced.

According to Ms. Bonita Holder, Executive Staff, Consumer Services, "the future will prove rewarding for those in our industry who recognize opportunities and respond to them. Those who do not will surely find that other, more far-seeing businessmen are ready to take their places."

These three case studies are by far exceptional in their conception and operation. They evolve a pattern of participation, exchange of perspectives, and high self-esteem all of which are sorely lacking in the majority of programs. The trend of passivity nurtured by electronic illiteracy can be counteracted by programs such as these.

There are, of course, political overtones involved in all of these programs, which are not revealed in the profile forms or included in the case study write-ups. Rather than analyze their political histories and social innuendos, however, these three programs were chosen as models with an emphasis on the positive ways in which the sponsoring companies attacked critical problems.

NON-CORPORATE INVOLVEMENT

The non-corporate sector of America is in the same bind as its corporate brethren. Organizations, trade associations, citizen groups, and government agencies are in the business of social betterment. The corporate dilemma of how to make a profit and yet be socially responsive is not a problem for the social agency. However, many organization programs share the lack of imagination, creativity, and root effectiveness that plague corporate involvement. Coalitions between profit-making corporations and non-profit organizations are a powerful alternative to corporations "going it alone."

The Board for Fundamental Education is a private, non-profit, non-political organization. It is dedicated to helping the disadvantaged to help themselves and in doing so, contributing to the maximization of the human resources potential in the U.S.

The Education and Training Division of B.F.E. directs education programs for states, communities and industrial firms throughout the country. B.F.E. sponsors a series of In-Plant Education courses in companies to prepare illiterate and semi-literate workers for the demands of a technologically sophisticated economy. Dr. Cleo Blackburn, President of the Board, says, "you can't get them back into school—they've already failed there. But many have jobs so the easiest place to educate them is at work."

A second division of B.F.E. is Flanner House. A United Fund Agency in Indianapolis, Flanner House is a laboratory center for B.F.E. It operates as an autonomous agency meeting the needs of the community around it.

B.F.E. shares in its publications the sentiment of Kipling:

The wisest thing I would suppose,
That a man can do for his land,
Is the job that lies under his nose,
With the tools that lie under his hand.

The National Alliance of Businessmen is another example of a corporate-organization coalition. The N.A.B. was originated in 1968 by presidential mandate to attack the problem of jobs and job training for the disadvantaged in America. Through the N.A.B.'s program of Job Opportuni in the Business Sector (JOBS), chronically unemployed and underemployed persons have been placed in private industry jobs; summer jobs have been provided for needy youth; and as of June 1971 the Alliance assumed the additional responsibility of helping Vietnam veterans find civilian jobs.

A new governing board of directors is elected at each annual meeting. They are top executives from corporations across the country.

Such coalitions are viable and potentially powerful vehicles for social action, but the same qualities are needed here as in the corporate sector to make such action effective. Furthermore, such coalitions have their own internal conflicts, external critics, and are thus the subject of much controversy.

THE ARTICLES

In March, I sent many letters to corporations asking them to send me copies of recent speeches given by major executives, dealing with corporate social responsibility. The response I received was tremendous. In addition I spoke with public relations directors, corporate executives from all levels, consumer activists, government representatives, economists, and lawyers. I wanted to get as broad an overview as possible of opinions and ideas.

I chose four speeches from the field by Hazel Henderson, Robert Lilley, Robert Theobald, and Ian Wilson. My choice was based on two criteria: their articulateness, freshness, and insight, and their contribution to a broad and diversified whole.

I also asked four people from the field, Theresa Abbott, Saul Alinsky, Wayne Owens, and Elmer Young to write original pieces for *Profiles of Involvement* dealing with any aspect they chose of the broad spectrum of corporate social involvement. Beyond this there was no interference on my part as to what they wrote.

The articles as a whole, undeniably bear out the pattern that emerged from the corporate profiles. All the pieces are concerned with participation. They vary in style, point of view, and nomenclature, but the overall message is clear: corporations can no longer afford to seclude themselves from critical social pressures. There is a necessity for corporations to allow greater participation on all fronts in their efforts to redefine a feasible and constructive relationship with the society at large. Such participation may be as conservative as the hiring of a private researcher to poll public opinion on a particular issue. Or, it may be as radical as an open-ended dialogue between community leaders with a grievance. Participation is the concern of the day and the first

 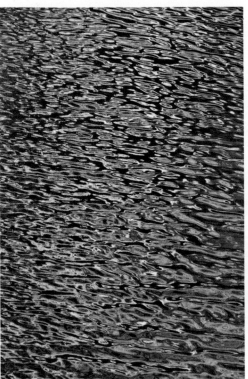 

step to an exchange of perspectives and the strengthening
of self-esteem.

History bears out the necessity of sharing resources
and the exigency of participation in any society.
Many revolutions have been caused in part by those people
who are denied participation in their governance and
denied access to channels of communications. They are
people of low esteem and weakened identity with no
stake in the society and thus no reason to let it live.

Futures researchers have already predicted that
unless radical changes are made in the interaction
between business and society, by 1985, internal industrial
sabotage will be an on-going reality. Corporations must
share their resource potential.

Real participation ultimately focuses on human resources.
Man is distinguished by his ability to act as a *source*
as well as a resource: he can independently generate ideas
and use these ideas to activate other resources.

The pragmatics of involvement dictate a change from
passivity to action on an individual level. But the
conscience of involvement dictates a transcendence from
the individual to the collective.

by Muffet Russell Shayon

REDEPLOYING CORPORATE RESOURCES TOWARD NEW PRIORITIES "THE NEW CONSUMER DEMAND"

Let me begin by briefly reviewing what I consider as America's emerging social values. They might well be termed the "post-industrial values" espoused by a growing number of our more affluent, politically-influential citizens who are disenchanted with many of our existing institutions and priorities, but for the most part, still believe that their objectives can be reached by restructuring business and government machinery through constitutional means.

They include environmentalists, militant consumers, students and young people, middle and upper income housewives newly activated by the consciousness of the women's rights movements or the boredom of suburban life, the public interest lawyers, scientists, engineers, doctors, social workers and other politicized professionals, the joiners of extra-political organizations such as Common Cause, the activist stockholders and the various crusaders for "corporate responsibility."

The new "post-industrial values" of such groups are to a great extent needs described by humanistic psychologists Abraham Maslow, Erich Fromm, and others as transcending the goals of security and survival. These values are less materialistic, often untranslatable into economic terms, and in turn, beyond the scope of the market economy and its concept of "homo economicus." They constitute a new type of "consumer demand," not for products as much as for life-styles, and include yearnings which Maslow referred to as "meta-needs" for meaning and purpose in life, a closer sense of community and cooperation, greater participation in social decision-making, as well as a general desire for social justice, more individual opportunities for self-development and more options for defining social roles within a more esthetic and healthful environment.

Ironically, these new values attest to the material successes of our current business system and represent a validation of a prosaic theory of traditional economics which holds that the more plentiful goods become, the less they are valued. For example, to the new "post-industrial consumers," the automobile is no longer prized as enhancing social status, sexual prowess, or even individual mobility which has been eroded by increasing traffic congestion. Rather it is seen as one component of a mode of transportation forced upon them by the particular set of social and spatial arrangements dictated by an interlocking group of powerful economic forces embodied by the auto, oil, highway, and rubber industries.

Such a consumer has begun to view the automobile as the instrument of this monolithic system of vested interests and client group dependencies, which has produced an enormous array of social problems and costs: decaying, abandoned inner cities, an overburdened law-enforcement system, an appalling toll of deaths and injuries, some 60% of all our air pollution, and the sacrifice of millions of acres of arable land to a highway system that is the most costly public works project

"The only universally valid statistical truth I know is that there is a direct correlation between the increase in statistics and the decrease in the pleasures of life."
Robert Hutchins

undertaken by any culture since the building of the Pyramids and the Great Wall of China.

It has become expedient of late for business spokesmen to excoriate such views as those held by such new consumers. At best, they are seen as esoteric, at worst, un-American; but certainly a luxury not affordable by the average American family, let alone those living in poverty. And yet it must be acknowledged that these views are increasingly validated by the realities of environmental degradation, decaying cities, unemployment, continued poverty in spite of a climbing Gross National Product and other visible evidence of the shortcomings of current social and economic arrangements.

At the same time, some of these "post-industrial values" are suprisingly congruent with some of those values being expressed by the poor and less privileged. Some of these groups, whether welfare recipients or public employees, less powerful labor unions or modest homeowners and taxpayers, seem to share the same demand for greater participation in the decisions affecting their lives and disaffection with large bureaucracies of both business and government.

Environmentalists find themselves agreeing with labor and minorities that human service programs, which also tend to be environmentally benign, should be expanded rather than cut; and that a federal minimum income program is more needed than ever. It would create purchasing power for instant spending on unmet basic needs, such as food and clothing, as well as permit the poor greater mobility to seek opportunities in uncrowded areas, thereby relieving the over-burdened bio-systems of our cities.

Although it is possible to dismiss these "post-industrial" consumers as irrelevant, and indeed they may well be less of a market for consumer goods, they nevertheless represent a new and different challenge of vital concern to corporations. Even though they are no longer willing to perform the heroic feats of consumption which have heretofore been successfully urged upon them by massive marketing barrages, their opinion-leadership roles and trend-setting lifestyles will continue to influence traditional consumer tastes. This is already apparent in the new anarchism and casualness in clothing fashions, the popularity of bicycling, the trends away from ostentatious over-consumption toward more psychologically rewarding leisure and life styles, reflecting the astounding growth of encounter groups and other activities associated with the human potential movement.

In addition, their "meta-needs" will express themselves in increasingly skillful political activism and advocacy as they continue to find in their more holistic concepts greater congruity between their own goals and the aspirations of the less privileged. Furthermore, their growing confrontations with corporations over their "middle-class" issues such as the environment and peace, have led them to discover the role of profit-maximizing theories in

environmental pollution and the role of the military-
industrial complex in defense expenditures and war.
These insights, together with their awareness of their
own privilege and their acceptance of guilt and concern
for social injustice are leading to the kind of con-
vergence with other socio-economic group interests so
much in evidence in the movement for corporate responsibility.

A growing understanding of the political nature of
economic distribution has naturally focused on the dom-
inant economic institution of our time: the corporation
and its political as well as economic role. Nothing
displays the political power of our large corporations
more vividly than their own managements' concepts of the
corporation as power broker, mediating the interests of
virtually all other constituent groups in the entire
society. Such an all-encompassing role is traditionally
ascribed to popularly elected governments in a democratic system such as our own, rather than to private,
special purpose organizations.

Such acknowledgement by both businessmen and their
critics in the corporate responsibility movement, of the
over-riding social power of the large corporation point
up the fallacy of Dr. Milton Friedman's argument that
corporations do not have the right to make social decisions but only maximize stockholders' profits. The
reality is that corporations in pursuing their profit
motives, regularly make ipso facto social decisions of
enormous consequence. All the movements in pushing for
their goals sooner or later find themselves in conflict with corporations.

One might conclude that if our corporations remain
as they are today, many business analysts believe that
this power in the multi-national corporation will
soon dominate or even supplant that of many nation
states. Then we might also expect it to collide more
extensively with that of other social forces. This
will lead to unprecedented challenge to corporate activities based on traditional economic theories, and
greater numbers of confrontations with citizens radi-
calized as they are more closely affected by corporate
efforts to expand, apply new technology, increase
production, or move into new areas such as large scale
agri-business operations with specifically severe
social repercussions. It is to be hoped that these
confrontations, whether boycotts, picket lines, or pol-
iticizing annual meetings and proxy machinery, will
eventually find civilized channels for expression and
will lead to new structures of social mediation.

As technology assessment methods improve and become
democratized at every level of government by public demand,
we can expect that these former areas of management preroga-

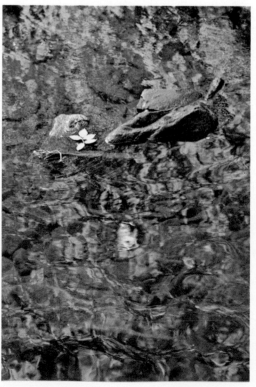

"We travel together, passengers on a little space-ship, dependent on its vulnerable reserves of air and soil; all committed for our safety to its security and peace; preserved from annihilation only by the care, the work, and, I will say, the love we give our fragile craft. We cannot maintain it half fortunate, half miserable, half confident, half despairing, half slave to the ancient enemies of man, half free in a liberation of resources undreamed of until this day. No craft, no crew can travel safely with such vast contradictions. On their resolution depends the survival of us all." Adlai Stevenson

tive will give way to a more open, consultative public decision-making process. Similarly, we may also expect the fruits of currently stepped-up funding will produce workable sets of social indicators of human well-being, as well as better documentation of social and environmental diseconomies generated by current production.

As macro-level social indicators are developed and begin to reformulate and enhance the accuracy of current narrowly-defined economic indicators, the information that individual companies base their decisions upon will also change. As social and environmental costs are factored into the Gross National Product, company decisions will be framed in terms of a much more slowly-growing "Net National Product." As these externalities become more explicitly quantified and publicly disseminated, there will be further pressure to internalize these formerly unacknowledged costs of production and add them to the market price of products. This will change the definition of profit to apply to only those activities which create real added wealth rather than private gain wrung from social or environmental exploitation.

The inevitable result of the reassessment of economic concepts and quantification methods will be the popular realization that economics is not much more than a set of unacknowledged assumptions parading as a "value-free" hard science. This realization will further politicize economics, and one would expect to see the growth of "public interest economics groups" to join those in public interest law and science. Such groups will eventually find foundation and other institutionalized support as citizen groups learn that they must have their own economist present testimony on the dis-economies of one-way bottles to counter the testimony of the container companies' economists at public hearings.

Similar insights will lead to demand for interest-group representation on all governmental economic decision-making bodies, such as the Federal Reserve Board, the Treasury, and the President's Council of Economic Advisers, which consumer, environmental and minority groups have already sought to expand so as to include member economists representing their interests.

For the corporation there will be similarly stepped up demands for interest group representation on their boards of directors or "public interest directors" as suggested by many corporate critics. It is also likely that other corporate publics, particularly stockholders, consumers and environmentalists, will organize themselves into coherent negotiating blocs and engage in annual bargaining with corporations just as labor unions do today.

One of the most vital and far-reaching corporate strategies must be that of learning to live with the new

"THE NEW POST-INDUSTRIAL CONSUMERS ARE NOT LUDDITES, THEY ARE REALISTS"

definition of profit and the internalizing of the full social
and environmental costs of production. This will alter mar
and production as it more rationally assigns such costs to
the consumer rather than the taxpayer. For instance, it
is highly likely that in the face of the coming energy
squeeze, current promotional rates for electricity will be
restructured to include external costs and remove subsidies
from heavy users such as the aluminum industry. One outc
would be the wholesale replacement of aluminum in many
consumer products; another might be the disappearance of
throwaway aluminum can.

Another consequence of such a more realistic definition
profit would be the discontinuance of many consumer iten

whose production was only profitable with formerly hidden social or environmental subsidies; and, as resources become scarcer, the gradual replacement of high energy/matter input goods with low energy/matter input goods and the continued growth of services in the public and private sectors that is already evident.

All of this may be initially inflationary while readjustments are occurring and may cause many American products to face even stiffer competition in world markets.

In view of such conditions, it would seem that three general areas for future profits exist: 1.) *Better energy-conversion ratios.* We will no longer be able to afford the thermal inefficiencies of the current generation of light water nuclear fission reactors or the internal combustion engine. It is now becoming clear that adding pollution control equipment, such as cooling towers or catalytic converters on cars, may on a total-energy basis leave us with a trade-off. Only by developing inherently more efficient energy-conversion systems such as fuel cells or nuclear fusion can we hope to achieve actual economy and environmental benefits.

2.) *Better resource management and rehabilitation* Production loops must be closed by recycling, but the current mode of volunteer recycling of bottles and cans does not constitute a valid negative feedback loop for the container industry because it permits them to continue externalizing the severe costs of collection.

3.) *Better "market failure research" into those areas where individual consumer demand is inoperable unless it can be aggregated.* There are potentially enormous public-sector "markets" where the backlog of unmet group consumer needs is greatest for such services as mass transit, health care, clean air and water, education, retraining, parks, and all kinds of public amenities. Many of these needs might well become coherently aggregated with a little corporate support of the necessary political activities of coalitions of potential consumers now working to underpin them with government appropriations. And yet many companies, blind to these new market opportunities, continue to oppose such citizens' efforts and even lobby against mass transit or clean air because they still identify with past vested interests in old, rapidly saturating markets.

If corporations can lobby to procure government contracts for military and space products, they can also learn the methodologies of the new multi-stage public sector marketing. Companies interested in developing new markets in the public sector must first contact citizen organizations pushing for new priorities in public spending and assess which new needs they might be best equipped to serve. Only these grass roots coalitions of potential consumers can create enough genuine political steam to capitalize these new economic activities, and corporations must learn to see these groups as indispensable allies instead of enemies. The companies must then determine the citizens' expectations for the performance of the new public sector goods and services. Together they can begin formulating the design criteria and functional goals with the companies providing technical and other supporting services to develop more detailed plans.

Meanwhile the real needs wait. The ripest public sector market is for mass-transit, which will need massive infusion of federal, state and local funds. The aerospace companies' heads are still in the clouds, trying to push monorails and hovercraft; the riders are ready to begin now, mounting the effort to encourage funds for express bus routes, open lanes on freeways, jitneys for congested inner cities, upgraded subways and commuter trains, and fast airport-to-center-city transit.

Another ripening public-sector market is in waste disposal of all kinds. Some companies are beginning to think creatively about how to handle this massive problem, and General Electric has offered an interesting proposal for large regional waste-handling "utilities" which would separate and recycle every salvagable component and then incinerate the remainder to produce usable energy for heating.

The grass roots coalition is in place: environmentalists, inner city dwellers, suburban commuters, public health groups, the aged and infirm and all others disenfranchised by current transportation patterns, as well as the workers who see tomorrow's job opportunities. They are waiting for companies to show an interest, to start earmarking those wasted advertising dollars to build public support for the new priorities, and to offer citizens the support they so desperately need in shifting the old system and its client dependencies into a new and more productive system.

Other opportunities await in housing, health, environmental control, communications and human development. But business must learn to play by the new rules: real, not false profits, technology assessed by human and environmental criteria, with full public participation in design and accountability in its operation.

The new post-industrial consumers are not Luddites, they are realists. They do not reject technology, because current population levels in industrialized nations clearly preclude such a course. Rather, they seek an end to the gross, wasteful, "meat-axe" technology which has characterized our receding industrial age. They envision a second generation technology, more refined, miniaturized and organically modelled along biological analogies. Buckminster Fuller calls this process of doing more with less "ephemeralization."

The new consumers understand that just as computers and mass communications can be used to manipulate people's buying habits or intimidate them politically by government surveillance and data banks, so they can be used individual citizen back into the central nervous system of the body politic. Then he can use the very hardware of participatory democracy: electronic town meetings, instantaneous polling and eventually voting in referenda to model public problems and issues. Reformulating our concepts of "capital," "return on investment" and "resources" will help us see that all such uses of technology to inform our citizens and improve public decision-making are profitable.

The new consumers are aware how narrowly-based economic decisions control current allocations of resources and that large corporations and the business system in general are predominant forces in our society and much of the rest of the world. Therefore, they also understand that they must deal with it and work within it because they are , in reality, within it and a part of it. But they also believe that with sufficient creative, vigorous and uncomfortable public pressure, the productive forces within capitalism can be adapted to the needs of the immediate present as well as the next two decades and redeployed away from their current preoccupation with our "death-industrial complex" toward a new "life-industrial complex."

by Hazel Henderson

This article is based on a paper given before the White House Conference on the Industrial World Ahead: A Look at Business in 1990, February 8, 1972.

CORPORATE COMMITMENT:

A MATTER
SURVIVAL

The intermittent riots of 1964 to 1968 brought the poverty and deprivation of America's ghettos into focus. Extensive newspaper, radio and television coverage disclosed with dramatic impact the sordid living conditions of most of the nation's blacks and large numbers of immigrant Mexicans and Puerto Ricans. The social and economic injustices suffered by blacks for 300 years were brought out for the American public to view.

The institutional racism which had for years deprived blacks of equal employment opportunities and inadequate housing conditions were revealed. De facto school segregation, the natural outcome of blacks being relegated to ghetto neighborhoods, was uncovered. And the difficulties encountered by minority group members in trying to secure either personal or commercial loans were exposed.

Minority group frustration, made deeper by increased awareness, led to the black separatist movement. The more militant black leaders argued that America had always provided two sets of rights and two kinds of opportunities, one for whites and the other for blacks, and they contended that as a nation, the United States would continue along this same course. Rejecting further struggle to assume a partnership at the helm of the national economy, the separatists vowed to become totally self-dependent. They assured all blacks that as a race they would be more successful starting their own businesses, building their own economy—in short, forming their own nation.

But at the same time, the white business community responded. Those business leaders who realized that their enterprises depended upon blacks as a work force and as a consumer outlet, initiated efforts to help ease inner-city tensions. Suddenly white businessmen recognized that the health of their institutions rested upon the development of the communities which they served. Industry then determined that bold attempts must be made to reach the unreached with a new kind of massive training program, leading not only to salable skills, but to the birth of self-pride and productive attitudes.

The temper of this country called for immediate action. Fortunately or unfortunately, the urgency of the situation did not permit lengthy planning sessions and well

"We businessmen can put together more sheer power for good or for evil than all the rest of the elements of the community combined. Call it power . . . call it influence . . . call it clout. By any name it is the ability to get things done. Whatever personal comfort you may get from the individual approach, it won't do a thing toward curing problems of such great dimensions. I believe the job can only be done by an organized, unanimous, massive assault by businessmen." Elisha Gray II, Chairman of the Board, Whirlpool Corporation

developed solutions. As a result, the untested ground of corporate responsibility became dotted with numerous "band-aid" programs. Attempts were made to finance minority entrepreneurs, to upgrade minority living conditions, to improve the quality of education for black children, and so on. A few of these early efforts established records of achievement and community acclaim, despite the lack of time available for advance planning. Some of these are still in operation today.

But most of the early remedies were dismal failures. These hastily planned programs, the majority of which had not correctly identified root problems, effected only surface cures. Too often the projects were geared to teach what established white institutions felt the blacks should learn, to provide what these same institutions felt the blacks should have, to prepare the blacks for a future predicated on white expectations.

Specifically while minority entrepreneurs now found that they could borrow the necessary dollars for business development, they frequently found it difficult to obtain management counselling, an essential ingredient for success. And black children, while they had the opportunity to go to school, did not have the chance or the means to attend integrated classes.

The failure of these early programs forced business into an extended period of self-examination. Honest analysis concluded that corporate involvement in urban affairs was on the whole a misunderstood phenomenon. Appraisal of programs frequently led to the unequivocal conclusion that ends and means were both quite simply off-target.

Major corporations across the nation are still re-examining their involvement in socially oriented programs, trying to come to grips with the changing role of business in contemporary society. Now is the time, then, to challenge industry to expand the scope and to refine the content and tone of urban affairs policies. Above all, industry must be urged to move away from participation in socially responsible "projects" toward adoption of on-line urban affairs functions which represent significant forces in day-to-day operating procedures.

This transformation of an idea to a workable blueprint for daily implementation requires the sincere and on-going commitment of top management. It also demands that the men and women who are responsible for the initiation of corporate policies include representatives of the minority community, from the board of directors on down. The "top of the house" must communicate a real spirit of commitment through the ranks of middle management and employees. They must establish specific methods of measuring the success or failure of urban affairs guidelines, and must make it unmistakably clear that the cooperation

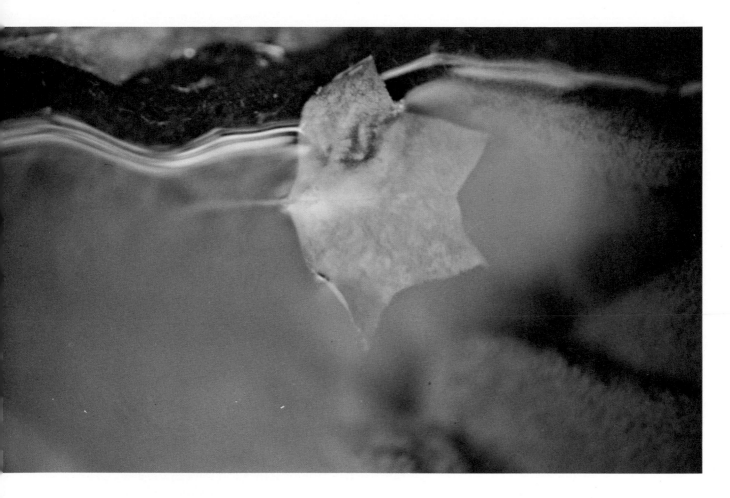

of all personnel in executing the company's goals is expected. Performance evaluation must be as real in this area as it is in budgeting, product development, profit planning and the like.

At First Pennsylvania Bank, for example, the Urban Affairs Committee, made up of members of senior and executive management, calls for each major department to submit a quarterly report detailing numbers and positions of minority employees. Similar term reports are required to measure commercial and personal minority loan portfolios. Funds which have been set aside for advertising in black media and dollars allocated for purchasing from black contractors or suppliers are monitored. All these figures are plotted against programmed goals. But what is most important is that the people responsible for achieving these goals are well aware of the fact that their performance in these areas is carefully assessed.

Events of the past decade have forced business to recognize that it no longer operates in a vacuum. Minority demands for increased corporate responsibility are merely an indication of a far broader-based American consumer awareness. The black experience is just one dimension of a multi-faceted urban dilemma.

The American people, as a whole, have begun and will continue to insist that business be held accountable. The demand for corporate involvement is not limited to any single interest group. It comes from young and old, black and white, rich and poor. The widespread philosophy of Ralph Nader, the vigor of the organized disadvantaged, and the power of the anti-establishment youth movement strike out against the traditional corporate system. These forces make it increasingly evident that the American consumer is not convinced that the "business of business is business."

Reflection of that fact can be seen in the recent trend to evaluate a company's stock not only on the ground of profitability, but also on the company's record of corporate involvement. There has been much discussion about the development of a social "scorecard," an audit of urban affairs activities. Such a system would provide comparative figures for potential investors and would give current stockholders a means to measure their company's progress in urban affairs.

The concept of quantitatively demonstrating social responsibility could well change the direction of the entire American business system. When it becomes clear that companies involved in urban affairs are more profitable than those which are not, previously uninvolved businesses will expend great energies attempting to solve social problems.

The question then ultimately rests with the American consumer. Through effective and selective use of purchasing power, he may influence the future direction of the American corporate system. For in order to survive and prosper, business *must* be responsive to his demands.

by Elmer Young

communities and business : expectations and frustrations

How many mountain-climbers have failed to reach their summit simply because they didn't plan their approach adequately? Many have been turned back by choosing the wrong face of the mountain or by too steep an ascent path only to find that their real failure was inadequate advance planning.

How many worthy community projects have failed to secure the support of neighboring businesses because the group failed to plan its approach adequately— either through lack of knowledge or lack of experience? Many potentially productive projects have floundered, never making the ascent to corporate sponsorship or assistance through the wrong choice of a means of access.

WHAT IS THE COMMUNITY . . . . TO WHICH BUSINESS MUST RESPOND?

Setting aside the necessity of motivating businesses to be responsive to their communities through such external forcing—functions as market acceptance, consumerism, equal-opportunity compliance and community pressures— assume that a business, large or small, wants to involve itself with its community. How does it define community? How can it look at the staggering needs of any city and delineate an appropriate "bite-sized chunk" with which to deal?

In virtually every major city is a contiguous collection of locales each distinctively a "community." Usually clusters of these "communities" form an area or geographically identifiable unit. To a Philadelphian, for example, West Philadelphia, South Philly, North Philadelphia and the Northeast are designations which form a handy index of the types of community needs probable in each section which is comprised of hundreds of smaller "communities."

Yet "community" also may refer to dozens of special segments of society (e.g. the student community or the black community). It may refer to various systems within the life of a city (e.g. the educational community or the business community). At times a vociferous individual may speak for "the community" and examination shows that, in those cases, "the community" may mean "me." It may even be necessary to work simultaneously with communities which are in conflict with each other (e.g. between the black community and a police department or between two adjacent community areas competing for the same funds).

Only a knowledgeable and well planned community relations program will enable a business to make appropriate responses to requests coming from "the community." This kind of information and planning is requisite for setting priorities and for definition of the "ball park" in which business-community interaction should take place. There is no substitute for a personal company representative listening to and sharing with the community groups empathetically.

MISTAKEN ASSUMPTIONS AND THEIR RESULTS

When businesses and community groups have insufficient contact with each other and attempts are made by the community to secure business support or involvement for community concerns, each tends to operate on some mistaken assumptions about the other and, frequently, each concludes certain things about the other. Often these misconceptions cause the potentially cooperative venture to become abortive. Here are a few of the more frequent assumptions and their results—viewed from the perspectives of business groups and from the vantage of communities.

(see opposite page)

WHAT SHOULD COMMUNITIES EXPECT OF BUSINESSES?

All public groups in the neighborhood have the right to expect a business to be genuinely interested in the community and its problems. It should find each business has designated someone to be the person who can and will listen with understanding to the community's concerns. One commodity which business ought to provide and communities should expect is imagination. No matter how

ON THE PART OF BUSINESS

Mistaken Assumptions	*Results*
1. The best or only way to respond to requests is with money.	1. Other resources such as services, equipment, know-how, manpower, or jobs aren't considered in lieu of money.
2. Selection of a primary community target area is too risky because of leaving some areas unaided.	2. Dilution of resources, as the thinly spread "something for everyone" way of responding, spills beyond the neighborhood of the business.
3. Community groups can't or won't try to understand the problems and limitations of businesses.	3. Lack of candor by business spokesmen introduces an artificial quality to relationships, undercutting trust.
4. Community groups really believe the requests they make will be granted in full.	4. There is an over-response or lack of discretion by businesses when weak or "flaky" proposals are met without checking.

ON THE PART OF COMMUNITY GROUPS

Mistaken Assumptions	*Results*
1. Small businesses and large firms operate and respond in the same manner.	1. The "blanket approach" (a mimeographed "Dear World" letter, for example) turns off recipients, both large and small.
2. Business owes an affirmative answer to every request.	2. Presumptuousness in advance is guaranteed to lead to frustration and a sloppy preparation of proposals.
3. It (i.e. the particular group) represents "the community."	3. There is lack of perspective and objectivity on the part of the community group.
4. Its project or request is unique, or more valid or worthy than others under consideration by a business.	4. Illusory confidence and baseless optimism may lead to unwarranted disappointment and/or unfair resentment against business.
5. Because business personnel may not reside in the ghetto or the inner city, they aren't knowledgeable or really concerned about those who do.	5. There is thwarting of the intentions to help and lessening of the interest of those in the business world most likely to be of genuine assistance.

"If you plant for years,
plant grass.
If you plant for decades,
plant trees.
If you plant for centuries,
plant men."
(an ancient proverb)

hard the problem or how formidable the obstacles, innovative thought and effort can help.

Communities can and should view businesses as a *resource*. To most this only means cash, but that's often not what's most needed. Services (such as photography, printing, or photocopying), know-how, manpower and equipment are all ways companies can aid communities—frequently with better results than giving cash.

Perhaps the most important thing communities can and do expect from businesses is an honest response. "Snow-jobs" are unacceptable now and never really were in order. Whether the response be positive or negative, there's no substitute for leveling with responsible community representatives.

WHAT SHOULD BUSINESSES EXPECT OF COMMUNITY GROUPS?

As the mountain-climber has to plan his approach, so the community group must plan its ascent up the mountain of credibility by doing its homework thoroughly. Every public affairs or community relations director sees dozens of poorly conceived and ill-prepared proposals each year. In many cases, the first point of aid to a group is to assist it in re-preparing its proposal or statement of its project. To spark the response of business, community groups must show that they know their own community and that they know what they are doing.

Business can expect community groups to take time to note the differences in the companies they are approaching. Whether a business is a research and development or a manufacturing shop, whether it's large or small, union or non-union, owned or leased, merchandising wholesale or retail—all these things make the ways a business can respond to its community different from other businesses.

Community groups should be as willing to listen as they are desirous to be heard. What's the state of the business from which they're seeking assistance? What's the real nature of the business being done and how do businessmen feel they can be of assistance?

Although key leadership in community groups is often changing for a variety of reasons, some attempt should be made to provide continuity in order to maintain an efficient level of communication between business and community groups.

Finally, business can and should expect and receive neighborliness from its community. The old adage, "to have friends, a man must show himself to be friendly," is certainly apropos of the relationships between businesses and their neighbors.

WHAT IS THE ROLE OF THE PUBLIC AFFAIRS (COMMUNITY RELATIONS) STAFF?

To be the eyes and ears of management in the community, absorbing the real concerns and needs of the

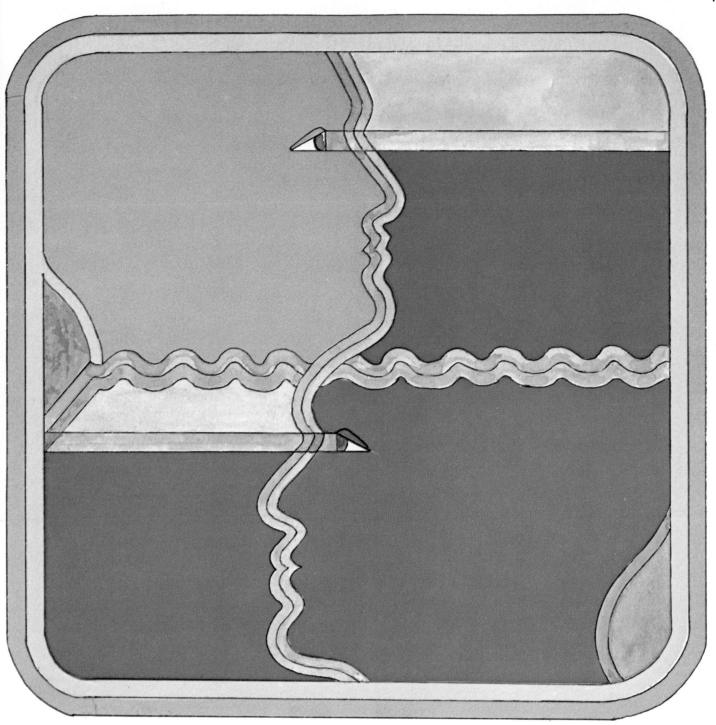

people who make up the city and its component communities, is the first priority. To do this requires hours of personal commitment as well as a flexible schedule within the business context. It is indispensible to generate the trust and credibility needed for good long-range relationships.

The mandate and authority to be a spokesman for the business and its management in and to the community is also vitally necessary. While everyone understands that some cases or requests require checking back with the office, no one will accept with good grace the company representative who can say nothing on his own and who can never make a decision on the spot. The business representative must understand his company and its positions sufficiently so as to be able to explain, inform and defend when appropriate; yet he cannot be just a "company man." He walks the delicate line of advocacy in the tradition of an ombudsman.

The continuous two-way educational task of helping the community to understand business and its capabilities and limitations, while at the same time providing business management with insight and recommendations for meaningful community participation, is the crux of the Public Affairs function. Since both community leadership (and the relative effectiveness of groups) and the top leadership and key staff members of businesses are continuously changing, this is a never-ending function, never to be overlooked.

Employee involvement in any community program is crucial to long term success in keeping business working with the numerous projects. Not only is high interest maintained within the business, but also personal commitment and involvement does wonders for the apathetic and the previously uninformed or prejudiced person. The community also likes employee participation in its projects.

The public affairs/community relations director or staff must be capable of innovation and leadership. The kaleidoscopic demands of major metropolitan areas and continuously shifting structures of relationships within the sectors of the broad community demand imagination and bold new attempts to harness the energies and resources of the nation's businesses to improve the quality of life for those whose lives are lived out within the walls of the city.

Leadership within the business, among fellow businessmen, within the community and all up and down the line is desperately needed. So few leaders lead! Whether in urban relations, government relations, community relations or in the informal relationships built up over the years with the key opinion-makers of a city, the public affairs staff should always be a catalyst, even a gadfly to stimulate invention and improvement in the ways people and groups of people work together in business and the community.

EPILOGUE

With the carefully thought-out approach, with the appropriate homework in hand, and with the access provided by concerned corporate citizens, there can be an infinite amount of progress in American cities for communities who will seize and use the opportunity to build relationships with businesses who care.

by Wayne L. Owens

SOCIETY AND THE BALANCE SHEET

The social role of the corporation is a subject that commands a lot of attention, and from some very distinguished people. Statements on corporate social responsibility have flowed in recent years from such eminent people as John Kenneth Galbraith, the economist and author; former Harvard Law School Dean, Eugene J. Rostow; and consumer advocate Ralph Nader.

Why is there all this concern about the social role of the corporation? Probably the principal reason for this concern is the activities corporations are engaging in today. Partly due to the failure of other institutions, corporations have felt compelled, for example, to train poorly educated blacks; to assist in the development of black-owned businesses; to build or provide mortgage money for ghetto housing; to operate child care centers; to help strengthen the management of urban school systems; and to make direct contributions to all kinds of efforts and agencies directed toward social improvement.

Many people believe, and perhaps with justification, that such activities go well beyond the classic function of the business corporation. Some people go so far as to say the corporation, by engaging in such activities, actually undermines our economic system and threatens to preempt the role of government.

As I interpret the current debate, the issue is not so much whether or not the corporation has a role to play or a contribution to make toward social improvement, but what should that contribution be and under what circumstances should it be made.

Milton Friedman, for example, contends that the social responsibility of business is "to use its resources and engage in activities designed to increase its profits." But even he concedes self-interest might dictate that corporations engage in limited kinds of socially directed activity.

Friedman essentially has two objections to corporate "social responsibility." He contends that corporate leaders are hypocritical when they cloak their social actions

with the phrase "social responsibility." He states that these so-called social actions are, or could be, legitimately taken in the interests of the corporation and its shareholders. Friedman feels this is the only proper basis for a corporation to take social actions.

When a corporation makes actions taken in its own self-interest appear altruistic, this, according to Friedman, gives support to those who feel that profit is a dirty word, and who feel anything done in the name of profit must be wrong. Friedman is saying that when corporations fail to defend their social actions on economic grounds, they undermine the vitality and integrity of the American economic system.

Friedman's second objection to corporate "social responsibility" is that under this concept corporations are, in effect, substituting their judgment of what is best for society for that of elected political representatives. He concludes that corporate social responsibility is a move toward acceptance of "the socialist view that political mechanisms are the appropriate way to determine the allocation of scarce resources to alternate uses."

Economist Paul Samuelson takes the position that the large corporation today has little choice. Not only is it able to engage in socially directed activities as a result of court rulings and established business norms, but it is expected to.

According to Samuelson, it is no longer possible for a large corporation to ignore the public interest and operate on the basis of immediate profit. If it did, it would be in trouble not only with other businesses but also with the Stock Exchange and the Securities Exchange Commission.

This doesn't mean corporations can engage unrestrained in social improvement. A corporation would, according to Samuelson, be ill-advised to go out and decide unilaterally, for example, to try and wipe out inflation or to rectify inequities in income distribution through manipulation of its own internal wage and pricing policies. It would be wiped out by its competitors.

Another viewpoint is expressed by Eugene Rostow who has stated, in effect, that business has enough to do just taking care of business. He feels we should concern ourselves solely with the maximization of profit and remain indifferent to the public interest. Mr. Rostow some years ago contended that the public does not regard the corporation as an appropriate institution through which to set public policy.

This statement may have been true five or six years ago, but public opinion changes. In 1969 a third of Americans, about 34%, were of the opinion that elimination of poverty was a responsibility of government and business. One out of every eight were of the opinion that this was entirely the job of business.

In November 1970 a poll by the Opinion Research Corporation indicated that 60% of the general public considered a main responsibility of business to be keeping the environment free of pollution. They rated this right alongside taking care of customer needs.

In the same year 47% of Americans felt another important responsibility of business was to help sustain full employment. Thirty-eight per cent felt a main responsibility of business was to hire and train the disadvantaged. Another 29% included among the major responsibilities of business that of assisting in cleaning up and rebuilding big city ghettos.

It seems clear that we are witnessing a shifting of public expectations. Most feel that business has a social responsibility, and they expect this responsibility to be discharged.

A final point of view to be considered is that of the corporation's owners—the shareholders. Stockholders, according to a recent Opinion Research Corporation poll, generally want corporations "to attend to business, stay honest and pay dividends."

There is some agreement and some truth in all of these points of view. Our position in the Bell System reflects some elements of most of them. However, much of the reasoning at the base of the more conservative views appears to be untenable and almost totally irrelevant to the world we live in today.

Several years ago, the Bell System came to grips with this problem of just what should be our involvement in helping to improve social conditions. Whatever this involvement was to be, it needed justification in terms of our business and in terms of the unique resources we had to contribute.

In seeking our justification, it became increasingly apparent that our business was overwhelmingly dependent on the health of the cities. We were, in effect, an urban business. Our resources of people, land and facilities

were centered largely in the cities, and the cities were
decaying.

Our business depends on people. At last count there
were about a million people working for Bell System
companies. We have estimated that half of the people we
will hire in the next decade will come from the school
systems in the big cities. We depend on these cities
as the major source of entry labor for our craft jobs.
A large and growing percentage of their inhabitants
are black.

Black people today account for 25% of the total
labor force in central cities. Thirteen of these
central cities where 37% of the blacks in the United
States live probably will be more than 50% black by 1984.
Two of these cities, Washington, D. C. and Newark,
already are.

I don't mean to suggest that the adjustments to be
made are solely within these eastern cities which
have a growing black population. We are
somewhat unique among corporations in
that our business is spread geographically throughout the nation.
In California which contains 40% of
our Spanish-surnamed employees and
in southwestern cities like Santa
Fe, Phoenix, and Albuquerque, we
have had to adapt both our service
and our labor market requirements
to a large Mexican-American and
American Indian population.

More than one-third of the
employees of telephone companies come
from the thirty largest cities in
the United States. These same thirty
cities contain more than 25% of the Bell
System's physical plant and generate
25% of its revenues.

It seemed logical for us to
focus our involvement on city problems,
particularly the "people" problems
that arise from conditions in the
cities. This has led to programs of
training and remedial education
for the un- and underemployed. It
has led some Bell System companies to
experiment with child care centers
as a potential means for improving
employee retention and reducing
absenteeism.

Companies in some cities also work
with school systems in setting up work-
study programs, remedial reading programs, vocational

training programs and guidance programs for students, and business management programs for school administrators. In addition, they donate financial and technical assistance to agencies working to improve communities and to meet the needs of people, particularly in the cities.

However, the point is not what the Bell System is doing, but the rationale that helped to influence our decisions. We are not being influenced blindly by the immutable forces of the marketplace. Instead, we and many other large corporations are guided by reality, by a need to develop workable solutions to the problems we encounter as we try to fulfill our obligations to customers and shareholders. This is perhaps where we part company with some economic theorists.

Those of you who have followed the debate over the corporate role in society probably have noticed two things: the commentary includes phrases like "the free market," "the free enterprise—private property system." Everything is "free." The discussions often are hypothetical or based on what economists call economic "models," and on theoretical concepts.

These theoretical concepts are used by some critics of corporate social action to justify maximizing profits to the exclusion of the public interest. This approach may be useful in reducing extremely complex problems to manageable form just for the sake of arguments that prove nothing. But theoretical concepts don't begin to describe the real world we live in today or the problems corporations face.

The American economy today is a curious mixture of public and private activity. This mix has evolved as a pragmatic way of getting things done. Whatever else it is, the economy is not purely private and it never has conformed identically to the classic, elegant, generalized model of a free enterprise, free market system that is used by some critics of corporate social involvement.

Whatever else the market is, it is not free. The oil men, the farmers, the textile manufacturers and other businessmen who clamor for the imposition of government controls, government subsidies, and import quotas probably couldn't live with it if it were completely free. The decision-making mechanism in our economy, far from being the invisible forces of the marketplace, really is a combination of market forces plus government and private manipulation and initiative.

In short, the economy, as it exists in the minds of many who defend the maximization of profits, is no more than a classic abstraction.

For corporate leaders faced with such social issues as crime and vandalism, pollution, racial discrimination, declining labor markets, high costs, consumerism, and rising demands for service—this abstraction offers no realistic solutions. For the management of a major corporation today to "stick to knitting"—to pursue profits to the exclusion of the public interest—is to isolate the operations of the company from life itself.

This does not mean we can ignore the need for profits. It is absolutely fundamental that a corporation be healthy and successful financially in order to discharge its social responsibilities. It does not mean there are no limits on how far corporations can go in fulfilling a socially responsible role.

There is, for example, much to think about in the counseling of those who warn of the danger of business preempting or seeking to preempt the role of government. I'm not suggesting that I am so much concerned about business threatening to supercede government. Rather, I see a greater threat to business in that the general conception of what corporations can actually and properly accomplish may become inflated. This could result in public pressures for corporations to respond to so many problems that they become diverted from their essential role, which ultimately is economic, into areas where they have little competence.

This danger, while not immediate, is implicit in the corporate accountability movement. This movement, which should not be confused with corporate responsibility, seeks to pressure corporations on social issues. In connection with this movement, companies have been pressured on issues ranging from pollution, discrimination against blacks and women, safety, all the way to economic sanctions against South Africa and ending the war in Southeast Asia. The rationale guiding this movement is a belief in the preeminent power and influence of the American corporation.

Ralph Nader best exemplifies the thinking of people who support this approach to social reform. Nader has described the large corporation as a "kind of private government." He states that, collectively, large corporations "constitute the most powerful, consistent and coordinated power grid that shapes the actions of men in public and private sectors."

In February, 1970 in his public statement launching Campaign GM, a movement described as being designed to make General Motors "responsible," Nader referred to it as "an effort which is dedicated toward a new constituency for the corporation that will harness these powers for the fulfillment of a broader spectrum of democratic values."

There are other such movements. The Council on Economic Priorities describes itself as the "socially concerned Dun and Bradstreet." It gathers and publishes information about the activities of some one hundred companies in such matters as pollution, hiring practices, foreign investments, and defense contracts. This information is passed on to investors.

"Arthur Koestler refers to creativity as an 'actualization of surplus potentials.' When we review the tremendous strides that technology has made in actualizing the potentials of our material resources, it is difficult for us to believe that the development of the most important resource of all — the human one — has not kept pace. Unused material resources, Jerome Wiesner points out, are not necessarily wasted; unused human resources are." Sidney J. Parnes, President, Creative Education Foundation, Inc.

What we have today, in effect, are not only government pressures, but pressures from private individuals and groups, many of them working skillfully within lawful channels, like the courts and share-owner meetings, in an attempt to move the corporation toward *their* concept of social responsibility. There are both positive and negative elements in these movements. Movements such as Nader's are seeking institutional change through lawful, proper means. This suggests that social protest may be becoming more sophisticated and that there is emerging at last an effective alternative to violent confrontation.

The danger is that the accountability movement through pressure may push the corporation into areas where it does not belong. This could weaken not only the corporation's ability to achieve its essential mission, but the viability of our political institutions as well.

We know something about these pressures. The Bell System has been petitioned to take positions and to use its resources to influence the outcome on just about every imaginable issue. We have had to give a great deal of thought to what our role should be and how we should respond to such pressures.

These are not simple issues to deal with. Most of us have both public and private views on all the major issues. Sometimes we feel compelled to adopt views as officials of publicly-owned corporations that cannot be reconciled easily with our views as private citizens.

We have had to come to grips with this problem in connection with the war in Southeast Asia. We received a number of letters seeking an expression either for or against extension of the Vietnam War into Cambodia.

Essentially, our response made two points:

1.) The corporation essentially is an economic rather than a political institution.

2.) There is a real question as to whether a business organization, even if it were inclined to express strictly political viewpoints, is a fit vehicle for the achievement of political objectives.

Because of the size and economic influence of some of our large corporations, people tend to ascribe wisdom to them in areas well beyond the relatively narrow spectrum of their competence.

People also tend to see complex political issues in very simplistic terms. The right action to take may be evident to them. But even if we had the power as a corporation to take actions that would influence the outcome on major political issues, we scarcely have the wisdom or the experienced judgement to decide which action is the right

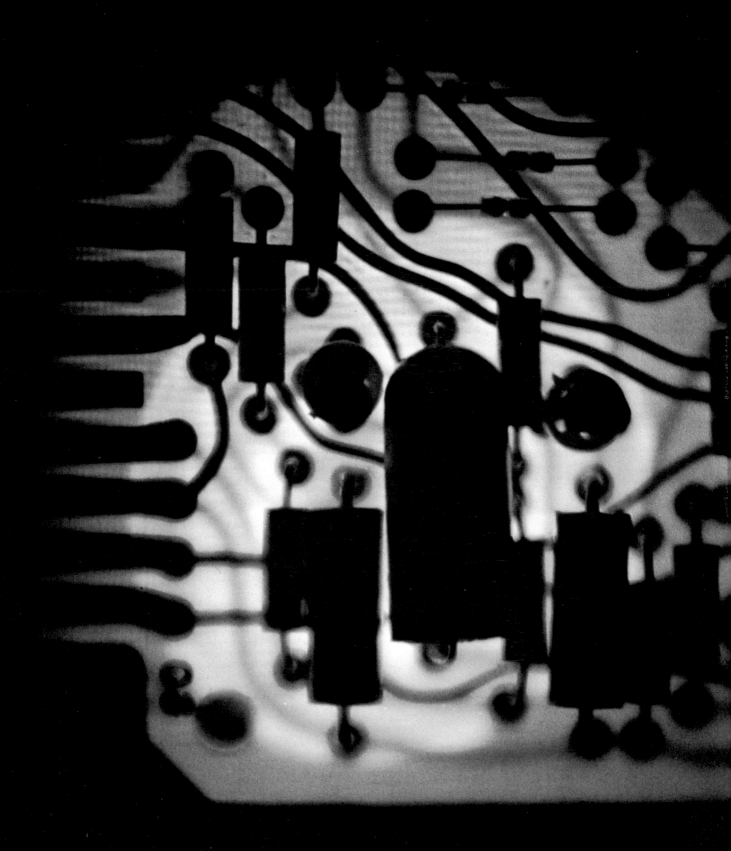

action. It is the public tendency to ascribe a kind of omniscience and power to corporate leaders and then to demand that they exercise this presumed power and wisdom that creates great risks.

Looking at the other side, a risk equal to the risk of corporations overextending themselves is that their full potential for making a contribution to the solution of social problems will go unrealized.

It is one thing to have a socially aware management; it is another thing to convince shareowners to deal with social problems. One of the constraints acting against a wider corporate involvement with social problems is that it is almost impossible for the corporation to assure its shareholders that they will benefit directly from contributions it makes for such purposes as education, health and welfare, or improving conditions in the nation's ghettos.

Because of this, many firms don't contribute anything to environmental improvement. Others contribute far less than would be the case if they could indicate to their shareholders a more immediate or direct return.

From 1936 to 1969 the per cent of net corporate income for philanthropic purposes has increased very little. It has gone from less than one half of one per cent to only slightly more than one per cent. This is despite the fact that the deductibility of corporate contributions for tax purposes established in 1935 has been sustained by several court rulings.

At the present time, most direct corporate financial contributions are going to education, hospitals, and to other health and welfare agencies. Such activities seem to be the easiest to rationalize; companies can argue that the availability of good schools, hospitals and other community institutions help industry attract good employees to the community.

It is easier for companies to argue this. But even in these areas where the need for corporate support is so well established, shareholders don't always buy the argument. There has been some opposition from some shareholders on this at recent annual meetings. In fact, a resolution was introduced to amend our Certificate of Incorporation so as to restrict contributions to purposes that directly further the company's interests.

What many shareholders fail to realize is that the present level of our contributions have virtually no impact on dividends. Total Bell System contributions amount to approximately three-tenths of one per cent of Bell System income. If we were to flow through to dividends the total amount of our contributions, it would amount to less than one penny a share per quarter.

Given the "tend to business, stay honest and pay dividends" attitude of most shareholders, it is no surprise that many companies find it difficult to contribute to an inner city street academy, to establish training or remedial programs for the hard-core, to support housing policies, or improvements in transportation that will make it possible for inner city residents to get where the jobs are.

In the long run all industry benefits from efforts to improve social conditions. They benefit in lower taxes, in better markets, and in more stable communities. The problem is that these are long-range benefits, and they are not always easily quantified.

Obtaining corporate support for programs of social improvement will continue to be difficult until the public, particularly the shareholder public, can be made to understand that social problems, if left unsolved, do as much damage to balance sheets as unsolved production and sales problems.

No business, no group of businesses, acting alone, can do the job that has to be done in our cities and communities. It must be a cooperative effort. All segments of American society must be involved, but the leadership and direction must come from government.

When we as citizens allow government to falter in its obligations to any segment of the community, when government fails to provide constructive leadership, the quality of life in the entire community suffers. Yet government won't provide the necessary leadership unless it has from the public a political mandate for a different set of social priorities.

If this is forthcoming, I believe more corporations will come forth with the kind of energies, talents and resources that will help bring us closer to the solution of our most pressing social problems.

by Robert D. Lilley

the corporation & social change:

a new relationship ...

a new dimension to planning

It is safe to say that there was, in the corporate world in the mid-to-late Sixties, a growing awareness of a need for a new type of futures planning. In large measure this need was caused by a change in the character of change itself. By that I mean that change was not only accelerating, but shifting from a purely quantitative and physical mode to an increasingly qualitative and psychological mode. We started to realize that we were being confronted with a much greater incidence of discontinuities in our society, and so in our business system and business operations. These discontinuities can be, and have been, caused by:

1. technology;
2. trends such as affluence or education "going critical"—that is, old trends taking on new and almost revolutionary force, as a nuclear reactor goes critical;
3. value system changes (whether these are a dependent or an independent variable is a philosophical question which we can defer for the moment).

To attempt to provide some advance warning of such discontinuities, General Electric established, in 1967, a so-called Business Environment Studies component. It was perhaps logical that this "people-oriented" futures research, or policy analysis, should first emerge in the "people-oriented" function of the company—the relations function. Our Business Environment component was assigned responsibility for:

1. Identifying and analyzing the broad social, political and economic trends (mostly in the U.S.), with 1980 as our time horizon.

2. Deriving the planning implications for the Relations function (which, just as much as technology and marketing, needs a future orientation).

With the inertia of any large organization you need to "buy time" if you are going to change the system; and it was predictable that this was exactly what we would have to do, if we believed that even half of what was being said at that time about the way people and society were changing. In other words, you needed to start thinking in 1967 about the Relations policies of 1972-1975—the way work was to be organized; the way people should be managed; the way people would be motivated. You need that sort of lead time to develop systemic corporate change.

3. Catalyzing responsive action, inside and outside the company, to deal with these trends and implications. I don't minimize the difficulties of our first function—

trying to make predictions: Alvin Toffler was right
when he cited that probably apocryphal Chinese proverb,
"To make predictions is very difficult—particularly with
respect to the future." However, I suggest that "changing
the system," trying to catalyze action in anticipation
of, rather than in blind and ultimate reaction to developing
trends, may be the more difficult assignment.

In our initial study we reviewed a broad spectrum of
changes that might develop in the U.S. over the next ten
years. It was an attempt, through identifying these forces
for change, to make sense of change, to see a pattern in
the kaleidoscope of events and trends. This was a broad
study, derived from a wide range of external inputs—
interviews and literature—and we re-evaluated the
forecasts a year later, largely because merely
publishing our study produced a whole new set of
inputs and comments which we felt should be factored
into our work.

One purpose in conducting this study had been to
establish our own priorities for future research. It
is scarcely surprising that the study identified
the urban/minority problem as the principal
domestic problem of the next decade. (You can
argue that this is really two problems—"urban," in
the sense of renewal of our cities; and "minority," in
the sense of race relations.) With our position in the
Relations function, it was only natural for us to
make the future minority environment our first target for
detailed study.

We focused on the long-term forces at work in the
minority environment, rather than on the immediate and
very obvious issues of 1967-68 when our cities were ablaze.
In this study we made abundantly clear the long-term
persistence of the problem, the complexity of the
problem, and the inadequacy of any corporate response that
had been so far developed, inside General Electric or
elsewhere, to deal with it.

Up to then (1967-68) we had focused on our first
two responsibilities—identifying trends, and deriving
business implications. From this point we started
to become involved in catalyzing action. In 1969 General
Electric established for the first time at the
corporate level an Equal Opportunity/Minority Relations
component to translate into action the long-term
comprehensive commitment our study had predicted would
be necessary. Then we in Business Environment worked
with this newly-established component in what I think can
justifiably be termed the first "systems approach"
(by a corporation, at least) to the minority problem.

There was no doubt in our minds about the
inadequacy of the typically piecemeal corporate response

to the problem in 1967-68. But translating the very general guidelines offered by our minority environment study into specific programs that really change the system is a hard, slogging, time-consuming, sometimes frustrating—but exciting—challenge. It took a task force of 27 people a year to take apart the manpower system of the company, piece by piece; analyze each piece to determine how far it impeded or helped the attainment of true equality of opportunity; and then put the pieces together again into an integrated system.

Translating some of these developing constraints and new expectations into systemic change in the corporation is, as John Gardner has said, "a task for the tough-minded and the competent"—and, I might add, for those who will persevere.

We were justified, I think, in appropriating the term "systems approach" from the aerospace field to the Relations field. We considered the problem as a system-wide problem, which obviously, as a "people problem," it must be. We also considered the fact that there is an inextricable linkage between the internal environment of a company and its external environment: there are elements of the problem which are caused outside the plant walls, but which the corporation cannot ignore—can, in fact, help to solve. To take a purely internal view of the problem would, therefore, inevitably be inadequate.

One key point in changing the system is a change in the management measurement and reward system. If society is re-writing its "charter of expectations" of corporations, if society is going to judge business performance by new criteria, then we must start to measure our own performance by new criteria. Otherwise all the best laid plans, all the most eloquent and sincere policy statements, will founder on the rock of inadequate performance. Managers are rational human beings—"economic men," if you will—who will perform as they know they are to be measured. If you measure them on profitability, they will strive for an increase in net earnings. If you measure them on market share, they will strive for an increased percentage of the available market.

We have not, in General Electric, totally changed our measurement system. We have, however, succeeded in grafting on to the present system a new set of measurements which, in effect, say that managerial and corporate performance in this particular aspect of corporate social responsibility *is* important, and will be evaluated and rewarded accordingly.

A few months later we predicted that we would be confronted with similar challenges, similar expectations, on a different front of this drive for equality—namely, the women's rights movement and the demands for the

elimination of sex discrimination. I think it says
something for the basic validity of our systems
approach that the same sort of principles, the same
sort of analyses, were transferable from one
area to the other. Interestingly, as a result of this
"early warning," General Electric issued
its own internal guidelines on "affirmative action" to eliminate sex
discrimination a full year
before the Federal
government did so.

In 1970 we came to a
transition point in our
Business Environment
history—a move from the
Relations function to the
field of strategic
planning. By 1968 we had
become convinced that
there is a broader appli-
cation for this socio-
political forecasting
than just in Relations.
We felt that experience
had shown a payoff in the
"here-and-now," so that
you could command the
respect and attention of
managers who are managing
quarter by quarter. However,
we felt that the sort of questions raised by our studies
translated into potential policy
decisions far *beyond* the Relations
area, and concerned the whole scope, relationships and purpose of the corporation, and, therefore, the
whole "gut" issue of what corporate planning is all about.

Well before the end of 1969, we were arguing that a
"four-sided framework" was essential for strategic
planning. Typically, corporate plans have been derived from
inputs from two main sectors—technology and economics.
(Fig. 1)* We have had economic forecasting which has produced projections and hard data about Gross National Product,
consumer spending patterns, personal savings, per capita
income and so on; while marketing research has given us
analyses, at the micro-economic level, of existing and
developing markets. Technological forecasting, too,
has produced, in tangible data form, projections about
the probable development cycle of new products, new
systems, new materials, in your own laboratories and in
competitors' laboratories, domestically and world-wide.

*For Fig. 1 and Fig. 2 (p. 100) see p. 103.

**"Men are disturbed not by
things, but by the views
which they take of them."
Epictetus**

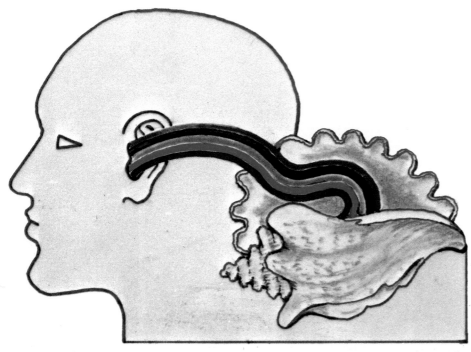

And these inputs have been the prime—indeed, the sole—bases for corporate plans.

We had, all of us, fallen into the trap—a trap which had become very evident by the end of the Sixties—of making the explicit or implicit statement, in our planning, "other things being equal." If we have learned one thing from the tumultuous Sixties, it is that we can no longer make such gross assumptions. "Other things" have had an uncomfortable habit of *not* being "equal." A perfectly logical plan based on these two conventional inputs can be very vulnerable to attack on its open flanks—the social and political flanks. (Fig. 2) To give ourselves protection on *all* sides, we need to develop a social and political dimension to our forecasting, and to make this a *required* part of the planning process.

We needed to change the system, *not* merely to change the organization, to add on another component—though that may be needed, for one must commit resources to the task if the objective is to do more than play at it. In the course of 1970, General Electric did a number of things—some of them organizational, some of them system changes in the planning process:

> - We established, as a separate component at the corporate level, a Corporate Executive Staff exclusively responsible, under four Senior Vice-Presidents, for strategic planning and long-term policy making.* Among the diverse experience, background and viewpoints of these four men and their staffs, we hoped to integrate the *full* range and diversity of inputs that the "four-sided planning framework" really needs.

> - We changed the planning system in many ways, but in particular we made it an *explicit* requirement that the first step in the planning process is development of a long-term environmental forecast.

*A separate and much larger group, the Corporate Administrative Staff, was established to be responsible for the short-term, functional operating work that has to be done at the corporate level.

In developing this required long-term forecast, we first produced nine separate views of aspects of the future business environment—"tunnel visions" of the future—dealing with probable developments in international, defense, social, political, legal, economic, technological, manpower and financial affairs. In each of these segments we tried to (a) give a brief historical review (1960-70) as a jumping-off point for our analysis of the future; (b) analyze the major future forces for change—a benchmark forecast for 1970-80; (c) identify the potential discontinuities, events which might have low probability, but high significance for General Electric; and (d) raise the first-order questions and policy implications suggested by these forecasts.

These were, by definition, *segmented* views of the future, and so inadequate as a final product. So we proceeded to a "cross-impact analysis," selecting out of the hundreds of trends/events that those nine environmental "slices" gave us the 75 or so that had the highest combined rating of probability and importance. On these 75 trends/events, we performed a cross-impact analysis asking, "If event A occurs, what will be the impact on the other 74? Will the probability of their occurrence increase? Decrease? Remain the same?" In effect, this process enabled us to build sets of "domino chains," with one event triggering another, and then to construct a small number of consistent configurations of the future.

The final step in the environmental forecasting process was the development of scenarios as an integrative mechanism for our work, pulling together the separate forecasts of the nine "slices," and blending quantitative and qualitative data. We developed multiple scenarios; we did *not* take a single view of the future. In fact, we ended up with four alternatives:

- A benchmark forecast, which combined the "most probable" developments from the nine environmental "slices";

- Three variants which, in effect, were derived from varying combinations of discontinuities.

Significantly, we rated even the benchmark forecast no more than a 50 percent probability. That, at least, is a measure of our own uncertainty about the future. Two of the scenarios—a "greater consensus" world and society, and a "greater disarray" world and society—were drawn up mainly as polar extremes to demonstrate the wide spread of possible results from the occurrence of divergent discontinuities at home and abroad.

The real value of these scenarios was to be found

in the fact that they provided us with bases for:

- making alternative long-term economic forecasts through computer modeling of the various scenarios' assumptions;

- analyzing General Electric results in alternative environments;

- testing out alternative corporate strategies in these environments;

- evaluating the probable outcome of competitors' strategies in these environments.

In short, they were useful, not only as integrative mechanisms for the diverse forecasting inputs, but also as "test beds" for planning corporate strategies.

Our experience to date has taught us important lessons.

1. Corporate planning must be developed within the parameters of "the four-sided framework" if it is to keep up with the pace and diversity of change, and protect the corporation from attack on an exposed flank. Planning must become as much at ease with the soft data of socio-political forecasting as it is now with the hard data of economic, marketing and technological forecasting.

2. Monitoring the future business environment must be both systematic and continuous. To be systematic, it must be a required part of the planning process; to keep abreast of change in a fast-moving world, it must be a continuous operation using feedback to modify forecasts.

3. We need to develop much more explicit and detailed contingency plans to deal with alternative futures. To take a single view of the future is to be overly simplistic and to court disaster. We have to accept the fact of uncertainty (which is something more than risk-analysis) and the probability of major discontinuities. Our plans must, therefore, be prepared to commit strongly to "most probable" trends while maintaining flexibility to deal with uncertainties.

4. We have to conceive of "strategy" as something more than marketing plans. The sort of strategy that alone seems adequate to the demands of the Seventies starts with a re-definition of corporate

purposes, mission and objectives; proceeds to an analysis of the new constraints and opportunities in the changing public expectations of corporate performance; and embraces both the external aspects of strategy (marketing, relationships) and its internal implications (the structure, governance and life-style of the corporation).

In the brief history of our experience with this form of futures planning, we can see the beginnings of a solution to the problem of outmoded planning concepts, and a dynamism toward systematic change that is encouraging in its signs, if not yet complete in its realization.

by Ian H. Wilson

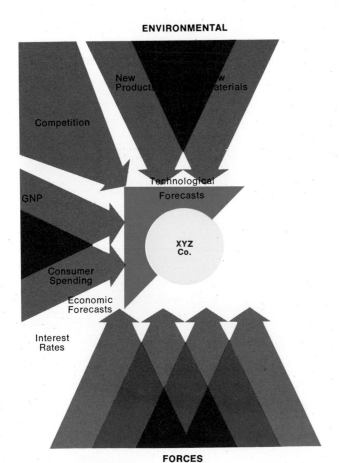

Figure 1

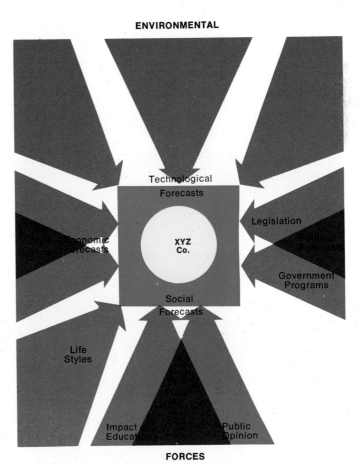

Figure 2

HOW TO MAKE SOCIAL RESPONSIBILITY PROFITABLE

We are at the point where it might be possible to catalyze a significantly new view of the corporation and its role. I believe that it in fact already exists but it needs to be made visible. It is crucially important that it be made visible as rapidly as possible because I am convinced that the major potential leaders of the present change process are to be found in business. It is equally clear, however, that the lack of a theory—and justification—for new styles of management is getting in the way of needed activity.

Increasingly, in recent years, corporations have been caught in an apparent double-bind. They have argued on the one hand that their freedom of action is limited by excessive government intervention. They also argue, however, that they are unable to carry through desirable social actions because, unless a law is passed and their competitors are compelled to follow it, they cannot afford to behave in a socially responsible way.

Managers have, in effect, far greater freedom of action that they are prepared to recognize. It is possible for them both to benefit the society and to increase their profits by careful choice of new areas of activity. These choices will not necessarily be obvious or easy, but in the changed climate of today, it is possible to behave in socially conscious and personally conscious ways without losing one's shirt. Such management would require higher levels of competence than presently exist, but this is absolutely necessary if a firm is to survive in the increasingly dif-ficult conditions which are inevitable in the immediate future.

From my point of view capitalism rests on a simple statement: that the combination of factors of production in imaginative and creative ways produces satisfactions which are such that all the factors of production can be compensated fairly with something left over for the manager who achieved the production. It is this thesis which makes nonsense of the "exploitation" argument.

However, we have failed to perceive the full implications of this thesis and the possibilities it raises for us. Instead of seeing the worker, consumer, community and environment as potential allies in our struggle to

increase satisfactions, we have all too often seen them
as enemies against which we should struggle. Managers
have used a win-win model in their internal planning but
retrogressed to a win-lose model in their relationships
with the rest of the world.

I do not intend to argue whether this was valid in the
past, but it is certainly a bad model for action in the
future. The thesis I am putting forward here is that
there are far wider areas for cooperative activity than we
have realized. Each business will have a greater or
lesser opportunity in each of the areas, but every business
needs to consider all of them.

The Worker. It is increasingly clear that a crisis is
brewing in this area. The remaining standards which insure
adequate work effort are due to the survival of a Puritan
ethic, but this is rapidly decaying. An increasing
number of workers believe that they have no
obligations except those that management
successfully enforces. Nor do they see
stealing—under a variety of more "acceptable"
names—as wrong.

It is possible that efforts to
increase productivity through "rationalization" of jobs have become counter-
effective. There is increasing evidence
that breakthroughs in effectiveness
are going to occur when people are given
responsibility for larger areas of
activity, for scheduling their time and
that of others in the system and when
they are treated as full human
beings rather than as replaceable cogs
in a machine-system. Today's human being
needs more challenge than he can find in the typical job,
and the lack of the challenge is destructive to him as
an individual and also reduces the gain of the firm
who pays him.

Once one has perceived that effectiveness depends on
the individual being able to deal with his problems,
cost effectiveness may suggest totally new patterns.
People are capable of extraordinarily greater effort than
they make most of the time. In effect, productivity in
an increasing number of jobs depends on whether people enjoy
their work. What can we do today, as opposed to the past,
to insure that most people enjoy their jobs? My guess
is that we have not even touched the surface of this issue.

(One pattern. A factory recently put its employees
on a 12-hour 3-day week. Result: a "new" factory for no
money and the employees thought this was the best thing
that had ever happened to them.)

The Consumer. "Let the buyer beware." In the end an
enormous amount of business still rests on this state-

ment—blatantly at one extreme and less blatantly at the other. What would our policies look like if we really believed that we should serve the buyer?

Paradoxically, I am not suggesting that the buyer is always right. I am suggesting that it might pay to work closely with the buyer, to meet his legitimate complaints but to refuse to deal with his illegitimate complaints. One needs to create a loyal clientele but not to preserve a clientele that will continue to make trouble.

The argument has often been that the dissatisfied customer will turn off other potential customers. But this once again assumes that all customers are stupid and cannot distinguish between the legitimate complaint and the try-on.

In the retail field, there would appear to be a case for a consumer ombudsman to sort out legitimate complaints from those which are invalid.

The Environment and the Community. There has been a tendency to assume that responsible behavior toward the environment and community will necessarily result in direct deductions from profit. I would suggest that views of responsible behavior are shifting so rapidly that this is no longer necessarily true.

Looked at only from the negative side, more and more groups are developing clout, annoying at least and potentially damaging at worst, in terms of socially irresponsible activities. But there is also increasing evidence that responsible behavior may make it easier to raise capital. In the recent past, four mutual funds have appeared, each premised on the idea that there is a substantial public which, given the opportunity, would prefer to put money into a fund, which in addition to producing a return on investment, applies social criteria in choosing its stocks. The four funds are Social Dimensions, Dreyfus Third Century, Pax World, and First Spectrum.

The social rhetoric is changing and the ways in which one is seen to be successful by the general public are changing also. I am attempting to develop a dialogue around this issue. Those who are interested should write to me: Box 1531, Wickenburg, Arizona, 85358.

by Robert Theobald

BIOGRAPHIES

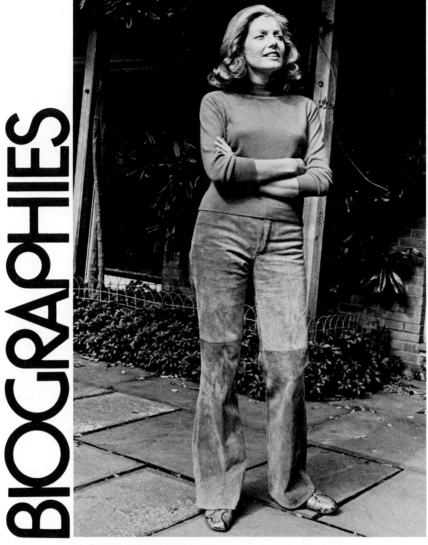

HAZEL HENDERSON
Writer, Lecturer, Environmental Activist
Photograph courtesy of NEW YORK TIMES, William E. Sauro

Ms. Henderson met with us at her home in Princeton. We sat on the patio and talked for two hours about many of the poignant and alarming "dis-economies" that plague our country. Ms. Henderson is a dynamic, warm, and articulate woman—an astute critic of the relationship between business and society. She was born and educated in Great Britain and became a U.S. citizen in 1962. She has given lectures across the country to a wide variety of consumer activists, scholars and businessmen. Her articles have appeared in many publications including, *The Nation, Harvard Business Review, The Futurist, Business Economics,* and the *Columbia Journal of World Business.* She is a member of the Board of Directors, Council on Economic Priorities; Board of Directors, Institute for Public Transportation; Board of Directors, Institute for the Study of Economic Systems; Member, National Programming Council for Public Television.

ELMER YOUNG, JR.
Vice President, Urban Affairs
First Pennsylvania Bank

Elmer Young is a strong and independent thinker dedicated to adjusting the inequities that have been dealt out to minority peoples and the poor by mainstream America. Young worked closely with the Reverend Dr. Leon Sullivan in the organization and development of Zion Investment Associates, Inc. Zion is a community-based investment organization which provides capital for minority enterprises. Prior to his employment with First Pennsylvania, Young served as the executive director of the Entrepreneurial Development Training Center engaged in teaching minority businessmen ownership and management principles. He was also general manager of Progress Plaza Shopping Center, a black owned and operated shopping mall in Philadelphia. Young holds directorships with H.O.P.E. Development Corporation, Zion Federal Credit Union—President, Philadelphia Council for Community Advancement, and Greater Philadelphia Venture Capital Corporation.

WAYNE L. OWENS
Public Affairs Director, General Electric Company
Re-entry & Environmental Systems Division

Wayne Owens bears the arduous burden of having both a community and a corporate conscience. He has a foot in each world and the difficult responsibility of stimulating communication and an exchange of perspectives between the two. Owens' work has resulted in increasing cooperation with community groups in finding workable ways to apply the total resources of industry to such problems as drug addiction, racial tensions, rat-control, recreation, area development and planning, educational needs, and the economic problems of the disadvantaged and minority groups of the city. Owens' community affiliations include Mantua Industrial Development Corporation, University City High School: Organizing and Advisory Committee, Philadelphia Adult Basic Education Academy, and Citizens' Committee for the Improvement of Justice. Owens is in the business of breaking down traditional barriers between people. He is willing to extend himself beyond the norm—the boy he is holding in the picture has the measles.

ROBERT D. LILLEY
President, American Telephone & Telegraph Company

Robert Lilley has been "people-oriented" since his early experiences working as a mining engineer in West Virginia. Now as the new president of a company employing over a million people, his concern counts. Much of his Bell career has been spent as a production man. While Lilley was president of New Jersey Bell and Newark was in flames in 1967, Governor Hughes named him to head the Select Commission to Study Civil Disorder. After six months of working long night hours, the Commission published a hard-hitting, controversial report which led to a radical change in minority hiring policies, as well as prosecution and conviction of corrupt local officials. More recently, Lilley has headed AT&T's new Human Affairs Organization—including departments of personnel, information, and environmental affairs. "More than ever, people count," says Lilley, and his unassuming manner, according to one newspaper, "suggests calm authority in the crunches."

IAN H. WILSON
Consultant—Business Environment Research & Planning
General Electric Company

Ian Wilson is tomorrow's man—a corporate futures-planner. He advocates the necessity of broad perspective and long-term planning on the part of the corporation if it is to effectively meet the challenges of the future. Wilson was educated in England, receiving his M.A. from St. John's College, Oxford University. From 1954-1963 he held a variety of jobs in the public relations field, including research on public issues affecting business and a position in corporate press relations. For the next four years he was involved in the planning of management education and development activities. At present, his futures research places emphasis on an analysis of environmental trends which will affect corporate management in the future. Wilson is a member of the World Future Society, The American Association for the Advancement of Science, The Institute on Man and Science, and the Industrial Relations Research Association. He is co-author of *The Business Environment of the Seventies.*

ROBERT THEOBALD
Writer, Futurist, Communicator

Robert Theobald is a master of diversity. He has lived in India, England, and France, and presently resides on a ranch in Arizona. Although he has an M.A. in Economics from Cambridge, England, he has since branched out to a number of other areas such as communication theory, system theory, and ecology. Theobald believes in the challenge of dialogue and has worked on an intensive basis with many groups from business, labor, education, government, and the churches. In 1970 he carried out a study for the United Nations on the patterns which might be effective if the second Development Decade were to have any chance of success. His conclusions were published in *The Challenge of a Decade: Global Development or Global Chaos.* As a result of his varied experiences, Theobald is convinced of the necessity of increasing diversity of concepts in the world of the future. His other books include *Teg's 1994* (with J.M. Scott), *Habit and Habitat, Futures Conditional, The Guaranteed Income,* and *The Economics of Abundance.*

TWO PERSONAL REFLECTIONS

The following two comments were written especially for *Profiles of Involvement.* They are personal opinions that represent feelings about corporate social involvement.

We had hoped to include a spokesman for the conservative point of view to round out a broader picture. It was very difficult to find a corporation that would openly speak out against corporate social involvement.

I contacted a corporation in Michigan and spoke personally with the Chairman of the Board who gave me a verbal commitment that he would be that spokesman. He had three weeks to prepare a brief comment for *Profiles of Involvement.* I was in constant contact with his secretary who assured me that something was being prepared. A few days before our final press deadline, his corporation withdrew.

This in itself, perhaps, is a comment on the conservative spokesman's hesitancy to defend a point of view that is still prevalent in business circles, but increasingly unpopular in the public forum.

Ms. Theresa Abbott is Director, Community Relations, National Welfare Rights Organization. The motto of NWRO is "Adequate Income, Dignity, Justice, Democracy." Ms. Abbott signed her letter to me, "Bread, peace, justice."

COMMENTS ON CORPORATE SOCIAL INVOLVEMENT

The National Welfare Rights Organization is an association dedicated to the premise that poor people, as American citizens and human beings, have the right to equal justice, dignity and adequate income. The majority of NWRO members are people who have been forced, by various circumstances of misfortune, into the country's welfare system for the poor. The programs have always reflected the American view of inequality towards the poor. *Their* plight is viewed as *their* fault, and a deliberately placed flaw in the country's self concept of a rich land of democracy and equal opportunity for all. Therefore, they should be treated accordingly.

This view places poor people at the opposite end of the spectrum with the corporate structure. Money and a material value system is the name of the game for success in the United States.

The struggle by poor people today is to overcome hunger, malnutrition, poor health care, poor housing, poor education, economic exploitation and social deprivation. These are the conditions of the social community of poor people—the children, the aged, the sick, the handicapped, the unskilled, the uneducated.

The prospect of real corporate social involvement as it would relate to this kind of social community would stretch the imagination, and yet, for the eventual welfare of the corporate structure as well as the poor society, such involvement is necessary.

The corporate structure would have to put aside the value of dollars as success and measure dollars as a means for successful change in the human condition. Anything less would be an empty gesture which would not appease even the conscience nor justify the involvement of dollar-minded philanthropic corporations.

One approach for corporate involvement in the social community for the poor would be to utilize their expertise on welfare programs for the rich and apply it to welfare programs for the poor; direct their power toward adequate legislation and sufficient funding for programs that would alleviate the nation's problems inflicted upon the poor society. Corporations should exercise some restraint from "social involvement" unless it can be valid.

June 8, 1972   **Theresa Abbott**

From "PLAYBOY Interview: Saul Alinsky"
March, 1972; copyright 1972 by Playboy.

Saul Alinsky needs little introduction. His activism as a professional radical organizer, and the work of his Chicago-based Industrial Areas Foundation clearly illustrate his commitment to a revolution of powerless people throughout the country.

Alinsky was a very busy man. A typical day started in Chicago, paused in New York, dined in Los Angeles, and stopped-over in Philadelphia. And yet, he took the time to answer my request for a contribution to *Profiles of Involvement*—probably one of the last things he wrote—proving his fundamental belief in and personal commitment to communications.

His comment speaks for itself, but it speaks to *Profiles of Involvement* and to corporate America as a clear and articulate challenge.

Is Alinsky's assessment right, or will this book, as a start, prove that corporate America will effectively rise to the challenge of social involvement?

INDUSTRIAL AREAS FOUNDATION
EIGHT SOUTH MICHIGAN AVENUE
TELEPHONE 236-1931
CHICAGO, ILL. 60603

June 8, 1972

EXECUTIVE DIRECTOR
SAUL D. ALINSKY

Miss Muffet Russell Shayon
Editor
Human Resources Network
2010 Chancellor Street
Philadelphia, Pennsylvania   19103

Dear Muffet:

How could I possibly turn you down. You caught me at a bad time with
at least six different deadlines for this month. Hence a brief comment
rather than a 15 to 2500 word exposition. One of my old college professors who was that rare specie, an educator, and one who really got me
turned on used to say, "Until you can express your idea in one, or at the
most, two sentences, you just haven't thought it through." I have found
that time has repeatedly verified the validity of that comment.

Now for your "Profiles of Involvement" on your section, "The Corporate
Section" - ready?

A Profile of Involvement of Corporate America would shape up in the
form of the latter's buttocks. From the ecological view these buttocks
have been strangers to toilet paper. I have always maintained that the
establishment can never hear you through their ears but only up their
rears and that any approach or tactic to involve corporate America
should be designed not for a mystical altruistic high road but always the
anal avenue. The establishment, like any other establishment - government, religious institution, any power group - only responds in the face
of a threat.

For various tactical reasons we of the anti-establishment coined the
phrase and myth of a so-called "corporate conscience" or "community
responsibility" to provide the necessary moral clothing to cover the
nakedness of the threat which is the sole compelling reason for the
corporation getting "involved" on the side of the people. Make no mis-
take about it and never forget that corporations have always been
"involved" but against the people from the very beginning when they
were referred to as the Robber Barons to now when they are the robber
lords of the world; where before the highjacking was limited to Cincinnati
it is now expanded to include Saigon. When we use the term "involvement"
here, it carries the meaning of any other word which is relative and here
it means involved socially on the side of the people.

Similarly for tactical reasons the corporate structure has found it difficult
to disavow the obvious absurdity of its having a conscience or a public
commitment since it is constantly at war with the central federal government, fearful of and constantly accusing the government with intrusion
upon the domain of the mythical so-called "private sector". Obviously a
corporate structure claiming a particular power domain must admit to
a responsibility and to conscience for its necessary rationalization.

Realistically the only commitment which corporations have is to make a
profit. The Friedman school of economics at the University of Chicago
and Barron's Weekly Magazine are correct in taking that position. The
fact is that the profit motive is the motivation, the beginning and the end
all for our corporate structures. Realistically the only way to get our
corporations involved in cleaning up pollution would be to show them how
they could make more of a profit in eliminating pollution rather than in
continuing to cause it or get the kind of legislation and implementation of it
to put them out of business. Social involvement or the corporate morality
is a very simple one - moral principle = financial principal and therein
lies the whole "Profile of Involvement."

Cordially,

Saul D. Alinsky

SDA:gh

The earth
belongs
always to
the living
generation.
Thomas
Jefferson

corporate profiles

Corporate Profiles:

The following pages contain the corporate profiles—brief case studies of those programs which corporations have implemented in an effort to fulfill their roles as responsible corporate citizens.

We have printed the information as we have received it from the participating companies. Our only editorial changes have been in grammar and format.

The section is divided into sixteen topic areas as follows:

General Community Affairs	Health
Consumer Programs	Minority Enterprise
Drug Abuse	Urban Development
Education	Consumer Safety
Environment	Youth
Housing	Volunteerism
Employment Opportunities	The Arts
Job Training	Miscellaneous

Topics are grouped by related areas and companies are listed alphabetically within each topic. Since certain programs, particularly those relating to young people, were applicable to two topic areas, we have reprinted these programs under both headings for your convenience. In addition, the book contains (in Volume III) three indices which cross-reference the information by topic, company and geographic area.

Obviously, a complete analysis of each program is beyond the scope of this work. Our intent has been to stimulate the interchange of ideas concerning the ways in which business can effectively contribute to solving social problems.

Our reactions to the programs have been varied. We consider some of them to be band-aid efforts to cope with gaping social wounds. Others are half-hearted attempts to develop a good corporate image, while still others are sincere, useful efforts which significantly apply available resources to social problems. The profiles speak clearly for themselves. They are reasonably representative of the corporate community's view of social commitment.

We realize that much of this information will elicit reactions. We welcome this, and have provided reader response cards at the end of the section to help you voice those reactions. But whether the dialogue is between you and us, or you and others, we hope the end result will be to promote the development of more effective, imaginative programs. All of us are searching for the answers.

The complex questions raised by the issue of social involvement are many. We do not suggest that these pages reflect final answers, but they can offer direction to the search for them. They are, in short, a starting point.

general
community affairs

COMMUNITY RELATIONS COMMITTEE OF SALEM, N.J.

ANCHOR HOCKING CORP.
109 N. Broad Street
Lancaster, Oh. 43130

Business: Glass and Plastic Containers,
   Metal Closures, Plastic Closures, Food Service
   Components and Glass Tableware
Sales: 293.2mm
CEO: Roger H. Hetzel   Employees: 14,700

Contact: N. H. Facer
Address: Anchor Hocking Corp., Salem, N.J. 08079
Telephone: (609) 935-4000
Program Reaches: 150-200 directly, 10,000 indirectly
When Started: 1967
Budget: no financial budgeting, only time and office
   supplies, and occasional contributions which are part
   of the general contribution budget

Program Outline:

The purpose of this program is to relieve racial tensions and to involve large numbers of citizens in identifying and solving community problems. In conferences with representatives of city government, civic, social and industrial organizations and citizens at large, positive factors affecting community life and race relations are identified first. Negative factors or problems are later identified, followed by group problem-solving sessions and assignment of project groups for in-depth investigation and implementation of solutions. Plans include training more people in the techniques of conference leading and problem solving in order to reduce heavy dependency on industrial leadership, therefore transferring visible leadership to private citizens and groups. The program is co-sponsored by H. J. Heinz, Mannington Mills and the National Bottle Company.

Co. Personnel Involved: 3-10; Industrial Relations Manager operates as leader and representative of the town's largest industry.

Measure of Success: There have been no riots or civil disturbances in this small community (10,000) 45% Black, in spite of rioting in communities 20 miles away; the first community swimming pool has been built; there have been 4 new Black volunteer firemen in 4 years; a day-care center has been expanded and improved; playground and recreational facilities have been created; churches are actively involved in community relations; teenagers are still willing to talk about problems and needed improvements; there is a current effort to organize Boy's Club of America; the mayor has established "Town Meetings" in which project groups are formed for problem solving.

PARENT, CHILD, COMMUNITY

BANK OF AMERICA
P. O. Box 37000
San Francisco, Cal. 94317

Business: Banking   Sales: not applicable
CEO: A. W. Clausen   Employees: 31,700

Contact: Jack L. Gescheider, Asst. V.P.
Address: Area Development 4120
   555 Flower Street
   Los Angeles, Cal. 90071
Telephone: (213) 683-3241
Program Reaches: 75 children and parents
When Started: 1971
Budget: n/a

Program Outline:

This program attempts to provide community and cultural awareness in predominantly Mexican-American populated East Los Angeles through parent-child shared learning experiences. The program provides an educational experience for these minority group individuals who, on consecutive Saturdays, visit a dairy, a local library, California State Polytechnic Institute, police and fire stations, the California Museum of Science and Industry, Olvera Street and the Plaza (restored center of old Los Angeles). Emphasis is on person-to-person relationships benefitting both volunteers and participants.

Co. Personnel Involved: Twenty bilingual employees serve as volunteers and counselors.

Measure of Success: The Spring, 1971 program was so successful that the Bank issued a special report for the benefit of communities throughout the state.

CRISPUS ATTUCKS YOUTH CENTER

BORG-WARNER CORP.—YORK DIVISION
P.O. Box 1592
York, Pa. 17405

Business: Manufacturing Air Conditioning, Heating, Refrigerating Equipment, Automatic Ice Makers, Oxygen Chambers, and Air Purifiers
Sales: 1,115mm
CEO: James F. Bere   Employees: 41,500

Contact: Ralph G. Meisenhelder
Address: same as above
Telephone: (717) 843-0731
Program Reaches: 2,300
When Started: 1969
Budget: $1,300,000

Program Outline:

This program's purpose is to lend assistance in the forms of money, equipment and personnel to the community-wide task of relocating and revitalizing the Crispus Attucks Center in York, Pa. The facility would provide constructive and recreational opportunities for the Black Youth of the City in an effort to alleviate racial tensions in the City.

Careful consideration of several worthwhile community projects led to the conclusion that the purpose could be best served by supporting the Crispus Attucks re-development project. The Center was originally conceived in 1931 and by 1969, when the city of York was torn by racial dissent and strife, was sorely in need of revitalization. In fact, post-strife investigations indicated that the racial conflict was due, in part at least, to the fact that young people had no recreational and constructive opportunities. York initiated its involvement by seeking the support of Borg-Warner's Foundation and by taking a leadership role in a city-wide fund-raising effort to build a new community center.

Co. Personnel Involved: Four York Division of Borg-Warner Corporation employees were involved in this project. Initially, a group of 5 key employees evaluated the merits of the Crispus Attucks project and other community efforts. Subsequently other employees joined the effort filling various volunteer roles.

Measure of Success: n/a

COMMUNITY RELATIONS/UNIVERSITY STUDENTS

CASTLE & COOKE, INC.
Drawer 2990
Honolulu, Hi. 96802

Business: Food Products, Land Development, Manufacturing and Merchandising
Sales: 507mm
CEO: Malcolm MacNaughton   Employees: 15,000

Contact: Emil A. Schneider, P.R. Dir.
Address: same as above
Telephone: (808) 548-6611
Program Reaches: about 60 outside company
When Started: n/a
Budget: $500/year

Program Outline:

The program aims, through informal meetings with business students, to give them a better idea of how a major company operates and to let the company learn about the student viewpoints. Face-to-face meetings of this kind are the most valuable means of reaching a better understanding between business and college students who think that business is composed of nothing but robber barons.

Three to 4 sessions are held per school year with groups of 12-15 students per meeting, along with 1 or 2 professors; all from the business college. The program involves a half-hour slide presentation depicting the company's varying operations followed by a question and answer session. This is followed by a tour and lunch with question and answer sessions with 2 or 3 of the company's top executives. The purpose of these sessions is not recruiting. They provide not only an opportunity for the students to learn more about business, but for our business executives to learn more about the student viewpoint and why that viewpoint exists.

Co. Personnel Involved: 12-15 people, 3-6 hours/year/person on the average

Measure of Success: Desired expansion is a result of favorable reaction on all sides.

STREET BANKER PROGRAM

CHEMICAL BANK
20 Pine Street
New York, N.Y. 10015

Business: Banking　　　　　Sales: not applicable
CEO: Howard W. McCall, Jr.　Employees: 12,523

Contact: C. Douglas Ades, Dir.
Address: Urban Affairs Dept., 14th fl., same as above
Telephone: (212) 770-4725
Program Reaches: approx. 25% of city's 8,000,000
When Started: May, 1970
Budget: n/a

Program Outline:

The purpose of the program is to develop, recommend and direct the Bank's programs aimed at solving the most critical social and economic problems in New York City's underprivileged areas. Particular emphasis is placed on assisting the Black and Spanish Speaking communities.

The program takes an aggressive approach to assisting the most troubled areas of the city. The street banker goes out to meet with the business and community leaders rather than waiting for them to come to the Bank. He attends all community functions and meetings and develops a confidence among businessmen. Having had previous exposure to banking services, the street banker is able to offer facilities which the community people are not aware of. In addition to the prime contact made by the street banker, the Bank has support personnel in all the major service departments who are trained to give any assistance needed to minority members in meeting the Bank's regular criteria.

Co. Personnel Involved: Eight full time members of the Urban Affairs Department as well as 3 employees in the minority loan staff are involved. There are many specialists in the Bank who assist on individual projects.

Measure of Success: In the economic area, Chemical Bank has greatly increased the loans to minority businessmen and for low-income housing. Social activities, i.e. Drug Educations Programs, etc., are more difficult to evaluate.

URBAN AFFAIRS

CHRYSLER CORP.
P.O. Box 1919
Detroit, Mich. 48231

Business: Automotive Manufacturing
Sales: 7,000mm
CEO: John J. Riccardo　　　Employees: 228,000

Contact: Albert J. Dunmore
Address: same as above
Telephone: (313) 956-2566
Program Reaches: citizens where Chrysler plants are located
When Started: November, 1969
Budget: n/a

Program Outline:

The purpose of the department of Urban Affairs within the company's operation is to counsel and guide the company in its actions relative to urban issues affecting both its internal and external environments. Aside from arranging financial contributions to minority-oriented organizations, Chrysler has assigned some 20 executives and management personnel to work with the urban coalition—New Detroit. Cars, vans and trucks are loaned for varying periods of time to many organizations involved in inner city projects. Drugmobiles are on loan for an anti-drug campaign in Washington, D.C. Employees serve on board of a number of organizations. In addition, many Chrysler experts have devoted much time and effort to Junior Achievement programs for the inner city youth. Internally, the department endeavors to keep the needs of minority employees constantly before management.

Co. Personnel Involved: 4 persons on department staff

Measure of Success: The successes are not readily measurable except in terms of public acceptance of the product and the institution.

COMMUNITY DEVELOPMENT CORP.

CITIZENS AND SOUTHERN NATIONAL BANK
99 Annex
Atlanta, Ga. 30399

Business: Banking   Sales: not applicable
Total Assets: $2,065,374,460
CEO: Mills B. Lane, Jr.   Employees: 3,550

Contact: William J. Van Landingham
Address: same as above
Telephone: (404) 588-2774
Program Reaches: all major Georgia cities
When Started: 1968
Budget: Currently CDC has a $3 million capital base.

Program Outline:

Community Development Corp. is a wholly-owned subsidiary of Citizens and Southern National Bank, founded for the purpose of providing minority business loans and low-income business loans, home mortgages for low-income families and low-income housing.

Business loans are made to those individuals who qualify, taking into consideration character, ability, and potentially profitable business projections. Home mortgages are provided to families who have never owned a home. Down payment financing is provided through second mortgages; first mortgages are placed in C&S National Bank or with other lenders. Five low-income housing projects have been built or renovated throughout Georgia. The businesses are provided managerial assistance by a young bank officer or management trainee on a continuing basis. Families purchasing their homes are given budgetary counseling. The housing projects have all been approached with the concept that environmental change and upgrading can substantially improve a family's present status and outlook.

The lending function of CDC is now being administered by the Bank's Term Loan Department to enable a broader managerial and technical assistance. However, all business loans are still being made by CDC.

Co. Personnel Involved: approximately 20 people on a statewide basis involved with CDC

Measure of Success: To date, 210 businesses have been financed with a total investment of $2.3 million. Over 300 home mortgages have been provided with over $800,000 currently outstanding. The 5 housing projects have produced over 200 living units.

SPRING CLEAN-UP

CITIZENS AND SOUTHERN NATIONAL BANK
99 Annex
Atlanta, Ga. 30399

Business: Banking   Sales: not applicable
Total Assets: 2,065mm
CEO: Mills B. Lane, Jr.   Employees: 3,550

Contact: William J. Van Landingham
Address: same as above
Telephone: (404) 588-2774
Program Reaches: all disadvantaged citizens in 44 Georgia cities
When Started: 1968
Budget: $500,000 in the first 2 years

Program Outline:

The purpose of the plan is to coordinate community forces for the solving of common community problems. The first step was a 2-day massive clean-up of selected target areas in Savannah, Georgia, followed by similar clean-ups across the state.

The organization of the clean-up campaign was built around individual homes, local churches and schools. An effort was made to coordinate as much of the community as possible. The business community pledged trucks, wreckers, and equipment and the Bank provided residents with free fencing, garbage cans and an American flag for those who did a good job.

The target areas that were cleaned were the low-income, predominantly Black communities that were in need of incentive to attack and solve some of their problems. The clean-up, through the coordination of various segments of the community for this common goal, provided some of that incentive. Most importantly, lines of communication between the minority community and the community-at-large were opened.

The Bank hopes that this type of project will continue on an on-going basis. Many independent clean-ups have been organized on a volunteer basis, sparked by the original clean-ups.

Co. Personnel Involved: The Bank's president was the initiator of the project, the Bank's Community Development Corporation staff was intimately involved in the planning and coordinating.

Measure of Success: The clean-up activities across the state were considered to be an overwhelming success. In one city (Savannah) alone, over 150 tons of debris and 78 junk autos were removed from a 109 square block area. A different aspect of success was gained by all participants who felt an increased pride in community spirit, a feeling that previously impossible problems could be solved.

CITIZENS AND SOUTHERN NATIONAL BANK SPRING CLEAN-UP PROGRAM

BEFORE

AFTER

SPRING SWING TO PLAYGROUNDS

CITIZENS & SOUTHERN NATIONAL BANK
99 Annex
Atlanta, Ga. 30399

Business: Banking   Sales: not applicable
Total Assets: 2,065mm
CEO: Mills B. Lane, Jr.   Employees: 3,550

Contact: William J. Van Landingham
Address: same as above
Telephone: (404) 588-2774
Program Reaches: hard to estimate
When Started: 1971
Budget: $250,000

Program Outline:

The purpose of this program is to provide Georgia cities with new playgrounds and to upgrade existing sites which have been neglected through a lack of municipal funds.

C&S undertook to provide this improvement through the coordinating of manpower and money from all segments of the community. In Savannah, 7 out of 10 banks and savings and loan institutions provided funds and volunteers to build new playgrounds. Existing city and county property was utilized as playground sites in addition to some privately owned property. Through the coordination of churches, schools, the U.S. Army and the Bank, over 3,500 pieces of equipment were erected in I day across the state to create 155 playgrounds.

Co. Personnel Involved: Public Affairs Department of the Bank coordinated the effort.

Measure of Success: The playgrounds are a reality and the community spirit in putting them together was a measurable quality in that people from all levels of the community were actively, physically involved in putting the equipment together, laying down turf and all the other aspects of building a playground.

AGRICULTURAL LABOR PROGRAM

THE COCA-COLA CO. (FOODS DIVISION)
P. O. Drawer 1734
Atlanta, Ga. 30301

Business: Manufacturing Syrups and Concentrates for Soft Drinks
Sales: 1,606
CEO: J. Paul Austin   Employees: 24,600

Contact: Mr. Garth Hamby
Address: same as above
Telephone: (404) 897-2676
Program Reaches: approximately 1,000
When Started: 1970
Budget: n/a

Program Outline

The Agricultural Labor Program is a program of total redevelopment, short-term improvement and long-term objectives toward the goal of assisting and improving the lives of agricultural workers employed by the company.

The program, which affects the agricultural workers employed in the harvesting crews and groves and their families, is based on 5 underlying principles that guide its activity: (1) involvement of people, (2) emphasis on long-term accomplishment rather than promises, (3) assurance of economic viability, (4) emphasis on self-help, (5) integrated total systems approach. The program incorporates 5 main areas of activity which are: employment and income; housing; health, education and social services; organization development and support; and, community relations and support.

The project is still underway with the emphasis on improving the overall quality of life for the workers through self-improvement in all of the above interrelated fields. Positive action towards the goal is particularly evident in the creation of new housing communities in which workers own their own homes.

Co. Personnel Involved: n/a

Measure of Success: More than ½ of the company's agricultural workers are now year-round, full time employees of Coca-Cola, with all the accompanying benefits. An 85-home community has been partially built and occupied by employees; day care centers have been established. There have been organization development seminars held for all grove and harvesting management from assistant foreman up, involving 115 persons. Written practices consonant with Agricultural Labor Projects objectives have also been established.

DETROITER-OR-DETRACTOR

DETROIT BANK & TRUST
Fort at Washington
Detroit, Mich. 48230

Business: Banking   Sales: not applicable
Assets: 2,400mm
CEO: C. Boyd Stockmeyer   Employees: 2,711

Contact: Charles J. Snell, V.P. & Dir.
    Ret. Marketing
Address: same as above
Telephone: (313) 222-3380
Program Reaches: 4.5 million
When Started: June, 1970
Budget: No new funds were appropriated for the program; rather, monies from the regular advertising and PR budget were diverted to this special program.

Program Outline:

The purpose of this program is to remind Detroiters of the many things which are taking place in the city and especially to reawaken interest in the many activities which take place in only downtown Detroit. The advertising staff develops ad materials for daily newspapers and outdoor advertising. The public relations staff inaugurates public relations programs, principally calendars of activities taking place in downtown Detroit and kiosks promoting these activities in selected central city offices.

Phase I involved a series of newspaper ads, later expanded to outdoor advertising, and the introduction of COD (Center of Detroit) calendars and the installation of the kiosks. Phase II involved the Bank's mid-year earnings statement being transformed into a special 4-page section in 2 Detroit daily newspapers which updated the information on the good things happening in the city.

The initial full-scale program has now evolved into a reminder-type project. Plans are underway for still additional projects in 1972.

Co. Personnel Involved: Marketing staff and advertising agency carried most of the responsibility after approval was given by senior management.

Measure of Success: Good response from the public and from many government officials and community leaders.

COMMUNITY RELATIONS TEAMS

EASTERN AIR LINES, INC.
10 Rockefeller Plaza
New York, N.Y. 10020

Business: Transportation, Hotels,
  Distribution Services
Sales: 971mm
CEO: Samuel L. Higginbottom   Employees: 31,500

Contact: M. L. Lethbridge, Staff V.P.—Civic Affairs
Address: same as above
Telephone: (212) 956-7838
Program Reaches: impossible to estimate
When Started: n/a
Budget: n/a

Program Outline:

The purpose of the program is to encourage Eastern personnel to serve their local communities by participating actively in local civic and charitable organizations. Under the auspices of the Public Affairs Department, community relations teams made up of Eastern employees have been formed in 75 cities. Each team adopts appropriate local action and members serve as individuals in local civic, charitable, educational and service groups. The teams may also take group action in these areas.

Co. Personnel Involved: approx. 1,350

Measure of Success: number of people involved

URBAN ECONOMIC ANALYSIS

FIRST NATIONAL CITY BANK
399 Park Avenue
New York, N.Y. 10022

Business: Banking   Sales: not applicable
CEO: William I. Spencer   Employees: 31,700

Contact: Nathan Bloom, S.E.
Address: same as above
Telephone: (212) 559-4725
Program Reaches: 15,000
When Started: 1966
Budget: staff time and printing cost

Program Outline:

The purpose of this program is to make a significant contribution toward the public understanding of the economic and social strength and problems of New York City and the New York Region, and to influence improved policy implementations.

During the past 5 years, the Bank has published the following studies: Metropolis New York; the Port of New York; Poverty and Economic Development in New York; Public Education in New York City; Housing in New York City; The Financial Position of the City of New York in Long-Term-Perspective; Transportation in the New York Region; and Pollution. In addition, pertinent articles on the problems of New York, as well as urban areas in general, are published in the Bank's Monthly Economic Letter.

Co. Personnel Involved: 5 people full time and 2 people part time

Measure of Success: Some of the recent policy changes—such as housing, education and economic development—have been consonant with recommendations of the Bank's studies. In addition, each study has evoked favorable responses from the highest level of government leadership at the Federal, State and Local levels.

CENTRO LATINO

FOREMOST-MCKESSON, INC.
Crocker Plaza
One Post Street
San Francisco, Cal. 94104

Business: Foods, Drugs, Liquor, Chemicals,
    Home Building
Sales: 1,738mm
CEO: William W. Morison   Employees: 17,400

Contact: Susan Huch or James Wills
Address: same as above
Telephone: (415) 391-6161
Program Reaches: over 500
When Started: Foremost-McKesson took up the project
    in October, 1971.
Budget: Centro Latino receives approximately $40,000
    annually from the United Bay Area Crusade and other
    mentioned sources. Foremost-McKesson and the em-
    ployees' support comes to $6,000/year. There is a
    standing bank account for approximately $80 for
    miscellaneous materials for the Center. The various
    fund raising activities cannot be estimated.

Program Outline:

Centro Latino provides essential community services to
the people in San Francisco's outer Mission District,
predominantly of lower socio-economic levels. These
activities range from free food programs for school
children to weaving classes. Since Centro Latino is part of
a relatively young program called Involvement Corps, it
also provides a medium for involvement for the employees of Foremost-McKesson at corporate headquarters
office in San Francisco. Centro Latino receives direct
financial support from the United Crusade, the CYO and
the Episcopal Church, and Levi Strauss. This money is
used to pay the staff and provide office materials for the
various activities. Centro Latino serves as a branch of the
International Child Art Center of San Francisco and as
the editorial office for a bi-lingual (Spanish/English)
community newspaper. Foremost-McKesson employees
have become involved primarily in the feeding program,
assisting in various field trips, painting projects and fund
raising. The money from the fund raising is used to buy
materials for the various activities of Centro Latino. As
the Corpsman on the project leaves, it is possible that the
areas of involvement will expand from the food and field
trip programs into other sectors.

Co. Personnel Involved: approx. 40 individuals at corporate headquarters

Measure of Success: The food program, through various
donations from employees of corporate headquarters, is
feeding breakfast to approximately 100 children a day at
Centro Latino. The corporation and the employees
(through voluntary payroll deductions) are presently
sustaining the Corpsman and providing administrative
funds for the Involvement Corps.

INSTANT PARK

GAC CORP.
825 S. Bayshore Drive
Miami, Fla. 33131

Business: Holding Company, Retail Automobile Parts,
    Manufacturing Truck Trailers and Heavy Machinery
    and Equipment
Sales: 1,760mm
CEO: S. Hayward Wills   Employees: 12,000

Contact: Richard Warner, Dir. of P.R.
Address: same as above
Telephone: (305) 358-3330
Program Reaches: n/a
When Started: 1971
Budget: n/a

Program Outline:

The purpose of the Instant Park program is to participate
in a community effort in the "instant" building of a park
in the Liberty City area of Miami, and to demonstrate
what people working together can do.

The park was to be built in 30 hours, from the morning
of July 23 to the afternoon of the 24th. When the dust
had settled on the second day, there was a concrete
wading pool with a multi-sprinkler fountain. In one
corner was a climbing system of columns of varying
heights. There was a slide, sand, grass, trees, benches and
a miniature amphitheatre complete with stage.

The deadline of 30 hours was set up to show in a
dramatic fashion what a group of well-intentioned individuals can achieve with a great deal of determination in a
very short period of time.

Co. Personnel Involved: Many in originating, planning
and coordinating the various sponsors; others volunteered
their time during the actual 30 hours of construction.

Measure of Success: The park was built in 30 hours.

COMMUNITY AFFAIRS TV PROGRAMS

General Foods Corp.
250 North Street
White Plains, N. Y. 10625

Business: Processed Food   Sales: 2,500mm
CEO: Tex Cook   Employees: 44,000

Contact: J. H. Singer
Address: same as above
Telephone: (914) 694-2417
Program Reaches: millions
When Started: 1969
Budget: approx. $2 million

Program Outline:

See article.

Co. Personnel Involved: 5, picking programs and evaluating them

Measure of Success: more than 140 different programs in various areas of the country on 40 different TV stations; Television Bureau of Advertising special award to General Foods for its "Commitment to better community involvement through sponsorship of meaningful local programs;" 1971 duPont-Columbia University Award for GF-sponsored documentary, "Warrior Without a Weapon," on KU-TV; Salt Lake City, Utah, program on the problems of the Gosiute Indians.

GOING TO THE PEOPLE

By sponsoring local programs, a giant corporation becomes involved in community affairs

By Richard K. Doan

What's a big corporate giant like General Foods doing spending money to sponsor a high school quiz show every week on a Schenectady, N.Y., TV station?

Or a live phone-in program with Oklahoma's governor David Hall on an Oklahoma City station?

Or a panel discussion on a Washington, D.C., station at the height of the My Lai controversy, assessing the question "Lt. Calley: Right or Wrong?"

Or dozens of other local public-affairs specials and series like these, all across the country—oftentimes without commercials?

Call it do-goodism, corporate responsibility, good-exampleism. General Foods people insist it's just good business. It even sells groceries, they claim.

In any case, they're so pleased with the way the public responds to these uncommon ventures in local sponsorship—there have been more than 130 on a total of 35 different stations so far—that they are continuing, they say, to seize such opportunities as fast as they turn up.

It all started about three years ago when a Los Angeles station, CBS's KNXT, came up with a "Black on Black" special examining the causes of the Watts race riots, and invited General Foods, on a long shot, to sponsor it. "We recognized the public-service value of it and decided to buy it," recalls F. Kent Mitchel, GF's vice president for corporate marketing.

Impressed with a batch of thank-you letters from viewers, GF officials put out word that they would be receptive to sponsoring such programming in other cities.

Upshot: General Foods credits began turning up in city after city on locally produced news and public-affairs telecasts. The programs ranged from such innocuous items as coverage of the Ohio State Fair and a Los Angeles Halloween parade to a Phoenix prime-time documentary on "Desert Survival" and a New York station's inquiry into "Methadone—Escape from Heroin."

None of these programs, to be sure, was outrageously controversial. And General Foods makes no secret of shunning public-issue programs where the views expressed are not "balanced" and which in any manner "damage the reputation of the sponsor as a responsible corporate citizen" (a seemingly unlikely development).

Still, Bob Gillespie, GF manager of "local media services," who handpicks the local sponsorships, and Joe Singer, who as public-relations director helps decide what

GF will buy, feel that they've tackled a few mildly risky ones. They were "nervous," says Singer, about a quickly arranged forum on a New York channel debating whether the Pentagon Papers should have been published. (Instead, all GF got were several letters of appreciation.)

General Foods admittedly, too, seldom runs a risk of seeing something on the air under its sponsorship that it had not anticipated. "Nearly all of the time," according to Gillespie, GF officials have an advance, approving look at the local programs, a practice the networks sternly forbid.

Even so, the GF local-TV efforts have been productive of unusual recognition. The judges of the 1971 Alfred I. duPont-Columbia University Awards thought enough of a GF-sponsored Salt Lake City documentary on the Gosiute Indians, "Warrior Without a Weapon," to give it one of seven awards.

Last November the Television Bureau of Advertising, an industry group, bestowed a special award on General Foods for its "commitment to better community involvement through sponsorship of meaningful local programs."

"We would hope—even pray—that this award would cause other sponsors . . . to look deeply and seriously into the benefits of local public-service programming," GF's Mitchel avowed in accepting the award. Recently he conceded nobody else seemed yet to have bought the idea.

GF, he adds, is prepared "to hang in there" despite low ratings for some of these efforts, and indeed anticipates increasing its participation in such entertainment-plus-education shows next fall. One prospect: an animated-cartoon special on geology called "Dig," to be aired April 8 on CBS, may become a GF-sponsored series.

GF's notion of local involvement, however, could well be the most significant recent development in TV sponsorship, if the enthusiastic view of it at one station is any criterion. Oklahoma City's KOCO-TV has just embarked on a second year of GF-sponsored public-affairs programming, including a monthly prime-time documentary, a weekly late-evening local-issues forum, and instant news specials.

"The response here toward General Foods has been terrific," reports Arthur D. Glenn, KOCO-TV's general manager. "People feel that a major manufacturer has become a good local neighbor."

Even GF executives admit this sort of TV do-gooding is just a drop in their ad budget: "Less that 5 per cent" of GF's total TV spot expenditure of some $40 million annually goes into it. At that, Mitchel claims GF buys just about "all there is" that really looks attractive in such local programming.

Roughly two-thirds of the programs carry hard-sell commercials for GF cereals, coffee and other products. "We don't view it as throwing our money away," Gillespie says. "These programs do sell products."

If all this works so well at the local level, does General Foods propose to take such an enlightened approach at the national level?

Oh, but it already does, insists Mitchel, citing GF's full sponsorship on NBC several years ago of *Julia*, the series that made Diahann Carroll TV's first black female star. Last summer, GF was part-sponsor of CBS's surprisingly popular airing of the BBC dramas *The Six Wives of Henry VIII*.

And most notably of all, 40 per cent of GF's advertising in children's programs currently is going into such recent entries as NBC's *Take a Giant Step*, CBS's *You Are There* and ABC's *Curiosity Shop*. Mitchel says proudly: "We're in every program on the networks that could be called 'upgraded.' We feel a responsibility to support this sort of thing."

And if General Foods up until recently has not been noted for raising any hackles in its local public-affairs sponsorships, it's possible the corporate giant is embarking now upon a somewhat more venturesome approach. In reply to the question of whether General Foods seemed to shun controversial programs. KOCO-TV's manager remonstrated: "On the contrary, they've been urging us to get more involved in local issues."

These days, word like that from a sponsor is rarer than a happy TV critic.

GREAT WESTERN UNITED FOUNDATION

GREAT WESTERN UNITED CORP.
Equitable Building
17th and Stout
Denver, Colo. 80202

Business: Marketing (Real Estate, Sugar, Pizza)
Sales: 241mm
CEO: William M. White   Employees: 4,497

Contact: Michael C. Moore
Address: same as above
Telephone: (303) 893-4327
Program Reaches: several hundred
When Started: November, 1968
Budget: 1% pre-tax profits of Great Western United
    Corporation ($150,000-330,000/year)

Program Outline:

The purpose of the foundation is to establish a philanthropic arm of the corporation which is responsive to social issues contributing most significantly to the breakdown of social order, confrontation and violence. The program is aimed toward helping Blacks, Chicanos, American Indians, young people with drug problems and the environment. Approximately 2/3 of the grants which are made by the Foundation emerge out of the initiatives of Foundation staff working with individuals or groups who appear to have the capability to effectively address the specific social problems in which they are concerned. The remaining 1/3 of the grants are in response to requests from promising organizations to address similar kinds of problems.

Co. Personnel Involved: 4 corporate officers (Chairman of the Board, Great Western United Corporation; President, Great Western Sugar Co.; President, Shakey's, Inc.; Vice President, Planning and Development, Great Western Cities Company) are the Trustees of the Foundation. The Director of Social Planning, Great Western Cities Company is the Program Director of the Foundation.

Measure of Success: Many of the organizations to whom seed money grants have been made available have subsequently become economically viable by finding support from other sources.

COUNTERPART

HEWLETT-PACKARD CO.
1501 Page Mill Road
Palo Alto, Cal. 94304

Business: Electronic, Medical, Analytical and Computing Instruments
CEO: William R. Hewlett   Employees: 16,000

Contact: Kemp Miller
Address: 1010 Doyle Street
    Menlo Park, Cal. 94025
Telephone: (415) 325-0075
Program Reaches: n/a
When Started: 1966
Budget: n/a

Program Outline:

Counterpart is an organization of Blacks and Whites working together to solve the problems of the primarily Black communities of East Palo Alto and East Menlo Park.

This organization has played a progressive role in improving the area's economic, educational, cultural and social environments. Counterpart's primary objective of achieving total development for the area necessitates its becoming involved in a wide variety and range of projects—everything from painting homes and finding jobs to purchasing and renovating an entire shopping center.

While HP is not involved in policy-making decisions in Counterpart, company officials are available as advisors and consultants. The organization was established by Kemp Miller, an HP employee, who sought and received initial financial backing from the company. Miller was given a paid 6-month's leave of absence to direct Counterpart activities. At the end of this period, it was felt that he should be on a "loaned executive" status, and he currently is directing Counterpart full time while continuing to receive his salary from HP.

Co. Personnel Involved: Kemp Miller and an unknown number of volunteers. Some public relations pieces (brochures and a film, for example) have been produced for Counterpart by HP personnel on company time and with company funds.

Measure of Success: In 1971, Paint up/Clean up operations were completed on about 50 houses and yards, summer jobs were provided for about 50 young men, a $200,000 renovation of the Nairobi Shopping Center was completed (including carpentry, plumbing, electrical work and painting involving all shops and offices in the 80,000-square-foot complex), ground breaking ceremonies were held for Kelly Park in East Menlo Park (climaxing 3 years of planning for this 5,000 square foot Girls' Club facility, restrooms were constructed at the EPA Little League Park built by Counterpart (now 90% complete), and various funds were disbursed for a myriad of projects such as a student Assistance Fund and a children's fund for breakfast and lunch programs. Other programs are in the planning and development stages and Counterpart sponsors various events and fund raising activities.

INVOLVEMENT CORPS

HEWLETT-PACKARD CO.
1501 Page Mill Road
Palo Alto, Cal. 94304

Business: Electronic, Medical, Analytical and Computing Instrumentation
Sales: 375mm
CEO: William R. Hewlett   Employees: 16,000

Contact: Harley Halverson or John Nidecker

Address: same as above
Telephone: (415) 493-1501
Program Reaches: community
When Started: n/a
Budget: n/a

Program Outline:

The purpose of this program is to provide a convenient means for persons to become involved in a variety of community interest programs and projects.

Essentially, the Palo Alto-based Involvement Corps encourages people to band together in task forces that can be set about doing something active and concrete in an area of common concern or interest. Ideally, each task force is made up of 50 or more persons who pledge to underwrite the activity of a full-time corpsman who represents them in the field. Often the corpsman is a young college graduate who commits as least 2 years of part or full time service on a particular problem in the community where his or her abilities can be applied. The Involvement Corps itself provides a central clearinghouse and communications center for the various task forces.

The Involvement Corps is a volunteer community organization, but some companies do sponsor a task force, either formally or informally.

Co. Personnel Involved: about 15 persons

Measure of Success: One task force headed by an HP individual has become involved in rehabilitating an abandoned grocery store in East Palo Alto, hoping eventually to put it into the hands of Black ownership and management to better serve the primarily Black community. Another force headed by an HP person was instrumental in establishing Ecology Action of Palo Alto, a waste recycling center serving the Palo Alto community. Many other projects currently are underway.

EL MODENA

HUNT-WESSON FOODS, INC.
1645 W. Valencia Drive
Fullerton, Cal. 92634

Business: Manufacturing Foods and Matches
Sales: 400mm
CEO: Edward Gelsthorpe   Employees: 6,800

Contact: Kenneth J. Ward, Dir. Corp. Rel.
Address: same as above
Telephone: (714) 871-2100
Program Reaches: 3-5,000
When Started: May, 1970
Budget: $5,000

Program Outline:

The El Modena Program is a community project, designed to help Spanish families at the community level. This entails sending a team of home economists to El Modena to help Spanish families translate and write up recipes that have been passed along for generations by word of mouth. Translating measurements such as 2 or 3 handfuls of flour, and pinches of salt, etc. into actual measurements, and putting together a recipe booklet in both Spanish and English was involved. The booklets were then given to the community so that they could be sold and needed funds raised through them.

Co. Personnel Involved: 5 translating recipes and designing and printing the booklets

Measure of Success: The booklet was composed and successfully utilized as a fund raiser.

KAISER BAUXITE'S COMMUNITY PROGRAMS

KAISER ALUMINUM & CHEMICAL CORP. (KACC)
Kaiser Center
300 Lakeside Drive
Oakland, Cal. 94604

Business: Aluminum, Chemicals, Specialty Metals
and Refractories Products, and
Diversified Operations
Sales: 881mm
CEO: Thomas J. Ready, Jr.   Employees: 26,000

Contact: R. L. Spees, Corp. Dir. of Pub. Affairs
Address: same as above
Telephone: (415) 271-3967
Program Reaches: over 1,000
When Started: 1953
Budget: unable to accurately estimate

Program Outline:

Kaiser Bauxite, a subsidiary of KACC, in mining bauxite on the North Coast of Jamaica, has pursued and is continuing a comprehensive community involvement program so that the people of the area, mostly small land farmers, can understand the mining operation and the company behind it.

As part of this program Kaiser Bauxite donated a good portion of the money that has built a new hospital wing at St. Ann's Bay. This hospital serves the Jamaicans of the area and, in addition, Kaiser Bauxite's own health clinic is open for public use and training purposes for medical professionals on the island. In the area of community services, the company has been a leader in the development of beaches and restoring artifacts and historical parks.

Co. Personnel Involved: Company involvement in the whole community involvement program includes: 5 management personnel; liason and support from the parent company in Oakland is supplied by 4 senior management personnel. This does not include the 150 Kaiser Bauxite salaried people working directly and indirectly with the various Jamaican communities.

Measure of Success: 90% of the supervisory personnel employed by the company are Jamaicans, indicating acceptance by the local people of the company presence.

COMMUNITY INVOLVEMENT

MARCOR (MONTGOMERY WARD & CO., INC.)
Box 8339
Chicago, Ill. 60680

Business: General Merchandising
Sales: 3,500mm
CEO: Leo H. Schoenhofen   Employees: 126,000

Contact: Hugh Tassey
Address: same as above
Telephone: (312) 467-6649
Program Reaches: an estimated 100,000
When Started: n/a
Budget: an estimated $20-30,000 annually

Program Outline:

The purpose of the program is to involve the company in tasks to seek solutions to some of the problems of urban communities. Marcor aids communities through its support of local United Funds and Community Chests, YMCA's, 4-H Clubs and other community organizations. Responding to the special problems of inner city communities, the company has expanded its support to the Urban League, the NAACP, the Urban Coalition and other local and national agencies that conduct effective inner city programs, including Youth Organizations and "grass roots" community groups. The company also provides leadership and use of company facilities for youth and adults for personal development activities; facilities and teachers for evening instruction in typing and consumer education; parking lots and playground equipment for summer recreation programs; company employees serve as volunteer tutors to local youngsters. More than 50 employees serve as board members or consultants to inner city community organizations. These various programs may become more structured so that the extent of involvement may be accurately measured.

Co. Personnel Involved: an estimated 100 on a part time basis, 4 on a full time basis

Measure of Success: impossible to estimate

NASHUA CORPORATION FUND, INC.

NASHUA CORP.
44 Franklin Street
Nashua, N.H. 03060

Business: Diversified Coating
CEO: William E. Conway

Sales: 130mm
Employees: 3,480

Contact: Michael A. Horrigan
Address: same as above
Telephone: (603) 883-7711
Program Reaches: undetermined
When Started: 1951
Budget: n/a

Program Outline:

The purpose of the program is to supply resources to projects and programs of community benefit in those communities where the company has production facilities. The Fund acts as a non-profit distributor of funds to non-profit organizations in certain communities and to certain select regional and national organizations for the purpose of bettering the social conditions in areas where the company operates. Potential recipients are screened carefully prior to receiving funds.

Co. Personnel Involved: Many executives are involved with a variety of community endeavors supported through the company Fund.

Measure of Success: n/a

COMMUNITY RESOURCE BANK

RAYBESTOS-MANHATTAN, INC.
205 Middle Street
Bridgeport, Conn.

Business: Friction Materials, Asbestos Textiles,
    Plastics and Industrial Rubber Products
Sales: 146mm
CEO: William S. Simpson

Employees: 7,400

Contact: Frank Williams
Address: same as above
Telephone: (203) 367-8661
Program Reaches: 60,000 community citizens
When Started: October, 1971
Budget: monetarily none

Program Outline:

The purpose of the program is to provide resources to community in a wide variety of areas. The people of Raybestos-Manhattan are available as a resource and community service to citizens of Bridgeport. They list businesses, community organizations and communications assistance between groups to narrow gaps where they might exist. If a service is not listed and is needed the personnel in the company's corporate office are available to help find other sources of aid.

Co. Personnel Involved: services rendered by 27 volunteers

Measure of Success: evaluation of services rendered, diversity of services rendered and number of services rendered

OPERATION BETTER BLOCK

ROCKWELL MANUFACTURING CO.
400 N. Lexington Avenue
Pittsburgh, Pa. 15208

Business: Metal Fabricating   Sales: 300mm
CEO: A. Clark Daugherty   Employees:12,900

Contact: James Givner, Exec. Dir.
Address: 807 N. Homewood Avenue
    Pittsburgh, Pa. 15208
Telephone: (415) 731-0565
Program Reaches: approx. 4,000
When Started: 1970
Budget: approx. $89,000

Program Outline:

The purpose of this program is to rehabilitate and revitalize the physical as well as mental and moral fiber of the ghetto-like neighborhood in Homewood-Brushton, Pittsburgh, on a block-by-block basis.

Operation Better Block was designed as a model of a similar New York City effort. Through the combined efforts of the business, industrial and community residents, an advisory group to guide the community effort was set up. Better Block seeks to work with block associations where they exist and set new ones up where they do not.

A grant of $500 is made to each association with no stipulations on its use except that it must be for the benefit of the entire block. The money is used for basic block improvements. Operation Better Block also loans tools for purposes of fixing up homes. Residents work with the organization to buy paint for repair at a wholesale price. It is hoped that the program can be extended on a statewide basis.

Co. Personnel Involved: Two or 3 as Board Directors; there are 5 staff members of Operation Better Block.

Measure of Success: increase of general community involvement of residents through block associations

COMMUNITY IMPROVEMENT PROGRAM

SEARS, ROEBUCK & CO.
303 E. Ohio Street
Chicago, Ill. 60611

Business: Retail and General Catalogue Merchandising
Sales: 9,262mm
CEO: Arthur M. Wood   Employees: 359,000

Contact: Mrs. Wendell Winger
Address: 242 N. 100 East
    Springville, Utah 84663
Telephone: (801) 489-5263
Program Reaches: n/a
When Started: 1955
Budget: $43,000 approx.

Program Outline:

The purpose of this program is to provide an incentive and a vehicle for community self-help programs.

The program offers national and international awards for community improvement programs. Federated Women's Clubs affiliated with the General Federation of Women's Clubs stimulate projects to analyze community needs and work with cooperating groups to meet those needs. Suggested projects in metropolitan areas: physical and social planning of volunteer or sub-professional services. Rural: area development and cooperation, job opportunities, upgraded housing, and improving availability of health care.

Co. Personnel Involved: n/a

Measure of Success: In June, 1972, winners were announced at the GFWC Annual Convention. Winners unavailable at press date.

CITIZENS FOR ACTING NOW, INC.

SCOTT PAPER CO.
Scott Plaza
Philadelphia, Pa. 19113

Business: Manufacturing Sanitary Paper Products
Sales: 756mm
CEO: Charles D. Dickey, Jr.   Employees: 21,700

Contact: Sam Ross
Address: 2108 W. Third Street
    Chester, Pa. 19013
Telephone: (215) 497-1747
Program Reaches: 4,000 residents of Tract 57 in Chester,
    Pa.
When Started: July, 1970
Budget: $150,000 for 1972

Program Outline:

The purpose of this program is to upgrade persons of Census Tract 57 in Chester, Pa. in the areas of education, housing, employment, health and recreation. The project has a Community Board that sets policy. This program is set up to get specific directions from the community and to move in these 5 general areas. Presently in operation are a day care center, a tutorial program, counseling and referral programs and a youth recreational program. Changes will occur as the community responds and as their needs change.

Co. Personnel Involved: 1 person involved directly, a great number involved indirectly as company supporters

Measure of Success: a new ray of hope for an apathetic population

SK&F INFORMATION SERVICES CENTER

SMITH KLINE AND FRENCH LABORATORIES, INC.
1500 Spring Garden Street
Philadelphia, Pa. 19101

Business: Pharmaceuticals and Other Health Products
Sales: 347mm
CEO: Thomas M. Rauch   Employees: 10,000

Contact: Carver Portlock
Address: 1720 Mt. Vernon Street
    Philadelphia, Pa.
Telephone: (215) 564-2400
Program Reaches: 2,000/year
When Started: 1966
Budget: n/a

Program Outline:

The role of the Information Services Center is to provide whatever assistance it can to enable the community to help itself, making it possible for residents to develop their own sense of direction.

The center provides information and referral services to some 2,000 Spring Garden area residents each year and also serves as a "nerve center" sponsoring and supporting block organizations, Boy, Girl, and Cub scouts and similar groups. It is staffed with people from the local community and is under the supervision of trained and experienced community workers familiar with the neighborhood and its needs.

Co. Personnel Involved: 6

Measure of Success: difficult to measure

MINORITY CONSTRUCTION

UNITED CALIFORNIA BANK
600 S. Spring Street
Los Angeles, Cal. 90054

Business: Banking   Sales: not applicable
CEO: Norman Barker, Jr.   Employees: 10,000

Contact: Dr. Larry Wilson, V.P.
Address: same as above
Telephone: (213) 624-0111, ext. 2813
Program Reaches: n/a
When Started: n/a
Budget: no set budget; activity determined by request

Program Outline:

To aid construction projects by minority groups, the Bank has participated in financial help on various levels:

(1) a construction loan approved to a Black contractor in March, 1971, for the construction of a new postal facility in South Los Angeles. The facility will be owned by a Black corporation and leased back to the postal service ($500,000); (2) funds provided to the Watts-Compton Development Corporation to enable the company to purchase and rehabilitate a small supermarket near a housing facility needing the service; (3) in East Palo Alto, the Bank aided in financing construction of Nairobi Village Shopping Center, a Black-owned and operated facility; (4) White Front Stores, San Francisco, a new discount department store was built with the Bank's help in a mixed neighborhood where a condition of the loan was the substantial employment of minority workers.

Co. Personnel Involved: Depends on particular loan; sometimes a group effort and at other times the local lending officer handles it.

Measure of Success: n/a

SUPERVISOR SOUL TOUR

WESTERN MASSACHUSETTS ELECTRIC CO.
174 Brush Hill Avenue
West Springfield, Mass. 01089

Business: Public Utility   Sales: 66.9mm
CEO: Robert E. Barret, Jr.   Employees: 987

Contact: Mack W. Jacobs
Address: same as above
Telephone: (413) 785-5871, ext. 298
Program Reaches: 250 supervisors and 12 Black and
    Spanish people
When Started:1968
Budget: $2,500

Program Outline:
The purpose of the program is to aid in sensitizing Western Mass. Electric's first line supervisory staff to the problems, conditions and feelings of urban Springfield and its inhabitants first hand. The program also aims to show the Black and Spanish people of the area the company's commitment to equal opportunity by making them part of the project.

Company officers, managers, department-heads and supervisory staff were acquainted with the sights, sounds, smells and attitudes of ghetto life by first-hand experience. This was done by taking the group on a tour of Springfield, Massachusetts center city, talking to the Black and Spanish—speaking residents, listening to their problems, needs and desires. Then, the group ate with leaders of the Black and Spanish community who later formed a panel for a "no-holds-barred," "tell it like it is" question-and-answer period. This was initiated by some provocative planned questions.

Co. Personnel Involved: 10 in planning, 240 involved in participation

Measure of Success: There was very little turnover of minority persons during 1971. The company's minority employment percentage is very close to the company's service area minority percentage.

consumer programs

BETTER BUSINESS BUREAU TV COMMERCIALS

COMPTON ADVERTISING, INC.
625 Madison Avenue
New York, N.Y. 10022

Business: Advertising
CEO: Milton Gossett

Sales: 130mm
Employees: 486

Contact: Woodrow Wirsig, Pres.
Address: 220 Church Street, New York, N.Y. 10013
Telephone: (212) 349-0470
Program Reaches: maximally 200 million consumers in U.S.
When Started: Fall, 1971
Budget: Agency time

Program Outline:

The purpose of the program is the education and protection of the buying public.

The program consists of 10 TV commercials (5 of 60 seconds' duration and 5 of 30 seconds') distributed to TV stations for showing on a public service basis. The function of the commercials is to help consumers recognize the pitfalls most commonly encountered in buying products and services (e.g. bogus free offers, overeasy credit, fly-by-night vendors, etc.) and to encourage them to buy more prudently and thus avoid becoming entangled in the types of problems most often brought to the attention of the Better Business Bureau.

Co. Personnel Involved: The commercials were written by 2 men—a writer-art director team—and produced by these 2 with help of the agency's TV producer and 1 of his assistants.

Measure of Success: (1) Although prepared originally for the BBB of New York, the commercials were deemed so communicative and helpful that they have been adopted by the national BBB Council for distribution nationwide. (2) They have received tremendous play by the TV stations, reflecting, the Bureau believes, the creative excellence of the spots.

CONSUMER EDUCATION

FIRST NATIONAL CITY BANK
399 Park Avenue
New York, N.Y. 10022

Business: Banking
CEO: William I. Spencer

Sales: not applicable
Employees: 31,700

Contact: William G. Herbster, S.V.P.
Address: same as above
Telephone: (212) 559-4211
Program Reaches: publication, up to 80,000
When Started: 1970
Budget: staff and printing costs

Program Outline:

The purpose of the program is to provide people in the market area with a better understanding of consumer credit, consumer buying, family budgeting and other activities relating to wise individual money management.

The Bank publishes a monthly newsletter entitled "Consumer Views." The 4-page booklet, available free at the Bank's branches and distributed by many correspondent banks in other cities to their customers, offers information and advice in such basics as family money management, reducing utility bill costs, etc. A consumer education course is in the process of being designed with a local organization. Upon completion and after training of community people as instructors, the package will be made available to residents in the community.

The Bank has just started to publish their brochure in Spanish as well as English so as to benefit the numerous Spanish-speaking customers in New York.

Co. Personnel Involved: One person full time and 2 part time on the brochure. In addition, about 4 people are involved part time in the design and offering of the consumer education course.

Measure of Success: Because of the heavy demand, the number of copies of the brochure has had to be increased substantially since it first appeared.

CONSUMER PROGRAMS

GIANT FOODS, INC.
P.O. Box 1804
Washington, D.C. 20013

Business: Supermarket Chain   Sales: 477mm
CEO: Joseph B. Danzansky   Employees: 10,700

Contact: Esther Peterson
Address: same as above
Telephone: (202) 341-4365
Program Reaches: n/a
When Started: Mrs. Peterson's involvement began in
    September, 1970
Budget: n/a

Program Outline:

The purpose of this program is to give the consumer representation inside business and to protect the consumer's right to be informed, right to safety, right to choose, right to be heard, right to redress, and right to service.

Giant has provided the consumer with various shopping tools at the point of purchase, including unit pricing and open dating. The company is working toward complete nutritional labeling, full ingredient labeling, and percentage of ingredient labeling, so that consumers will know what is in the food they buy.

Giant also has CYCLE brand recycled paper products, Giant brand laundry soap, low-phosphate and phosphate-free detergents with ingredient listings as part of the company's effort to respond to environmental problems.

More accurate labels have been developed for fish which is now labeled "fresh" or "previously frozen"; and for ground beef, which is labeled according to fat content. Giant will soon introduce a bacon package that shows 70% of a slice, and hot dogs without nitrites or nitrates.

Co. Personnel Involved: Mrs. Peterson plus 3 full time and I part time staff

Measure of Success: n/a

"COMPARE-A-PRICE"

THE GRAND UNION CO.
100 Broadway
East Paterson, N.J. 07407

Business: Retail Food and General Merchandise Chain
Sales: 1,300mm
CEO: Charles G. Rodman   Employees: 26,000

Contact: Jean F. Judge
Address: same as above
Telephone: (201) 796-4800
Program Reaches: upwards of 1.3 million
When Started: November, 1970
Budget: n/a

Program Outline:

The purpose of this program is to help Grand Union customers more easily determine best price buys on the

basis of comparing price per pound, quarter, etc.

"Compare-A-Price" shelf markers under each of more than 4,000 items in Grand Union's 225 New York Region supermarkets show the total price on the right and the unit price—or price per measure—on the left. Window signs, in-store signs and bag stuffers have called attention of shoppers to the program, and explained how it works.

Grand Union is currently developing a standardized format for the shelf markers to comply universally with various state and local unit pricing laws. Unit pricing will also be expanded to other divisions of the company.

Co. Personnel Involved: n/a

Measure of Success: No formal study of success has been conducted, but informal feedback from some customers and consumer educators indicate the system is successful and Grand Union "Compare-A-Price" materials are being used.

PRODUCT LIABILITY LOSS PREVENTION AND CONTROL PROGRAM

Kaiser Aluminum & Chemical Corp.
Kaiser Center
300 Lakeside Drive
Oakland, Cal. 94604

Business: Aluminum, Chemicals, Specialty Metals, Refractory Products, and Diversified Operations
Sales: 904.5mm
CEO: Thomas J. Ready, Jr.   Employees: 26,000

Contact: J. G. Ainsworth, Dir. P.R. Serv.
Address: same as above
Telephone: (415) 271-3437
Program Reaches: in excess of 3,000 (an expanding no.)
When Started: 1971
Budget: for the commercial version, $5,000

Program Outline:

The purpose of the program is to make available to interested outside companies an audio-visual presentation which explains to an audience the hazards of liability due to a faulty process or product. The presentation was developed internally to make employees be more quality conscious and aware of the liability climate; then geared by demand to an outside group.

The audio-visual program is an educational tool whereby employees of user companies are made aware of product quality. The susceptibility of products to sources of liability is emphasized. In addition, the danger of loss stemming from product liability is explained. The presentation introduces a plan of preventative action wherein stress is placed on product reliability and performance.

Co. Personnel Involved: The presentation internally involved approximately 10 people and the version made available to other companies involved 5 people, not counting management support and Aluminum Assn. personnel.

Measure of Success: Presently over 60 firms have purchased the audio-visual presentation for use with their own employees. The Aluminum Association, 750 Third Avenue, New York City 10017 is also selling the presentation. The cost of producing the a/v presentation has been covered by the sales.

CONSUMER CREDIT COUNSELING SERVICE

SIGNAL FINANCE CORP.
1800 Three Gateway Center
Pittsburgh, Pa. 15222

Business: Consumer Finance
Sales: 77mm (loan volume)
CEO: Paul M. Hickox   Employees: 306

Contact: E. H. Van Alstyne, V.P., P.R.
Address: same as above
Telephone: (412) 471-1568
Program Reaches: residents of 5 counties; all economic classes
When Started: September, 1969
Budget: $50,000/year

Program Outline:

The aim of CCCS is to restore self-reliance, economic stature and family well-being to those involved in unfortunate financial circumstances and to help others to avoid the pitfalls of extravagant use of credit.

CCCS is a chartered, non-profit corporation established by business and civic leaders to provide free assistance to people who are over-burdened with debt. The service aids persons who already have debt problems (1) through advice and counsel on budgeting and family money management and (2) by developing and utilizing plans for orderly liquidation of their debts within the means of the clients and with the cooperation of their creditors.

CCCS also tries to prevent debt problems from arising by fostering and promulgating an educational program; teaching family money management and the wise use of credit.

Co. Personnel Involved: E. H. Van Alstyne, Jr. on the Executive Committee, Board of Directors and Chairman, Operations Committee

Measure of Success: In 28 months CCCS has helped 3,600 clients in distributing $359,328 to 770 creditors, giving relief from pressure on emotions and family life and helping the head of the house continue his job and be productive.

OFFICE OF CONSUMER INFORMATION

TRAVELERS INSURANCE CO.
One Tower Square
Hartford, Conn. 06115

Business: Insurance   Sales: 3,000mm
CEO: Morrison H. Beach   Employees: 30,000

Contact: Francis K. Holland
Address: same as above
Telephone: (203) 277-4079
Program Reaches: General Public
When Started: April, 1971
Budget: $2.5 million

Program Outline:

The purpose of the program is to provide a sounding board for the general public insofar as insurance related questions are concerned.

The OCI is staffed with knowledgeable employees and the back-up of the entire Travelers organization to answer insurance related questions and explain complicated problems. Watts-line telephones are available nationally as well as written answers to written requests for information.

All of Travelers' national media advertising in 1971 has been devoted to promoting the OCI.

Co. Personnel Involved: 4 full time and 7 part time members of the OCI staff.

Measure of Success: Current measure of success is the volume of phone calls (40,000 in 9 months) and voluminous but uncounted pieces of correspondence.

CONSUMER INFORMATION

UNION CARBIDE
270 Park Avenue
New York, N.Y. 10017

Business: Manufacturing   Sales: 3,026mm
CEO: William S. Sneath   Employees: 102,144

Contact: Marion Merrill
Address: same as above
Telephone: (212) 551-3770
Program Reaches: n/a
When Started: 1960
Budget: $50,000

Program Outline:

The purpose of this program is to provide helpful consumer information about Union Carbide products or products made with Union Carbide ingredients.

The corporation's consumer information program includes a quarterly newsletter, slide film, speakers, demonstrations and exhibits adapted to meet specific requests and situations and to make available practical information about products and processes that may affect the consumer but are not yet covered in the consumer literature.

Co. Personnel Involved: 1 person plus aid, advice and counsel of corporate departments and divisions

Measure of Success: letters of appreciation, increased use of materials and number of requests

CONSUMER CREDIT COUNSELING

WELLS FARGO BANK
464 California Street
San Francisco, Cal. 94120

Business: Banking   Sales: not applicable
CEO: Richard P. Colley   Employees: 10,500

Contact: Forest U. Naylor, Exec. V.P.
Address: 868 Paramount Road,
    Oakland, Cal. 94610
Telephone: (415) 451-0419
Program Reaches: 450 families
When Started: 1969
Budget: n/a

Program Outline:

The purpose of this non-profit community organization is to help consumers learn the proper role of credit and to help families prevent financial problems.

CCC's job is to avert financial ruin in a family that has gotten itself deeply into debt. This is done through the implementation of a money management plan which helps to get the average family that applies to CCC out of debt within 22 months. The cooperation of the creditors and the payment schedule worked out through the CCC leads to the family making payments to the CCC and the money going out to creditors through them. A further understanding of credit is also elaborated through the counselors to help avoid similar financial trouble in the future. Once the program has been arranged, there is an 85% follow-through by the applicants. The cost to the applicants is $10.00/month.

When a family in trouble comes to CCC they are asked to fill out an application detailing their debts, income and expenses. Next in an interview, the CCC decides if it can apply its help and it finds out if the family is willing to curtail its credit buying.

Co. Personnel Involved: A number of Bank managers and employees participate. The Bank also contributes money to this program.

Measure of Success: Since March of 1969, 450 San Francisco families have had programs set up to pay off $164,035,800 in debts to 271 different creditors. In June of 1970, the debtors through CCC had paid $243,733 on the total amount.

CARE-A-VAN

WHIRLPOOL CORP.
Benton Harbor, Mich. 49022

Business: Appliance Manufacturing
Sales: 1,200mm
CEO: John H. Platts   Employees: 28,280

Contact: William L. Kucera
Address: Admin. Ctr., U.S. 33 North
    Benton Harbor, Mich. 49022
Telephone: (616) 925-0651, ext. 7120
Program Reaches: over 1,500,000
When Started: 1969
Budget: At the outset, Whirlpool was prepared to invest
    more than $500,000 in this program.

Program Outline:

In trying to bridge the "information gap" between appliance manufacturers and consumers, Whirlpool introduced a 90-minute stage show featuring Broadway performers in songs and skits which concentrate on industry-oriented consumer information. The show provides information on how to buy, use and get service on major home appliances. The live performance is supplemented by films, slides, and special visual effects. Each attendant of the performance is offered a 16-page booklet, "Your Appliance Buy-Lines and Warranty Record," which spells out the important points to consider in shopping for each household appliance as well as facts about safety and warranties. Also offered is a letter which enables persons to write questions and comments to Leslie Paige, the spokeswoman for the show.

The show was promoted through newspaper and radio advertising, personal contact with schools, clubs and consumer organizations, cooperation with the Better Business Bureaus and appliance-oriented associations, etc.

Co. Personnel Involved: The amount of manpower varied throughout the program; however, on the average, it involved approx. 60% of 1 staff member's time.

Measure of Success: In order to fulfill the many requests for the show, the live presentation has been converted into a motion picture which is available to civic groups, theatres and schools throughout the country.

NEWSPAPER CONSUMER LINE SERIES

WHIRLPOOL CORP.
Benton Harbor, Mich. 49022

Business: Appliance Manufacturing
Sales: 1,200mm
CEO: John H. Platts   Employees: 28,280

Contact: William L. Kucera
Address: Admin. Ctr., U.S. 33 North
   Benton Harbor, Mich. 49022
Telephone: (616) 925-0651, ext. 7120
Program Reaches: Consumers of Major Home
   Appliances
When Started: 1971
Budget: The project cost approx. $8,000 to $10,000.

Program Outline:

Whirlpool Corporation has made available a booklet containing 31 articles on consumer advice, "Thirty-one Ways To Really Help Consumers," to be distributed to editors of weekly newspapers throughout the United States. The articles are non-commercial and are designed to give the homemaker helpful hints and information about appliances.

Written under the pseudonym of Leslie Paige, the spokeswoman and authority in the Care-A-Van program, over 7,000 copies of the booklet have been distributed to newspaper editors. The booklet is designed to enable the editors to easily cut the articles out and insert them in their papers. The articles cover such topics as How to Buy a Dishwasher, Vacation Care for Appliances, How to Avoid Unnecessary Service Calls, etc.

Co. Personnel Involved: Approximately 2 persons in the Public Relations Department were involved in the project—staff members.

Measure of Success: The Leslie Paige consumer article series has had a total pick-up of over 500 national newspapers. In addition, many schools and clubs have requested reprints of the articles.

drug abuse

ALCOLHOLISM PROGRAM

BETHLEHEM STEEL CORP.
Corporate Headquarters
Bethlehem, Pa. 18016

Business: Steelmaking and Related Activities
Sales: 3,000mm
CEO: Lewis W. Foy   Employees: 130,000

Contact: Medical Director
Address: same as above
Telephone: (215) 694-4306
Program Reaches: n/a
When Started: 1965
Budget: n/a

Program Outline:

The company regards alcoholism as an illness for which therapy is indicated. Through this program, the company insures each alcoholic employee proper consideration and treatment. Through this program, the Corporation makes its medical services available for assistance in the diagnosis of employees suspected or known to be alcoholics. In making these services available, the Company respects the employee's right to privacy.

Co. Personnel Involved: n/a

Measure of Success: In the 7 years of the program's life, over 60% of the enrollees have made dramatic progress toward recovery.

DRUG ABUSE CONTROL PROGRAM

BETHLEHEM STEEL CORP.
Corporate Headquarters
Bethlehem, Pa. 18016

Business: Steel Making and Related Activities
Sales: 3,000mm
CEO: Lewis W. Foy   Employees: 130,000

Contact: P. J. Whitaker, M.D.
Address: same as above
Telephone: (215) 694-4306
Program Reaches: all employees
When Started: October, 1971
Budget: n/a

Program Outline:

The program aims to detect and refer for treatment employees who are misusing drugs. Bethlehem recognizes that employees who become drug abusers have acquired an illness for which therapy is indicated. Any employee whose work performance, appearance, or behavior suggests drug abuse, will be referred to the Medical Director.

As part of the pre-employment examination, a urine screening for drugs is performed, after advising the employee of the purpose of the examination. Applicants found to be abusing drugs are not employed until the practice has ceased.

Co. Personnel Involved: All supervisory employees have received a copy of the written program, attended conferences on the subject and are expected to become involved as required.

Measure of Success: Program is presently too new to evaluate.

SOCIAL COUNSELING

BURLINGTON NORTHERN, INC.
176 E. Fifth Street
St. Paul, Minn. 55101

Business: Transportation   Sales: 953mm
CEO: R. W. Downing   Employees: 46,490

Contact: C. L. Vaughan, Jr.
Address: 567 Iona Lane, St. Paul, Minn. 55113
Telephone: (612) 484-1653
Program Reaches: available to all 46,000 employees
When Started: August, 1951
Budget: $140,000/year

Program Outline:

The purpose of this program is to identify and rehabilitate problem drinker employees. The program strives for early detection and endeavors to work with the personnel who are not yet in the desperate stages of alcoholism. In this way the program hopes to avert disastrous situations through early personal counseling, referral to other sources of assistance, guidance, education and intervention. Employees' wives and families are included in the rehabilitation effort and also receive counseling and encouragement.

Co. Personnel Involved: 9 on staff, supported by supervisory personnel

Measure of Success: 75-80% of cases successfully recovered, i.e. have attained physical sobriety and were restored to the best possible degree of general good health.

DRUG EDUCATION

CASTLE & COOKE, INC.
Drawer 2990
Honolulu, Hawaii 96802

Business: Food Products, Land Development
   Manufacturing and Merchandising
Sales: 507mm
CEO: Malcolm MacNaughton   Employees: 15,000

Contact: Emil A. Schneider, P.R. Dir.
Address: same as above
Telephone: (808) 548-6611
Program Reaches: 3-5,000
When Started: 1971
Budget: $2,000 to date

Program Outline:

The purpose of this program is to make available a series of films on drug education designed for use with students from about the 6th through 10th grades—an age range considered to cover those who have not yet turned on to drugs but may be wondering about it all.

Each film is 15 minutes in length and usage is accompanied by trained instructors who develop dialogue among the students. Each film treats a different subject: marijuana, LSD, amphetamines, barbituates, heroin and glue sniffing. All films are offered to the school system (public and private) for use in their drug education programs.

Co. Personnel Involved: 1 person—handles reservations and requests for films

Measure of Success: These are the only drug films of this type in Castle and Cooke's community. They receive heavy usage and have been highly praised by the instructors using them.

COMMUNITY DRUG PROGRAM

CLAIROL, INC.
345 Park Avenue
New York, N.Y. 10022

Business: Hair Color, Toiletries,
    Beauty Appliances
Sales: n/a
CEO: Bruce S. Gelb   Employees: 2,500

Contact: W. L. Tyson, Mgr. Comm. Rels.
Address: One Blachley Road
    Stamford, Conn. 06902
Telephone: (203) 325-1609
Program Reaches: ultimately 250,000
When Started: 1970
Budget: Upwards of $1 million/year, depending on NIMH
    approval

Program Outline:

The purpose of this program is to create a 4-town comprehensive community drug program which would help all residents and businesses in a 4-town (Greenwich, Stamford, Darien, New Canaan) area of Southwestern Conn. One man from Clairol, 1 from Pitney-Bowes and 1 community agency director began planning for a comprehensive drug program (education, prevention, treatment and rehabilitation). A Drug Liberation Program was created. Community representatives were brought in from the 4 towns to form a Board, and a staff was established. Agencies were brought together who dealt with drug problems and an application was initiated to NIMH.

Co. Personnel Involved: 1 Executive on Board (active), others expected to get involved with component groups as program matures

Measure of Success: support of local governments and agencies, citizen support, involvement of youth, good prospects for federal funding, some local government funding, some private funding

---

MILITARY DRUG ABUSE PROGRAM

COMPTON ADVERTISING
625 Madison Avenue
New York, N.Y.

Business: Advertising   Sales: 130mm
CEO: Milton Gossett   Employees: 486

Contact: David Hart, The Ad Council
Address: 825 Third Avenue, N.Y., N.Y.
Telephone: (212) 758-0400
Program Reaches: n/a
When Started: January, 1972
Budget: n/a

Program Outline:

The purpose of this program is to arrest the growth and spread of drug abuse in the military. Compton wants to reach the enlisted men and NCO's with the theme, "Come Home Clean." It is the hope that this campaign will convince the servicemen that they are not only letting themselves down if they take drugs, but that they're letting down family members and friends who are waiting at home hoping to see them return as they left. This campaign is designed as a multi-media campaign, involving TV, radio and posters.

Co. Personnel Involved: Four—creative supervisor, writer/producer, art director and account executive

Measure of Success: too soon to tell

DRUG ABUSE EDUCATION

DEERE & CO.
John Deere Road
Moline, Ill. 61265

Business: Farm and Industrial Equipment,
   and Consumer Products
Sales: 1,188mm
CEO: Ellwood F. Curtis   Employees: 41,700

Contact: George F. Neiley
Address: same as above
Telephone: (309) 792-4136
Program Reaches: n/a
When Started: 1971
Budget: cost of films; $1,360—other expense of per-
   sonnel in scheduling and maintaining films is minimal

Program Outline:

The purpose of this program is to assist schools, the local drug abuse council, law enforcement agencies and others in their drug educational programs. It is geared to both students and adults in the greater Moline (Illinois) area. Deere & Co. purchased 6-16mm motion pictures on various aspects of drug abuse: marijuana, amphetamines, barbituates, LSD and heroin. A letter was mailed to all local school superintendents informing them of the availability of the films for their use without charge.

Co. Personnel Involved: 3 people—Public Relations Director to get program started; 1 scheduling clerk; 1 audio-visual employee for maintenance of films

Measure of Success: not able to assess, although films are frequently requested throughout the community

DRUG ABUSE

ELI LILLY CO.
307 E. McCarty Street
Indianapolis, Ind. 46206

Business: Manufacturing Pharmaceuticals
Sales: 600mm
CEO: B. E. Beck   Employees: 23,450

Contact: H. W. Wallace
Address: same as above
Telephone: (317) 261-3167
Program Reaches: hard to estimate
When Started: Security has been enforced since the
   company's beginning; 1968 coordination of education
   programs.
Budget: There is no specific budget; monies come from
   departments throughout the country.

Program Outline:

The procedures followed at Lilly's loading dock are typical of the security system that prevails throughout every phase of the company's operations to prevent the diversion of its products for illicit use. At the loading dock, the driver and loader may know each other, but neither is aware until the truck backs into position, that the other will be on the job at that particular place, time and day. Within the company, a sealed plastic sack holds bulk Pulvules in a plastic case. The sack is closed with a tape that cannot be removed without tearing it. The tapes are color coded to indicate which department last handled the item. No department will accept an unsealed sack; a torn tape immediately sets off an investigation.

Lilly is also engaged in the educational aspects of combating drug abuse. The company has made films and exhibits on drugs available on loan to schools, civic, social, church, professional and other groups. Recently an unstructured session was organized in which 12 midwestern high school students talked about drugs. The result is a movie in which the young people themselves tell why drug abuse exists and what can be done about it. Also, Lilly speakers lecture on drug abuse before youth groups and other organizations.

Co. Personnel Involved: n/a

Measure of Success: hard to estimate

"11:59—LAST MINUTE TO CHOOSE"
(A film produced especially for T.V.)

THE FIDELITY BANK
1200 Lancaster Avenue
Bryn Mawr, Pa. 19010

Business: Banking   Sales: not applicable
                                Assets: 1,600mm
CEO: Carl K. Dellmuth   Employees: 2,200

Contact: Harris C. Aller, V.P.
Address: Room 1242, Broad & Walnut Streets
    Philadelphia, Pa. 19109
Telephone: (215) 985-7003
Program Reaches: approx. 1 million
When Started: April, 1971
Budget: n/a

Program Outline:

The purpose of this program is to support a movement to help curb the alarming increase in drug abuse in the Nation's youth, and to heighten public awareness of one of our society's most complex problems. The Fidelity Bank sponsored as a public service the television premiere in the Greater Philadelphia area of this starkly realistic film. Produced in color especially for TV audiences, the film portrays not only the horrifying effects, but also the excruciating experiences the overdosed undergo during drug emergency treatment and tapering off periods. The film features actual youth addicts and the filming itself took place in the treatment centers and emergency rooms where the overdosed are treated.

Letters and posters promoting the film were sent to educators and community leaders throughout the Greater Philadelphia Area. A spokesman for Gaudenzia, Inc. provided a special introduction for the film.

Co. Personnel Involved: initially 8; presently 3

Measure of Success: The enthusiastic acceptance of the film has resulted in a constant flow of requests for it from schools, community relations divisions of police departments, both in the city and surrounding counties, drug abuse councils, business and industrial firms, civic, service and other concerned community organizations. The demand is continuing.

EMPLOYEE DRUG PROGRAM

J. L. HUDSON CO.
1206 Woodward Avenue
Detroit, Mich. 48226

Business: Retail   Sales: 356mm
CEO: Joseph L. Hudson, Jr.   Employees: 14,000

Contact: George Greer, ACSW
Address: Employee Consultation Center, same as above
Telephone: (313) 223-5100, ext. 2684
Program Reaches: 14,000
When Started: 1971
Budget: n/a

Program Outline:

The purpose of this program is to reduce the incidence of drug abuse. It provides counseling to individual drug abusers within the company, provides referral service to outside sources for drug abusers as needed, provides information to employee and management as to effects of drug abuse on individuals, groups, and company as a whole.

Co. Personnel Involved: 30 people—training and referral and direct treatment

Measure of Success: (1) referrals of drug abusers by supervisors; (2) reduction of usage in individual clients; (3) improved functioning and job performance of individuals

DRUG ABUSE
ALCOHOLISM IN EMPLOYMENT

KEMPER INSURANCE GROUP
Long Grove, Ill. 60049

Business: Insurance	Sales: 275mm
CEO: n/a	Employees: n/a

Contact: Jess Wilson, Pers. Mgr.
Address: P. R. Dept., same as above
Telephone: (312) 540-2000
Program Reaches: n/a
When Started: April, 1971
Budget: n/a

Program Outline:

The purpose of this program is to establish a policy of non-discrimination in the employment of rehabilitated drug users and alcoholics.

Kemper is attempting to aid the drug user and alcoholic in finding a suitable substitute for drugs and alcohol, namely a job, so that complete rehabilitation can occur. This will eliminate the stigma, "once a junkie, always a junkie" or "once an alcoholic, always an alcoholic." The company's formal policy on hiring and drug abuse/alcoholism is presented in their public service pamphlets, "What about Drugs and Employees?" and "Management Guide on Alcoholism and Other Behavioral Problems." Both pamphlets are authored by Lewis F. Presnall, nationally recognized authority in the areas of drug abuse and alcoholism and Director of Rehabilitation Services for Kemper. The booklets provide guidelines for industrial supervisors confronted with employee drug/alcohol dependency. Kemper recommends a close analysis of the employee's relation to the company and how he can be helped. In keeping with this policy of non-discrimination and the desire to educate and inform other businessmen of the need to help drug abusers and alcoholics, Kemper has run an extensive national ad campaign to this effect. Hopefully, this will help to break the cycle of unemployment and return to addiction by the drug user/alcoholic.

Co. Personnel Involved: No exact number—numerous people from community and public relations and personnel committees are involved in this area.

Measure of Success: Since its printing in early 1971, nearly 100,000 free copies of "What About Drugs and Employees?" have been distributed through the company's Public Relations Department. Eleven employees have been hired at Kemper Branch offices around the country. More than a million booklets on alcoholism have been distributed by the Kemper Organizations.

IT TAKES A LOT OF HELP

KEMPER INSURANCE
Long Grove, Ill. 60049

Business: Insurance	Sales: 275mm
CEO: n/a	Employees: n/a

Contact: George P. Ducharme, Adv.
Address: same as above
Telephone: (312) 540-2000
Program Reaches: over 20 million
When Started: November, 1970
Budget: n/a

Program Outline:

The film, "It Takes a Lot of Help," offers a comprehensive guideline for groups and individuals concerned with developing constructive programs to combat local drug abuse within a community.

Produced by Kemper Insurance Group in cooperation with the National Coordinating Council on Drug Abuse Education and Information, this is a 27-minute, full color documentary film narrated by television and movie personality, Lorne Greene. The film, focusing on Cedar Rapids, Iowa, avoids medical and moral debate and concentrates on programs of prevention and rehabilitation. It is made available on a free loan basis to any interested organization, and, when ordered, has with it a kit containing a press release, speech, order form for window display unit, a pamphlet answering the most frequently asked questions about drugs, and a copy of the Council's book on organizing community drug programs.

Co. Personnel Involved: exact figure not available

Measure of Success: In less than a year and a half, the film has been seen by more than 20 million people.

DRUG TRAINING INSTITUTES

PFIZER, INC.
235 E. 42nd Street
New York, N.Y. 10017

Business: Pharmaceuticals, Fine Chemicals,
Cosmetics and Toiletries
Sales: 870.4mm
CEO: Edmund T. Pratt, Jr.   Employees: 5,000

Contact: Barry J. Fry, Ph.D.
Address: same as above
Telephone: (212) 573-3435
Program Reaches: 1,500 directly/year
When Started: 1970
Budget: $100,000

Program Outline:

The purpose of this program is to train physicians and students to cope with the current drug abuse problem through professional, scientific discourse. Company conducts 1- or 2-day symposia, nationwide, on an average of once per month. Topics like pharmacology, methadone programs, the changes in the drug scene, treatments of overdose, attitudes, etc. are discussed by nationally-known experts. Symposia are completed through further cooperation with medical participation in a drug-abuse clinic in Norwalk, Conn.

Co. Personnel Involved: 2 full time, 1 part time

Measure of Success: Follow-up evaluations (questionnaires, etc.) have shown good response from participants asking for more specific help in their areas. Several participants have begun their own drug abuse clinics.

TIP (TURN IN A PUSHER)

TEXAS CITY REFINING, INC.
P.O. Box 1271
Texas City, Tx. 77590

Business: Petroleum Refining   Sales: 140mm
CEO: William H. Fetter   Employees: 535

Contact: James Luhning
Address: Mainland Savings Assoc.
   1221 6th Street, N.
   Texas City, Tx.
Telephone: (713) 948-2546
Program Reaches: countywide
When Started: September 23, 1971
Budget: no budget yet; too new a program

Program Outline:

The purpose of this program is to make the environment of Galveston County so unpleasant for drug pushers that they discontinue the practice or leave the area. The program was copied from a similar project in Tampa, Florida.

A reward is provided for information leading to the arrest of a drug pusher. A toll-free number was set up for citizens with information leading to arrest. Citizens who have information can call and be assigned a code name and number. If the information the citizen gives leads to the arrest and conviction of a pusher, the citizen receives a reward. The company provides up to $100 reward for an indictment and $500 for a conviction. The crime squad in the police department work with the citizens on an anonymous basis throughout the whole process.

Co. Personnel Involved: Two—requirement varies; most time spent in original organization

Measure of Success: In the first 2 months, 148 bona fide phone calls have been received on the TIP phone. Fourteen arrests have been made as a result of the information provided.

IT'S YOUR CHOICE

TRAVELERS INSURANCE CO.
One Tower Square
Hartford, Conn, 06115

Business: Insurance
Sales: 3,000mm
CEO: Morrison H. Beach   Employees: 30,000

Contact: Francis K. Holland
Address: same as above
Telephone: (203) 277-2779
Program Reaches: 100 million plus potential
When Started: July, 1971
Budget: $11,000

Program Outline:

The purpose of the program is to provide—in the vernacular of young people and reflected in their own opinions—suggestions regarding the avoidance of drug use. A 1-minute film, "It's Your Choice," was sent to 500 TV Stations across the United States.

The spot uses 2 voice-overs, 1 a teenage girl, the other a teenage boy—both using the vernacular to point out to the young man in the film that, in effect, drug abuse is "out." An adult voice-over closes the spot saying "Life without drugs is the way it's getting to be. It's the way it's going to be. It's the way it's got to be."

Co. Personnel Involved: 8 in preliminary brainstorming sessions; 1 program manager thereafter

Measure of Success: "It's Your Choice" was released on 1/7/72. In the next four months, it was telecast 3,291 times by 132 stations in 124 cities in 42 states. Estimated viewers number 216,362,207. Total time spot was on the air is 54.13 hours.

NEED FOR DECISION

UNION CARBIDE CORP.
270 Park Avenue
New York, N.Y. 10017

Business: Diverse Manufacturing
Sales: 3,026mm
CEO: William S. Sneath   Employees: 102,144

Contact: Dr. J. J. Welsh
Address: same as above
Telephone: (212) 551-3101
Program Reaches: n/a
When Started: 1968
Budget: $30,000

Program Outline:

The purpose of the program is to help supervisors understand their role concerning an alcoholic employee. By bringing to light cases of alcoholism, while they are still salvagable, the corporation's employees, business operations, and stockholders are benefited.

Union Carbide, working with the National Council on Alcoholism and Alcoholics Anonymous, commissioned a 12-minute film entitled, "Need for Decision." The film was produced to help Union Carbide supervisors carry out the corporation's alcoholism program. It was made available to supervisors throughout Union Carbide, to be kept and used as a teaching aid.

Co. Personnel Involved: In the making of the film, 3 members of the Medical Department plus other departments and division specialists acted as advisors.

Measure of Success: The film has been widely acclaimed and the corporation has made it generally available to other companies. Over 400 companies have requested it.

DRUG EDUCATION PROJECT

UNITED TELECOMMUNICATIONS, INC.
(formerly UNITED UTILITIES, INC.)
2330 Johnson Drive
Shawnee Mission, Kan. 66205

Business: Telecommunications   Sales: 570mm
CEO: Paul H. Henson   Employees: 24,371

Contact: Forrest Ehrenman
Address: same as above
Telephone: (913) 236-9900
Program Reaches: 100,000-200,000
When Started: Winter, 1970-71
Budget: $25,000

Program Outline:

The purpose of this program is to acquaint United's employees and customers with the drug problem, particularly among young people, and through this educational process, to make them better able to recognize and deal with this problem in their families and communities. The first phase of the project was the publication of a special issue of the UNITED SYSTEM QUARTERLY devoted entirely to the drug problem. This was distributed to all employees and to the daily, weekly and college newspapers in the country.

The second phase was to make available to high schools and civic organizations copies of the film, "The Trip Back." This widely acclaimed film dealing with the problems of drug addiction is available free of charge from the headquarters of each of the 9 subsidiary groups.

Co. Personnel Involved: Four persons devoted most of their time for several months to put out the QUARTERLY issue on drugs. Approximately 10 persons are responsible for distributing the drug film when it is requested.

Measure of Success: many letters, telephone calls and personal expressions of appreciation for the information, and various testimonies as to its favorable impact on people

education

MEMORIAL FOUNDATION OF ALLIED VAN LINES

ALLIED VAN LINES, INC.
P.O. Box 4403
Chicago, Ill. 60680

Business: Household Goods Carrier
Sales: 170.2mm
CEO: S. S. Steckler   Employees: 600

Contact: E. R. Calzaretta, Controller
Address: same as above
Telephone: (312) 344-8700
Program Reaches: n/a
When Started: 1960
Budget: based on contributions to fund by Allied Corporate office, and agents

Program Outline:

The purpose of the program is to provide financial aid to young men and women seeking a college education. Under this program, which is administered at John Hopkins, Notre Dame and Stanford Universities, respective students may apply directly to the universities. Each of the three universities select candidates for scholarships which are awarded only when the need for financial assistance has been displayed by the candidate. The number of scholarships distributed is left to the discrimination of each university.

Co. Personnel Involved: n/a

Measure of Success: Program has helped approximately 30 students graduate from the above 3 universities. Currently, 14 students enrolled at the 3 schools are receiving financial assistance from Allied.

COOPERATIVE WORK-STUDY

BELL OF PENNSYLVANIA
201 Stanwix Street
Pittsburgh, Pa. 15222

Business: Communications   Sales: 698mm
CEO: William S. Cashel   Employees: 34,300

Contact: Richard E. Thorn
Address: 8th fl., same as above
Telephone: (412) 633-3670
Program Reaches: about 50% of all seniors and juniors in Fifth Avenue High School
When Started: 1970
Budget: n/a

Program Outline:

The program is designed to give juniors and seniors at Fifth Avenue High School, Pittsburgh, Pennsylvania, exposure to the world of work.

Students are assigned meaningful jobs and are expected to make some contribution to the work group. High school juniors work 2 hours/day, 5 days/week for 6 weeks. Seniors work a full half-day tour the entire school term. Both juniors and seniors are paid basic starting salaries for whatever job they are doing.

Each student is assigned to a supervisor who provides continuing counseling service, supervision and required job training. Supervisors are required to complete an evaluation of students on completion of the program. During the 6-week period, students are given the opportunity to take Bell's employment exam. If the students are interested, and the employment situation permits, the scores they make on the test can be considered if they apply for full time employment after graduation.

Co. Personnel Involved: One management person coordinates this and other activities at the school. Other employees are involved to the extent that they have work-study students working for them.

Measure of Success: According to the school counselor, students who have participated in the work-study program are more readily placed following graduation from high school.

EMPLOYMENT READINESS TRAINING

BELL OF PENNSYLVANIA
201 Stanwix Street
Pittsburgh, Pa. 15222

Business: Communications   Sales: 698mm
CEO: William S. Cashel   Employees: 34,300

Contact: Richard E. Thorn
Address: 8th fl., same as above
Telephone: (412) 633-3670
Program Reaches: entire senior class of Pittsburgh's Fifth
    Avenue High School each year
When Started: 1969
Budget: n/a

Program Outline:

The purpose of this program is to inform the students of qualifications and information needed to apply for a job.

Students come to the Telephone Company building in groups of 20 for 2 half-day sessions of job readiness training. During the 6-hour session, the students fill out applications and counselors discuss in detail each item on the application. Problems that most new employees face are discussed. The goals of the program are to develop job qualifications, encourage students to present themselves well, encourage initiative, develop an awareness of a company's need for qualified employees, impart knowledge required for job application and employment interviews, and discuss employee responsibilities.

Co. Personnel Involved: Three people conduct the program and are involved 1 or 2 days each year. A coordinator spends additional time organizing the program so that it meshes with school schedules.

Measure of Success: Feedback from students indicates they felt better prepared during job interviews.

LEADERSHIP SEMINAR

BELL OF PENNSYLVANIA
201 Stanwix Street
Pittsburgh, Pa. 15222

Business: Communications   Sales: 698mm
CEO: William S. Cashel   Employees: 34,300

Contact: Richard E. Thorn
Address: 8th fl., same as above
Telephone: (412) 633-3670
Program Reaches: n/a
When Started: 1969
Budget: under $500

Program Outline:

The purpose of this program is to develop leadership among the students of the Fifth Avenue High School, Pittsburgh, Pennsylvania.

Bell Telephone and school administrators conduct an annual leadership seminar for students and/or teachers. Items such as public speaking, how to conduct meetings, administrative details and procedures, self critique and motivational sessions are conducted during a weekend seminar held on a camp location somewhat removed from the school surroundings.

Each year this program changes slightly to meet the present needs of the students or teachers, but the format itself will not be changed.

Co. Personnel Involved: 3-6 people including the company administrator for the school project

Measure of Success: The student council has been somewhat more active and effective following this type seminar.

READING LABORATORIES

BELL OF PENNSYLVANIA
201 Stanwix Street
Pittsburgh, Pa. 15222

Business: Communications
CEO: William S. Cashel

Sales: 698mm
Employees: 34,300

Contact: Richard E. Thorn
Address: 8th fl., same as above
Telephone: (412) 633-3670
Program Reaches: about 85% of the student body
When Started: 1970
Budget: n/a

Program Outline:

The purpose of this program is to improve the reading ability of high school students at the Fifth Avenue Junior and Senior High School, Pittsburgh, Pennsylvania.

The Bell Telephone Coordinator researched various reading laboratories and assisted school administrators in preparing a recommendation to install a reading laboratory for use by all students in the school.

All students are tested and trained in the reading laboratory. An interdisciplinary approach is used so that students may develop ability in reading and various other subjects simultaneously.

Co. Personnel Involved: the company coordinator, who is responsible for the entire school project

Measure of Success: The reading laboratory is not equally successful with all students but there are some who show great progress.

TUTORING PROGRAM

BELL OF PENNSYLVANIA
201 Stanwix Street
Pittsburgh, Pa. 15222

Business: Communications
CEO: William S. Cashel

Sales: 698mm
Employees: 34,300

Contact: Richard E. Thorn
Address: 8th fl., same as above
Telephone: (412) 633-3670
Program Reaches: 75-100 students/year
When Started: 1969
Budget: no out-of-pocket expense

Program Outline:

The tutoring program assists individual students in various subjects and is the program that launched Bell Tel's various activities at Fifth Avenue High School, Pittsburgh, Pennsylvania.

In its effort to help students who are not progressing as well as they should, tutors have been made available in a variety of different courses of study. Student participation is strictly voluntary and is available to all students requesting it. The tutors, volunteers, are local Bell employees who offer their services (2 wives of Bell employees are also participating).

Co. Personnel Involved: The coordinator who administers other projects in the school for Bell also administers this program. Generally, about 10 company tutors are involved on released time.

Measure of Success: The success of the tutoring program has been shown in the fact that at least 50 of the students showed improvement, some as much as 4 grade levels. More important has been the development of a 2-way street of understanding, insight and respect between the tutors and students.

DETROIT STREET ACADEMY

BUNDY CORPORATION
333 W. Fort Street
Detroit, Mich. 48226

Business: Tubing Manufacturing and Fabricating
Sales: 90mm
CEO: Wendell W. Anderson, Jr.
Employees: 2,700

Contact: William Howard
Address: 7434 Harper, Detroit, Mich. 48226
Telephone: (313) 964-4100
Program Reaches: 150/year
When Started: May, 1970
Budget: $175,000/year

Program Outline:

Purposes are to:

1. Establish street academies in ghetto neighborhood to educate teenage dropouts and enable them to develop their talents;

    2. Provide sufficient education for students to pass primary or high school equivalency tests;

    3. Provide training in certain skills such as drafting, typing and photography;

    4. Attempt to provide part time or summer employment while student is going to school.

This program was initially started and funded by H.E.W. and U.S. Postal Service, Street Academy and is now trying to obtain local community assistance. Bundy Corporation is assisting in this effort.

Co. Personnel Involved: Divisional Vice President on Consulting Board, photo lab equipment supplied, business advice and guidance provided, several part time jobs provided, financial support provided and solicited

Measure of Success: The term ending June, 1971 saw 125 students completing the term out of 145 who started. A general equivalency diploma (G.E.D.) was obtained by 23 of the students who took this test.

CARNATION TEACHING INCENTIVE AWARDS

CARNATION CO.
5045 Wilshire Boulevard
Los Angeles, Cal. 90053

Business: Food Processing   Sales: 1,148mm
CEO: H. Everett Olson   Employees: 18,100

Contact: J. Edward Atkinson
Address: same as above
Telephone: (213) 931-1911, ext. 193
Program Reaches: impossible to estimate
When Started: 1969
Budget: $5,000

Program Outline:

The program's goal is improved education for center-city school children. Unemployment, over-crowded housing, drugs, sex, alcohol and disease present almost insurmountable obstacles to good education for ghetto children. This program offers gifts of $500 each as an incentive to dedicated and talented teachers to begin their careers in center-city schools where the real challenges to educate exist. The awards are 10 in number and are given in cities where Carnation has a fresh milk and ice cream plant and where there is a neighboring university or college.

Carnation plant managers contact the colleges, and the selection of candidates is the responsibility of school's education departments. Carnation's people present the awards. Most of the schools will issue a local news release; Carnation sends news stories to selected black newspapers.

Co. Personnel Involved: 9

Measure of Success: Positive responses from schools, education and interested civic groups and citizens across the country. Many requests to sponsor the program in other areas have been received. Intention was to participate in cities where company has plants. It is hoped that other companies would adopt similar projects.

EDUCATION PROGRAMS FOR DISADVANTAGED EMPLOYEES

CARSON PIRIE SCOTT & CO.
1 S. State Street
Chicago, Ill. 60603

Business: Retail   Sales: 250mm
CEO: Norbert F. Armour   Employees: 12,100

Contact: J. Gordon Gilkey, Jr.
Address: same as above
Telephone: (312) 744-2152
Program Reaches: 100
When Started: 1968
Budget: $15,000/year

Program Outline:

The purpose of the program is to provide education for those lacking same and to produce better equipped employees. The program is aimed at Black, Spanish speaking, ethnic and disadvantaged white employees. Scholarships are made available at the University of Illinois (Circle Campus) for employees of at least 12 months seniority, who apply, meet admission require-ments and do not have other resources. They are given "leaves of absence," retain benefits, seniority and are given part time work.

Money is made available to Chicago High School to establish career-oriented curriculum including work experience at Carson's for students not academically motivated. Approximately 70 students are involved at Carson's and other business firms enrolled in the program.

The scholarship program is being continued on a minimal scale at this time because it has been found that most employees were older, had families and it did not make any sense for the employees or Carson's. Fifty per cent of the students were lost in the 1st semester or 2 because it was too demanding and pulled them away from Carson's. Carson's has been changing to in-house training; bringing teachers into the company who will teach courses more applicable to work, as well as tuition reimbursement.

Co. Personnel Involved: Coordinator, Store Manager, Students

Measure of Success: About 20 persons have gone through; 1 is in her senior year, and several are juniors at this time.

CUNY VOLUNTEERS

CELANESE CORP.
522 Fifth Avenue
New York, N.Y. 10036

Business: Chemicals, Textiles   Sales: 1,300mm
CEO: John W. Brooks   Employees: 36,000

Contact: David A. Gardner
Address: same as above
Telephone: (212) 867-2000
Program Reaches: 650
When Started: 1970
Budget: no direct expense

Program Outline:

The purpose of this program is to provide training and classroom assistance to the City University of New York, in response to its open admission program. Celanese provides classroom tutors for compensatory subjects at the college level in numerous academic fields, ranging from business administration, economics, foreign languages, English, etc.

When the program was first conceived, 120 Celanese employees volunteered to participate in it. Their backgrounds ranged over varying academic disciplines and they held degrees ranging up to Ph.D.'s. Employees tutor on released company time. The program is to be expanded from model presently at one campus to 170 other CUNY campuses.

Co. Personnel Involved: 35-70; varies each semester, approximately 2-4 hours per teacher. Time is released company time.

Measure of Success: The tutor program has been successful in terms of better academic performance of students and students have specifically requested Celanese tutors due to their competent instruction.

STEP PROGRAM

CELANESE CORP.
522 Fifth Avenue
New York, N.Y. 10036

Business: Chemicals, Films, Coatings,
    Manufacturing
Sales: 1,300mm
CEO: John W. Brooks   Employees: 36,000

Contact: S. J. Brockman
Address: same as above
Telephone: (212) 867-2000, ext. 3155
Program Reaches: 12-16/year
When Started: 1967
Budget: $18,000

Program Outline:

Celanese sponsors each summer at Hampton Institute a program to train selected female minority high school graduates to be efficient and resourceful office workers at various Celenese plants and facilities. The students receive an 8-week scholarship to Hampton.

Co. Personnel Involved: primarily 1; for about 8% of his time in summer months

Measure of Success: The program will run again in 1972 for the 6th consecutive summer. The retention rate for 5 years has been about 60%.

ONE-TO-ONE PROGRAM

CENTRAL PENN NATIONAL BANK
5 Penn Center
Philadelphia, Pa. 19101

Business: Banking   Sales: not applicable
CEO: Harold F. Still, Jr.   Employees: 1,115

Contact: Cecil W. Bond, Jr., Asst. Cashier
Address: 4th Fl., same as above
Telephone: (215) 854-3137
Program Reaches: 20
When Started: September, 1970
Budget: no planned budget

Program Outline:

The purpose of the program is to improve reading levels and arithmetic skills of children in the city's inner schools, specifically, Bartlett Junior High School, 11th and Catherine Streets, Philadelphia.

The program gives these children, many of whom come from fatherless families, individual attention which usually is lacking at home or in the classroom. In addition, it exposes them to situations which they would not ordinarily encounter in the inner city, in the form of field trips to the seashore, to the Art Museum, Central Penn's executive offices and other points of interest in the Philadelphia area.

Central Penn plans to increase the number of tutors participating in the program and thus increase the number of children reached.

Co. Personnel Involved: Ten employees serve as tutors with 13 more serving as alternates.

Measure of Success: The children have come to rely on the tutors and look forward to the individual attention they are receiving and to sharing experiences with the tutors. In addition, the tutors enjoy the sessions with the children and feel they are "becoming involved."

NEIGHBORHOOD LIBRARY PROGRAM

CITIZENS AND SOUTHERN NATIONAL BANK
99 Annex
Atlanta, Ga. 30399

Business: Banking   Sales: not applicable
Total Assets: 2,065mm
CEO: Mills B. Lane, Jr.   Employees: 3,550

Contact: William J. Van Landingham
Address: same as above
Telephone: (404) 588-2774
Program Reaches: Albany minority community
When Started: 1971
Budget: $23,000

Program Outline:

The purpose of the program is to stimulate and encourage reading by children in low-income areas of Albany, Georgia. The Neighborhood Library program, established in Albany, provides 3 new libraries which are housed in mobile home units. The books are all paperbacks and cards have been issued to over 1,000 individuals as library members. Follow-up is not rigidly kept up since the scope of the program was to get as many books into as many neighborhood homes as possible.

Additional community assistance has provided such adjuncts as movies, story telling sessions, remedial reading programs and volunteer staff members. A remedial reading program for first graders has also been initiated in Albany. Over 200 children enrolled in classes which met for 6 weeks with students identified by local educators as in need of reading help.

Co. Personnel Involved: 65 or 70

Measure of Success: Over 2500 people in the disadvantaged neighborhoods have registered for library membership since last spring. Over 1,200 books are being checked out each month by the area's residents.

BLACK TREASURES

THE COCA-COLA CO.
P. O. Drawer 1734
Atlanta, Ga. 30301

Business: Manufacturing Syrups and Concentrates for
    Soft Drinks
Sales: 1,606mm
CEO: J. Paul Austin   Employees: 24,600

Contact: Kevin A. Wall, V.P. and Market Dev. Mgr.
Address: same as above
Telephone: (404) 897-2676
Program Reaches: est. 2 million direct; more through TV
    and radio
When Started: February, 1969
Budget: n/a

Program Outline:

The purpose of this program is to make people aware of the importance of Negro history in America, to highlight works of Negro historians and to dramatize the importance of knowledge of Black history by both Black and White people.

Black Treasures history kits are distributed to schools, libraries and civic organizations. The kits contain a film strip, a record, a teacher's guide and 3 copies of the GOLDEN LEGACY illustrated books on Negro history. Materials were presented to school boards and formally accepted in major cities around the nation including Atlanta, Washington, D.C., Chicago, Detroit and Baltimore. The books were produced by Fitzgerald Publications, a Black-owned publishing firm.

Co. Personnel Involved n/a

Measure of Success: Six months after the introduction of the program, there had been an estimated 50,000 showings in more than 1,000 cities throughout the country and nearly 200 bottlers of Coca-Cola participated. Distribution to more than 9,000 schools and organizations and the program's formal acceptance have made the kits one of the most widely used classroom tools for teaching the importance of Negro history and the work of Negro historians. Four hundred kits were distributed by the NAACP to its branches.

MAN IN HIS ENVIRONMENT

THE COCA-COLA CO.
P. O. Drawer 1734
Atlanta, Ga. 30301

Business: Manufacturing Syrups and Concentrates for
Soft Drinks
Sales: 1,606mm
CEO: J. Paul Austin   Employees: 24,600

Contact: Marketing Services Department
Address: same as above
Telephone: (404) 897-2676
Program Reaches: n/a
When Started: n/a
Budget: n/a

Program Outline:

The purpose of this program is to help children: (1) become more aware of their environment; (2) appreciate their interdependence on the environment; (3) realize that, as human beings, they can make decisions which can affect their environment for better or worse.

The program is in the form of 2 games with accompanying teachers' guide for children to play. "Rescue in Space" is designed to help children understand this ecological principle: resources of the planet Earth are limited—to achieve a stable world, we must use our resources wisely and reuse them where possible. "Make Your Own World" is designed to teach students this ecological principle: all elements of the environment are interrelated and interdependent. When man changes the environment, there are conspicuous consequences not only for himself, but for other forms of life and for the soil, air and water.

Co. Personnel Involved: n/a

Measure of Success: n/a

REMEDIAL EDUCATION PROGRAM

COCA-COLA CO.
P. O. Drawer 1734
Atlanta, Ga. 30301

Business: Manufacturing Syrups and Concentrates for
Soft Drinks
Sales: 1,606mm
CEO: J. Paul Austin   Employees: 24,600

Contact: Bonita Holder
Address: same as above
Telephone: (404) 897-2121
Program Reaches: n/a
When Started: n/a
Budget: n/a

Program Outline:

The purpose of this program is to help prepare unskilled employees for better jobs through remedial education programs.

Several of the syrup branch plants conducted free adult education programs for unskilled employees in cooperation with local educational systems. When the company enlarged its product line to include a number of soft drinks and package sizes, it was found that unskilled plant employees were having difficulty reading labels or stacking different size containers. An elementary education course was established to teach the basic skills needed to accomplish these jobs.

Co. Personnel Involved: n/a

Measure of Success: The first elementary education course was successful enough to lead to the implementation of a more advanced course for additional personal development in techniques of how to instruct and how to get along with people.

PROJECT INVOLVEMENT

CONNECTICUT GENERAL LIFE INSURANCE CO.
Hartford, Conn. 06115

Business: Insurance
Sales: Premium Income: 1,680
   Investment Income: 322mm
CEO: Henry R. Roberts   Employees: 6,000

Contact: James N. Mason, Jr.
Address: same as above
Telephone: (203) 243-8811
Program Reaches: estimated 200
When Started: 1969
Budget: 1971, $20,000—1972 budget is not yet official

Program Outline:

The purpose of this program is to support self-help efforts of inner city residents in solving problems and achieving goals, to encourage CG employees to participate with inner city adults and young people in community activities, to make use of various company resources, including office facilities, company grounds, printing and photographic capacities, recreational facilities and others for the benefit of certain inner city programs.

Field trips by elementary school pupils to CG offices for tours and lessons are offered as well as printing and photographic service for 2 schools in CG's "school partnership" program. CG supplements limited school budgets for special education and recreational programs in these schools. Also, CG supplies volunteers (partly company time, mostly their own) to work with about 40 children during winter months under special American Youth Hostel inner city program. Staff time of a CG investment expert is contributed for South Arsenal Neighborhood Development Corporation (SAND), a ghetto citizen's group which is redeveloping its neighborhood. Funds and fund raising efforts were also supplied for SAND's experimental "Everywhere School."

The company's community service efforts will be evaluated this summer with intensification of some and reduction of others. No decisions have been made yet, however. The general trend is toward greater involvement.

Co. Personnel Involved: n/a

Measure of Success: Success in these programs is hard to measure. Teachers report that children respond enthusiastically to educational and recreational programs. CG volunteers say they are more sensitive to inner city problems.

PROJECT EARLY BIRD

CROWN ZELLERBACH CORP.
One Bush Street
San Francisco, Cal. 94119

Business: Forest Products   Sales: 955mm
CEO: C. R. Dahl   Employees: 26,700

Contact: G. R. Sherrill
Address: same as above
Telephone: (415) 823-5544
Program Reaches: 600 children to date
When Started: October, 1969
Budget: $6,200 for 4 locations

Program Outline:

This program aims to provide vocational information to elementary school children in the 5th, 6th or 7th grades at selected inner city schools, on the various aspects of industry and Crown Zellerbach in particular, and the importance of continued education to qualify for wage and salaried jobs in industry.

The company provides tours of local facilities and classroom speakers to cover the various work activities in the company. Company speakers focus attention on the wage and salary employment opportunities that can be achieved by students with educational levels of high school and above, discussing the various occupations from beginning job to top supervisor in their work area. In addition, specific information is correlated with the regular program of the teachers (i.e. paper-making kits as part of a science unit, accounting problems as part of a math unit, salesmanship as part of a public speaking unit, etc.). By providing experiences outside the student's regular environment, the company hopes to aid in broadening the scope of the child's awareness of the world.

The program allows for local variations and for specific requests from the teachers.

Co. Personnel Involved: 1 headquarters coordinator, 150 employee-speakers, 8 Crown facilities

Measure of Success: It is difficult to measure the success of a program such as this. Since the company is hoping to encourage children to stay in school, the effectiveness of the program will not be tested until the first group graduates from high school. In addition, the company has found that many of the children in these schools move around and it has been hard to trace them even into the upper grades.

FAMILY FINANCIAL EDUCATION PROGRAM

CONTINENTAL ILLINOIS NATIONAL BANK
AND TRUST CO.
231 S. LaSalle Street
Chicago, Ill. 60604

Business: Banking   Sales: not applicable
CEO: Tilden Cummings   Employees: 8,138

Contact: Thomas B. Hanchett
Address: Second V.P., Pub. Affairs Div.
Telephone: (312) 828-2345
Program Reaches: n/a
When Started: February, 1970
Budget: The Bank's out-of-pocket investment was ap-
prox. $100,000

Program Outline:

This program was designed to provide personal financial
management to:
   1. students in public and non-public secondary schools
   2. out of school groups of adults with low income who
have limited knowledge of personal money management
   3. gainfully employed adults who are overextended
financially

Designed to help schools comply with the Illinois Partee
Bill requiring consumer education for public school students, grades 8-12, the materials issued by the Bank in
the program are used as supplemental teaching aids and
are provided at no cost to the Chicago area. The total
program consists of a teacher's guide and student pro-
blem-workbooks for each 2 units (Unit 1-Managing Personal Income; Unit II-Accepting Credit Responsibility).
Materials for out-of-school use are implemented through
adult education programs and social training programs
sponsored by labor groups, corporations and other interested consumer education organizations. These materials approach situations more realistically and present
problems which serve as springboards for group discussion.

The program is made available at no charge to local
service agencies and materials are distributed at nominal
cost outside Chicago. The Bank also sells directly to
industries, labor unions, government agencies, and the
program has been extended to other communities
through banks at a small charge (student workbooks
$.35; teacher guides, $.60).

Co. Personnel Involved: n/a

Measure of Success: The Bank has distributed more than
35,000 student workbooks without charge and sold
almost 100,000 copies. The total number of banks
cooperating has reached 175. Extensive classroom use of
the material is the best measurement of the program's
success.

NORTHWESTERN HIGH SCHOOL PROJECT

CHRYSLER CORPORATION
P.O. Box 1919
Detroit, Mich. 48231

Business: Automotive Manufacturing
Sales: 7,000mm
CEO: John J. Riccardo   Employees: 228,000

Contact: A. J. Dunmore
Address: same as above
Telephone: (313) 956-2566
Program Reaches: n/a
When Started: January, 1968
Budget: n/a

Program Outline:

The primary goal of the comprehensive cooperation program between Chrysler and Northwestern High School is to upgrade student achievement levels and to motivate and prepare Northwestern students for the career of their choice. The program draws upon the expertise and facilities of both the school and the corporation. From the beginning, the approach has been to build a bridge between the world of the classroom and the world of commerce and industry, but not at the expense of overemphasizing vocational education.

A unique reading improvement program has been developed. All students are placed at a level where they can succeed and then improve. Audio and visual aids are used. A program for students interested in medical careers enables them to spend 6 weeks observing various activities in a hospital. Also a warehouse was converted into an auto repair shop and classroom. A center for keypunch instruction was set up as well as a model job placement office.

Co. Personnel Involved: n/a

Measure of Success: The voluntary reading program has seen reading skills of some improve as much as 3 to 3½ grades during one academic year. More programs are being planned and some expanded due to the responses.

NATIONAL ALLIANCE OF BUSINESS CLUSTER PROGRAM

DEERE & CO.
John Deere Road
Moline, Ill. 61265

Business: Manufacturing of Farm, Industrial and
    Consumer Products equipment
Sales: 1,188mm
CEO: Ellwood F. Curtis   Employees: 41,700

Contact: C. W. Toney
Address: same as above
Telephone: (309) 792-4540
Program Reaches: theoretically, the entire student body
When Started: Deere has been participating since 1968
Budget: Deere support has totaled $15,000 the past two
    years (total contributions have exceeded $250,000)

Program Outline:

The purpose of the College Cluster Program is to improve the ability of minority college graduates to compete for private sector jobs and to move up to higher positions of professional and executive responsibility. The Cluster Program is a cooperative organized effort by business and industry and the university to upgrade the quality of education at predominantly black colleges. The Southern University Cluster Program has 36 nationally and locally based (Baton Rouge, La.) business firms participating in that program. Business and industry input into the Cluster Program has been in the form of men, money and materials. A statistics laboratory has been equipped at Southern University. A computer was donated to the university. An executive is on loan to help structure computer programming and computer operation. Equipment has also been procured for the School of Engineering from member companies of the Cluster.

Co. Personnel Involved: The chairman of the Cluster Program is a Deere & Co. employee. Other personnel have contributed time as guest lecturers, and have procured equipment.

Measure of Success: Several professors from this university have had summer experience in business and industry. The College of Engineering has been accredited. Students have received summer training in business and industry. The establishment of the Cluster Program has enlarged the employment opportunities for co-op students.

ASSISTANCE TO URBAN EDUCATION

DUPONT CO.
1007 Market Street
Wilmington, Del. 19898

Business: Diversified Manufacturing
Sales: 3,800
CEO: Charles B. McCoy   Employees: 110,865

Contact: John Burchenal
Address: same as above
Telephone: (302) 744-2036
Program Reaches: n/a
When Started: Began in 1920s
Budget: $270,278 contributed to Wilmington area schools in 1971

Program Outline:

This program is designed to aid urban education at the elementary and secondary school levels. To do this, DuPont has undertaken a number of efforts. These include weekly seminars and counseling by DuPont people for the Bayard Middle School students; cooperative work-study employment of high school vocational students; providing summer employment for science teachers in the company's laboratories; providing summer industrial experience for guidance counselors; summer instruction programs for city youngsters in suburban schools and numerous gifts of property made to the school system.

Co. Personnel Involved: more than 70 to varying degrees

Measure of Success: evaluation by administrators and teachers based on annual company reassessment

UPWARD BOUND

DUPONT CO.
1007 Market Street
Wilmington, Del. 19898

Business: Diversified Manufacturing
Sales: 3,800
CEO: Charles B. McCoy   Employees: 110,865

Contact: John Burchenal
Address: same as above
Telephone: (302) 774-2036
Program Reaches: n/a
When Started: 1967
Budget:: $41,000 in 1971; $140,800 since 1967

Program Outline:

Dupont was one of the nation's pioneer sponsors of the Upward Bound Program designed to bring under-achieving, deserving high school students into college—students who would ordinarily not get to college. For example, in the high school class of 1966, 50 high school students were selected, some of whom had no intention or chance to go to college. These rising seniors spent the summer before their senior year on the campus of the University of Delaware, getting accustomed to campus life, attending special classes and receiving intensive guidance. In addition, DuPont assumed responsibility for providing and finding summer employment for those youngsters who needed the money. Other companies are now being asked to participate.

Co. Personnel Involved: about 4-6 involved in planning, funding, handling procurement of summer jobs

Measure of Success: Of the 50 seniors selected from the class of 1966, 46 were accepted by and entered college. Today 33 are still in college, 8 different colleges. In subsequent years, 45 out of 50 entered college and 33 are still enrolled. This year, out of 40 seniors and 16 high school graduates, making a total of 56, 55 were admitted to 10 different colleges last fall.

PROJECT BEACON

EASTMAN KODAK CO.
343 State Street
Rochester, N.Y. 14650

Business: Manufacturing Photographic Equipment
Sales: 2,976mm
CEO: Walter A. Fallon   Employees: 110,700

Contact: Kenneth Howard, Dir. Urban Affairs
Address: same as above
Telephone: (716) 724-4620
Program Reaches: n/a
When Started: n/a
Budget: n/a

Program Outline:

Project Beacon is a camera-in-the-classroom program developed in the Rochester schools under the guidance of Dr. Keith Whitmore, a Kodak research scientist on loan to the school system as a full time consultant. The project stresses self-expression, the organization of complex material, and the communication of it in an understandable way. This is accomplished through the use of film cameras by children in 5 Rochester inner city schools on the first grade level. The children participate in the filming and editing of movies, expressing themselves in pictures even when written and spoken words are difficult for them. Kodak loaned the cameras and contributed the film used in the program. Teachers were given short courses in filmaking.

The basic concept behind this experiment is the fact that today's children are the first children to grow up with television and they understand visual communication intuitively. The over-all goals of the project are: building the child's self image, early success in language arts, cultural enrichment, development of new materials and presentation of programs on minority history and culture.

Co. Personnel Involved: In addition to Dr. Whitmore, several persons from Learning Systems Laboratory of Kodak Research Labs, as required by the project, are involved.

Measure of Success: Dr. Whitmore says that the average child in Project Beacon has advanced his skills level 1½ years. A by-product of the program is the way the films have drawn parents from the inner city neighborhoods into closer contact with the schools. For example, PTA meetings, which otherwise might have drawn sparse attendance, bring many parents to see the films which the children have made.

CO-OP PROGRAM WITH
HARRY E. WOOD HIGH SCHOOL

ELI LILLY & CO.
307 E. McCarty Street
Indianapolis, In. 46206

Business: Pharmaceutical Manufacturing
Sales: 600mm
CEO: B. F. Beck   Employees: 23,450

Contact: Juan C. Solomon
Address: same as above
Telephone: (317) 261-3229
Program Reaches: 2,100
When Started: earliest programs, 1969
Budget: approx. $15,000

Program Outline:

The program's purpose is to assist the Wood High School administration and student body in meeting expressed educational and cultural needs. Lilly has helped implement several programs: the Big Brother and Big Sister programs with employees joining in as the big brothers and sisters, and an Auditorium Series in which guest performers are brought in as part of the cultural enrichment program. Also, four Neighborhood Playgrounds were built in needed areas, Lilly has sponsored a Neighborhood scout troup which is run by Lilly volunteers, and an Industrial Cooperative Training program provides on-the-job work experience for students and many others. Some programs have worked; others will be dropped or changed; new approaches will be taken. Continuous review of various programs are built in.

Co. Personnel Involved: 73 for 10 hours/month

Measure of Success: student interest and participation, enthusiasm of school administrators; no quantitative measures possible

PUBLIC EDUCATION SUPPORT

FIRST NATIONAL CITY BANK
399 Park Avenue
New York, N.Y. 10022

Business: Banking
CEO: William I. Spencer

Sales: not applicable
Employees: 31,700

Contact: Dr. Norman Willard, V.P.
Address: same as above
Telephone: (212) 559-0459
Program Reaches: directly, 10,000 plus
When Started: about 1968
Budget: n/a

Program Outline:

The purpose of the program is to participate effectively in broad private sector programs to supplement the activities of the New York City Board of Education in upgrading the quality of education in the city. The program primarily helps a handful of public schools; ultimately, a much broader base of schools at all levels. Through the commitment of both money, full time and part time personnel, and management expertise, the Bank has played a substantial role in a number of experiments aimed at improving secondary education in the city, including the New York Urban League Street Academy program, the Economic Development Council High School Partnership, and the Board of Education/Urban Coalition Mini-School program at Harlem High School. As an ongoing objective, the Bank aims to introduce some more "independent" projects toward more meaningful relationships with the public school system.

Co. Personnel Involved: 1 high-level individual full time and 6-8 high-level individuals part time

Measure of Success: The EDC program has resulted in significant improvements in administration, teacher performance, student involvement and parent interest. Under the coalition program, a complete high school was converted into a mini-school with improvements in administration-teacher-student rapport.

SCHOLARSHIP PROGRAM

FOOD FAIR STORES, INC.
Food Fair Building
3175 John F. Kennedy Boulevard
Philadelphia, Pa. 19101

Business: Supermarkets
CEO: Jack M. Friedland

Sales: 2,000mm
Employees: 30,000

Contact: J. Arvid Johnson, Exec. Dir.
    Food Fair Stores Foundation
Address: same as above
Telephone: (215) 382-9500
Program Reaches: n/a
When Started: 1952
Budget: $72,000/year approx.

Program Outline:

The program is directed to the support of higher education and to the provision of educational opportunities for capable students. Through the program, college and university scholarships are made available to the company's employees, their children and members of the community served by Food Fair Stores. The Food Fair Stores Foundation annually grants some 60 scholarships, each renewable over a 4-year period. Preference is given to qualified Food Fair employees and their children.

In establishing these grants, the Foundation has given complete freedom to the institutions concerned in making the awards and in continuing them in accordance with their academic standards. In all cases, colleges award the scholarships, not the foundation.

Scholarships are awarded annually. Grants range in value upwards of $250/year. No restrictions are placed on the areas of study the scholarship recipient may wish to pursue.

Co. Personnel Involved: Exec. Dir., Scholarship Secy. primarily

Measure of Success: numerous graduates, many of whom have gone into professional fields

THE COLLEGE CLUSTER PROGRAM

FORD MOTOR CO.
The American Road
Dearborn, Mich. 48121

Business: Automotive Manufacturing
Sales: 15,000mm
CEO: Lee A. Iacocca   Employees: 431,000

Contact: Richard Ruddell, Mgr. Ed. Affairs
Address: same as above
Telephone: (313) 322-2420
Program Reaches: 60,771 (population of the 20 colleges
    the program is working with)
When Started: 1969
Budget: n/a

Program Outline:

The purpose of the program is to augment the growth
and development of minority colleges which it is hoped
will improve the ability of minority college graduates to
compete for private sector jobs and advance to more
responsible professional and executive positions. Ford has
actively participated in the Cluster Program for a little
more than one year. Grants totaling some $90,000 have
been awarded to Cluster Colleges. Areas of involvement
have included curriculum development, faculty development, organization and administration, student loans
and scholarships, fund raising and student career counseling through campus visits. One of the more notable
functions of this program has been Ford's sponsorship of
a Cluster College Roundtable Program. The primary
aspect of the program is a series of small, informal group
discussions between college students and Ford representatives.

Co. Personnel Involved: One employee is assigned full
time as a project coordinator. He calls upon other
company personnel for assistance in specialized programs.

Measure of Success: the reactions (verbal and written)
from college administrators, faculty and students

AEROSPACE AND AVIATION ACADEMY

GENERAL ELECTRIC
RE-ENTRY & ENVIRONMENTAL
SYSTEMS DIVISION
3198 Chestnut Street
Philadelphia, Pa. 19101

Business: Aerospace and Environmental Systems
Sales: n/a
CEO: Otto Klima, Jr., V.P. and Div. Gen. Mgr. RESD
Employees: 4,000

Contact: Hank Koenig
Address: Phila. Urban Coalition
    1512 Walnut Street, Phila., Pa. 19102
Telephone: (215) 841-5568
Program Reaches: n/a
When Started: January, 1970
Budget: RESD invested approx. $8,000

Program Outline:

The purpose of this program is to provide educational
opportunity to high school students in Philadelphia's
depressed areas to improve their career potential through
skills in highly sophisticated aerospace and aviation
industries.

RESD acted as a catalyst at the inception of the
acedemy, bringing together representatives of aerospace
and aviation to lay the groundwork to develop a
curriculum that would ensure the readiness of students in
facing job challenges in industry. Designed as a school
within a school for non-college bound students, the
academy was developed under the auspices of
Philadelphia's Urban Coalition and held in cooperation
with South Philadelphia and Benjamin Franklin (Malcolm
X) High Schools so that students could gain a high school
diploma and basic wage earning skills.

Co. Personnel Involved: about 5 persons—1 man full
time for 5 months

Measure of Success: RESD trained 10 students. Upon
graduation, at least 3 of the students were placed in
G.E.'s Philadelphia Works.

PHILADELPHIA ADULT BASIC EDUCATION ACADEMY

GENERAL ELECTIRC
RE-ENTRY & ENVIRONMENTAL
SYSTEMS DIVISION
3198 Chestnut Street
Philadelphia, Pa. 19109

Business: Aerospace and Environmental Systems
Sales: n/a
CEO: Otto Klima, Jr., V.P. and Div. Gen. Mgr., RESD
Employees: 4,000

Contact: Sven H. E. Borei
Address: 3723 Chestnut Street, Phila., Pa. 19101
Telephone: (215) 382-3700
Program Reaches: at present about 150/year
When Started: 1968
Budget: $22,000 last year

Program Outline:

The purpose of this program is to enable functionally illiterate adults (reading below 4th grade level) to read with enough skills to achieve their personal goals.

With one-to-one tutoring as the primary modus operandi, the Philadelphia Adult Basic Education Academy (PABEA) uses volunteer instructor/tutors to teach basic reading (and some basic math skills) to adults who cannot read beyond 4th grade level. Using literacy training methods used by Dr. Frank Laubach in many illiterate overseas countries, the Academy trains tutors and gets them prepared to help students read. While not a "Laubach Project" in the formal sense, PABEA does use some of their printed texts and other materials as well. Students select their own reading goals (some select the Pennsylvania driver's manual). G.E. provides funds and administrative support for the academy, prints the PABEA annual report and provides assistance in publicity and public communications through its Public Affairs Staff.

The company hopes to increase the number of available tutors, and through contractual services (e.g., in prisons) to better undergird the project financially.

Co. Personnel Involved: Public Affairs Staff and the treasurer is a G.E. Finance Manager/Volunteer

Measure of Success: There are 100s of individuals waiting to enter the academy. In 1971, G.E. sponsored a "Conference on Literacy" for PABEA at which Governor Milton J. Shapp was the featured speaker and about 100 business and educational leaders met to discuss involvement with this problem which affects both.

THE GENERAL FOODS FUND, INC.

GENERAL FOODS CORPORATION
250 North Street
White Plains, N.Y. 10602

Business: Major Consumer Goods Manufacturing
   (particularly food)
Sales: 2,200mm
CEO: Tex Cook   Employees: 44,000

Contact: L. F. Genz
Address: same as above
Telephone: (914) 694-2345
Program Reaches: n/a
When Started: 1953
Budget: varies annually

Program Outline:

The purpose of this program is the support of higher education. The Fund matches individual General Foods employee gifts to institutions of choice. It also supports the United Negro College Fund, Council for the Advancement of Small Colleges and other state and regional college associations, as well as supplying individual student scholarships. In this way the colleges, universities and the individual students receive aid.

Co. Personnel Involved: n/a

Measure of Success: impossible to calculate

LINCOLN LEARNING CENTER

GENERAL MILLS, INC.
P.O. Box 1113
Minneapolis, Mn. 55440

Business: Foods, Crafts, Games, Toys, Fashions,
   Direct Marketing, Chemicals, Restaurants
Sales: 1,120mm
CEO: James A. Summer   Employees: 28,412

Contact: Dr. Frank C. Hildebrand
Address: same as above
Telephone: (612) 540-3105
Program Reaches: 40-50/year
When Started: April, 1965
Budget: $123,000—Since 1968, General Mills has pro-
   vided $100,000 for support of the Lincoln Learning
   Center.

Program Outline:

The Lincoln Learning Center, a specialized branch of the
Minneapolis Public Schools, is devoted to providing a
meaningful education for inner-city youth. Students
selected for the project have been designated as
"academic under-achievers" or have failed to make a
healthy emotional adjustment to the routine Junior High
School. The project is geared to 7th, 8th, and 9th grade
boys who are students in the northern area of Minneapolis.

The boys involved have rejected conventional classroom
techniques and curricula; the Lincoln Learning Center
emphasizes increased skills in mathematics and language
for them. Small classes and individual instruction are
provided. Each student receives three hours of classroom
instruction per day, and a production laboratory provides
the students with an opportunity to participate in a work
experience, applying the basic skills they have learned.
On-the-job work experience in many phases of business
and industry is provided for selected students. General
Mills supports the program with money, equipment and
both financial and technical knowledge.

Because the project is frankly experimental, it will be
continually modified in the light of experience. Its basic
approach is expected to remain constant, however.

Co. Personnel Involved: The number varies from month
to month and year to year. Eleven General Mills employees are or have been active by consulting on programs, providing technical assistance, arranging job experiences, lending help with public information and
assisting with financial affairs.

Measure of Success: Demonstrated increases in the
reading and vocabulary skills of students and improved
attendance with a parallel decrease in tardiness indicate
the Lincoln Learning Center's high level of success. In the
1969-70 school year, for example, Lincoln Learning
Center students showed improved reading vocabulary
skills of 1.4 grade levels and improved reading comprehension skills of 1.9 grade levels. Eighty to 90% of
Lincoln Learning Center students are motivated to
continue in the public school system.

GENERAL MOTORS INSTITUTE

GENERAL MOTORS CORP.
3044 W. Grand Boulevard
General Motors Building
Detroit, Mich. 48202

Business: Automotive Industry   Sales: 28,264mm
CEO: Edward N. Cole   Employees: 696,000

Contact: GMI Admissions Officer
Address: 1700 W. Third Avenue, Flint, Mich. 48502
Telephone: (313) 776-5000
Program Reaches: 3,000 enrolled
When Started: n/a
Budget: n/a

Program Outline:

The purpose of this program is to recruit Black high school students for engineering education. It helps members of minority groups, particularly Black high school students, who desire to study engineering, to achieve their goal. General Motors Institute is a private, degree-granting engineering college operated by GM with elective study in Black Culture, Black instructors, and a Black admissions counselor.

To assist high school students who apply for admissions to GMI but who do not have sufficient formal education, a program known as Pre-Engineering and Management has been developed. Under its auspices, disadvantaged students are enrolled in a 1-year cooperative program of alternating work-study periods. The academic periods are devoted to remedial math, science and communications courses and a study of blueprint reading, mechanical drawing and shop practices. As further assistance, they are paid regular wages while in the work periods of the Pre-EM program. Students who successfully complete the courses are enrolled as GMI freshmen. Any students who do not complete the course satisfactorily are candidates for salaried positions, apprentice programs or production employment.

Co. Personnel Involved: Approximately 280 faculty members are involved in the co-op course.

Measure of Success: As of April, 1972, GMI has enrolled 128 minority students; matriculated 12.

COLLEGE SCHOLARSHIPS

GEORGIA-PACIFIC CORP.
900 S.W. 5th Avenue
Portland, Ore. 97204

Business: Forest Products of All Kinds
Sales: 1,400mm
CEO: William H. Hunt   Employees: 37,000

Contact: R. O. Lee
Address: same as above
Telephone: (503) 222-5561
Program Reaches: 457 to date
When Started: 1960
Budget: $750,000 to date

Program Outline:

The program aims to provide outstanding high school seniors, in areas where Georgia-Pacific has major operations, finances to obtain college educations. Four-year college scholarships are awarded to outstanding high school seniors on the basis of student's need, scholastic achievement, intellectual ability, character and promise of future contribution to society. Selection is without discrimination as to race, creed, country of origin, but recipients must be U.S. citizens. Selection is made by local school officials, not by Georgia-Pacific personnel. Student must fulfill bachelor degree requirement in 4 years and the school chosen must be accredited. For tax supported schools, annual scholarship is $1,500 and for non-tax supported, $2,000 annually.

Co. Personnel Involved: Approximately 25 employees work with selection committees of local school authorities.

Measure of Success: The program has been successful. There have been a few young people who have failed because of lack of effort, but in the main, those receiving scholarships have performed above average and in some cases (quite a few) have been outstanding in their academic achievement and later accomplishments.

BFG AID TO HIGHER EDUCATION PROGRAM

THE B.F. GOODRICH CO.
500 S. Main Street
Akron, Ohio 44318

Business: Rubber   Sales: 1,236mm
CEO: W. B. Warner   Employees: 47,900

Contact: Gary J. Rine, P.R. Dept.
Address: same as above
Telephone: (216) 379-3411
Program Reaches: 1000s
When Started: 1956
Budget: n/a

Program Outline:

The purpose of this program is to encourage young people to seek higher education and to assist them in obtaining it, and to assist colleges and universities in providing better instruction and facilities. The program includes 4-year scholarships to qualifying high school graduates (through the means of the National Merit Scholarship Corp.), sharing of tuition costs with BFG employees for job-connected courses, matching of colleges and universities for special studies, and other assistance and grants to selected educational institutions and their staffs. This program is continually evaluated and adjusted to be most effective.

Co. Personnel Involved: Several departments within the company are involved in the administration of various phases of the program.

Measure of Success: Thousands of students and scores of colleges and universities throughout the U.S. have benefited through the various phases of the program.

SCHOLARSHIP TRUST PROGRAM

HEWLETT-PACKARD CO.
1501 Page Mill Road
Palo Alto, Cal. 94304

Business: Electronic, Medical, analytical and computing
    instrumentation
Sales: 375mm
CEO: William R. Hewlett   Employees: 16,000

Contact: George Climo
Address: same as above
Telephone: (415) 493-1501
Program Reaches: 370 to date (1972)
When Started: 1952
Budget: To date, scholarships totaling $184,000 have
    been awarded

Program Outline:

The purpose of this program is to assist graduating high school seniors in pursuing higher education at the college or university of their choice.

The awards are made under the HP Employees' Scholarship Fund to sons and daughters of HP employees. In 1972, more than 50 corporate scholarships were given. Awards are made on the basis of scholastic achievement, financial need, participation in activities and educational objectives. An increasing number of awards have been made each year, and scholarships are now valued at $750. Funds are derived from employee contributions (usually payroll deductions) and from annual contributions by the company to a trust fund handled by a trust officer in a local bank. Scholarships are awarded primarily from the earnings of the trust.

Co. Personnel Involved: n/a

Measure of Success: n/a

TUTORING PROGRAM

HEWLETT-PACKARD CO.
1501 Page Mill Road·
Palo Alto, Cal. 94304

Business: Electronic, Medical, Analytical and Computing
  Instrumentation
Sales: 375mm
CEO: William R. Hewlett   Employees: 16,000

Contact: Ena Yale
Address: same as above
Telephone: (415) 493-1501
Program Reaches: no official count
When Started: 1968
Budget: n/a

Program Outline:

The purpose of this program is to allow HP persons to take time off with pay to serve as teaching assistants at local junior high schools in order to assist primarily minority students in East Palo Alto who need assistance in reading and other subjects.

Originally, the program was operated in conjunction with 3 junior high schools in East Palo Alto. Volunteers go 2 days per week to help tutor minority children who need help with reading problems. The tutoring project always has been an informal program which depends upon the individual efforts of HP persons rather than company involvement. Individuals pay their own expenses for travel, but HP does allow paid time off so they can participate and provides some supplies and use of duplicating and related equipment.

Although past participants feel it would be beneficial to initiate this program at the lower grades, no plans have been made for this at this time. They may be introduced at some future date.

Co. Personnel Involved: n/a

Measure of Success: There have been many individual successes, but the program as a whole has not worked satisfactorily. Of the 30-40 persons originally participating, the number has dwindled to only a few. The primary difficulty concerns the age level of the students being tutored. All participants agreed that it would have been much better to be with younger children (3rd and 4th graders for example). The most-mentioned negative factors were lack of discipline and interest on the part of the 7th and 8th graders. Mrs. Ena Yale—most active of the tutors—now spends more time performing various support functions (preparing special assignments, etc.) than she spends in actual tutorial sessions. She feels there still is a need for this type of program at the junior high level, but that untrained persons such as those volunteers from HP could perform a more valuable service in the lower grades.

LOW COST COOKERY

HUNT-WESSON FOODS, INC.
1645 Valencia Drive
Fullerton, Cal. 92634

Business: Manufacturing Foods and Matches
Sales: 400mm
CEO: Edward Gelsthorpe   Employees: 6,800

Contact: Kenneth J. Ward, Dir. Corp. Rel.
Address: same as above
Telephone: (714) 871-2100
Program Reaches: n/a
When Started: 1968
Budget: About 2.5mm was spent in advertising and
  material preparations.

Program Outline:

This program is a campaign to show women how they could shop and prepare more nutritious meals for less money. It could help anyone who cooks meals for themselves or their families. The program involved a series of newspaper ads over a period of 9 months. The campaign told how to select various cuts of meat, poultry, fish, etc. and gave preparation tips, recipes and meal planning ideas. It also published the USDA Plentiful Foods for that month and offered a special low cost cookery cookbook published by Hunt-Wesson.

Additionally, the company did a special campaign on the Low Cost Cookery idea which was expanded into Black media such as EBONY and Black newspapers in selected cities. This campaign was entitled "The Little Cookbooks" and featured Esther Coley, one of the company's home economists.

Co. Personnel Involved: n/a

Measure of Success: Because of the excellent results experienced with the Lost Cost Cookery program, the company knew it wanted to build a similar program for the next year. They wanted one that could do an even better job in helping the American consumer understand that he could buy food inexpensively, and more important, that inexpensive food could be both nutritious and interesting. As a result, Hunt-Wesson's Computer Menu Program was created.

"WE'LL HELP YOU MAKE IT" COMPUTERIZED MENU PLAN PROGRAM

HUNT-WESSON FOODS, INC.
1645 W. Valencia Drive
Fullerton, Cal. 92634

Business: Manufacturing Food and Matches
Sales: 400mm
CEO: Edward Gelsthorpe   Employees: 6,800

Contact: Kenneth J. Ward, Dir. Corp. Rel.
Address: same as above
Telephone: (714) 871-2100
Program Reaches: so far, 1,300,000
When Started: 1970
Budget: Over 1 million was spent on the preparation of the plan and its distribution.

Program Outline:

The program's purpose is to provide women with specialized menu planning in accordance with their family's needs and budget. Women are asked to give Hunt-Wesson the number of people in their family in certain age groups along with their weekly food budget. In return, they receive a personalized computer menu plan covering a menu for breakfast, lunch and dinner for 30 days. All the meals are designed to feed the particular family size within the specified weekly food budget.

In total, the company prepared and offered 3 separate menu plans and as of January 1972, 1,300,000 requests have been received and filled. Each day's menu is nutritionally balanced, as well.

Co. Personnel Involved: 15-20 people ranging from home economists, marketing personnel, management people, etc.

Measure of Success: This plan was endorsed by the US Department of Agriculture and has been commended by consumers and the grocery trade alike. The program received Congressional Commendation and was read into the Congressional Record.

FACULTY LOAN PROGRAM

IBM Corp.
Old Orchard Road
Armonk, N.Y. 10504

Business: Information Handling
Sales: 7,500mm
CEO: T. Vincent Learson   Employees: 269,291

Contact: Mike Halford
Address: same as above
Telephone: (914) 765-4030
Program Reaches: several hundred students
When Started: Fall, 1971
Budget: n/a

Program Outline:

In its effort to help support Black Colleges by loaning the services of IBM employees for teaching in subjects requiring assistance, 18 scientists, engineers, and other volunteers from IBM's professional staff, on paid leaves from their regular jobs, are spending an academic year teaching at 18 different Black colleges in the South. Each participating college had previously identified skill and curriculum needs. These were matched with the abilities and experience of IBM volunteers. The IBM people are now teaching undergraduate and graduate courses in physics, mathematics, business, chemistry, computer science and engineering. In many cases, these courses are being offered for the first time because there is now someone to teach them. The program provides added business professional expertise for the Black college faculties and administrations, and assists the colleges in offering quality education.

Co. Personnel Involved: 18 employees on loan for 1 academic year

Measure of Success: Positively received by students and Black educators to date, although overall conclusions can only be reached at the end of the academic year. Statements from Black educators indicate the program will help Black colleges: (1) provide quality education; (2) attract promising students and faculty and (3) attract increased financial support from private sources.

ENGLISH AS A SECOND LANGUAGE

JOHN HANCOCK MUTUAL LIFE INSURANCE CO.
200 Berkeley Street
Boston, Mass. 02117

Business: Insurance
CEO: Frank B. Maher

Sales: 1,760mm
Employees: 22,554

Contact: Miriam Seiler, ESL instructor
Address: same as above
Telephone: (617) 421-2263
Program Reaches: approx. 70/semester
When Started: approx. 1968
Budget: n/a

Program Outline:

The purpose of this program is to upgrade the English language skills of non-English-speaking John Hancock employees from more than 20 countries.

ESL classes, which are offered to company employees on company time, employ modern aural-oral language teaching methods to encourage increased oral fluency as well as improved writing skills. A complete language laboratory supplements the classroom curriculum. Other employees attend labs, working independently with periodic consultation with the instructor. The class and lab curricula are flexible, to meet the different needs of the students, and include introductory as well as advanced books and tapes.

Class and lab materials are constantly evaluated and revised according to the needs of the students. However, the basic format of class and lab is expected to remain the same.

Co. Personnel Involved: One full time ESL instructor; other Career Development Program instructors are available for specialized needs beyond the ESL curriculum.

Measure of Success: Evaluation by instructor of programs during semester; increased job mobility; program is a resource for many outside ESL programs.

FLEXIBLE CAMPUS PROGRAM

JOHN HANCOCK MUTUAL LIFE INSURANCE CO.
200 Berkeley Street
Boston, Mass. 02117

Business: Insurance
CEO: Frank B. Maher

Sales: 1,760mm
Employees: 22,554

Contact: Marion L. Nierintz
Address: same as above
Telephone: (617) 421-4267
Program Reaches: 1,000
When Started: planning—mid-1971; implementation—
    early 1972
Budget: n/a

Program Outline:

John Hancock, in cooperation with the city of Boston and other firms and community organizations, has combined educational and business resources to provide high school students off-campus credit courses and internships.

In this new dimension of high school curriculum involving initially 1,000 students, the company donates its facilities and personnel for teaching courses such as electronic data processing, job instruction, effective communications and business organization. At John Hancock, 8 students from the Burke School are attending a 10-week course in business machines and meet at the company 3 afternoons a week. The rest of their time is spent at the high school where they are completing required courses. Also, 4 11th grade students attend a class in job instruction training which is also attended by John Hancock employees. In addition, John Hancock offers a basic computer programming course. Two boys attend all day, every day, for 2 months, while most other students in the program do have to report to school at least a few hours a day or 1 per week.

This is a pilot program; it is too early to fully evaluate yet. Changes will be made only in conjunction with Boston Public School personnel.

Co. Personnel Involved: approx. 10 (predominantly in-company instructors from education and training and EDP)

Measure of Success: Initial indications show that students have been able to meaningfully participate in classes and have expressed a high degree of enthusiasm. Boston Public School coordinators have also been pleased with the program.

PREP PROGRAM

JOHN HANCOCK MUTUAL LIFE INSURANCE CO.
200 Berkeley Street
Boston, Mass. 02117

Business: Insurance   Sales: 1,760mm
CEO: Frank B. Maher   Employees: 22,554

Contact: Karen Keep
Address: Career Dev. Programs, C-6, same as above
Telephone: (617) 421-2263
Program Reaches: over 700
When Started: 1968
Budget: n/a

Program Outline:

Extensive experience in offering employee career training has made adult education an important part of John Hancock's community service capability. The Prep Pro-gram assists the disadvantaged of greater Boston in receiving further education and training for improved economic standing.

Professionally staffed with teachers from the company's Education and Training Division and local schools, the Prep Program has given more than 700 people a chance to work towards high school equivalency certificates or to learn a meaningful business skill. "English as a Second Language," a company-instituted educational course for employees with language difficulties, has been modified for Prep Program participants as a Language Arts course of study.

Co. Personnel Involved: 27 in total: 1 clerk, 1 adminis-trator, 2 teachers, 4 teaching aides, 17 students

Measure of Success: number of equivalency certificates earned, teacher evaluation (written comment and mea-sure), number of peopel obtaining employment as a result of their training

KAISER BAUXITE'S COMMUNITY PROGRAMS

KAISER ALUMINUM & CHEMICAL CORP. (KACC)
Kaiser Center
300 Lakeside Drive
Oakland, Cal. 94604

Business: Aluminum, Chemicals, Specialty Metals
   and Refractories Products, and
   Diversified Operations
Sales: 881mm
CEO: Thomas J. Ready, Jr.   Employees: 26,000

Contact: R. L. Spees, Corp. Dir. of Pub. Affairs
Address: same as above
Telephone: (415) 271-3967
Program Reaches: over 1,000
When Started: 1953
Budget: unable to accurately estimate

Program Outline:

Kaiser Bauxite, a subsidiary of KACC, in mining bauxite on the North Coast of Jamaica, has pursued and is continuing a comprehensive community involvement pro-gram so that the people of the area, mostly small land farmers, can understand the mining operation and the company behind it.

As part of this program the company is involved in an educational and training support effort for the com-munity. In the course of its 20 plus years in Jamaica, Kaiser Bauxite has donated land for various educational institutions—including technical, vocational and scientific schools and laboratories. Kaiser Bauxite also conducts regular adult education courses to teach the basic skills, while other company sponsored programs offer vo-cational and technical training to young people. Pre-sently, the company is donating approximately $150,000 for technical training centers which are sponsored by the Jamaican Government. Also in this area of education, the company has donated property and greathouses for the 4-H demonstration centers and other youth development programs. A regular scholarship program is also sponsored by the company to enable Jamaican youths to further their education at home and abroad.

Co. Personnel Involved: Company involvement in the whole community involvement program includes: 5 management personnel; liason and support from the parent company in Oakland is supplied by 4 senior management personnel. This does not include the 150 Kaiser Bauxite salaried people working directly and in-directly with the various Jamaican communities.

Measure of Success: 90% of the supervisory personnel employed by the company are Jamaicans indicating acceptance by the local people of the company presence.

GUIDANCE COUNSELORS TRAVELING WORKSHOP

KIMBERLY-CLARK CORP.
N. Lake Street
Neenah, Wis. 54956

Business: Manufacturing Paper and Cellulose Products
and Wholesale Lumber
Sales: 869mm
CEO: Darwin E. Smith   Employees: 29,051

Contact: Robert H. Mott, P.R. Dept.
Address: same as above
Telephone: (414) 729-1212
Program Reaches: 25-30 counselors and their counselees
When Started: 1960
Budget: currently $2,250/year

Program Outline:

The purpose of the program is to give high school
counselors the tools they need to provide adequate
information in the area of vocational guidance. It helps to
close the communications gap between trade schools in
the company headquarters area and the high schools.

Each year, the company's Guidance Counselors Traveling
Workshop takes high school advisors on a 3-day tour of
selected trade schools within a 300 mile radius of
Neenah. Groups have visited Chicago, Milwaukee,
Minneapolis and Madison, attending sessions at about 6
schools per trip.

The company tries to schedule a balanced program so the
counselors can see schools of art, music, nursing and
education as well as vocational and technical institutes.

Kimberly-Clark pays the bills, including a fee for a
coordinator selected from among the guidance counselors
in the area, bus rental, room and board, and miscellaneous expenses.

Co. Personnel Involved: two: 1 works with coordinator
in developing the schedule and accompanies the tour.
Another provides the necessary clerical/stenographic services.

Measure of Success: The company is now planning to
extend the program to other communities where it
operates plants.

TRAINING FOR ENVIRONMENTAL TECHNICIANS

KIMBERLY-CLARK CORP.
N. Lake Street
Weenah, Wis. 54956

Business: Manufacturing Paper and Cellulose Products
and Wholesale Lumber
Sales: 869mm
CEO: Darwin E. Smith   Employees: 29,051

Contact: Mill Manager
Address: Peter J. Schweitzer Div.,
Kimberly-Clark Corp.
Lee, Mass. 01238
Telephone: (413) 243-1000
Program Reaches: n/a
When Started: n/a
Budget: n/a

Program Outline:

The purpose of this program is to give students technical
training as well as make them aware of industry's problems.

The students monitor the workday functions of a solid

waste disposal unit in the Peter J. Schweitzer Division at
Lee, Mass. They also learn about the costs of cleaning up.

The students include teen-agers and middle-agers, all of
whom are studying to become environmental technicians
under a federally-funded education program at Berkshire
Community College at Pittsfield. The curriculum is highly
concentrated: 7 hours daily, 5 days/week for 32 weeks.
Components include academic communications courses
(speech, literature, composition) plus instrumentation,
math, chemistry, contemporary environmental issues and
a helping of group dynamics.

Each student spends 27 hours over a 3-week period at the
disposal facility and laboratory. Working under supervision of technicians and others, he analyzes samples of
Housatonic River water, tests cleansed effluent and computes results of the investigation.

Co. Personnel Involved: Five persons take part in varying
degrees; participation may take 3-25% of a person's time.

Measure of Success: Measured in number of participants,
the college-company venture is small. As a meaningful,
valid enterprise, the effort takes on more weight. The
company is coming away with a better idea of how others
perceive it as owning up to its responsibility.

CLASSES FOR NON-ENGLISH SPEAKING EMPLOYEES

LEVI STRAUSS &'CO.
98 Battery Street
San Francisco, Cal. 94106

Business: Manufacturing Men's, Boys'
  and Women's Wear
Sales: 327mm
CEO: Peter E. Haas   Employees: 17,500

Contact: Thomas E. Harris, Dir. Comm. Affairs
Address: same as above
Telephone: (415) 391-6200, ext. 389
Program Reaches: to date, approx. 100
When Started: 1970
Budget: $23,700 for 1972

Program Outline:

The Community Affairs Department initiated a Conversational English class for employees at the San Francisco plant who wished to learn or improve their English. Instruction is offered in both spoken and written English in the classes.

Levi's is presently working with school districts in El Paso, Texas, San Jose and San Francisco to develop adult education classes leading to GED certificates for employees. Classes will be conducted in company facilities after work and will eventually be opened to the entire community.

Co. Personnel Involved: Community Affairs Department

Measure of Success: There are waiting lists of employees who wish to participate in the English classes. Also the adult education departments of the local school districts are assuming responsibility for these classes.

PROJECT S.E.E.D.

LEVI STRAUSS & CO.
98 Battery Street
San Francisco, Cal. 94106

Business: Manufacturing Men's, Boys',
  and Women's Wear
Sales: 327mm
CEO: Peter E. Haas   Employees: 17,500

Contact: Thomas E. Harris, Dir. Comm. Affairs
Address: same as above
Telephone: (415) 391-6200, ext. 389
Program Reaches: demonstration project for 2 classes
When Started: Fall, 1972
Budget: initial grant, $14,000

Program Outline:

The purpose of this program is to develop new approaches to elementary education. The company is working with an educator from Berkley, Dr. William Johntz, in developing this new approach: that of teaching advanced mathematics to elementary students in minority schools using Ph.D.'s from industry and universities. This program is to be introduced in Knoxville in 2 ghetto schools with teachers being drawn from Knoxville College, the University of Tennessee and Oakridge Atomic Energy Commission.

Co. Personnel Involved: Community Affairs Department

Measure of Success: Project SEED has been thoroughly researched by the University of Michigan.

SCHOLARSHIP ASSISTANCE

LEVI STRAUSS & CO.
98 Battery Street
San Francisco, Cal. 94106

Business: Manufacturing Men's, Boys',
  and Women's Wear
Sales: 327mm
CEO: Peter E. Haas   Employees: 17,500

Contact: Thomas E. Harris, Dir. Comm.
Address: same as above
Telephone: (415) 391-6200, ext. 389
Program Reaches: 75-100/year
When Started: 1971
Budget: initial grant, $1,000

Program Outline:

The purpose of this program is to provide scholarship assistance for the education of minority students. The company has given 4 scholarships to San Jose State College. In El Paso, the company challenged operation S.E.R. and launched a scholarship drive to assist minority students to enroll at El Paso Community College. Also, the Levi Strauss Foundation provided assistance to a consortium of colleges and universities, primarily for minority education programs; additionally, a scholarship fund for employees and families is provided as well as a "matching funds" program.

Co. Personnel Involved: function of the Community Affairs Department

Measure of Success: In the El Paso Scholarship Drive, 23 students have received assistance and will be attending school.

COOPERATIVE STUDENT PLAN

METROPOLITAN LIFE INSURANCE CO.
One Madison Avenue
New York, N.Y. 10010

Business: Insurance   Sales: 5,555mm
CEO: Richard R. Shinn   Employees: 57,000

Contact: J. G. Reiners
Address: same as above
Telephone: (212) 578-3440
Program Reaches: 300-400/year
When Started: 1947
Budget: varies according to employee needs

Program Outline:

Each year, hundreds of high school seniors, including large numbers of Negro and Puerto Rican students, work in Metropolitan's Home Office. In addition to providing needed financial help while attending school, this work experience also motivates them to remain in school until graduation.

Under this program, students work alternate weeks in pairs. At the time of graduation, if they remain with the company, they are given credit for their work service in terms of starting salary, vacation allowance, job assignment, etc.

Co. Personnel Involved: Difficult to answer since program is used throughout the Home Office. The individual supervisors provide on-the-job training, orientation and encourage self-development.

Measure of Success: Almost all qualify for permanent employment and about 70-80% continue in full time regular employment following graduation.

EDUCATIONAL OPPORTUNITIES AT METROPOLITAN

METROPOLITAN LIFE INSURANCE CO.
One Madison Avenue
New York, N.Y. 10010

Business: Insurance   Sales: 5,555mm
CEO: Richard R. Shinn   Employees: 57,000

Contact: R. F. Barry
Address: same as above
Telephone: (212) 578-2181
Program Reaches: some 6,000 participate
When Started: over 30 years ago
Budget: n/a

Program Outline:

A host of training and development activities is provided for Metropolitan employees at all levels without reference to race, creed, color, sex, age or national origin.

Skilled training is offered on company time in such areas as typing, keypunching, shorthand, secretarial practice and office machine operations. Courses in staff and supervisory skills are provided to further employee growth and development. Over a hundred self study programs are available in a wide range of general subjects in the company's Self Development Center. Consultation, testing and help is available as needed. However, enrolled employees study on their own time and at their own pace. Those located in detached offices are serviced through the mails. In addition, a number of study programs for those who wish to attain professional status in life insurance are available. Each year, the company helps hundreds of employees meet educational expenses at outside institutions for courses related to their assignments, and for undergraduate degree programs in evening colleges.

Co. Personnel Involved: full time training staff of 47

Measure of Success: yearly increase in participation

EMPLOYMENT QUALIFICATION PROGRAM

METROPOLITAN LIFE INSURANCE CO.
One Madison Avenue
New York, N.Y. 10010

Business: Insurance   Sales: 5,555mm
CEO: Richard R. Shinn   Employees: 57,000

Contact: R. F. Barry
Address: same as above
Telephone: (212) 578-2181
Program Reaches: 1,200 in past 5 years
When Started: 1966
Budget: n/a

Program Outline:

This program is designed to recruit, train, develop and qualify for employment disadvantaged minority group members. The New York State Employment Service and other agencies refer candidates who cannot meet normal employment qualifications. The training program is 13 weeks long and classes are limited to 8-12 trainees so that special attention can be given to each individual. Fifteen hours a week are devoted to basic clerical skills. After orientation, half of each day is spent working on a job in an operating area. On graduation, participants become regular, full time clerks.

Co. Personnel Involved: full time training staff of 9

Measure of Success: More than 2/3 of those participating qualify for regular employment.

HIGH SCHOOL SERVICE STATION TRAINING PROGRAM

MOBIL OIL CORP.
150 E. 42nd Street
New York, N.Y. 10017

Business: Petroleum Operations Sales: 7,261mm
CEO: William P. Tavoulares Employees: 75,600

Contact: A. L. Roe
Address: same as above
Telephone: (212) 833-3372
Program Reaches: from 25 to 100 boys/year
When Started: September, 1970
Budget: varies, depending on facilities and equipment already available at the school

Program Outline:

The purpose of this program is to reduce the high school dropout rate at inner city high schools.

A pilot program was instituted by Mobil at a New York City high school in which junior year boys are given automotive and service training plus paid work experience as service station attendants, attending school 1 week and working the next week throughout the school year. Emphasis is on providing an interesting classroom experience relevant to the world of work, and developing a marketable skill. Mobil trained the school system instructors who teach the course. Mobil also helped develop the course outline; supplies service station equipment used in teaching; provides text materials and visual aids and arranges for field trips and jobs with Mobil dealers.

Co. Personnel Involved: several people from headquarters and from 2 to 6 field offices for each project

Measure of Success: Success in achieving and maintaining a high level of class attendance at New York City schools, plus evidence of increased interest in other courses, e.g. math and reading, have resulted in introducing the program to a Los Angeles school in January, 1972. Initial results there are good. Further expansion to 2 additional cities is planned for September, 1972.

EDUCATION PROGRAMS

MOTOROLA, INC.
9401 Grand Avenue
Franklin Park, Ill. 60131

Business: Electronics Sales: 900+mm
CEO: Wm. J. Weisz Employees: 36,000

Contact: Judy Ressler, P.R.
Address: same as above
Telephone: (312) 451-1000, ext. 3692
Program Reaches: n/a
When Started: n/a
Budget: n/a

Program Outline:

The purpose of this program is to encourage a greater quality of educational enterprise.

Program function: (1) SPD gives 2 graduate fellowships at $2,400 each to support an outstanding student in the public interest; (2) Motorola encourages its employees to serve on educational boards, committees and commissions; (3) Motorola takes an active interest in forming curricula of universities, colleges, institutes and high schools by meeting with deans and other educational persons, and serving on curricula review committees; (4) pays tuitions for education of its full time employees; (5) employees are encouraged to lecture at universities; (6) puts out "Motorola Volunteers in Civic Affairs" on a quarterly basis which encourages Motorola employees to become involved with educational institutions, among other groups; (7) donates 1000s of dollars of electronics equipment to schools to give students a wider experience in their education; (8) offers in-plant courses (credit and non-credit) so employees may continue their education. Also encourages schools to offer a broader spectrum of courses to fulfill needs of industry's employees and the community; (9) donates a $10,000 unrestricted grant to Arizona State University each year; (10) sponsors or assists with research done by students or student groups (11) Motorola Chairman, Robert W. Galvin is one of 12 Fellows of the University of Notre Dame. Other officers and directors are trustees, etc. (12) There are a large number of other donations and cooperation between Motorola and educational institutions which are just too numerous to include.

Co. Personnel Involved: all the training employees and countless number of persons who lecture or teach, become involved on school boards or committees and work on special projects with schools

Measure of Success: A large percentage of Motorola employees receive degrees through the encouragement of the company. In Arizona State University's College of Engineering, about half of those receiving masters degrees are Motorola employees.

INDUSTRIAL SKILLS CENTER
CHICAGO BOARD OF EDUCATION

MOTOROLA, INC.
9401 W. Grand Avenue
Franklin Park, Ill. 60131

Business: Electronics
CEO: William J. Weisz

Sales: 900mm
Employees: 36,000

Contact: Ray Orth, Dir. Employee Svc.
Address: same as above
Telephone: (312) 451-1000, ext. 2025/6
Program Reaches: school enrollment of more than 300
When Started: 1969
Budget: Initial budget and investment in management time is approximately $50,000.

Program Outline:

The Motorola program at the Industrial Skills Center is a cooperative effort with the Chicago Board of Education to aid high school students in the inner city in relating their education to skills required in industry. Other companies, like Western Electric, have participated since 1969. Students in the program devote 4 hours per day to high school academic endeavors and 4 hours per day to industrial skills training. In the Motorola program, students learn to use electronic test equipment and perform electrical tests on radio component parts. As the student's experience broadens, he is acquainted with basic electronic theory and then learns to perform simple radio repair. The training is designed to help prepare the student for jobs typically found in the electronics industry and to motivate the student to continue his technical education so that he can maximize his aptitude and develop skills. Improvements in the format of the program will be implemented as developed.

Co. Personnel Involved: 1 person full time as a Coordinator of Training and 6 managers in part time support functions

Measure of Success: The response of the students participating in this program has convinced Motorola that this project fulfills the student's need to prepare himself for job opportunities when he completes his high school education. The company believes that it further motivates the student to continue his education, either in a technical school or in a college degree program, so that he can prepare to maximize his potential.

PROJECT UNITE

NATIONWIDE INSURANCE
246 N. High Street
Columbus, Oh. 43216

Business: Insurance
CEO: Dean W. Jeffers

Sales: 497mm
Employees: 8,860

Contact: Will Hellerman
Address: same as above
Telephone: (614) 228-4711, ext. 770
Program Reaches: when completed, all households in Columbus
When Started: December, 1971
Budget: The costs have been underwritten by 3 private foundations with an estimated total budget of $13,000. It should be pointed out that no public money has been used in the project.

Program Outline:

This broadly based active program is aimed at uniting and using the resources of the school system with those of the community to determine actions to be taken towards solving problems facing the Columbus Public Schools in 7 major areas: educational programs, finance, buildings, staff resources, urban problems, communications and organization. Volunteers, working in 7 "Search and Solve" teams, have spent some 36,290 hours researching each area of problems, and reading recommendations for their solutions. A printed report to be hand delivered to each Columbus home by the PTA and Model City groups will be followed by 9 public forums for discussion purposes. The final report will be turned over to the Board of Education on June 6 for action; their complete cooperation has been forthcoming throughout. Although the basic plans have been followed from the "kick-off" date, certain changes have been made in the program's format as it has progressed.

Co. Personnel Involved: Specifically from Nationwide: (1) community coordinator (general chairman) practically full time, (2) sub-committee chairmen; 2 working in areas of finance and special education, (3) secretarial assistance (5 to 8) and (4) occasional assistance by public relations personnel.

Measure of Success: Involvement of over 1,900 volunteers; almost 100% cooperation of the media; over 26,000 volunteer man-hours and, finally, the adoption of those recommendations by the school board at the conclusion of the program. As an incidental measurement, although the program was not envisioned to be a forerunner of a school bond issue in November, it is now very clear that the results of the program could very well contribute to a successful passage of any such issue placed before the public.

CLIFFORD SCOTT ASSISTANCE PROGRAM

NEW JERSEY BELL TELEPHONE CO.
540 Broad Street
Newark, N.J.

Business: Communications   Sales: 691mm
CEO: Robert W. Kleinert   Employees: 30,800

Contact: Donald F. McCormick
Address: same as above
Telephone: (201) 649-2810
Program Reaches: 220
When Started: September, 1971
Budget: $56,000

Program Outline:

The purpose of the program is to improve the reading ability of high school students. This program is an interdisciplinary, multi-media approach to learning and reading. Thematic units have been devised by 2 teams of teachers; 1 team works with business education freshmen; another team works with college preparatory freshmen. The units are based on the interests and needs of students and include common core vocabulary skills activities and reading material on many reading levels. This approach reduces the reading pressure placed on students and helps them to see the relationship of each subject to the other. Graduate interns are used to assist the teachers in implementing the program.

Co. Personnel Involved: 2 people—administrative duties only—approximately 20% of 1 person's time

Measure of Success: Success is relative to administrative commitment, careful teacher planning, availability of resources, and effective in-service planning. Standardized pre-tests and post-tests, reading and math scores; inventories; discipline and attendance records; records of books read by students; student projects; teacher attitudinal forms.

NEWARK SCHOOL BOARD BUSINESS STUDY

NEW JERSEY BELL TELEPHONE CO.
540 Broad Street
Newark, N.J.

Business: Communications   Sales: 691mm
CEO: Robert W. Kleinert   Employees: 30,800

Contact: Donald F. McCormick
Address: Room 801B, same as above
Telephone: (201) 649-2810
Program Reaches: n/a
When Started: April, 1970
Budget: Time of employees from 10 companies plus miscellaneous expenses

Program Outline:

Under the sponsorship of the Greater Newark Chamber of Commerce and the leadership of New Jersey Bell, this program was originated to bring together the talents of the business community and educators to assist the Newark School Board in identifying problems and applying, where possible, modern business methods, in an attempt to improve educational opportunity for the youth of Newark. The specific function was, using a task force approach, to study, recommend solutions and help implement programs in the non-curricular side of the Education System of Newark. Complete studies were made in the areas of supply management (purchasing, warehousing and distribution), personnel, school plant (custodial service, maintenance and repair, and architecture and engineering) and business activities (payroll, accounting, and data processing). Written and verbal reports were submitted to the School Board. The implementation process is still underway.

Co. Personnel Involved: 1 full time for 1 year, 1/3 time for 6 months

Measure of Success: the recommendations that have been implemented, resulting in improved services to the staff and students and the increased value of services received for dollars expended

SCHOOL SUPERINTENDENT SEMINARS

NORTHERN ILLINOIS GAS CO.
P.O. Box 190
Aurora, Ill. 60507

Business: Distributing Natural Gas
Sales: 365mm
CEO: C. J. Gouthier   Employees: 3,100

Contact: Ed Koska, Dir. P.R.
Address: same as above
Telephone: (312) 355-8000
Program Reaches: approx. 300 administrators, and through publicity, an undetermined number of the public
When Started: 1969
Budget: n/a

Program Outline:

The purpose of the program is to gather Illinois school superintendents together for discussion of topics relevant to them. For example, in 1971, the seminar featured a student panel, the purpose of which was to familiarize administrators with students' views on education. While the seminar programs differ each year, they are all designed to present a forum for the educators to exchange ideas and to hear discussions. In addition, they are designed to help the company and the educators understand each other's needs and goals.

Co. Personnel Involved: Approximately 25 persons help to organize the event and serve as hosts.

Measure of Success: As indicated by the excellent attendance each year, the administrators find the seminars informative and worthwhile. Wide print coverage of last year's speeches indicate the media view the program as newsworthy and relevant.

DUAL DEGREES PROGRAM

OLIN CORP.
120 Long Ridge Road
Stamford, Conn. 06904

Business: Chemicals, Metal Products,
   Packaging Materials
Sales: 1125mm
CEO: Gordon Grand   Employees: 3,200

Contact: M. A. d'Amelio, Mgr.
   Education and Support Programs
Address: same as above
Telephone: (203) 356-3173
Program Reaches: approx. 180 students to date
When Started: 1968
Budget: Olin Corp. Charitable Trust "seed money" $265,000 plus $90,000 for nationwide recruiting effort

Program Outline:

The program is a multi-college experiment by Olin Corporation Charitable Trust and other co-sponsors designed to increase the number of highly qualified Black engineers and aimed at minority students with technical potential. The Dual Degrees Program joins the resources of 2 Atlanta educational complexes; 1 with the world's largest private cluster-college Black student enrollment and Georgia Tech with the 3rd largest undergraduate engineering enrollment in the country. Under this program, students will attend 1 of the undergraduate schools at Atlanta University Center (Clark College, Morehouse College, Morris Brown College or Spelman College) for 3 years and then transfer to Georgia Tech for 2 additional years. Upon successfully completing the program at both institutions, the student will simultaneously receive two degrees, a Bachelor of Science or Bachelor of Arts degree awarded by the Atlanta University Center, affiliated college attended, and one of the bachelor's degrees in engineering awarded by Georgia Tech. Co-sponsors of the program are the Alfred P. Sloan Foundation, American Cyanamide Company, Westinghouse Corporation, Koppers Foundation, U.S. Steel Foundation, Kaiser Chemical and Aluminum Company of California, Honeywell Company, and General Electric Company.

Co. Personnel Involved: The program had its genesis in discussions with Atlanta University, Georgia Tech and Olin representatives, all still involved.

Measure of Success: Since the program was started, the number of students has increased from 85 to 180. The program is working out so well that it is attracting financial support from several major corporations and foundations, thereby giving the effort by far the nation's largest enrollment of Blacks in engineering.

McCALL SCHOOL TUTORIAL PROJECT

PENN MUTUAL LIFE INSURANCE CO.
Independence Square
Philadelphia, Pa. 19105

Business: Life Insurance   Sales: 354mm
CEO: Frank K. Tarbox   Employees: 1,860

Contact: Suzanne Kaplan
Address: same as above
Telephone: (215) 925-7300
Program Reaches: n/a
When Started: 1971
Budget: n/a

Program Outline:

The purpose of this program is to provide tutorial assistance to pupils at the McCall Elementary School in Philadelphia, in a variety of subjects including non-academically oriented areas such as astronomy and photography.

Employee volunteers spend up to 2 hours/week at the school helping pupils with academic problems on a one-to-one basis or in a group on topics of general interest. Another group of volunteers work with students involved in educational programs held in the home office.

With the financial difficulties of the Philadelphia school system, a program of this kind is definitely needed. It enables the Penn Mutual employees to assist teachers by taking charge of the students and acting as positive influences on them. It also enables the classes to be somewhat smaller in size, increasing teacher contact with students.

Co. Personnel Involved: The Manpower Planning and Development Division is responsible for this project.

Measure of Success: n/a

SOPHIA, INC.

PET, INC.
Pet Plaza
400 S. Fourth Street
St. Louis, Mo. 63166

Business: Processing and Packaging of Food Products
Sales: 658mm
CEO: Boyd F. Schenk   Employees: 22,500

Contact: Will McRoberts
Address: Sophia, Inc., 2568 W. Herbert Street
   St. Louis, Mo. 63106
Telephone: (314) 421-2640
Program Reaches: about 100
When Started: n/a
Budget: n/a

Program Outline:

The philosophy of Sophia is one of individualized education. The organization helps counteract the problems of Black students in inner city school systems, enabling individuals to achieve their academic potential including college preparation.

With inner city youth as the students, Sophia deals basically with the general high school program. Emphasis is placed on math, verbal communications and reading skills. The students are encouraged to develop at their own speed. Materials and approach are tailored to the individual needs and achieved through low ratio tutoring.

Co. Personnel Involved: Two Pet, Inc. executives have been very active in the affairs of Sophia, Inc.

Measure of Success: One hundred five Sophia alumni have been placed in college on full or partial scholarships. The first college graduates among Sophia students (10 inner city youth) will graduate in the class of 1972.

WINGATE PREP

PFIZER, INC.
235 E. Forty-second Street
New York, N.Y. 10017

Business: Pharmaceuticals, Chemicals,
    Cosmetics and Toiletries
Sales: 870.4mm
CEO: Edmund T. Pratt, Jr.   Employees: 5,000

Contact: Wil Crump
Address: same as above
Telephone: (212) 573-3334
Program Reaches: about 80 students/year
When Started: 1970
Budget: $100,000

Program Outline:

The purpose of the program is to provide an alternate means of secondary education for ghetto prep students on the basis of their "not functioning" in the feeder high school. Wingate Prep School is an experimental school that attempts to solve some of the problems of the New York school system. Predominantly Black and/or Spanish speaking students who show promise are selected for admission and Wingate provides teachers in small classes on an almost one-to-one basis and personal guidance counseling in an informal, unstructured educational setting. The program is a cooperative venture sponsored by Pfizer, the New York Urban Coalition and the Board of Education. These groups are interested in a program that involves not only professional educators, but also other interested parties such as community, parents, business. An attempt is being made to maximize the involvement of these diverse groups. Curricula are being assessed for greater relevance in various courses of study.

Co. Personnel Involved: directly 2, indirectly 7

Measure of Success: Current enrollment is 65, and 18 students have graduated, 5 of whom have gone on to college; one on a full 4-year scholarship to the School of Visual Arts.

ADULT EDUCATION COURSE

PHILADELPHIA ELECTRIC CO.
1000 Chestnut Street
Philadelphia, Pa. 19105

Business: Electric Utility   Sales: 504mm
CEO: James L. Everett   Employees: 10,500

Contact: Joseph F. Van Hart, Mgr. P.R. Dept
Address: 2301 Market Street
    Philadelphia, Pa. 19101
Telephone: (215) 841-4000
Program Reaches: employees of the company who do not
    have a high school diploma
When Started: n/a
Budget: n/a

Program Outline:

The purpose of this program is to sponsor an education program for employees of the company who do not have a high school diploma.

The program is designed to provide basic reading, writing and mathematics skills necessary to pass the tests of General Educational Development. Sessions are conducted by the School Extension Division of the Philadelphia Board of Education with all costs being paid by the company.

Co. Personnel Involved: n/a

Measure of Success: n/a

BUSINESS ACADEMY

PHILADELPHIA NATIONAL BANK
Broad and Chestnut Streets
Philadelphia, Pa. 19101

Business: Banking   Sales: not applicable
Earning Assets: $2.0 billion
CEO: G. Morris Dorrance, Jr.   Employees: 2,788

Contact: Thomas J. Patterson, Jr.
Address: same as above
Telephone: (215) 629-3620
Program Reaches: n/a
When Started: 1971
Budget: not yet determined

Program Outline:

In March, 1971, PNB granted a 3-year leave of absence to Mr. Patterson to work with the Philadelphia Urban Coalition to develop a business vocational program in the city. The Business Academy is expected to provide, at a minimum entry level vocational competence to high school students who might otherwise drop out or graduate unqualified for skilled or semi-skilled jobs. Mr. Patterson will develop the curriculum and organize and run the Academy during its first years.

Co. Personnel Involved: 1 person, full time, for 3 years; 2 others from time to time, in supportive activities

Measure of Success: being developed

OPERATION PREPARE

THE PHILADELPHIA NATIONAL BANK
Broad and Chestnut Streets
Philadelphia, Pa. 19101

Business: Banking   Sales: not applicable
Earning Assets: $2.0 billion
CEO: Morris Dorrance, Jr.   Employees: 2,788

Contact: Robert A. Evans, Asst. Pers. Officer
Address: same as above
Telephone: (215) 629-4707
Program Reaches: 35-45 students
When Started: 1968
Budget: n/a

Program Outline:

This is a cooperative work-study program that provides business awareness and experience to young men and women from inner city high schools. During the 1971-72 school year, 19 juniors and 19 seniors from 7 Philadelphia high schools go to school during the morning and work afternoons in various PNB departments. This provides valuable job experience and school back-up which emphasizes the learning of skills and good work habits. Job assignments normally are for periods of 6 months or a year to give depth of experience. During the summer, the students work full time at their assignments.

Co. Personnel Involved: Three persons are involved in program development and administration. Twenty-five department heads and immediate supervisors work with the student on the job.

Measure of Success: Of the 25 seniors in the 1970-71 program, 11 work for PNB full time, 9 went to college and 5 are in military service, married and not working, or unaccounted for.

READING IMPROVEMENT PROGRAM

THE PHILADELPHIA NATIONAL BANK
Broad and Chestnut Streets
Philadelphia, Pa. 19101

Business: Banking   Sales: not applicable
Earning Assets: $2.0 billion
CEO: Morris Dorrance, Jr.   Employees: 2,788

Contact: Robert A. Evans, Asst. Pers. Officer
Address: same as above
Telephone: (215) 629-4707
Program Reaches: all second, third and fourth graders at
    John Greenleaf Whittier Elementary School
When Started: 1971
Budget: $24,900

Program Outline:

The purpose of the program is to improve reading levels
and interest in education in line with a corporate goal.

At the Reading Center, a reading teacher and two
assistants teach reading fundamentals and improvement
to all second, third and fourth graders. In addition, 42
PNB employees are given release time to tutor children
with more severe reading problems.

Bank is now discussing with the school the inclusion of
an adult reading education program as well as the feasibility of reading education of preschool children.

Co. Personnel Involved: Basic reading program—2; one--
to-one tutoring—42 active tutors and 8 reserve tutors

Measure of Success: too early to tell

SCHOOL VOLUNTEER PROGRAM

THE PHILADELPHIA SAVINGS FUND SOCIETY
1212 Market Street
Philadelphia, Pa. 19107

Business: Savings Bank   Sales: not applicable
CEO: M. Todd Cooke   Employees: 828

Contact: Anne Ruasch, Com. Affairs Coordinator
Address: same as above
Telephone: (215) 629-2132
Program Reaches: approx. 100
When Started: September, 1969
Budget: $1,000 plus, and transportation costs for indivi-
    dual tutors involved

Program Outline:

The purpose of the program is to provide tutors as aids
for South Philadelphia's Meredith Elementary School
pupils in the elementary reading area. Through one-to-
one pupil ratio and in-class tutoring in the Volunteer
School Program, employees of the Bank work with
students of 1 local school, 2 hours, 1 morning per week,
for each of 20 tutors.

They work in class under the guidance of teachers, to
help pupils develop basic reading skills. Evaluation
meetings are held annually at the end of each tutoring
program to discuss satisfactoriness of efforts and develop
possible changes of direction or expansion of plans.

Co. Personnel Involved: A roster of 20 of the Bank's
employees participate each year, which represents a total
of 60 different employees involved over the 3-year period
of the program at the Bank. This represents over 700
man-hours.

Measure of Success: The volunteer tutors are enthusiastic
and have indicated good response to their efforts during
in-class sessions. The children are responding by exhi-
biting more interest in learning when a tutor concentrates
his or her efforts on the slow learner or pupil lacking
motivation.

SCHOLARSHIP PROGRAM

PIPER AIRCRAFT CORP.
Lock Haven, Pa. 17745

Business: Manufacturing of Aircraft
Sales: 65mm
CEO: Joseph M. Mergan   Employees: 2,998

Contact: W. T. Piper, Jr.
Address: same as above
Telephone: (717) 748-5963
Program Reaches: 52/year
When Started: 1958
Budget: $32,000/year

Program Outline:

The purpose of the program is to provide college scholarships for the children of Piper employees. Each year a total of 13 sons or daughters of Piper employees are selected to receive college scholarships to the school of their choice. These are based on college entrance examinations with the student receiving the highest grades being awarded the top scholarship. The sum total of the scholarships each year amounts to $8,000 and, assuming the students stay in college for the 4 years, this means that there are a total of 52 students receiving $32,000 annually in the way of financial help from the company.

Co. Personnel Involved: 2 people, not to any large extent

Measure of Success: This program is much appreciated by those employees whose children have been successful in obtaining scholarships for their college education and it seems to have been quite successful.

RHEEM NATIONAL MERIT SCHOLARSHIP PROGRAM

RHEEM MANUFACTURING CO.
400 Park Avenue
New York, N.Y. 10022

Business: Manufacturing—Appliances, Steel
   Containers, Pressure Vessels
Sales: 220mm
CEO: Clifford V. Coons   Employees: 4,500

Contact: William S. Noel
Address: same as above
Telephone: (212) 355-3400
Program Reaches: 5,000 Rheem employees and their
   families
When Started: 1960
Budget: $6,000 maximum/year

Program Outline:

The purpose of the program is to assist young people in gaining a college education through scholarships. Sons and daughters of any Rheem and domestic subsidiary company employee may qualify for a 4-year college scholarship. High School academic records, extra curricular activities, special tests administered by National Merit Scholarship Corporation and personal qualities are the basis on which scholarship winners are selected. Selection is entirely in the hands of the National Merit Scholarship Corporation. One Rheem scholarship is granted each year under the program.

Co. Personnel Involved: 3 work with the National Scholarship Corp.

Measure of Success: n/a

CO-OP EDUCATION PROGRAM
SUMMER WORK-STUDY PROGRAM

A. H. ROBINS CO., INC.
1407 Cummings Drive
Richmond, Va. 23220

Business: Pharmaceutical   Sales: 150mm
CEO: W. L. Zimmer, III   Employees: 4,000

Contact: John T. Terry
Address: same as above
Telephone: (703) 257-2309
Program Reaches: 2
When Started: 1968
Budget: n/a

Program Outline:

The purpose of this program is to help minority college students in scientific disciplines by mixing formal academic study with actual work experience. The individuals combine work experience with similar academic studies and receive wages commensurate with their experience or background. Each individual works in A. H. Robins's Research Center and is exposed to a number of scientific techniques, such as helping with investigation of compounds of new methodology to determine the pharmocological activity. With respect to the faculty member involved (from Virginia State College), this individual is assigned to Robins's Research Center and performs a variety of more sophisticated experiments which are designed to bridge the gap between business and institutions of learning.

Co. Personnel Involved: 1, direct supervision

Measure of Success: The company has employed 2 co-op students.

TUTORING

ROHM & HAAS CO.
Independence Mall West
Philadelphia, Pa. 19105

Business: Manufacturing of Chemicals, Plastics,
    Fibers and Health Products
Sales: 507mm
CEO: Vincent R. Gregory   Employees: 13,805

Contact: John M. Geisel
Address: same as above
Telephone: (215) 592-3863
Program Reaches: 50-100 students/semester
When Started: 1968
Budget: none

Program Outline:

The purpose of this program is to provide informal tutoring in basic learning (arithmetic, spelling, language, history, etc.) to elementary school children in a disadvantaged community. Volunteer employee-tutors visit the lower elementary school to provide individual help to students as recommended by instructors. Volunteers meet with students once a week for approximately 1½ hours. The project has temporarily been discontinued pending possible change in format.

Co. Personnel Involved: 50-60 volunteer employee-tutors in after-work sessions throughout the school year

Measure of Success: judged by school system instructors to be very helpful in enabling students to keep up with studies and to advance

ENGLISH CLASSES FOR FOREIGN SPEAKING EMPLOYEES

SIGNODE CORP.
2600 N. Western Avenue
Chicago, Ill. 60647

Business: Manufacturing Steel and Plastic Strapping
Sales: 200mm
CEO: J. Milton Moon   Employees: 5,084

Contact: J. J. Palen,
    Coord. Community Affairs
Address: same as above
Telephone: (312) 276-8500
Program Reaches: 20-30
When Started: 1970
Budget: minimal

Program Outline:

The purpose of the program is to help foreign speaking employees become more proficient in the use of the English language. Signode made arrangements with the Chicago Board of Education to supply a teacher to instruct foreign speaking employees in English. The classes are held on Signode property for both day and night shift personnel. Night shift classes consist of 2-hour sessions twice a week before the shift begins; day shift employees attend 2-hour classes twice a week after their shift.

Co. Personnel Involved: 1 in charge, Mr. Palen, and personnel department at Skokie, Ill. plant

Measure of Success: n/a

SCHOLARSHIP AND EDUCATION AID PROGRAM

SONESTA HOTELS
390 Commonwealth Avenue
Boston, Mass. 02215

Business: Managing Hotels   Sales: 121mm
CEO: Paul Sonnabend   Employees: 6,800

Contact: James T. Stamas
Address: same as above
Telephone: (617) 536-2700
Program Reaches: n/a
When Started: n/a

Program Outline:

The Scholarship and Education Aid Program is a project of the Sonesta Human Development Fund for children of employees who meet these general guidelines. children of low-income employees who have demonstrated the motivation to want to continue their education; children whose parent or guardian is employed by a Sonesta Hotel within the continental U.S.A.

The recipients must meet the acceptance criteria of a recognized institution of higher education. Financial aid is not available for studying toward a high school diploma. The parent or guardian of applicants is expected to have completed a minimum of 5 years service with Sonesta Hotels. It must be ascertained that adequate funds from other sources are not available.

Assistance is offered in the form of company grants. The maximum grant per applicant is $1,500/year. A total of $1,500 is available to applicants entering a 2-year education program. Scholarships cannot be granted to 1 individual for more than 2 years and priority is given to recipients for any available summer or part time jobs. While such employment cannot be guaranteed, every effort is made to provide a job with Sonesta Hotels. Counseling of employees on additional financial assistance, work arrangements, etc., is handled by the employee's supervisor and/or the hotel Personnel Department.

Co. Personnel Involved: selection committee consists of 3 permanent members

Measure of Success: presently too new to evaluate

ADOPT-A-SCHOOL

SUN OIL CO.
1608 Walnut Street
Philadelphia, Pa. 19103

Business: Diversified Oil Refining
Sales: 1,942mm
CEO: H. Robert Sharbaugh   Employees: 28,400

Contact: Robert A. Matteson
Address: 240 Radnor-Chester Roads
  St. Davids, Pa. 19087
Telephone: (215) 985-1600
Program Reaches: n/a
When Started: 1968
Budget: n/a

Program Outline:

The purpose of the program is to provide students at inner city high schools a one-to-one tutorial situation. The company adopted a predominantly Black inner city boys' high school, and Philadelphia employees began serving as tutors. A similar program was begun at a predominantly Black inner city girls' high school. The program also includes a work-study program for seniors and Sun provides some employment after graduation.

Co. Personnel Involved: 20 tutors

Measure of Success: n/a

COUNTERPART

SYNTEX CORP.
Stanford Industrial Park
Palo Alto, Cal. 94304

Business: Pharmaceutical Veterinary and Health Care
  Products
Sales: 100mm
CEO: George Rosenkranz   Employees: n/a

Contact: Frank Koch, Dir. of P.R.
Address: same as above
Telephone: (415) 855-6111
Program Reaches: n/a
When Started: n/a
Budget: n/a

Program Outline:

This local organization provides a starting or entry point for a variety of community initiated support programs. It is the catalyst for a variety of self-help projects in which both White and Black residents work together constructively and cooperatively with the financial support of all segments of the community. Syntex provided funds for the neighborhood "Clean-up, Paint-up" program; donated to the Counterpart Education Fund which financially assists the support of minority college students; provided monies for office expenses; and supplied funds for covering of the living expenses of the Principal Education Officer of British Honduras who participated in the Counterpart effort for a period of time in 1970.

Co. Personnel Involved: n/a

Measure of Success: n/a

MEXICAN-AMERICAN EDUCATION

SYNTEX CORP.
Stanford Industrial Park
Palo Alto, Cal. 94304

Business: Pharmaceutical, Veterinary and Health Care
  Products
Sales: 100mm
CEO: George Rosenkranz   Employees: n/a

Contact: Frank Koch, Dir. of Corp. P.R.
Address: same as above
Telephone: (415) 855-6111
Program Reaches: Mexican-American students
When Started: 1969
Budget: n/a

Program Outline:

Syntex and Lockheed provided funds for the establishment of cooperative living and eating quarters for 50 Chicano students at the University of California at Berkeley. This permitted the students to reduce their living costs greatly and provided a necessary focus for Mexican-American activities at the University. In addition, Syntex provided funds to purchase color printing equipment which is being used to train Mexican-American students at San Jose State in the photographic and film arts.

Co. Personnel Involved: none

Measure of Success: n/a

MEXICAN AMERICAN LEGAL DEFENSE FUND

SYNTEX CORP.
Stanford Industrial Park
Palo Alto, Cal. 94304

Business: Pharmaceutical Veterinary and Health Care
  Products
Sales: 100mm
CEO: George Rosenkranz   Employees: n/a

Contact: Frank Koch, Dir. of Corp. P.R.
Address: same as above
Telephone: (415) 855-6111
Program Reaches: n/a
When Started: 1967
Budget: n/a

Program Outline:

The Defense Fund adjudicates the constitutional and statutory rights of Mexican-Americans; operates a scholarship program to assist promising Mexican-Americans who desire to study law.

Co. Personnel Involved: n/a

Measure of Success: The Fund has awarded 455 scholarships to 231 students comprising over 30% of all Mexican-American students enrolled in law school.

MINORITY CHILD DEVELOPMENT

SYNTEX CORP.
Stanford Industrial Park
Palo Alto, Cal. 94304

Business: Pharmaceutical, Veterinary and Health Care
Sales: 100mm
CEO: George Rosenkranz   Employees: n/a

Contact: Frank Koch, Dir. of Corp. P.R.
Address: same as above
Telephone: (415) 855-6111
Program Reaches: minority children
When Started: n/a
Budget: n/a

Program Outline:

Syntex has provided funds for the Foundation for Research and Community Development to help purchase 2 portable classrooms for the Los Pequentitos Child Development Center in San Jose. The Center is designed to promote intellectual growth and enrichment for the disadvantaged pre-school Mexican-American child. In addition, each year the company sponsors a scholarship for a minority child to attend the Parents Nursery School of Palo Alto. This cooperative pre-school institution has been in existence for over a quarter of a century and aims to have 1/3 of its children from the minority community. A similar Syntex scholarship is available for a minority child at the Bing Nursery School of Stanford.

Co. Personnel Involved: n/a

Measure of Success: n/a

APPRENTICE SCHOOL
(NEWPORT NEWS SHIPBUILDING)

TENNECO, INC.
(Newport News Shipbuilding Division)
4101 Washington Avenue
Newport News, Va. 23607

Business: Construction, Modification and Repair
   of Ships
Sales: Tenneco Inc.: 2,883mm
CEO: N. V. Freeman   Employees: 60,000

Contact: Conrad H. Collier, P.R. Dir., NNS
Address: same as above
Telephone: (703) 247-4792
Program Reaches: 4,000 graduates
When Started: 1919
Budget: n/a

Program Outline:

The purpose of the program is to provide skilled craftsmen for Tenneco's shipyard located at Newport News, Virginia, and to provide job opportunities for residents of surrounding area. Shipyard has employment total of over 24,000.

This company-owned and operated school, with its own buildings and staff of 65, offers a full 4-year program of academic instruction and vocational training to an enrollment of approx. 800 students at a time. Students learn many types of technological skills and are paid for both their apprenticeship labor and time spent in school. Most remain in company's employ and many have become top level supervisors and executives. School also has full program of extra-curricular activities, including varsity sports.

Co. Personnel Involved: School has administrative and teaching staff of 65 people.

Measure of Success: Highly successful in providing corps of skilled craftsmen for complex manpower needs of shipyard, ranging from welders to technicians in nuclear propulsion and computer controlled machinery. Of approximately 3,000 graduates presently under 65 years of age, 60% are currently employed at the shipyard and 1/3 of these are in supervisory positions.

LEADERSHIP TRAINING SEMINAR

TRAVELERS INSURANCE CO.
1 Tower Square
Hartford, Conn. 06115

Business: Insurance
CEO: Morrison H. Beach

Sales: 3,000mm
Employees: 30,000

Contact: Wayne D. Casey, P.R. Dept.
Address: same as above
Telephone: (203) 277-2764
Program Reaches: 15, at present
When Started: October, 1971
Budget: $150—miscellaneous supplies

Program Outline:

The purpose of this program is to help to develop decision-making capabilities and constructive leadership within school student bodies. The 10-week, 1-hour seminars, now offered to the Student Council members of West Middle School in Hartford, are held at a Travelers building located near the school. The curriculum includes discussion of what leadership is, problem solving and decision making, how to conduct a meeting and public speaking. The program generated from visits made earlier in 1971 by Travelers personnel to all the elementary and middle schools in the Hartford School System. If judged to be effective, the present pilot will become a model for possible extension to other schools.

As a follow-up to the seminars, the Travelers Toastmasters are working with the school toward forming a junior toastmasters club to help the youngsters improve public speaking.

Co. Personnel Involved: 40 man-hours—preparations by the 2 instructors; 20 man-hours—classroom instruction; 10 man-hours—evaluation

Measure of Success: The final evaluation from the school is yet to be received. However, according to the guidance counselor, the day of the program was the one day of the week that all 15 participants were always present.

THE BED-STY STREET ACADEMY

UNION CARBIDE CORP.
270 Park Avenue
New York, N.Y. 10017

Business: Manufacturing
CEO: William S. Sneath

Sales: 3,026mm
Employees: 102,144

Contact: Dr. L. M. Cooke
Address: same as above
Telephone: (212) 551-6371
Program Reaches: 25 to 30/year
When Started: 1968
Budget: $74,000/year

Program Outline:

The purpose of this program is to motivate disadvantaged youngsters to complete school education and thereby prepare themselves for employment or for continuation into college. The program is aimed at minority youth in the 14-18 age level who have dropped out or have been forced out of the public school system.

Business in New York City is working toward improvement in urban education in several ways. The oldest of these is the New York Urban League Street Academy Program. This program provides an alternate route to education to ghetto youth who have dropped out of the regular schools. One of the most useful aspects in the street academy approach is to find ways to introduce certain street academy concepts into the regular school system to help prevent the potential drop-out from dropping out.

The street academy, sponsored by the Union Carbide Corporation in the Bed-Sty section of Brooklyn, is formally tied to nearby Boys High School and is used as an alternative method of education for students presently enrolled at Boys High as well as those who have already dropped out of the system. In this program, teachers from Boys High work with the regular staff of the Street Academy to exchange methods and ideas to motivate and teach youth who are in conflict or otherwise out of communications with the system. This should also lead to the development of changes in the system which will help the system itself better meet the needs of urban youth. The Academy is now affiliated with a public high school and a community college.

Co. Personnel Involved: 25% of 1 staff person's time

Measure of Success: Over 70% of the Street Academy students achieve high school equivalency level. About 40% go on to college.

SCHOOL PARTNERSHIP PROGRAM
(UNDER THE DIRECTION OF ECONOMIC DEVELOPMENT COUNCIL OF NEW YORK CITY,INC.)

UNION CARBIDE CORP.
270 Park Avenue
New York, N.Y. 10017

Business: Diverse Manufacturing
Sales: 3,026
CEO: William S. Sneath   Employees: 102,144

Contact: Dr. L. M. Cooke
Address: same as above
Telephone: (212) 551-6371
Program Reaches: staff and students at 4 city high schools
When Started: 1969
Budget: Union Carbide's contribution is about $25,000 in salaries and about $10,000 in contributions.

Program Outline:

Business employees are loaned to individual schools in an effort to bring skills, experience and resources of the business community to bear on school problems. The problems can relate to facilities, equipment, curriculum (especially as related to career guidance) and administration.

Two careful soundings were taken in intensive conferences with school principals, teachers, parents, community leaders and the pupils themselves to launch a school partnership. In this way problems were identified, priorities were determined and programs were agreed upon from the start. Programs are underway in 4 high schools in New York City. The primary aim of the "partnerships" is to motivate students toward education and opportunity, to help students learn of the places for them in the world of business.

Union Carbide has 1 employee stationed full time at George Washington High School. Here, with 2 other representatives from business, students are counseled, encouraged to achieve, and administrators and faculty are assisted in problem solving.

Specific achievements include reduction in violence, development of successful anti-drug programs led and managed by students, introductory courses in career exploration and guidance for 9th graders, initiation of alternative (street academy) affiliate programs in 2 schools, and strenghthening of curriculum for tens of thousands of Spanish-speaking youngsters who are deficient in English.

Co. Personnel Involved: 1 middle-management executive full time and 25% of a second staff person's time

Measure of Success: George Washington School was open every day in the 1971-1972 year. It was closed 20% of the time in the spring of 1970 because of violence. The attendance record of students in alternative programs at George Washington is now 88% as opposed to less than 20% 2 years ago. Student attitudes toward drugs have taken an about-face in Monroe and George Washington High Schools.

Management by objectives has been learned by 4 teachers at Monroe High School and these teachers are now training other teachers to manage their many tasks more effectively.

UCB SCHOLAR PROGRAM

UNITED CALIFORNIA BANK
600 S. Spring Street
Los Angeles, Cal. 90054

Business: Banking Sales: not applicable
CEO: Normal Barker, Jr. Employees: 10,000

Contact: Dr. Larry Wilson, V.P.
Address: same as above
Telephone: (213) 624-0111, ext. 2183
Program Reaches: 20 students
When Started: 1972
Budget: see below

Program Outline:

The purpose of this scholarship program is to provide financial assistance to minority students to enable them to continue their education on the college level.

This 4-year combination scholarship-employment pilot program will be instituted in 5 cities in California. The first selections will be made from June, 1972 high school graduates. The program will provide aid of $2,000 for 4 years/student to be disbursed in sums of $500/year for college work successfully completed ("C" average or above). The funds are designed to help pay incidental fees, purchase books and provide transportation money for students from low-income families who wish to attend a nearby college and live at home. The program provides part time employment at a local UCB branch office during the school year and full time employment at the office during the summer vacation period.

The program is aimed particularly at male students interested in pursuing a career in business, but not necessarily banking; however, females are not to be excluded. Candidates will be selected by the designated high school faculties and representatives of UCB, including the local branch manager.

Co. Personnel Involved: n/a

Measure of Success: n/a

ENGLISH CLASSES FOR EMPLOYEES

WEYERHAEUSER CO.
2525 S. 336th Street
Federal Way
Tacoma, Wash. 98002

Business: Sawmills, Manufacturing Hardwood, Plywood
  Containers, etc.
Sales: 1,233mm
CEO: George H. Weyerhaeuser Employees: 42,721

Contact: John Ketter
Address: same as above
Telephone: (206) 924-2345
Program Reaches: about 20 people
When Started: 1969
Budget: instructors fee

Program Outline:

In order to offer English language classes to non-English speaking employees who are anxious to learn the language, the company provided an instructor for English classes. The classes are taught during 1 hour of company time and 1 hour of non-company time per week.

Co. Personnel Involved: About 20 employees participated in the classes.

Measure of Success: The employees and the company were pleased enough with the first year of operation to continue the program.

environment

YES WE CAN

ALUMINUM CO. OF AMERICA
Alcoa Building
Pittsburgh, Pa. 15219

Business: Aluminum Producer   Sales: approx. 1,500mm
CEO: John D. Harper   Employees: 46,500

Contact: J. B. O'Donnell
Address: same as above
Telephone: (412) 553-2345
Program Reaches: 3,000,000
When Started: September 29, 1970
Budget: n/a

Program Outline:

The purpose of the program is to establish the feasibility (or lack of it) of reclaiming and recycling all-aluminum cans from the public.

Alcoa sets up centers for all-aluminum can reclamation at shopping centers and wholesale beer distributors. The public scours beaches, parks, roadsides and returns cans to the centers for 10 cents a pound. Professional scrap yards collect cans from the centers, bale the scrap and ship it to Alcoa's can sheet plant at Warrick, Indiana. There it is melted into ingot, and rolled into new can sheet.

Co. Personnel Involved: 4 full time, 40 to 50 part time

Measure of Success: This type of program can be self-liquidating and profitable. And such measures do noticeably reduce the number of all-aluminum cans in the environs of those areas where the company operates.

HOMESTAKE LEAD COMPLEX COOPERATIVE ENVIRONMENTAL CONTROL STUDY

AMERICAN METAL CLIMAX, INC.
1270 Avenue of the Americas
New York, N.Y. l0020

Business: Mining, Smelting, Refining
Sales: 841mm
CEO: Donald J. Donahue   Employees: 17,000

Contact: M. Norman Anderson, Gen. Mgr.
Address: Boss, Mo. 65440
Telephone: (314) 626-4211
Program Reaches: sparsely populated area (lead and smelter mine located in national forest)
When Started: January, 1971
Budget: Total direct and indirect costs of the co-op program are expected to exceed $300,000. The Company is financing $30,000.

Program Outline:

In the Missouri Ozarks, some 120 miles southwest of St. Louis, an AMAX subsidiary, government agencies and a university are working together to pinpoint the causes and find remedies for some discoloration that has appeared on trees and foliage in the area.

Missouri Lead Operating Company (an AMAX subsidiary) and Clark National Forest officials reacted to the potential problem by obtaining infra-red aerial photography of the area and thus set in motion the machinery of co-operative pollution research.

The company agreed to finance a $30,000 research program to be administered by the University of Missouri-Rolla, and a host of federal and state agencies offered their help in providing monitoring instruments, vegetative studies, background data and technical assistance, their aerial photography expertise, and the performance of biopsies and analyses of the effects of smelter emissions on the fauna of the area.

The research program started with data-collecting to determine the meteorological characteristics of the air-shed near the area in question. This information can then be corrolated with data from instruments monitoring emissions from smelting operations. The effects of air pollution on plant and animal life must then be evaluated by biological scientists studying leaf damage and animal tissue. Finally, a comprehensive geochemical study of soil samples and vegetation will be made. The University of Missouri-Rolla research scientists will correlate and interpret the data as well as devise methods and equipment to allow the Clark National Forest and the New Lead Belt to co-exist.

This study was planned for 1971 only; a $217,000 grant from the National Science Foundation to the University of Missouri will permit it to continue through 1972 and possibly longer if the grant is renewed. The enlarged study includes possible water pollution.

Co. Personnel Involved: n/a

Measure of Success: When the program is completed, the results will be published, thus making the findings available to other companies engaged in mining and processing sulfer-containing ores.

MEADOWLARK FARMS, INC.

AMERICAN METAL CLIMAX, INC.
1270 Avenue of the Americas
New York, N.Y. 10020

Business: Mining, Smelting, Refining
Sales: 841mm
CEO: Donald J. Donahue   Employees: 17,000

Contact: Irwin Reiss, Pres.
Address: same as above
Telephone: (812) 268-6337
Program Reaches: 1000s
When Started: 1945 (purchased by AMAX 1969)
Budget: not determinable as part is borne by AMAX Coal
    Co.

Program Outline:

Meadowlark was created with 2 goals in mind: to farm
the acquired coal lands before strip mining and to
develop the land's most productive resources after
mining, utilization being the key to both goals.

Utilization is effected in 3 ways: through farming, coal
harvest and reclamation. The reclamation program often
results in farming operations more profitable and more
productive than those prior to mining. Present operations
involve Ayrshire (an AMAX subsidiary) land that is yet to
be mined—$50,000 acres—as well as reclaimed pit areas
covering 35,000 acres. These 85,000 acres are spread over
16 counties in Indiana and Illinois. In this area, Meadowlark has 132 crop-share lease arrangements with local
farmers and 4 operations managed directly by the
company.

This forward-moving rehabilitation process of reju-
venating the land is never complete and changes with new
scientific and technological advances.

Co. Personnel Involved: several dozen part time; 12 full
time

Measure of Success: In 1970 the farms produced
360,000 lbs. of pork, 450,000 lbs. of beef and 600,000
bushels of grain. More than 40% of this production was
from land reclaimed from open pit mines. Also, on the
average, 50-60% of the lands were tillable prior to mining.
This percentage is increased, if possible, after mining.

PUBLIC SERVICE POSTERS—ENVIRONMENT

AMERICAN METAL CLIMAX, INC.
1270 Avenue of the Americas
New York, N.Y. 10020

Business: Mining, Smelting, Refining
Sales: 841mm
CEO: Donald J. Donahue   Employees: 17,000

Contact: Terry Fitzsimmons
Address: same as above
Telephone: (303) 486-2150
Program Reaches: 31,000
When Started: 1971
Budget: minimal

Program Outline:

As a public service, AMAX is now employing the graphic
arts in its concern with the environment.

A series of colorful posters are being distributed all over
Central Colorado. The posters, designed by a commercial
artist on the public relations staff of AMAX's Climax
Molybdenum Company Division, are being distributed by
Climax and several organizations and individuals concerned with keeping Central Colorado beautiful. One of
the posters urges vacationers traveling in campers not to
leave litter behind, another shows what abandoned cars
and other junk left along the handsomely forrested
highways can do and a third enlightens those who
somehow presume that highway littering is no crime in
winter because Colorado snow will soon cover the trash.

New posters are planned for 1972

Co. Personnel Involved: part time

Measure of Success: not determinable

URAD MINES

AMERICAN METAL CLIMAX, INC.
1270 Avenue of the Americas
New York, N.Y. 10020

Business: Mining, Smelting, Refining
Sales: 841mm
CEO: Donald J. Donahue   Employees: 17,000

Contact: Terry Fitzsimmons
Address: same as above
Telephone: (303) 486-2150
Program Reaches: as many as 10,000/year
When Started: 1967
Budget: Over $1 million is available to reclaim the area
   after mine is closed.

Program Outline:

In opening a mine in Urad, Colorado for the extraction of molybdenum, AMAX was presented with a challenge in environmental planning. The fresh water streams that flow through the area eventually become part of the water supply for the city of Golden.

This area had previously been mined by other companies which had not considered the mine's tailings' disposition and the safeguarding of streams against contamination from tailing and mine drainage. AMAX, in correcting the problems of the past and in preparing the area for new mining operations, had to resolve several environmental problems. In this effort, the engineers constructed diversion structures and 2 miles of underground pipeline so that the streams would flow around and under the mill and tailing areas and emerge from the property in uncontaminated condition.

To make certain that enough water would always be available for mining and milling of the Urad ore, as well as to be prepared for rare periods of flood water conditions, the company built an upper reservoir above the property. AMAX, working with the Colorado State Division of Game, Fish and Parks, as well as the US Forest Service, agreed to open this upper reservoir to the public for camping, fishing and the enjoyment of nature. In return, the agencies agreed to manage the area, including stocking the water with trout. AMAX put in and helps maintain an access road and has posted routing signs for motorists.

When the Urad operation is phased out sometime in the mid 1970s, AMAX will remove the mine and mill buildings, and will stabilize and re-vegetate the tailing ponds. Topsoil that was set aside during the construction will be used. The reservoir will remain for the enjoyment of the public.

Co. Personnel Involved: none now

Measure of Success: not determinable

AMERICAN MOTORS CONSERVATION AWARDS PROGRAM

AMERICAN MOTORS CORP.
14250 Plymouth Road
Detroit, Mich. 48232

Business: Manufacturer—Motor Vehicles
Sales: 1,300mm
CEO: William V. Luneburg   Employees: 22,769

Contact: Ed Zern
Address: same as above
Telephone: (313) 493-2177
Program Reaches: general public
When Started: 1953
Budget: n/a

Program Outline:

The purpose of the program is to encourage and stimulate citizen interest in preserving the nation's natural resources.

The program annually presents awards to ten outstanding professional conservationist employed by non-profit organizations. These awards consist of a check for $500 and an engraved bronze plaque. Ten non-professionals whose conservation efforts are a voluntary expression of good citizenship receive bronze plaques. Special awards of $500 and bronze plaques are made to non-profit organizations for outstanding achievement.

Co. Personnel Involved: Administered by Public Relations Department. Awards committee consists of five outstanding authorities in various fields of conservation who serve voluntarily.

Measure of Success: Program is widely recognized as the oldest and most prestigious in the field of conservation—one of the most coveted awards among conservationists.

PARKSIDE ENVIRONMENTAL QUALITY

AMERICAN MOTORS CORP.
14250 Plymouth Road
Detroit, Mich. 48232

Business: Manufacturer—Motor Vehicles
Sales: 1,300mm
CEO: William V. Lunburg   Employees: 22,769

Contact: Chancellor Wyllie
Address: University of Wisconsin—Parkside
    Kenosha, Wis.
Telephone: (414) 658-4861
Program Reaches: n/a
When Started: 1970
Budget: n/a

Program Outline:

The purpose of the program is to develop environmental quality index and information retrieval system for southeastern Wisconsin in which American Motors plants are located.

Its functions are: first, to compile into book form information relevant to the environmental quality in southeastern Wisconsin with updates as new material appears; second, to identify needs of the adjoining communities of Racine and Mount Pleasant as they relate to the Pike River Basin.

A newspaper archive on environmental issues and action was established. As time goes on, this archive will provide a background for those who want to implement various projects and for students here and in neighboring universities in political science, sociology, economics and applied ecology.

Co. Personnel Involved: staffed by designated members of University faculty and students

Measure of Success: Volume I of the environmental quality index is now ready. The collections of the newspaper archive extend from September, 1970.

ENVIRONMENTAL CONTROL DEPARTMENT

CHEMICAL BANK
20 Pine Street
New York, N.Y. 10015

Business: Banking   Sales: not applicable
CEO: Howard W. McCall, Jr.   Employees: 12,523

Contact: John S. Cook
Address: 770 Broadway, New York, N.Y.
Telephone: (212) 770-1726
Program Reaches: over 1000 firms to date
When Started: June, 1970
Budget: n/a

Program Outline:

The purpose of this program is to assist realtors and industry in meeting the clean air codes in New York City with loan assistance.

The Environmental Control Department finances the purchase of pollution control devices/equipment for residential real estate to help them conform to the legal air codes in New York. The loans are over a 7-year period at prime rates (5%). The Department also assists industry in the cost of pollution control with loans over 5-year periods at 1% over prime. The loans are usually for anti-pollution equipment on heating and incinerator units, and for real estate, can be advanced 100% of contract costs.

This Department expects to expand its pollution control loans to water pollution as well as air in the future.

Co. Personnel Involved: 2 in all phases of the operation of the Department

Measure of Success: With over 1,000 loans presently made since the inception of the Department, the reception has been good.

ENVIRONMENTAL SURVEY

DILLINGHAM CORP.
P.O. Box 3468
Honolulu, Hi. 96801

Business: Construction, Property Development;
Maritime Services; Resources (mining,
quarrying, rock products)
Sales: 1971 revenues 528mm, 1971 earnings from
operations 3.2mm
CEO: H. C. Cornuelle   Employees: 14,000

Contact: W. H. Stryker, Dir. P.R.
Address: same as above
Telephone: (808) 946-0771
When Started: major management meeting held, May,
1970
Budget: n/a

Program Outline:

The program is set up as a survey and guidance of Dillingham Corporation's environmental programs. Its purpose is to use the corporation as an instrument to create better approaches to environmental management, to review our operations—get "our own house in order" —to formulate corporate environmental policy and to translate words into action in an on-going program of review and enhancement.

Co. Personnel Involved: All. Affects all activities at Dillingham Corporation and its affiliated companies in Hawaii, Mainland U.S., Canada, Australia, and parts of Far East.

Measure of Success: Feedback from operations managers, response from community residents, national recognition in environmental awards programs (1971 award winner in The Environment Monthly Honor Awards).

DENVER PILOT RECYCLING PROGRAM

EX-CELL-O CORPORATION
P.O. Box 386
Detroit, Mich. 48232

Business: Manufacturing   Sales: 284mm
CEO: Edward J. Giblin   Employees: 14,500

Contact: Charles B. Brownell
Address: same as above
Telephone: (313) 868-3900
Program Reaches: 1 million
When Started: September, 1971
Budget: no basic appropriation

Program Outline:

The purpose of the program is to determine the success of a program to collect and recycle pure-pak paperboard milk cartons.

Milk cartons are returned to supermarket locations by consumers and are collected in Denver area school lunchrooms. These cartons are taken to a central point where they are baled. Bales are shipped to a converter in Santa Ana, California, where they are processed to remove their plastic coating, and the remaining pulp is then sold to paper products manufacturers to use in the production of such products as napkins, towels, plates, etc.

Co. Personnel Involved: 5 (no more than 10% of each individual's time)

Measure of Success: Company has proven the program works, but its implementation is still limited. At present, even under its limited scope, the people of Denver are returning 10 to 12% of the milk cartons used in the market.

GOOD EARTH CERTIFICATES AND LOANS

FIRST NATIONAL BANK IN ST. LOUIS
510 Locust Street
St. Louis, Mo. 63166
Business: Banking   Sales: not applicable
CEO: C.C. Barksdale   Employees: 1,024

Contact: Richard F. Ford, V.P.
Address: same as above
Telephone: (319) 421-1000, Station 422
Program Reaches: n/a
When Started: December, 1970
Budget: 1971—approximately $70,000; 1972—same
    amount projected

Program Outline:

The program encompasses an ecology loan fund of
$5,263,000 set aside to help St. Louis Metropolitan
businesses deal with existing pollution problems and to
assist organizations in developing, producing and supplying anti-pollution equipment, products and services.

Individuals participate by purchasing Good Earth Savings
Certificates from $25 to $100,000. These certificates
earn a 5½% interest rate for a two-year period. Good
Earth Certificate sales proceeds are added to the loan
fund and matched by the bank. Ecology projects during
1971 included a day of tree and flower planting in St.
Louis with the aid of 7,500 Girl Scouts and participation
with the St. Louis Junior Chamber of Commerce, Stations KSD and KSD-TV and other organizations and
groups involved in environment improvement programs.

Co. Personnel Involved: Top management—Chairman
and President—are personally involved but the details are
largely handled by a committee of 3 vice presidents and 4
other bank officers.

Measure of Success: To date there has been a relatively
low response to offer to make loans for environment
improvement. Many of Bank's prime rate customers
borrow on open lines and it is difficult to determine how
much of their borrowings are related to environment
improvement. Smaller firms have not been in much of a
borrowing mood in recent months. Therefore, so very
few loans have been made for this specific purpose.

POLLUTION ABATEMENT SUPPORT

FIRST NATIONAL CITY BANK
399 Park Avenue
New York, N.Y. 10022

Business: Banking   Sales: not applicable
CEO: William I. Spencer   Employees: 31,700

Contact: William G. Herbster, S.V.P.
Address: same as above
Telephone: (212) 559-4211
Program Reaches: indeterminate
When Started: 1971
Budget: management time

Program Outline:

The purpose of the program is to take whatever steps
Bank appropriately can in order to help foster better
understanding of the pollution problem and generate
sensitivity and positive responses to it.

To make employees aware of the daily opportunities to
reduce pollution on the job, Bank has started a special
"Environment Suggestion Program." Also, First National
has just completed a major economic study on pollution
in New York, and has prepared a slide talk on the types
and causes of pollution which has been packaged and is
being distributed to the New York City public schools by
the Environmental Action Coalition. Meanwhile, the
Bank's Branch system is actively promoting the "Trash is
Cash" program in New York.

Co. Personnel Involved: 5 part time

Measure of Success: too new to tell

AIR POLLUTION RESEARCH ADVISORY COMMITTEE OF THE COORDINATING RESEARCH COUNCIL, INC. (APRAC)

FORD MOTOR CO.
The American Road
Dearborn, Mich. 48121

Business: Automotive Manufacturer
Sales: 15,000mm (1970)
CEO: Lee A. Iacocca   Employees: 431,000

Contact: E. D. Marande
Address: 20000 Rotunda Drive, Dearborn, Mich. 48121
Telephone: (313) 322-7115
Program Reaches: n/a
When Started: early 1968
Budget: $12 million for three years

Program Outline:

The purpose of the program is to improve scientific knowledge of all aspects of automotive air pollution in order to provide a better basis for public policy and development of pollution control technology.

Atmospheric Projects: Determine why carbon monoxide concentration in atmosphere does not build up. Develop mathematical model of spread of automotive emissions in cities. Assess damage to vegetation caused by air pollution.

Engineering Projects: Develop typical vehicle driving cycles for use in evaluating emission control systems. Identify odor-causing constituents of diesel exhaust. Develop methods of assuring continued low emission performance of cars throughout useful life.

Medical Projects: Determine medical effects of carbon monoxide. Investigate toxicity of polynuclear aromatic hydrocarbons. Study effects of various combinations of atmospheric pollutants.

Co. Personnel Involved: Twenty-eight Ford Personnel are directly involved, as a portion of their total responsibility, in APRAC project work. A larger number are indirectly involved, and to a lesser degree.

Measure of Success: n/a

FAHKAHATCHEE ENVIRONMENTAL STUDIES CENTER

GAC CORP.
825 S. Bayshore Drive
Miami, Fla. 33131

Business: Holding Company, Retail Automobile Parts, Manufacturing Truck Trailers and Heavy Machinery and Equipment
Sales: 1,760mm
CEO: S. Hayward Mills   Employees: 12,000

Contact: Louis V. Wilcox, Jr., Dir.
Address: Fahkahatchee Environmental Studies Center
    P.O. Box 188, Goodland, Fla.
Telephone: (813) 394-2058
Program Reaches: n/a
When Started: n/a
Budget: n/a

Program Outline:

The center was founded to encourage study and research in the subtropical environment of South Florida. Its methods are intended to be creative and unique, both in the course of instruction and in research studies. Problems will be examined from the perspective of many disciplines.

The land is owned by GAC properties. However, the state is in the initial discussion stages of buying the land to preserve it as an undeveloped area.

The Center offers college-level instruction and research opportunities. Organized to provide maximum usage in a flexible manner, the Center also encourages the use of the facilities by colleges organizing their own programs. The facilities can be used by any group attempting to arrive at a better understanding of the environment.

Some of the programs offered are: the January Term— courses will be given on a wide range of environmental topics during this month; term and semester length courses will be offered with the faculty and topics varying from term to term; a program offered primarily during the summer for undergraduate research; a summer study program; and ongoing research programs. Courses may be taken for credit or non-credit. In addition to the physical sciences, the Center's curriculum includes courses in the social sciences and the humanities.

Co. Personnel Involved: n/a

Measure of Success: n/a

POLLUTION CONTROL

GENERAL DYNAMICS
Pierre Laclede Center
St. Louis, Mo. 63105

Business: Manufacturing Aircraft and Parts, Missiles, Navy and Commercial Vessels and Submarines, Communication Equipment and Building Materials, Coal and Asbestos
Sales: 2,000mm
CEO: Hilliard W. Paige   Employees: 80,000

Contact: David R. Lavalette
Address: same as above
Telephone: (314) 862-2440
Program Reaches: unknown
When Started: several years ago
Budget: anticipate spending over $2 million for these controls next year

Program Outline:

The purpose of this program is to assure that none of the operations of General Dynamics causes an adverse effect upon the environment. The key elements of this corporate-wide pollution control program include identification of potential sources, surveys of the environment and the imposition of controls as appropriate. Strong technical direction and survey capabilities are provided by the Corporate Bioenvironmental Control Center located at Fort Worth, Texas. Expert field engineers, supported by a comprehensive analytical laboratory capability, routinely visit General Dynamic's operation, make surveys and prescribe controls as appropriate.

In line with the program's purpose, the corporation has assigned a responsible health physicist at corporate level. As manager of Safety and Environmental Health, he ensures protection of not only employees at their work places, but also areas surrounding the corporate facilities.

Co. Personnel Involved: extremely variable

Measure of Success: Air filter systems which remove 99.8% of visible particulate matter have been installed at 4 operation plants; a 3-phase water pollution program eliminates sewage discharge into the Thames River near Electric Boat Division in Groton, Ill.; extensive anti-pollution projects completed at Material Service's Redimix Yard No. 3 on the Chicago River.

CONSERVATION IN ACTION

GEORGIA-PACIFIC CORP.
900 S. 5th Avenue
Portland, Ore. 97204

Business: Forest Products of All Kinds
Sales: 1,400mm
CEO: William H. Hunt   Employees: 37,000

Contact: R. O. Lee, V.P.
Address: same as above
Telephone: (503) 222-5561
Program Reaches: could reach all U.S. citizens
When Started: about 5 years ago
Budget: not budgeted—handled on a project basis

Program Outline:

The purpose of the program is to take direct action and a position of leadership in protecting and improving habitat of flora and fauna both for their preservation and for the enjoyment of the American people now and for the future.

The project encompasses the gift of large timber and wildlife areas (Redwood groves valued at $6 million, Florida wetlands valued at $1 million, etc.), plus establishing sanctuaries and refuges on company lands and working with conservation and agricultural agencies on preservation programs for such creatures as the American Bald Eagle, the Osprey, Red Cockaded Woodpecker, South Carolina Brown Bear, etc. Also establishment of Nature Study Tracts with trails and identification of flora plus a number of recreation areas for fishermen, hunters, campers, hikers, bird watchers, etc.

Company Personnel Involved: Several hundred employees have been directly involved.

Measure of Success: Accolades from Audubon Society, the Nature Conservancy and other conservation organizations—and various governmental agencies. Most important, however, has been response of public who have new opportunities for nature study. One must also consider the quiet dignity—not voiced in human terms—which has been preserved for the animal and plant life which has been given a place in the sun.

BIKE RACKS

GIRARD BANK
One Girard Plaza
Philadelphia, Pa. 19101

Business: Banking
Assets: 2,801.9mm
CEO: William B. Eagleson, Jr.
Employees: 3,032

Sales: not applicable
Deposits: 2,325.7mm

Contact: Donald C. MacFarland
Address: same as above
Telephone: (215) 585-3009
Program Reaches: n/a
When Started: 1971
Budget: n/a

Program Outline:

The purpose of the program is to improve the ecology in the Delaware Valley and elsewhere through the elimination of vehicular pollution and traffic congestion.

Girard's Bike Rack promotion is designed to stimulate greater public awareness of the importance of protecting the environment, and to encourage other companies' participation in the concentrated effort to eliminate vehicular pollution and traffic congestion. With the support of the Delaware Valley Citizen's Council for Clean Air, the bike racks have been designated "official" bike stops.

Co. Personnel Involved: 2 public relations officers (1 vice president and 1 administrator) involved completely; 1 vice president in the Trust division

Measure of Success: Other Philadelphia companies and organizations have requested bike racks.

NATURAL LANDS TRUST

GIRARD BANK
One Girard Plaza
Philadelphia, Pa. 19101

Business: Banking
Assets: 2,801.9mm
CEO: William B. Eagleson, Jr.
Employees: 3,032

Sales: not applicable
Deposits: 2,325.7mm

Contact: Donald C. MacFarland
Address: same as above
Telephone: (215) 585-3009
Program Reaches: n/a
When Started: 1961
Budget: n/a

Program Outline:

The purpose of this program is to improve the ecology in the Delaware Valley and elsewhere through the preservation of natural lands.

Girard's Natural Lands program is designed to enlist broad support for the preservation of lands in their natural state. Through publicity of the Trust, Girard seeks to make the public more aware of the importance of setting aside such lands, and the need for financial support to protect and maintain them. The Bank offers a method by which interested individuals and groups can contribute land, securities, cash or any other kind of property to preserve natural land areas throughout the U.S.

Co. Personnel Involved: 2 public relations officers (1 vice president and 1 administrator) involved completely: 1 vice president in the trust division who administers the Trust and accepts donations

Measure of Success: Considerable donations of money and land have been received by the Trust.

ANTI-POLLUTION PROGRAM

THE B.F. GOODRICH CO.
500 South Main Street
Akron, Ohio 44318

Business: Manufacturing Rubber Products
Sales: 1236.7mm
CEO: H. B. Warner   Employees: 47,900

Contact: Gary J. Rine, P.R. Dept.
Address: same as above
Telephone: (216) 379-3411
Program Reaches: residents in affected areas
Budget: estimated $24 million through 1974

Program Outline:

The purpose of this program is to make significant improvements in air and water quality and solid waste disposal at all BFG plants where such improvements are needed and to place greater emphasis on the environmental aspects of product development. BFG has passed the mid-point of this corporate-wide program. As one example of an individual project, conducted in co-operation with the Federal Water Quality Administration, BFG installed a waste treatment demonstration facility at its Pedricktown, New Jersey, polyvinyl chloride plant. Under this program, BFG developed a comprehensive treatment system and demonstrated it to other PVC manufacturers.

Co. Personnel Involved: An 8-man Corporate Environmental Control Department and numerous engineers at divisional and plant levels are assigned to the program.

Measure of Success: Improvements have been made in air and water pollution control and solid waste disposal in BFG domestic plants where needed.

GOODYEAR CONSERVATION AWARDS PROGRAM

THE GOODYEAR TIRE & RUBBER CO.
1144 E. Market St.
Akron, Ohio 44316

Business: Tires, Rubber Products Sales: 3601.5mm
CEO: Victor Holt, Jr.   Employees: 136,800

Contact: Ray Oviatt
Address: same as above
Telephone: (216) 794-3546
Program Reaches: 2,000,000
When Started: 1947
Budget: $75,000 in 1972

Program Outline:

Sponsored in cooperation with the National Association of Conservation Districts (NACD), the awards program provides incentive to the nation's more than 3,000 conservation districts and their more than 2 million cooperating landowners. The score sheets also provide a check list of district functions.

Conservation districts compete annually for first and second place awards in their states; winners receive plaques. Each first place district wins expense-paid, vacation-study trips for its outstanding cooperator and a board member. The 4-day trips are made to exceptional conservation projects. In addition, persons selected as outstanding cooperators in all competing districts receive framed certificates of merit.

Co. Personnel Involved: 3, year 'round; 12 others seasonally as the work load demands

Measure of Success: The growth of the conservation district movement has been attributed in considerable measure to the Goodyear Conservation Awards Program.

RECYCLING CENTER

HEWLETT-PACKARD CO.
1501 Page Mill Road
Palo Alto, Cal. 94304

Business: Electronic, Medical, Analytical and Computing
   Instrumentation
Sales: 375mm
CEO: William R. Hewlett   Employees: 16,000

Contact: Matt Schmutz
Address: same as above
Telephone: (415) 493-1501
Program Reaches: all HP employees at divisions and
   offices where a cycling center has been established
When Started: 1970
Budget: n/a

Program Outline:

A program for recycling waste computer paper printout
and cards has been started by the corporate Bay Area
Electronic Data Processing Center of HP. It is estimated
that more than 140 tons in printout and IBM cards can
be recycled during the coming year. One source reported
that each 115 pounds that is recycled will save 1 tree.
Most other HP divisions have their own recycling centers.
Recycling of company-generated waste paper materials in
many cases has resulted from the private initiative of
interested employees. One outgrowth of the recycling
project has been the use of used computer cards in the
Palo Alto's Association for the Retarded.

The donated used cards have both monetary and thera-
peutic value. Sale of the recyclable paper and cards has
brought in more than $1,000 a month to the association,
but the highlight of the program is the enthusiasm with
which retarded youngsters and adults take to the job of
sorting the cards by color. This activity increases the
recycle value of the cards significantly, and the money
the participants earn represents for many of them the
first success they've had in life. The twice monthly
payday is a big event.

Contact for the Card Donation Program:
   George Lewis, Personnel Manager
   HP Automatic Measurement Division
   Palo Alto Office
   (415) 326-1755

Co. Personnel Involved: almost all who are involved with
the use of recyclable computer printout paper and cards

Measure of Success: financially, the more than
$1,000/month earned by Palo Alto's Association for the
Retarded; on a more human level, the enthusiasm and
feeling of success experienced by the retarded children
and adults who participate

BRING A FOREST BACK TO LIFE

HUNT-WESSON FOODS, INC.
1654 W. Valencia Drive
Fullerton, Cal. 92634

Business: Manufacturing Foods and Matches
Sales: 400mm
CEO: Edward Gelsthorpe   Employees: 6,800

Contact: Kenneth J. Ward, Dir. Corp. Rel.
Address: same as above
Telephone: (714) 871-2100
Program Reaches: n/a
When Started: n/a
Budget: over $1 million

Program Outline:

This recently introduced new program offers consumers, in return for a label, the opportunity to plant a tree in a

national forest. The consumer receives a certificate signed by the president of Hunt-Wesson, and the Chief of the United States Forest Service, along with information on the importance of the Forest Service's reforestation program. Trees relating to the Forest Program are being planted in the Wenatchee National Forest in central Washington state. This was the forest selected by the U.S. Forest Service representing the greatest need at this time. This idea is an alternative to the usual cash or coupon refund offer associated with new product introductions. Because of the response to this offer, the program has been expanded to include other Hunt-Wesson products as well.

Co. Personnel Involved: 15-20

Measure of Success: The results of this program have generated to date (April, 1972) funds for the planting of over 1 million trees. It is expected that by the completion of the program, between 1,300,000 and 1,500,000 trees will have been planted. This represents 3-5,000 acres of new forest.

Your trees will be planted in the Spring of 1972.

Thank you for participating in our forest building program. The U.S. Forest Service has informed us that they will begin planting trees in the three Children's Forests in the Spring. Your tree or trees will be planted in the forest nearest your home. As you know, the three Children's Forests will be located in the following states:

San Bernardino National Forest   California
Mark Twain National Forest   Missouri
George Washington National Forest   Virginia

HUNT-WESSON FOODS, INC.

If you don't like what the world has done to your forests, start a new one.

Send us a label, and we'll have a tree planted in your name in a burned-out National Forest.

Last year, people and lightning ravaged more than 555,000 acres of National Forests. More often than not, it was people who started the fires.

Trees prevent erosion and hold back flood water. They keep silt from clogging streams and rivers. They fight back at air pollution. They keep wildlife alive. If people keep burning your forests, you'll be left without a future.

We'll help you bring a burned-out National Forest back to life by having a tree planted in your name.

This photo shows part of the San Bernardino National Forest in California. It burned to a char on November 13, 1970. With your help, we'll re-tree it and grow two more forests in sites chosen by the U.S. Forest Service: the George Washington National Forest in Virginia, and the Mark Twain National Forest in Missouri. They'll be for the future of young people. So we'll call them the National Children's Forests. We'll buy the trees in your name, and the Forest Service will have them planted right next to a full-grown forest, to give you something to look forward to.

We can plant 350 trees per acre. Share an acre with your school, club or Scout troop.

Bring your friends into our re-treeing plan, and the Forests will come to life faster. We can't think of a better way to counteract the damage the world has done.

We'll put your name in a time capsule in your National Forest.

We'll place a marker in each Forest site with a vault to hold the name of everyone who has a tree planted. And to show the world that this Forest is *your* doing. We're also blazing a nature trail specially constructed to make your Forest a special place for everyone, including the handicapped. To show the world you care.

When your tree is bought for planting, you'll know.

We'll mail you an ecology decal that says, "I helped save a forest." And a certificate with a map and legend of your National Forest, to show your tree has been bought and will be planted.

All we need is a label to start your new Forest.

Any of the products shown in the coupon will buy a tree. Just send us the labels or code numbers, along with the coupon. Nine labels buy nine trees (the maximum for each coupon request). Groups can share in a Forest by sending labels, coupons and names together.

Bring a forest back to life. And show the world how to do things better in the future.

TRAINING FOR ENVIRONMENTAL TECHNICIANS

KIMBERLY-CLARK CORP.
N. Lake Street
Weenah, Wis. 54956

Business: Manufacturing Paper and Cellulose Products and Wholesale Lumber
Sales: 869mm
CEO: Darwin E. Smith   Employees: 29,051

Contact: Mill Manager
Address: Peter J. Schweitzer Div.,
    Kimberly-Clark Corp.
    Lee, Mass. 01238
Telephone: (413) 243-1000
Program Reaches: n/a
When Started: n/a
Budget: n/a

Program Outline:

The purpose of this program is to give students technical training as well as make them aware of industry's problems.

The students monitor the workday functions of a solid waste disposal unit in the Peter J. Schweitzer Division at Lee, Mass. They also learn about the costs of cleaning up.

The students include teen-agers and middle-agers, all of whom are studying to become environmental technicians under a federally-funded education program at Berkshire Community College at Pittsfield. The curriculum is highly concentrated: 7 hours daily, 5 days/week for 32 weeks. Components include academic communications courses (speech, literature, composition) plus instrumentation, math, chemistry, contemporary environmental issues and a helping of group dynamics.

Each student spends 27 hours over a 3-week period at the disposal facility and laboratory. Working under supervision of technicians and others, he analyzes samples of Housatonic River water, tests cleansed effluent and computes results of the investigation.

Co. Personnel Involved: Five persons take part in varying degrees; participation may take 3-25% of a person's time.

Measure of Success: Measured in number of participants, the college-company venture is small. As a meaningful, valid enterprise, the effort takes on more weight. The company is coming away with a better idea of how others perceive it as owning up to its responsibility.

"LEARN TO LIVE"

MARINE MIDLAND BANK—WESTERN
237 Main Street
Buffalo, N.Y. 14203

Business: Banking   Sales: not applicable
CEO: John L. Hettrick   Employees: 2,250

Contact: William L. Martin
Address: P.R. Div., same as above
Telephone: (716) 843-4197
Program Reaches: n/a
When Started: March, 1971
Budget: not determinable

Program Outline:

This public service program is aimed at helping evolve workable solutions to environmental problems. In this effort, the program has endeavored to disseminate information through: (1) holding a seminar involving 5 national and a dozen area environmental specialists to discuss issues ranging from population control to proper planning of land use; (2) an environmental film festival; (3) cash awards for environmental documentaries filmed by students; (4) an ecology action youth forum; (5) ecological displays; (6) the sponsorship of an ecological crisis documentary on local TV; (7) a grant made to the Environmental Clearing House of Buffalo on a matching-fund basis; (8) a nationwide survey of industry, government and higher education to learn the amount of environmental action being generated; (9) bookshelves of 100 volumes each presented to 5 Western New York libraries.

This is a continuing program which will be tailored to specific aspects (i.e. "The Economics of Environmental Improvement") rather than the broad subject of the environment in total.

Co. Personnel Involved: Many departments have been and will be involved (i.e., improvement of the Bank's own ecological problems).

Measure of Success: attendance at events, requests for information

INDUSTRIAL WASTE WATER TREATMENT FACILITY

MCDONNELL DOUGLAS CORP.
ST. LOUIS FACILITIES
P.O. Box 516
St. Louis, Mo. 63166

Business: Aerospace Manufacturing
Sales: 2,088mm
CEO: Sanford N. McDonnell   Employees: 92,552

Contact: J. C. Patterson
Address: Dept. 191, Bldg. 32, same as above
Telephone: (314) 232-3319
Program Reaches: all area citizens
When Started: 1965
Budget: initial construction: $400,000; annual operations: $100,000

Program Outline:

The purpose of this program is to remove polluted industrial processing rinse waters from Coldwater Creek, normally a low-flowing storm water conveying stream.

The treatment plant at McDonnell Douglas receives rinse water from several metal-finishing operations. The St. Louis facility—a sewage treatment plant before con-version to handling industrial wastes exclusively—discharges approximately 700,000 gallons/day to district sewers.

Shortly after sewer service was made available in 1965, MD engineers recognized the need to treat waste that is not compatible with sewage. They embarked on a 2-year, $400,000 engineering and construction project to modify the existing but inactive sewage facility. This modified plant is not presented as an example of system sophistication. Rather, it illustrates how minimal capital expenditures, practical engineering and ingenuity of in-house personnel might be combined to solve waste-water treatment problems.

Co. Personnel Involved: The Environmental Pollution Control Unit consists of 3 engineers. The Treatment Plant has 2 full time operators. Additional support is supplied through Plant Engineering Design and Maintenance Departments.

Measure of Success: To date, McDonnell Douglas has had no trouble meeting effluent specifications imposed by the Metropolitan St. Louis Sewer District—an independent organization treating about 20 mgd. Its requirements: maintain pll between 5.5 and 10.5, BOD under 300 mg/l and suspended solids below 350 mg/l. In fact BOD and suspended solids generally are less than 10% of these values.

UNDERGROUND CONVERSION PROGRAM (UCP)

MEMPHIS LIGHT, GAS AND WATER DIVISION
P.O. Box 388
Memphis, Tenn. 38101

Business: Publicly-Owned Utility
Sales: 130mm
CEO: n/a   Employees: n/a

Contact: Carl Crawford, Dir. P.R.
Address: 220 South Main, Memphis, Tenn. 38103
Telephone: (901) 528-4736
Program Reaches: 723,000
When Started: approved September, 1970; budgeted, January, 1971
Budget: $1.5 million/year, unused part carried over

Program Outline:

The purpose of the program is to add to the esthetic quality of the Memphis environment by removing over-head power lines and utility poles through conversion to underground power cables.

MLGW became the first utility in the nation to establish a program aimed at systematically removing overhead electric distribution lines and utility poles and replacing them with an underground electrical system. Coupled with a policy of running underground service to all new commercial and residential customers, including all new subdivisions, the Division will eventually remove all overhead lines.

Co. Personnel Involved: Any of the 1,000 employees of the Electric Division of MLGW may become involved at any time, so it is impossible to give an accurate figure. An educated guess is that 40-50 people may be involved in the UCP at any one time.

Measure of Success: MLGW has not yet had sufficient time to make any significant progress. The UCP is a long-term project that will not show immediate change easily recognized by Memphis residents.

BRINK MIST ELIMINATION SYSTEMS

MONSANTO ENVIRO-CHEM SYSTEMS, INC.
10 S. Riverside Plaza
Chicago, Ill. 60606

Business: Pollution Abatement, Engineering Design
Sales: n/a
CEO: Edward J. Bock   Employees: n/a

Contact: Jack Burke
Address: 800 N. Lindbergh Boulevard
   St. Louis, Mo. 63166
Telephone: (314) 694-2768
Program Reaches: n/a
When Started: 10 years ago
Budget: n/a

Program Outline:

The purpose of this program is the design of a system to prevent escape of microscopic airborne pollutants in mists in exit gas streams of diverse industrial installations.

Mists carrying pollutants are channeled through a specially designed fiber bed system. Pollutants are captured for possible re-use or safe disposal, while clean gas emerges from the fiber bed. Collection efficiences have been rated up to 99.99%.

Co. Personnel Involved: n/a

Measure of Success: Brink systems are in use throughout the free world. There are now some 1,400 installations in operation on diverse industrial plants. These include sulfuric acid plants, wet and dry chlorine plants, plastic operations and mercury mist containment.

CAT-OX

MONSANTO ENVIRO-CHEM SYSTEMS, INC.
10 S. Riverside Plaza
Chicago, Ill. 60606

Business: Pollution Abatement, Engineering, Design
Sales: n/a
CEO: Edward J. Bock   Employees: n/a

Contact: Jack Burke
Address: 800 N. Lindbergh Boulevard
   St. Louis, Mo. 63166
Telephone: (314) 694-2768
Program Reaches: n/a
When Started: 1961
Budget: n/a

Program Outline:

The purpose of this program is to control sulfur dioxide emissions from power generating stations with a system capable of producing marketable sulfuric acid as a by-product to help offset cost.

Following extensive research and development on the Cat-Ox system, the feasibility of such a system was established in a pilot operation and, later, a prototype plant was developed to develop engineering information. This prototype handled 6% of the flue gas from a 250Mw boiler—or the equivalent of a 15Mw power generating station. Prototype performance of 3 years proved its ability to solve the SO_2 pollution problem of power generating facilities.

The system removes all of the fly ash and 85-90% of the SO_2 emission problem is solved. The sale of the sulfuric acid collected by this process will help offset the operating costs.

Co. Personnel Involved: Experience indicates that operation of the facility can be controlled by existing operating manpower from a console in the control room.

Measure of Success: Prototype unit operated over a 3-year period at Metropolitan-Edison Co. site at Portland, Pa. Full scale demonstration unit funded by the Environmental Protection Agency and the Illinois Power Company is now under construction at Illinois Power's Wood River site. The anticipated start-up date is July 1972.

LANDGARD

MONSANTO ENVIRO-CHEM SYSTEMS, INC.
10 S. Riverside Plaza
Chicago, Ill. 60606

Business: Pollution Abatement, Engineering Design
Sales: n/a
CEO: Edward J. Bock   Employees: n/a

Contact: Joe P. Orr
Address: 800 W. Lindbergh Boulevard
   St. Louis, Mo. 63166
Telephone: (314) 694-2866
Program Reaches: n/a
When Started: n/a
Budget: n/a

Program Outline:

The Landgard waste disposal system was developed as a solution to the solid waste disposal problem of municipalities without adding to pollution.

The system is designed to handle municipalities sufficiently large to generate a minimum of 250 tons of refuse/day, and to turn that refuse into useful by-products.

In the Landgard system, using a process based on py-rolysis (chemical change brought on by the action of heat), refuse is decomposed by heating in an oxygen deficient atmosphere with the resulting gases burned in a separate chamber. The remaining char residue is odorless, innocuous and may be further processed to recover iron, glass and carbon. The system emits no combustible material to the atmosphere and the particulate content of the exiting gas is cleaner than the existing federal law guidelines. The process does not permit a build-up of nitrogen oxide. Process water is treated and recycled in a closed system.

The system handles all typical municipal wastes including large bulky items such as stoves and matresses and may be designed to handle sewage sludge. Steam for heating/cooling or electrical generation can also be produced. Volume reduction with the ferrous metals removed is approximately 94%.

This system is fully guaranteed as to plant capacity, ability to meet pollution control codes, volume reduction and quality of residue.

Co. Personnel Involved: n/a

Measure of Success: A 35-ton/day pilot plant was built and operated in St. Louis County, Missouri. All types of municipal refuse was processed with success—sewage sludge, wet grass, plastics, oil sludge, tires, etc. This was a demonstration unit only.

LOPAC CONTAINER SYSTEM

MONSANTO COMMERCIAL PRODUCTS CO.
800 N. Lindbergh Blvd.
St. Louis, Mo. 63166

Business: Agricultural Products, Electronics, Packaging,
   Environmental Control Systems
Sales: 500mm+
CEO: Edward J. Bock   Employees: n/a

Contact: Jim Rollins, P.R. Mgr.
   Fabricated Products Division
Address: same as above
Telephone: (314) 694-2893
Program Reaches: small number now because it is developmental; ultimately millions daily
When Started: mid 1960s
Budget: n/a

Program Outline:

The purpose of this program is to develop, produce and sell to beverage industries a new type of container which is lighter, safer, consumer-preferred and ecologically desirable.

Because the container is made of a completely new kind of plastic material, it is the first plastic to successfully contain carbonation, resist escape of flavor components and intrusion of outside contaminants, while maintaining its original shape. The bottle is safely breakable (won't explode dangerously, broken pieces not likely to cut), more than 80% lighter in weight than glass, and can be disposed of harmlessly by any conventional method and is recyclable. The final cost will be competitive to that of conventional containers.

Co. Personnel Involved: n/a

Measure of Success: In market tests involving more than 3 million containers and more than a year of continuous store sales, performance of container and acceptance by consumers has been very favorable.

MOTOR VEHICLE CLEAN AIR TEST PROGRAM

NEW JERSEY BELL TELEPHONE CO.
540 Broad Street
Newark, N.J. 07101

Business: Communications   Sales: 691mm
CEO: Robert W. Kleinert   Employees: 30,800

Contact: Alan B. Goetze
Address: Room 805b, same as above
Telephone: (201) 649-2481
Program Reaches: residents of New Jersey
When Started: 3rd quarter, 1971
Budget: $12,000

Program Outline:

The purpose of this program is to reduce harmful motor vehicle exhaust emissions from the company's light trucks and passenger cars to a practical minimum. Each passenger car and light truck will be tested for exhaust emissions (carbon monoxide and unburned hydro-carbons). Where emissions are found in excess of the proposed New Jersey Motor Vehicle exhaust emissions standards for 1973, the vehicle is adjusted for minimum emissions. Where vehicles fail to meet standard after adjustments, PCV valve and air cleaners are checked and replaced if necessary. Vehicles still above accepted standards are considered for major repairs based upon economic consideration of age, past maintenance history and vehicle condition.

Co. Personnel Involved: 2 staff personnel, 5% of the time; 24 motor vehicle supervisors on a part time basis as the vehicles in their charge are being tested.

Measure of Success: Initial sampling of results indicate that 42% of the vehicles pass initial tests, 42% pass on adjustment, and 12% pass following replacement of PCV valve or air filter. It is estimated that emissions of carbon monoxide and hydrocarbons have been reduced between 45-50% on those vehicles tested and adjusted.

ENVIRONMENTAL IMPROVEMENT

NORTHERN ILLINOIS GAS CO.
P.O. Box 190
Aurora, Ill. 60607

Business: Distribution of Natural Gas
Sales: 365mm
CEO: C. J. Gouthier   Employees: 3,100

Contact: Ed Koska, Dir. P.R.
Address: same as above
Telephone: (312) 355-8000, ext. 333
Program Reaches: Because this is a continuing program which includes many areas of the company's work, the number of persons reached cannot be estimated.
When Started: n/a
Budget: n/a

Program Outline:

The purpose of this program is to improve the environment through company programs and by supporting the environmental improvement efforts of others.

The objectives of NI-Gas's environmental improvement efforts are: that construction projects include scenic and functional restoration; that NI-Gas-owned land be used for purposes which preserve natural resources; that regulator stations harmonize with their surrounding environment and that NI-Gas support the environmental improvement efforts of others. This last objective has been reflected in leadership in the 1970 anti-pollution bond act and in 1972 through an ecology contest for school children.

Co. Personnel Involved: The 4-point environmental improvement program requires the coordinated efforts of many specialists in the company. While public relations and corporate development representatives organize the clean water campaign, real estate men coordinate land use and engineers work on station design.

Measure of Success: The best indicator of the success of NI-Gas's efforts was a first place award in an Environmental Improvement Contest sponsored by Petroleum Engineers's Publishing Company.

BOILER CONVERSION

OSCAR MAYER & CO.
910 Mayer Avenue
Madison, Wis. 53701

Business: Meat Processing Sales: 651mm
CEO: P. Goff Beach Employees: 11,800

Contact: Walter S. Brager
Address: same as above
Telephone: (608) 241-3311
Program Reaches: residents of affected area
When Started: continuing effort
Budget: $1.2 million for gas turbine; $425,000 for boiler conversion

Program Outline:

The purpose of this program is to reduce emissions from Oscar Mayer's power plant, which has long used coal as a fuel and relied upon it exclusively until February, 1970. In March, 1970, a gas turbine generator was installed and in the Spring of 1971, a converted boiler was put into operation. The coal boiler was converted from coal firing to natural gas firing with oil standby when the local utility company had to interrupt service due to residential needs during cold months. Presently the power plant is provided electricity by the gas turbine, the converted boiler and one coal boiler. The company plans to convert all equipment to natural gas when it is available.

Co. Personnel Involved: power plant personnel and plant engineers

Measure of Success: Since February, 1970, with the installation of the gas turbine and conversion of the coal boiler to natural gas, coal usage has been cut in half, thereby decreasing emission by one-half.

BURKE WASTEWATER TREATMENT PLANT

OSCAR MAYER & CO.
910 Mayer Avenue
Madison, Wis. 53701

Business: Meat Processing Sales: 651mm
CEO: P. Goff Beach Employees: 11,800

Contact: Walter S. Brager
Address: same as above
Telephone: (608) 241-3311
Program Reaches: residents of affected area
When Started: n/a
Budget: $18,000 for spray system; $440,000 for water filtering system

Program Outline:

The purpose of this program is to reduce and eventually eliminate an odor emanating from the Burke Wastewater Treatment plant, ¼ mile from Oscar Mayer's manufacturing plant. In March, 1970, a deodorizing spray system was installed in an attempt to neutralize the odor while a more permanent solution was researched. During 1971, two separate tests were conducted of equipment designed to replace existing wastewater treatment operations and thereby reduce odors. The possibility of completely eliminating the Burke plant operations was also investigated. As a result of one of the 1971 tests, the company is now building a $440,000 wastewater filtering system on the grounds which will reduce Burke plant odors by 50%. Methods are now under study to eliminate the other 50% and the company continues to study the possibility of completely by-passing the Burke operation and going to the Madison Metropolitan Sewerage District.

Co. Personnel Involved: sanitary engineers of the company

Measure of Success: The waste filtering system will reduce odors in part and it is hoped that they can be eliminated altogether in the near future.

ENVIRONMENTAL CONTROL: EVERYONE'S CONCERN

REX CHAINBELT
P.O. Box 2022
Milwaukee, Wis. 53201

Business: Manufacturing Mechanical Power Transmission
    Equipment
Sales: 300mm
CEO: Robert V. Kirkorian   Employees: 11,142

Contact: E. L. Satola, Dir. P.R.
Address: same as above
Telephone: (414) 384-3000
Program Reaches: n/a
When Started: 1971
Budget: n/a

Program Outline:

This is a book intended as a baseline from which to learn, discuss and finally decide on satisfactory solutions for some of the environmental problems.

The book provides background information on the environment and its problems. It includes an article by Rene Dubos, "Life Is An Endless Give-And-Take With Earth And All Her Creatures." Also, there is a listing of regional pollution problems, information on water quality standards, indices of pollution and its visible signs, zones of degradation and recovery, etc. There are charts of pollution control devices which are easily understood by the layman and further made clear by a glossary of commonly used terms to help understand the water pollution problem, as well as a list, by state, of pollution abatement incentives offered.

Co. Personnel Involved: n/a

Measure of Success: n/a

REX RESOURCE BUREAU

REX CHAINBELT, INC.
P. O. Box 2022
Milwaukee, Wis. 53201

Business: Manufacturing Mechanical Power Transmission
    Equipment
Sales: 300mm
CEO: Robert V. Kirkorian   Employees: 11,142

Contact: E. L. Satola, Dir. P.R.
Address: Rex Resource Bureau, same as above
Telephone: (414) 384-3000
Program Reaches: national program
When Started: 1970
Budget: n/a

Program Outline:

Rex feels that in order to insure progress in the solution of the environmental prises, a working partnership must be fashioned between an aroused public armed with facts, a sensitive and responsive business community, and enlightened and aggressive public officials at all levels of government.

The bureau endeavors to be a chief resource for factual information about water pollution control. It offers a Kit for Concerned Citizens which contains material that can form the basis for study and action program to evaluate and improve water quality in a community. This kit contains background information on the environmental problems including water and air pollution, a list of regional water pollution problems, a glossary of pollution problem terms commonly used and ways to start at home and in groups to help solve the environmental problems.

Co. Personnel Involved: n/a

Measure of Success: At the end of the first year, the Rex Resource Bureau had received 24,007 inquiries and 34,056 Kits for Concerned Citizens had been distributed.

REYNOLDS ALUMINUM RECLAMATION PROGRAM

REYNOLDS METALS CO.
6601 West Broad Street
Richmond, Va. 23261

Business: Aluminum Manufacturing
Sales: 1,093mm
CEO: Richard S. Reynolds, Jr.
Employees: 37,300

Contact: L. E. Whitehead
Address: same as above
Telephone: (703) 282-2311
Program Reaches: 75 million
When Started: January, 1967
Budget: n/a

Program Outline:

The purpose of the program is to reclaim all-aluminum beverage cans and other household aluminum scrap for recycling and reuse, to help solve litter and solid waste problems and conserve natural resources.

Public is paid 10 cents per pound for all-aluminum cans and other clean aluminum scrap brought to 12 permanent redemption centers, 11 mobile redemption centers and more than 700 satellite centers in areas of the country where there is substantial distribution of all-aluminum beverage cans (31 states in 1971). Reynolds reprocesses the collected aluminum and recycles it into new aluminum products. Program enables individuals and groups such as the Boy and Girl Scouts, civic, service and garden clubs, schools, towns and cities to clean up litter at a profit.

Co. Personnel Involved: Fifty are involved totally in the program and another 250 in ancillary functions.

Measure of Success: (1) Each year, since 1969, there has been a 4-fold increase in number of cans collected over the previous year (1971 collections, 418 million cans); (2) Increase in number of collection stations from one in 1968 to over 700 in 1972; (3) Widespread official recognition, praise or awards from city, state and federal officials and ecology, anti-litter and beautification organizations.

ENVIRONMENT IMPROVEMENT PROGRAM

SEARS, ROEBUCK & CO.
303 E. Ohio Street
Chicago, Ill. 60611

Business: Retail and General Catalogue Merchandising
Sales: 9,262mm
CEO: Arthur M. Wood   Employees: 359,000

Contact: Donald A. Deutsch
Address: same as above
Telephone: (312) 661-3100
Program Reaches: n/a
When Started: 1971
Budget: $42,000

Program Outline:

The purpose of the program is to encourage action programs and projects aimed at improving the quality of the environment.

The Environment Improvement Program established by National Council of State Garden Clubs, Inc. in cooperation with Sears, Roebuck & Company. In an effort to restore beauty to the environment, Garden Clubs will undertake various 2-year projects in areas such as Air and Water Pollution, Solid Waste Disposal, Environmental Education, Noise Abatement, Anti-Litter and Clean-Up campaigns, Billboard Control, Vest Pocket Parks, and Converting Vacant Lots Into Tiny Playlots.

Co. Personnel Involved: n/a

Measure of Success: Program runs until 1973, at which time awards will be given for the best and most effective projects.

LOCAL ECOLOGY PROJECTS

SYNTEX CORP.
Stanford Industrial Park
Palo Alto, Cal. 94034

Business: Pharmaceutical, Veterinary and Health Care
   Products
Sales: 100mm
CEO: George Rosenkranz   Employees: n/a

Contact: Frank Koch, Dir. of Corp. P.R.
Address: same as above
Telephone: (415) 855-6111
Program Reaches: n/a
When Started: n/a
Budget: n/a

Program Outline:

The company is involved in several local ecological
programs on various levels: matched employee contributions to provide food supplies for volunteers working
during the San Francisco Bay oil spill crisis in 1971; a
grant was given to the Nature Conservancy to assist in the
acquisition of an 80-acre shore-bird sanctuary in the
south of San Francisco Bay called the Morse Baylands;
grants were made to the Sempervirens Fund to provide a
campsite at Castle Rock in the redwoods area of the
Santa Cruz Mountains in 1970, and to purchase several
acres of the Rancho Del Oso which hopefully will be a
2,300-acre addition to the Big Basin Park in the same
area; a grant to the Trianon Foundation to assist in the
rehabilitation of "Le Petit Trianon," a Santa Clara historical landmark on the campus of DeAnza College in
Cupertino; financial support was provided to the Ecology
Center Foundation to help establish an ecology center in
San Francisco; a grant was made to the John Muir
Institute covering production costs for the preparation of
a half-hour film based on a successful environmental
teach-in at Cubberly High School in Palo Alto which was
subsequently aired on television in the Bay Area.

Co. Personnel Involved: n/a

Measure of Success: n/a

THORNE ECOLOGICAL FOUNDATION

SYNTEX CORP.
Stanford Industrial Park
Palo Alto, Cal. 94304

Business: Pharmaceutical, Veterinary and Health Care
   Products
Sales: 100mm
CEO: George Rosenkranz   Employees: n/a

Contact: Frank Koch, Dir. of Corp. P.R.
Address: same as above
Telephone: (415) 855-6111
Program Reaches: all types of community leaders
When Started: n/a
Budget: n/a

Program Outline:

Syntex has supported the seminars of the Thorne Ecological Foundation which are held in the West each year
for top businessmen, government officials, educators,
student leaders, union officials and other community
leaders. The purpose of the seminars is to acquaint these
individuals with the basic principles of ecology, to provide interaction among all segments of society concerned
with environmental reform, and to encourage these
leaders to commit themselves to action programs in their
own sphere of influence.

Co. Personnel Involved: n/a

Measure of Success: reports

METROPOLITAN BOTTLE & CAN RECYCLING CENTER

THEODORE HAMM CO.
(A SUBSIDIARY OF HEUBLEIN, INC.)
720 Payne Avenue
St. Paul, Minn. 55101

Business: Brewing and Marketing Beer, Malt Beverages
Sales: n/a
CEO: n/a   Employees: n/a

Contact: John Geisler
Address: same as above
Telephone: (612) 776-1561
Program Reaches: n/a
Budget: approximately $150,000 for establishing the Center and for the first year of operation

Program Outline:

The purpose of the program is to aid the cause of environmental preservation by reducing littering and through the re-use of glass and metal packaging materials.

Also, to provide jobs and job training for the handicapped.

The recycling Center, which accepts virtually all types of glass and metal containers, was set up in a large former factory building in St. Paul. It is operated by the Occupational Training Center, a non-profit organization offering jobs and job training to handicapped. The Center pays a specified amount for each pound of glass or metal collected by individuals or organizations. The materials are then re-sold to container manufacturers. The necessary equipment (crushers, compactors, etc.) was purchased with the financial aid of the Theodore Hamm Co. and Coca-Cola Midwest, Inc.

Co. Personnel Involved: n/a

Measure of Success: Public awareness of the Recycling Center and participation in its program has been growing steadily. Materials have been brought in for recycling from 100s of miles away. Based on its steady growth in volume, the Center is expected to become self-sustaining relatively soon.

TOTAL ENERGY CONCEPT

TRANS WORLD AIRLINES
605 Third Avenue
New York City, N.Y. 10016

Business: Airline Transportation
Sales: 1,150mm
CEO: Charles Tillinghast   Employees: 60,000

Contact: Mr. Robert Hall
Address: TWA, 5 Penn Center Plaza
    Philadelphia, Pa.
Telephone: (215) 923-5200, ext. 684
Program Reaches: 6,800 people at the center
When Started: n/a
Budget: $5 million

Program Outline:

To generate electric power for TWA's aircraft overhaul base and nearby administrative facilities on the edge of the new Kansas City International airport, TWA utilizes 2 converted Boeing 707 jet engines to generate kilowatts. The surplus Pratt & Whitney jet engines have been modified in a pollution-free "total energy" concept to provide all of TWA's energy requirements for power, heating and air-conditioning of its buildings from 1 single source of energy and fuel. The jet engines drive gas turbine engines, gas compressors, and heating recovery units use the engines' hot exhaust gases to produce saturated steam for heating and air-conditioning. Natural gas supplies a major source of fuel for the jet engines.

Co. Personnel Involved: n/a

Measure of Success: TWA expects a financial savings during the first year of operations of some $500,000. This figure is expected to increase in later years.

POLLUTION CONTROL

TRAVELERS INSURANCE CO.
One Tower Square
Hartford, Conn. 06115

Business: Personal and Casualty-Property Insurance
Sales: 3,000mm
CEO: Morrison H. Beach   Employees: 30,000

Contact: David E. Nash
Address: same as above
Telephone: (203) 277-3359
Program Reaches: hard to estimate
When Started: n/a
Budget: $260,000

Program Outline:

The purpose of the program is to prevent loss of property or life, and damage to health by the emission or discharge of materials considered pollutants. To facilitate the implementation of pollution controls, the following steps are taken: review insured's activities in the area of pollution and their controls; define deficiencies and formulate regulations; present recommendations to insured; follow-up and encourage compliance.

Travelers fulfills a consulting function without going into the design phase of a system. The company makes customers aware of the available technology and recommends alternate methods to choose from for solving their specific problems.

Co. Personnel Involved: Approximately 500 people are involved, 2% of their time; 9 people, 25% of their time; and 1 person, 75% of his time.

Measure of Success: Compliance with recommendations, customer satisfaction and reduction in losses to customers. Our success is measured first by the degree of compliance with Traveler's recommendations; second, by the loss record of the insured.

RIDE 'N BANK

UNITED BANK OF DENVER
1740 Broadway
Denver, Colo. 80217

Business: Banking   Sales: not applicable
CEO: John D. Hershner   Employees: 966

Contact: Sharron Landeck, Mgr/Communications
Address: same as above
Telephone: (303) 244-8811
Program Reaches: over 20,000 during the months of February and March, 1972
When Started: February 1, 1972
Budget: approx. $25,000, including full advertising campaign

Program Outline:

The purpose of this program is to contribute to the alleviation of air pollution problems through encouraging the population to utilize available mass transit rather than private transportation.

When a customer opens a checking or savings account at the Bank, he is given a stack of 10 bus tickets, each good for a 1-way fare on the Metro-Transit.

The Bank offered a fare reimbursement program during the months of February and March, 1972. Every time a customer made a transaction at the Bank, if he advised the teller that he rode the bus, he received a special ticket good for 25 cents on his next ride to or from downtown.

The Bank also arranged a "Bus Fair" in the lobby with people available to give information that may be needed about schedules, routes, etc.

Co. Personnel Involved: Employees were treated just like customers, so the only people directly involved were the public affairs staff, the communications manager (for publicity), marketing (for advertising) and 3-4 people in the personal banking (for the mechanics of distribution).

Measure of Success: n/a

This 2-door hardtop takes 47 people to work.

This 2-door hardtop takes 1 person to work.

Next time you take a deep breath of some downtown pollution, stop and think about the alternatives to the car you're driving.

Like the bus.

One Metro Coach can take 47 times as many people downtown as most cars take.

As more people ride the bus, fewer people will drive cars. Which will mean less congestion. And fewer pollutants in the air.

We're trying to help things along. With a special February offer designed to introduce you to the notion of commuting by bus.

To start with, if you'll open a checking or savings account at United Bank of Denver, we'll give you a stack of 10 bus tickets. Each one is good for a one-way ride on Metro Transit. (That's a whole week's worth of commuting.)

To continue, we're starting a new fare-reimbursement program, too. Every time you make a transaction at our bank, let the teller know you ride the bus. You'll get a special ticket good for 25 cents on your next ride to or from downtown. That means you ride the bus for a dime.

We know as much as anyone that our bus fare program isn't going to solve the pollution problem.

But it just may be a start. With your help, of course.

Don't you think it's about time?

⊗ United Bank of Denver
We'll pay you to ride the bus.

ENVIRONMENTAL LOAN PROGRAM

UNITED CALIFORNIA BANK
600 S. Spring Street
Los Angeles, Cal. 90054

Business: Banking
CEO: Norman Barker, Jr.

Sales: not applicable
Employees: 10,000

Contact: Lloyd B. Dennis, P.R.
Address: same as above
Telephone: (213) 624-0111
Program Reaches: n/a
When Started: September, 1971
Budget: no special budget

Program Outline:

The purpose of the program is to offer preferred rates of credit to help finance capital expenditures for the fight against pollution.

After extensive research into how it could effectively contribute to the fight against environmental pollution, the Bank established this program aimed primarily at small and medium size businesses to encompass investments in numerous environmentally related areas. The program offers preferred credit rates of up to 1½ points off the prime normal lending rate and/or double the normal repayment period. A broad outline of eligibility was created to assist lending officers in determining whether a company would qualify for the program.

At the same time the Loan Program was put into effect, the Bank initiated the distribution of 100% re-cycled paper litter bags through its branch system. These bags are available outside the branch system and are enclosed with an issue of THE CALIFORNIA ANTI-LITTER LEAGUE NEWSLETTER, distributed at the Watts Summer Festival, and mailed to California subscribers of ENVIRONMENTAL QUALITY MAGAZINE.

In addition, UCB is presently studying the feasibility of the use of fully re-cycled or reclaimed, or non-wood, paper products for internal operations.

Co. Personnel Involved: the lending officers who make the loans plus certain Bank personnel who belong to an ad hoc technical committee

Measure of Success: In Kern County, California, a company called Environmental Protection Corporation is implementing a system meeting the strict 1970 Porter-Cologne Water Quality Act standards for disposing of liquid wastes derived from local oilfield operations. Another company receiving special credit considerations is Tork-Link, whose electronic division specializes in developing electric motor conversion systems for downtown mini-bus transportation. These are just 2 examples of the success of the loan program.

PAPER RECYCLING

WELLS FARGO BANK
464 California Street
San Francisco, Cal. 94120

Business: Banking
CEO: Richard P. Colley

Sales: not applicable
Employees: 10,500

Contact: Gary Tanaka, Asst. Opr. Off.
Address: Data Processing Adm.
　62 First Street
　San Francisco, Cal.
Telephone: (415) 396-2531
Program Reaches: n/a
When Started: in its present form, August 1970
Budget: salary of 2 part time employees

Program Outline:

The purpose of this program is to lead in an area of environmental concern, providing as much recyclable paper as feasibly possible; to reduce scavenger costs by deriving revenue from the sale of paper while also providing new jobs in the local job market; and to save natural resources by using recycled paper in more Bank applications.

Waste paper from the Bank's computer center and from the subsidiary, Wellsco Data Corporation, are now recycled. Recycled paper is being used on some internal bulletins and publications. As of January 1972, all Bank checks will be printed on "Bagasse" paper, a sugar cane by-product. It would take 8,000 trees to provide 200 million checks which are now being produced from the sugar cane by-product.

A long range plan to administer and control the flow of computer generated reports within the Bank's major volume users could possibly add a substantial future resource for more recyclable paper.

Co. Personnel Involved: Two part time employees and one supervisor are currently performing the functions of paper segregation and salvaging supplies at the Computer Center. Supervisor performs other duties pertaining to record keeping.

Measure of Success: Success is measured in terms of the percentage of total paper waste sorted for recycling. Currently, this averages 55-60%; up from 25-30% in 1970.

"INVOLVEMENT MONEY"

WINTERS NATIONAL BANK & TRUST CO.
Winters Bank Tower
Dayton, Ohio 45401

Business: Banking   Sales: not applicable
CEO: Robert A. Kerr   Employees: 700

Contact: James Hubbard, V.P.
Address: same as above
Telephone: (513) 449-8740
Program Reaches: n/a
When Started: July 1, 1970
Budget: n/a

Program Outline:

In an effort to encourage involvement in pollution abatement by young and old and to help meet needs of area firms in financing pollution control equipment, Winters National Bank and Trust Co. offered to match up to $2.5 million of its own funds with any amount the public would raise. The total would be dedicated to loans for Dayton businesses in financing pollution-control programs. To enable more citizens to participate, the Bank lowered its usual minimum deposit amounts and created special "youth involvement accounts" to encourage young people to participate. In addition to the youth accounts, 3 special types of accounts were set up, in which the Bank lowered the required minimum deposit from $5,000 to $1,000.

Youth accounts attracted $31,000 and were nearly ½ the accounts opened. Deposits as small as $10 could be made by young people in a 4½% passbook account with no withdrawal restrictions.

Co. Personnel Involved: n/a

Measure of Success: On August 25, 1970, the Bank announced that 2 anti-pollution loans had been made for loans ranging up to $200,000 at the special interest rates. Kuhns Brothers Company and the Miami Conservancy District were approved for $200,000 each. Kuhns Brothers, one of the 10 worst polluters in the county, used the funds to purchase smoke-abatement equipment. The Miami Conservancy District loan was to help finance a $500,000 aeration project for the Great Miami River.

During the 3-month program, over $900,000 was raised from the public. The Bank matched these funds and made available some extra funds so that a total of $2 million was available for loans. By the end of 1970, all of the funds had been committed for low-cost loans to area firms for pollution abatement programs.

housing

MIDDLETOWN GIANT STEP, INC.

ARMCO STEEL CORP.
P.O. Box 600
Middletown, Ohio 45042

Business: Basic Steelmaking   Sales: 1,700mm
CEO: Calvin William Verity, Jr.   Employees: 51,236

Contact: B. C. Huselton, V.P.
Address: Church of the Ascension,
    Middletown, Ohio 45042
Telephone: (513) 425-2564
Program Reaches: not yet known
When Started: March, 1970
Budget: $25,000 budgeted for first two years of
    operation

Program Outline:

The purpose of the program is to develop, with other participating corporations, improved housing in any area of Greater Middletown that needs help, without regard to neighborhood, race or religion. Giant Step will help low-income Middletown people qualify for grants or loans that may be available from government agencies to help them improve their own homes, build low-cost housing or improve their neighborhoods. This program was started to fill a local need. Many families in the community own their own homes and have need of improving them, but cannot get assistance because these needs exceed the $3,500 limit established by law as the maximum grant. This non-profit, church- and business-sponsored organization is providing supplemental help so these families can bring their homes up to minimum levels. The organization is also set up to accept tax deductible gifts of real estate, building materials, or labor which can be developed into improved housing and sold, rented or used to house families in need.

Co. Personnel Involved: Eight to 10 management people have served on the governing board to get the group organized and continue to serve on the racially-mixed board that approves projects, raises funds, etc.

Measure of Success: The first rehabilitated home assisted by Giant Step is nearing completion.

NEW OPPORTUNITY HOME LOANS

BANK OF AMERICA
P.O. Box 37000
San Francisco, Cal. 94137

Business: Banking   Sales: not applicable
CEO: A. W. Clausen   Employees: 31,700

Contact: Frank Toner, V.P.
Address: Bank of America Center, Urban Affairs 3762,
    555 S. Flower Street, Los Angeles, Cal. 90071
Telephone: (415) 622-6598

Program Reaches: so far, over 7,000 families
When Started: 1968
Budget: $200 million

Program Outline:

The purpose of the program is to make money available for housing in low-income areas in order to promote local, not absentee, ownership within minority communities. In the past few years, Bank of America has increased its efforts to provide additional funds for low- and moderate-income housing and as a result, has established this program. The loans can be used to construct, buy or improve one- to four-family dwellings. Mortgages are available on terms approved by the FHA or VA. In the process of extending credit through the program, a special team of lending officers has been trained in the problems of making home loans in low-income areas. In addition, the bank has revised its minimum standards for homes in an effort to increase the volume of sound housing loans in minority communities.

Co. Personnel Involved: about 500 lending officers and supporting staff responsible for implementing the program

Measure of Success: By mid 1971, the original $100 million goal had been passed with loans going to more than 6,100 families. In August, 1971, the bank announced it would commit another $100 million to the program.

CINDERELLA NO. 2

BROOKLYN UNION GAS CO.
195 Mantague Street
Brooklyn, N.Y. 11201

Business: Public Utility
CEO: Gordon C. Griswold

Sales: 143mm
Employees: 3,150

Contact: Frederic H. J. Rider
Address: same as above
Telephone: (212) 643-3881
Program Reaches: n/a
When Started: n/a
Budget: over a 5-year period averaged about $50,000/year, exclusive of staff time

Program Outline:

Brooklyn Gas encourages the renaissance of Brooklyn. Not only have its officers participated vigorously in businessman's organizations especially set up for this purpose, but the company has participated in 2 home renovation projects which are having noticeable effects.

The first of these is the renovation of a dilapidated brownstone house at 211 Berkely place which attracted national attention. Thousands toured the house by appointment and there was a general revival of the whole neighborhood.

At the suggestion of a local community group, Brooklyn Union then undertook a second project, the renovation of a whole block not far from the original project. Here the company tried to pursuade builders and bankers that the abandoned houses on the periphery of a redeemable neighborhood represent a good business opportunity.

Co. Personnel Involved: n/a

Measure of Success: All the participants in this program believe that other similar neighborhoods can be brought back from decay if the company continues to take the leadership to bring the right parties together and provide the promotional muscle.

CAMDEN HOUSING IMPROVEMENT PROJECTS

CAMPBELL SOUP CO.
Campbell Place
Camden, N.J. 08101

Business: Food Processing
CEO: Harold Shaub

Sales: 965mm
Employees: 30,149

Contact: Jerome I. Weinstein
Address: 562 Benson Street, Camden, N.J.
Telephone: (609) 966-4555
Program Reaches: approx. 35,000 residents of North and South Camden
When Started: October, 1967
Budget: $622,000

Program Outline:

The purpose of the program is to provide sound housing and make home ownership possible for low-income families. Utilizing vacant and/or abandoned properties for housing helps stop the spread of this blight and further deterioration to the neighborhood. The project purchases vacant, vandalized houses, re-builds them to high quality standards (the value of the improvements is often ten times the purchase price of the house) and re-sells them to low-income families. Generally, these families cannot obtain sound housing for either rental or purchase on the open market. A major effort is made to work with small, local contractors in order that the financial and employment benefits of the program remain within the city.

Co. Personnel Involved: Eight people are concerned in one way or another and spend a few hours every week on CHIP.

Measure of Success: Company has submitted its 400th individual house to FHA for approval before construction is started. Thus far, the program has re-housed approximately 2% of the population of the city, has arrested the spread of blight on many blocks in neighborhoods in which the company is working and has been able to stay current with the rate of vacancy.

STAMFORD DEVELOPMENT CORP.

CLAIROL, INC.
345 Park Avenue
New York, N.Y. 10022 and
One Blachley Road
Stamford, Conn. 06902

Business: Hair Color, Hair Care,
   Toiletries, Beauty Appliances
Sales: n/a
CEO: Bruce S. Gelb   Employees: 2,500

Contact: W. L. Tyson, Mgr., Com. Rels.
Address: One Blachley Road, Stamford Ct. 06902
Telephone: (202) 325-1609
Program Reaches: initially 89 families
When Started: 1966
Budget: Clairol contributes to S.D.C. on annual basis S.D.C. has revolving capital fund of just under $200,000 and an annual operating budget of around $60,000.

Program Outline:

The purpose of the program is to assist in production of moderate-income housing in the Stamford area, which has one of the lowest housing vacancy ratios and is one of the highest-cost housing areas in the nation. The program helps families with incomes up to $15,000 (depending on family size) including a large number of minority group families. The program began with a $22,000 grant to New Hope Corp. (a black, church-sponsored, non-profit housing organization) to provide land-aquisition write-down for an 89-unit housing project. It now includes financial and manpower support for Stamford Development Corp., an "umbrella" agency formed by the private sector to provide financial and technical assistance to non-profit housing sponsors.

Co. Personnel Involved: Two company executives serve as directors of S.D.C., one as director of New Hope Corp.

Measure of Success: 89-unit project now occupied, 36-unit S.D.C. project about to be occupied. Through S.D.C., have assisted in advancing from other projects with 204 units.

RIVERSIDE GARDENS REDEVELOPMENT

CITIZENS AND SOUTHERN NATIONAL BANK
99 Annex
Atlanta, Ga. 30399

Business: Banking   Sales: not applicable
 Assets: 2,065mm
CEO: Mills B. Lane, Jr.   Employees: 3,550

Contact: W. F. Ottinger
Address: same as above
Telephone: (404) 588-2485
Program Reaches: 400
When Started: 1969
Budget: Approximately $800,000 has been spent on acquisition and renovation thus far.

Program Outline:

The purpose of the program is to redevelop an apartment complex that was built during World War II to house dockworkers, and had become one of the worst areas of the city. The 132-unit apartment complex was purchased in Savannah in 1969. It had been neglected by its former owner who was an absentee, and the lack of maintenance contributed to the area's reputation as one of the worst in Savannah. Prostitution, crime, etc. were prevalent.

The Bank renovated the units, inside and out. A laundromat, a recreation hall, and playground were also built. A church, kindergarten and Boy Scout Troup have also been established. Crime in the project, according to local police, has dropped significantly. Rents have been raised only approximately 10% since purchase. All renovation work was handled by minority contractors financed by the Community Development Corporation.

Co. Personnel Involved: 10-15

Measure of Success: The greatest measure of success has been the decreased crime rate in the project. It has decreased significantly according to the City Police Department.

RIVERSIDE GARDENS REDEVELOPMENT

Before

After

RIVERSIDE GARDENS REDEVELOPMENT

Before

After

REHABILITATION HOUSING SUBSIDY PROGRAM

DUPONT CO.
1007 Market Street
Wilmington, Del.

Business: Diversified Manufacturing
Sales: 3,800mm
CEO: Charles B. McCoy   Employees: 110,865

Contact: John Burchenal
Address: same as above
Telephone: (302) 774-2036
Program Reaches: too early to tell
When Started: November, 1971
Budget: $400,000 for the first year

Program Outline:

The program plans for a privately financed program to make possible rehabilitation of 400 homes in Wilmington and New Castle County over the next 4 years. It will subsidize the cost of rehabilitating houses so that they can be sold in a price range for moderate income families. The program will be carried out through Community Housing, Inc. and will provide subsidies up to $4,000 per house for the 400 homes to be rehabilitated over a 4-year period. Persons qualifying for federal programs will be able to purchase these homes for $200 down and mortgage payments for $75-$90 a month. A $200,000 "challenge" grant has been committed by DuPont to be used as a matching fund to help raise the full $400,000 needed for the program's first year.

Co. Personnel Involved: DuPont's President and Chairman, Charles McCoy headed the campaign to raise funds. James A. Grady, Director of the DuPont Central Systems and Services Department, is President of Community Housing, Inc., and there are other employees involved on an ad hoc basis.

Measure of Success: too early to tell

CHICAGO'S BEST LANDLORDS

THE FIRST NATIONAL BANK OF CHICAGO
One First National Plaza
Chicago, Ill. 60670

Business: Banking   Sales: not applicable
Assets: 9,514mm
CEO: John E. Drick   Employees: 5,100

Contact: Norman Ross, V.P. Public Affairs
Address: same as above
Telephone: (312) 732-4090
Program Reaches: 200-300
When Started: 1971
Budget: $205,000 for rehabilitation; $30,000 for the park

Program Outline:

A group of welfare mothers was given a slum property for the purposes of rehabilitating a 12-flat apartment building on Chicago's west side and the construction of an adjacent mini-park. They represent Aid for Dependent Children, welfare residents and neighborhood mothers and children. The group approached the Bank for a $205,000 loan to rehabilitate the apartment building. This was eventually granted through a loan from the FHA. Then the Bank put an additional $30,000 into the building of the park adjacent to the property.

Co. Personnel Involved: 12

Measure of Success: The success of giving this type of property to a group of welfare individuals has been sufficient enough so that a Chicago judge has offered to turn others of the 10,000 properties in the housing court over to Chicago's Best Landlords. The park is now in operation and the rehabilitation project will be completed by the fall of 1972.

GREATER MINNEAPOLIS METROPOLITAN HOUSING CORPORATION

FIRST NATIONAL BANK OF MINNEAPOLIS
120 S. Sixth Street
Minneapolis, Minn. 55480

Business: Banking
CEO: George H. Dixon

Sales: not applicable
Employees: 1,500

Contact: Charles R. Krusell
Address: 1030 Midland Bank Bldg.
   Minneapolis, Minn. 55401
Telephone: (612) 339-0601
Program Reaches: n/a
When Started: 1970
Budget: n/a

Program Outline:

The purpose of the program is to provide financing for low-income housing. The Bank provides technical assistance to non-profit sponsors from the initial conception of a project through technical processing, construction and management. The corporation further makes non-interest or interest-bearing seed-money loans to non-profit housing sponsors to cover costs incurred before project feasibility determination by the Federal Housing Administration and until the initial Federal Housing Administration closing. The corporation makes training grants to persons selected by community non-profit sponsors to be project coordinators and managers. The Bank, in addition, sponsors housing development through new construction or rehabilitation where no community sponsor is available, and sponsors housing demonstrations for new and innovative methods for construction.

Co. Personnel Involved: 1 (the Bank president)

Measure of Success: The Bank is working with at least a dozen non-profit sponsors and has provided technical and financial assistance to them. Plans are for 1000-dwelling units of housing. Currently, 250-dwelling units of housing for low- and moderate-income families and individuals are under construction.

LOW- AND MODERATE-INCOME HOUSING

FIRST NATIONAL CITY BANK
399 Park Avenue
New York, N.Y. 10022

Business: Banking
CEO: William I. Spencer

Sales: not applicable
Employees: 31,700

Contact: William W. Panitz, V.P.
Address: same as above
Telephone: (212) 559-3575
Program Reaches: directly, 20,000/year
When Started: late 1970
Budget: annually committed, $125 million of funds (plus
   management time)

Program Outline:

In response to the critical shortage of decent housing for low and moderate income families in New York City, FNCB aggressively pursues opportunities to finance the construction of low- and moderate-income housing, predominantly in the committing of loans for the construction of new housing. The Bank committed to lend approximately $125 million in 1971, and expects to perform similarly in 1972. This enables close to 5,000 units to be built each year.

Co. Personnel Involved: The major share of the time of a senior officer and one other officer, and about 10% of the time of 5 other officers.

Measure of Success: Of the 14 projects to which the Bank committed funds since the program began, two are essentially completed, and most of the others should be completed this year. So far, dollars committed, housing accomplished and various cost factors have gone according to plan.

URBAN MORTGAGE LENDING

THE FIRST PENNSYLVANIA BANK & TRUST CO.
15th & Chestnut Streets
Philadelphia, Pa. 19105

Business: Banking   Sales: not applicable
Deposits: December 31, 1971—2,900mm
CEO: John R. Bunting   Employees: 4,323

Contact: C. H. Whittum, Jr.
Address: same as above
Telephone: (215) 786-8116
Program Reaches: n/a
When Started: 1971
Budget: initially $4 million—future amount to be determined

Program Outline:

The program is designed to provide specialized attention to low-income group members attempting to secure mortgage loans for residential or commercial properties.

To ensure special consideration in the area of mortgage lending to people in low-income brackets, the Bank's Real Estate Department created a new urban mortgage lending division responsible for these loans. The Urban Affairs Committee, made up of members of the Bank's senior executive management, earmarked an initial $1 million fund for mortgage lending on residential properties and a $3 million fund for commercial and non-profit properties.

Co. Personnel Involved: The Urban Mortgage Lending Division, the unit most directly involved, is made up of approximately 6 people. The real estate staff and the Bank's management team are involved in a supportive manner.

Measure of Success: To date, only 6 months from the program's start, over $1.1 million of the earmarked funds have been used.

URBAN LOW-INCOME HOUSING

GENERAL MOTORS CORPORATION
3044 West Grand Boulevard
General Motors Building
Detroit, Mich. 48202

Business: Automotive Industry
Sales: 28,264mm
CEO: Edward N. Cole   Employees: 696,000

Contact: C. V. Hagler, P.R. Staff
Address: same as above
Telephone: (313) 556-2394
Program Reaches: n/a
When Started: n/a
Budget: $1 million/project

Program Outline:

General Motors has provided interest-free loans to 2 non-profit community organizations for the purpose of acquiring land for low-income housing projects. This seed money, the donated talents of attorneys, real estate men and architects has been the impetus needed to make self-determination a reality. These programs have provided business experience for black contractors while creating employment for local minority laborers and tradesmen. The result will mean above-average housing for hundreds of minority persons. Harambee (Swahili for "Let us work together") is the name of one such project in Pontiac, Michigan which was established through a spirit of cooperation among citizens, industry and government.

Co. Personnel Involved: Several General Motors realty company employees act as advisors.

Measure of Success: project presently under construction

HOUSING OFFICE

MCDONNELL DOUGLAS CORP.
P. O. Box 516
St. Louis, Mo 63166

Business: Aerospace   Sales: 2,088mm
CEO: Sanford N. McDonnell   Employees: 92,552

Contact: David T. Birge
Address: same as above
Telephone: (314) 232-9811
Program Reaches: 29,000 employees
When Started: 1952
Budget: $23,500/year

Program Outline:

The purpose of the Housing Office is to increase the availability of non-discriminatory housing for employees.

The Housing Office assists employees and temporary representatives of government agencies, foreign governments and sub-contractors in finding suitable housing by rental, lease or purchase. The office makes referrals only to real estate agencies, housing developers and apartment and mobile home agents and managers who have submitted notification of compliance with the Federal Fair Housing Act. Individual home owners must agree to comply with FFHA before their listing will be accepted by the corporation.

Co. Personnel Involved: 2 full time employees

Measure of Success: Of the 729 requests for assistance received during the past year, over 95% of the individuals have been placed in housing of their choice. During this period, 69 requests were received from minorities; 66 have been placed in housing of their choice and 3 requests are still open.

LOW RENT HOUSING PROGRAM

THE NEW YORK BANK FOR SAVINGS
280 Park Avenue, South
New York, N.Y. 10010

Business: Banking   Sales: not applicable
                       Assets: 2,500mm
CEO: Arthur J. Quinn   Employees: 620

Contact: William P. Schweickert
Address: same as above
Telephone: (212) 473-5656
Program Reaches: n/a
When Started: April, 1968
Budget: no budget (funds are made available as needed)

Program Outline:

The New York Bank for Savings, together with the Bowery Savings Bank, joined together to develop low-income housing in Harlem and other ghetto areas. The banks help low-income Blacks and Puerto Ricans of these areas by working with the local community groups and supplying the development funds and expertise. The banks supply the funds to purchase land, either privately or from the city, demolish buildings, employ architects, hire contractors, finance the construction and, upon completion, the property is either transferred to the New York City Housing Authority for operation as a public housing project, or deeded to the local non-profit community group with 100% FHA financing provided by the banks. The banks accept the same return on their funds as they would receive on an FHA mortgage.

Co. Personnel Involved: 2 full time officers and part of three other officers' time plus two other full time employees

Measure of Success: 300 completed apartments; 400 additional apartments to be completed this year; recognition from community groups

LOW INCOME LOAN PROGRAM

NORTH CAROLINA NATIONAL BANK
200 South Tryon Street
Charlotte, N.C. 28201

Business: Banking
CEO: Thomas I. Storrs

Sales: not applicable
Employees: 3,200

Contact: W. W. Owens or J. B. Perkins
Address: P.O. Box 21848, Greensboro, N.C.
Telephone: (919) 378-5320
Program Reaches: n/a
When Started: 1971
Budget: Goals will not be set until more experience is
obtained

Program Outline:

The purpose of the program is to provide loans to
deserving low-income families.

A pilot study has been completed to test the idea that
large banks can give financial aid, in the form of loans
and financial counseling, to lower-income families and
individuals to encourage better financial planning and to
improve their standard of living.

Under this program, these people receive extensive
counseling in financial management from the Bank in an
effort to keep the same problem from recurring. NCNB
will extend credit or offer counseling based on the
following criteria: the participant has a definite need to
improve his financial condition or standard of living, he is
sincere and the repayment schedule can reasonably be
worked into his budget if credit is extended. In this way,
debt consolidation and home improvement may be
initiated, necessary furniture and major appliances may
be purchased, an automobile may be purchased if needed
for school or work, necessary education may be financed
and adequate health care will not have to be delayed for
lack of funds.

Co. Personnel Involved: All consumer loan officers of
the Bank in the 5 larger cities of North Carolina are
involved. One loan officer in each city is responsible for
the program and reports to the division office in Greensboro.

Measure of Success: Since the program is new, there is
no way of measuring success with previous experience.

LOW- AND MODERATE-INCOME HOUSING PROGRAM

NORTHWEST BANCORPORATION
1200 Northwestern National Bank Building
Minneapolis, Minn. 55480

Business: Bank Holding Co.

Sales: not applicable
Assets: 4,500mm

CEO: Henry T. Rutledge

Employees: 7,868

Contact: Dennis W. Dunne, V.P.
Address: same as above
Telephone: (612) 372-8656
Program Reaches: 4,000 families
When Started: July 1, 1970
Budget: In addition to mortgage commitment, advertising
and public relations expenditures were approximately
$25,000.

Program Outline:

The purpose of this program is to allocate assets
to provide low- and moderate-income housing for the
consumers in the Bank's trade area. Northwest Ban-

corporation, through its 78 affiliated banks and mortgage banking company, made a commitment to supply
at least $30 million for low- and moderate-income
housing for families in the upper Midwest. These projects were to be financed under FHA 235 and 236
loans with each of the affiliated banks making specific
commitments. The commitment was announced at the
annual stockholders' meeting and communicated throughout the entire area by TV video tapes, through news
stations and followed up by extensive news releases
inviting low- and moderate-income families to visit their
local bank. Seminars were held with real estate officers
from the affiliated banks to discuss procedures for handling these type loans and the mortgage banking company
was used as a clearinghouse for questions.

Co. Personnel Involved: Approximately 200 real estate
loan officers of affiliates were directly involved.

Measure of Success: The original goal was to reach over
$30 million commitment in 18 months. This goal was
exceeded in the first 3 months of the program and at the
end of the first year, over $60 million worth of 235 loans
were closed.

BILLION DOLLAR INVESTMENT PROGRAM
(LIFE INSURANCE INSTITUTE)

NORTHWESTERN MUTUAL LIFE INSURANCE CO.
720 E. Wisconsin Avenue
Milwaukee, Wis. 53202

Business: Life Insurance   Sales: 2,000mm
CEO: Francis E. Ferguson   Employees: 2,150

Contact: William Cary
Address: same as above
Telephone: (414) 271-1444
Program Reaches: n/a
When Started: completed 1970
Budget: $2 billion; NML has pledged $71 million

Program Outline:

The industry's program is concerned with the improvement of inner city housing and the development of job-creating facilities. A result of this commitment is the Hillside urban renewal area where construction crews have completed 112 new homes—the Plymouth Hill Apartment Project. The apartments qualify under the federal rent supplement program and attract small, low-income families and elderly persons.

In addition to the Plymouth Hill project in Milwaukee, MNL has commited itself to other loans which will help build low-income apartments in Corpus Christi, Texas, and will help inner city residents in Chicago, Detroit, Los Angeles, and San Francisco to purchase their own homes. Two blocks from the Plymouth Hill project is one of the company's job-creating projects, the Central City Development Corporation complex. It is Black-sponsored and operated and has all Black stockholders. When completed in September, 1972, it will house 11 businesses, all Black-owned and operated, a 54-room motel, 12-lane bowling alley, restaurant and cocktail lounge, supermarket, barber shop, drug store, laundry and dry-cleaning facility, merchandise mart, liquor store, a law firm, a certified public accounting firm. NML is providing long-term financing.

Co. Personnel Involved: n/a

Measure of Success: The project is entirely occupied.

LIFE INSURANCE INDUSTRY'S
$2 BILLION INVESTMENT PROGRAM

THE PENN MUTUAL LIFE INSURANCE CO.
Independence Square
Philadelphia, Pa. 19105

Business: Life and Health Insurance
Sales: 345mm
CEO: Frank K. Tarbox   Employees: 1,860

Contact: William Dikeman
Address: same as above
Telephone: (215) 925-7300
Program Reaches: n/a
When Started: n/a
Budget: Penn Mutual's is nearly $30 million, of which almost $20 million has been advanced or committed.

Program Outline:

The purpose of this program is to help increase the standard of living in inner cities through the financing of homes and apartments, jobs and services.

As a result of Penn Mutual's investment program in inner city mortgages, over 280 Philadelphia families have moved into better neighborhoods and become homeowners. The San Francisco complex is one of 9 new apartments financed by the company under the program and provides modern living quarters for 910 families and single persons in core city areas of West Virginia, New Jersey, Texas, Alabama, Florida, Arkansas and Pennsylvania. To help create new jobs, the company is helping a medical clinic operated by Temple University to provide medical care as well as jobs for nearby residents. When renovations are completed, the center will offer medical, dental, mental health, pharmacy and laboratory services to community residents. It will be staffed by 228 full-time and 63 part time professional employees.

The Life Insurance Industry's program is structured so that each participating company makes its own investment decisions.

Co. Personnel Involved: n/a

Measure of Success: So far, under the industry's program, over 86,000 housing units have been financed and 46,000 jobs created. The success of the Urban Investment program established it as a model for plans which could be developed by other industries.

HOPE (HOUSING OPPORTUNITY PROGRAMS WITH EDUCATION)

PHILADELPHIA ELECTRIC CO.
2301 Market Street
Philadelphia, Pa. 19101

Business: Electric Utility   Sales: 504mm
CEO: James L. Everett   Employees: 10,500

Contact: Joseph F. Van Hart, Mgr. P.R. Dept.
Address: 2301 Market St.
    Philadephia, Pa. 19101
Telephone:(215) 841-4000
Program Reaches: inner city residents
When Started: n/a
Budget:n/a

Program Outline:

In order to maintain a stable community, the principle of home ownership as opposed to rental is the goal of HOPE.

To help solve inner city housing problems, HOPE builds or rehabilitates for sale minimum cost housing. The program includes assistance in home maintenance and budgeting. In 1969, HOPE became actively involved in the planning of new construction and rehabilitation of homes in East Frankford, Kensington and North Philadelphia.

Co. Personnel Involved: n/a

Measure of Success: n/a

LOW INCOME HOUSING

PITTSBURGH NATIONAL BANK
1 Oliver Plaza
Pittsburgh, Pa. 15230

Business: Banking   Sales: not applicable
CEO: Merle E. Gilliand   Employees: 2,311

Contact: Wallace Abel, Dir.P.R.
Address: same as above
Telephone: (412) 355-2000
Program Reaches: n/a
When Started: n/a
Budget: n/a

Program Outline:

The purpose of the program is to provide aid in housing to low-income families and the elderly.

The Bank has loan commitments outstanding of $9,500,000 to cover construction of 756 multi-family housing units. The Bank is committing an additional $4,000,000 to help finance, with other lenders, another 1,000 units, which require loans totaling $17,000,000. Further, the Bank is in the preliminary stages of approving an additional $9,750,000 in loans for construction of 494 units. These loans are extended at below-market interest rates, under various Federal Housing Administration programs. During the last 2 years, the Bank has lent in excess of $13,000,000 at these below-market rates to assist in the financing of more than 1,600 multi-family units currently occupied by either the elderly or families with low income.

Co. Personnel Involved: n/a

Measure of Success: Objectively, the wide acceptance of specialized services. Subjectively, the value of establishing Free Clinics, opening channels of communication, etc.

LIFE INSURANCE INDUSTRY
BILLION DOLLAR PLEDGE

PHOENIX MUTUAL LIFE INSURANCE CO.
One American Row
Hartford, Conn. 06115

Business: General Life Insurance
Sales: not applicable   Assets: 1,249mm
CEO: R. T. Jackson   Employees: 2,000

Contact: C. Russell Noyes, V.P., P.R.
Address: same as above
Telephone: (203) 278-1212
Program Reaches: n/a
When Started: late 1967
Budget: $16 million dollar pledge

Program Outline:

The purpose of this program is to aid American cities through money commitments in high-risk areas normally not considered for insurance company investment. Phoenix Mutual has contributed $16 million to the life insurance industry's $2 billion dollar pledge in these areas: $4 million invested in 8 apartment developments in Hartford, Atlanta, Norfolk, and in Charlotte and Thomasville, North Carolina; $400,000 has gone into mortgages to finance purchase of 591 living units; $2.2 million has helped build new shopping centers and office buildings in Hartford, Chicago, and East Palo Alto, California. The East Palo Alto loan was made through that town's unique Black-White cooperative organization, Counterpart, Inc. The single biggest loan so far was a $5 million one which went to Harper Hospital in Detroit. Located in a ghetto area, the hospital will provide for expanded and modernized health care facilities for the area residents, and several hundred jobs.

Co. Personnel Involved: n/a

Measure of Success: n/a

BETTER RICHMOND, INC.

A. H. ROBINS CO., INC.
1407 Cummings Drive
Richmond, Va. 23220

Business: Manufacturing Pharmaceuticals
Sales: 150mm
CEO: W. L. Zimmer, III   Employees: 4,000

Contact: John Orgain
Address: 7th and Franklin Bldg., Richmond, Va. 23219
Telephone: (703) 643-2861
Program Reaches: 51 to 500 families
When Started: 1968
Budget: Ranges from $171,000 to $903,000; base operating fund available at beginning of program $522,000

Program Outline:

The purpose of this program is to provide new, single-family dwellings at a reasonable price to low- and low to medium-income families in deteriorating urban areas and to provide a vehicle through which minority contracts in building business can achieve experience and status. Single-family dwellings are financed, constructed and sold to persons in the $4,000 to $8,000 income range in 2-, 3- and 4-bedroom units, using minority constructors and laborers. Homes are located in the inner city, replacing delapidated property and other usable land with former occupants receiving first choice of new units. Assistance is given in all transactions to enhance the opportunity for those desiring to own a home. This corporation is governed by a bi-racial board with technical and financial advice given to community business.

Co. Personnel Involved: Executive Vice President is member of Executive Committee and is involved as much as is required.

Measure of Success: Total success has been realized as a result of input from clientele served. Fifty-one family units have been built, 51 sold and properly financed.

PLUMLEY VILLAGE EAST

STATE MUTUAL LIFE ASSURANCE CO. OF AMERICA
440 Lincoln Street
Worcester, Mass. 01605

Business: Life Insurance   Sales: 270mm
CEO: W. Douglas Bell   Employees: 1,550

Contact: Paul J. Foley, V.P.
Address: same as above
Telephone: (617) 852-1000
Program Reaches: 430 families
When Started: 1968
Budget: $15 million

Program Outline:

The purpose of the program is to provide comfortable housing for low- and moderate-income families in a new neighborhood designed to meet all the needs of the people who reside there—people with large numbers of children who, in the past, have been relegated to shabby, blighted housing. Strong emphasis in this housing project is placed on the design of the physical structure. A 16-story tower surrounded by 49 3-story buildings, all constructed with concrete and steel, curve gracefully around old trees, lawns and playgrounds. All auto traffic is kept on the perimeter of the neighborhood. A tenant's committee and a social services referral center in the neighborhood assists in solving the social problems of the residents. In addition, a day-care center has also been established.

Co. Personnel Involved: One State Mutual full time employee, 3 part time employees and a management staff of 9 individuals from State Mutual work closely in the neighborhood.

Measure of Success: the opinions of people who live in Plumley Village East

CONNECTICUT HOUSING INVESTMENT FUND

TRAVELERS INSURANCE CO.
One Tower Square
Hartford, Conn. 06115

Business: Life Insurance   Sales: 3,000mm
CEO: Morrison H. Beach   Employees: 30,000

Contact: James R. Miller, II
Address: same as above
Telephone: (203) 277-2906
Program Reaches: n/a
When Started: 1970
Budget: Travelers has $1 million invested in this fund.

Program Outline:

This program is actually a corporation that will buy or arrange financing for suburban homes for Negro and other minority families trapped in the Hartford ghetto, and, on occasion, help a white family buy a home in a racially-mixed neighborhood.

Co. Personnel Involved: 3 man-months

Measure of Success: n/a

TWO BILLION DOLLAR PROGRAM

TRAVELERS INSURANCE CO.
One Tower Square
Hartford, Conn. 06115

Business: Life Insurance   Sales: 3,000mm
CEO: Morrison H. Beach   Employees: 30,000

Contact: J. G. Page
Address: same as above
Telephone: (203) 277-2545
Program Reaches: n/a
When Started: 1967
Budget: $54 million for Travelers's share of the program

Program Outline:

The Life Insurance Industry has committed itself to a $2 billion program to provide housing and job opportunities. This program provides mortgage financing on single-family and multi-family housing, office buildings, fast food service facilities, etc.

Co. Personnel Involved: approximately 15 involved part time in connection with originating, processing, underwriting and servicing these mortgage investments

Measure of Success: Financing for approximately 3,700 units of housing has been supplied thus far.

FINANCIAL ASSISTANCE TO MINORITY CONSTRUCTION/HOUSING

UNITED CALIFORNIA BANK
600 S. Spring Street
Los Angeles, Cal. 90054

Business: Banking   Sales: not applicable
CEO: Norman Barker, Jr.   Employees: 10,000

Contact: Dr. Larry Wilson
Address: same as above
Telephone: (213) 624-0111, ext 2813
Program Reaches: n/a
When Started: n/a
Budget: see program outline

Program Outline:

The purpose of the various projects UCB is participating in is to aid in the construction of numerous low-income housing developments.

These projects are conducted in several areas of California and on many different levels: (1) UCB's Real Estate Department provided approximately $100,000 to a Black contractor for construction of 11 units of housing in the Watts area; (2) UCB has processed 100 loans insured under FHA 221 for rehabilitation housing in Southeast Los Angeles sponsored by Mead Housing Trust; financing has also been provided for 2 apartment house projects for the same sponsor ($2 million and $700,000 consecutively); (3) UCB (Florence-Central) has contracted with the Los Angeles County's Model Cities Program to process over 500 applicants for loans and grants from property owners in the Florence-Firestone community for housing rehabilitation; (4) in Northern California, UCB aided in the construction of Midtown Terrace, a multi-family housing complex located in San Francisco; (5) in San Diego, an interim construction loan on a small tract of 13 homes was made under FHA 235 ($225,000); (6) UCB, Beverly Hills, made a construction loan for 400 units (Villa Nueva Apts.) occupied mostly by Mexican-Americans, sponsored by the Augustinian Fathers ($5,810,000) also in San Diego; (7) in addition, UCB San Diego provided interim financing for construction of 20 units in Riverside, California ($40,000); (8) in Orange County, the Bank provided financing for a tract of 20 homes under FHA 235, called "New World" ($40,000).

Co. Personnel Involved: Depends on loan—sometimes a team effort, sometimes the lending officer from the nearest branch handles the activity.

Measure of Success: In terms of what UCB has done, good. In terms of community need, the needs are tremendous.

Before

CITY HOMES, INC.

WASHINGTON GAS LIGHT CO.
1100 H Street, N.W.
Washington, D.C. 20005

Business: Natural Gas Utility   Sales: 135mm
CEO: Paul F. Reichardt   Employees: 3,000

Contact: Sanford Wiesenthal
Address: same as above
Telephone: (202) 624-6213
Program Reaches: n/a
When Started: November, 1969
Budget: n/a

Program Outline:

The purpose of this wholly-owned subsidiary of Washington Gas is to help stop the trend of urban decay by giving inner city residents a chance to own their own homes. City Homes purchases deteriorating homes, rehabilitates them and resells them to low and middle-income families.

In the rehabilitation process, quality in materials and workmanship is emphasized. Each house receives major rehabilitation and modernization with special emphasis being given to practicality. Special attention is given to kitchens, baths, wiring, plumbing and heating to provide for a minimum of maintenance.

City Homes has made a special effort to seek qualified minority group contractors to do the rehabilitation work, and so far, only minority contractors have been used.

The company would like to increase the volume of houses and also become involved in some of the depressed housing areas in the suburbs.

Co. Personnel Involved: 1—heavily involved, 2—moderately involved, and 4—slightly involved

Measure of Success: The 6 homes completed so far have been very successful and have stimulated further improvement in their neighborhoods. All are excellent examples of fine rehabilitation work. Additional improvement is needed over cost control, contractor dependability and government housing authority cooperation.

After

Before

After

Reprinted from WONDER FLAME,
a publication of Washington Gas & Light Company

A HOME FOR HOUSING

UNITED STATES NATIONAL BANK
OF OREGON
321 S.W. Sixth Avenue
P.O. Box 4412
Portland, Oregon 97208

Business: Banking   Sales: not applicable
CEO: E. L. Dresler   Employees: 3,998

Contact: John D. Mills, V.P.—Urban Affairs
Address: same as above
Telephone: (503) 225-6111
Program Reaches: n/a
When Started: August, 1968
Budget: $7 million ceiling for financing

Program Outline:

The purpose of the program is to support and actively
participate in several major housing programs, which,
when taken together, provide a strong base or "home"
for housing programs in the Portland region. The program is aimed at low and moderate income families in
need of better housing, either through rehabilitation of
old units or new dwellings.

Through a $5 million dollar pledge for financing low-
and moderate-income families in new and rehabilitated
multi-unit dwellings in the Portland area, the Bank serves
as a central coordinator for financing housing development. With a stress on guiding individuals through the
paperwork after securing proper forms USNB seeks to
further increase the standard-of-living-housing unit, with
an average $10,000 investment per unit.

The projects led to the Bank providing office space to
various Community Action Program groups as headquarters for screening and processing applications for
housing loans. The Bank assumed a leadership role in
getting other businesses to participate in the Portland
Housing Development Corporation, a non-profit development corporation, in the planning stages.

Co. Personnel Involved: n/a

Measure of Success: Of the $7 million dollars approx-
imately $4 million had been allocated for specific pro-
jects by the end of 1971—2/3 for new multi-family
dwellings and 1/3 for new units providing approximately
400 families with housing. There has also been a noticeable increase in the success of recruiting college graduates, due to the Bank's social commitment.

EXPERIMENTAL COMMUNITY

WHITTAKER CORP.
10880 Wilshire Boulevard
Los Angeles, Cal. 90024

Business: Manufacturing, Distribution, Housing
Sales: 566mm
CEO: Joseph F. Alibrandi   Employees: 22,500

Contact: R. W. (Bob) Murray
Address: same as above
Telephone: (213) 475-9411, ext. 383
Program Reaches: 120 directly
When Started: January 31, 1972
Budget: $12,000

Program Outline:

Whittaker Corp. is sponsoring the construction of a
120—unit experimental community on the campus of
California State Polytechnic College, Pomona, in which
students (who designed the community) will live, investi-
gating the social, psychological and ecological implications.

The idea is to take a total community concept developed
by freshmen of the Environmental Sciences school from
the idea stage to reality, allowing students to live in the
completed 120—unit project for a period of weeks, and
thus experience the "real world" problems faced by
urban planners. The community will be self-sustaining,
producing no waste materials. Students will govern themselves and create their own model society in the physical
community. They will actually manufacture their own
dwelling unit which will fit together into a "mega-
structure."

Co. Personnel Involved: 4 directly, 8 indirectly

Measure of Success: The program is just starting.

employment opportunities

BEECHCRAFT PROGRAM ON EQUAL EMPLOYMENT OPPORTUNITY

BEECH AIRCRAFT CORP.
9709 E. Central
Wichita, Kan. 67201

Business: Manufacturing Corporate and Private Aircraft
Sales: 150mm
CEO: Frank E. Hedrick   Employees: 4,974

Contact: J. E. Isaacs
Address: same as above
Telephone: (316) 685-6211, ext. 2661
Program Reaches: tens of 1000's
When Started: n/a
Budget: n/a

Program Outline:

(1) The enunciation of company policy to employees, potential employees, employment services, employment agencies, technical schools and universities.

(2) Communication with supervisory and management people which results in their satisfactory support of the company policy involved.

(3) A continuing follow-up to determine that equal employment opportunity is accorded all concerned without regard to sex, age, race, color, or religious creed.

(4) Maintenance of a comprehensive, goal-centered administrative policy designed to achieve a comprehensive equal employment opportunity policy.

Co. Personnel Involved: several 1000's

Measure of Success: high morale among the several age levels, satisfactory morale among the minority groups, satisfactory morale and cooperative and helpful attitude among those not considered members of minority groups

AFFIRMATIVE ACTION

CLARK EQUIPMENT CO.
324 E. Dewey Avenue
Buchanan, Mich. 49107

Business: Capital Goods Manufacturing
Sales: 675mm
CEO: Bert E. Phillips   Employees: 21,600

Contact: Don Klinkhamer
Address: same as above
Telephone: (616) 697-8529
Program Reaches: varies with location
When Started: 1969
Budget: varies with each facility

Program Outline:

The purpose of the program is to achieve a utilization of minorities equal to or greater than their numerical representation within the communities in which the company has facilities.

Available qualified minorities are determined for each community. On the basis of turnover and expansion, goals are set each year to hire or promote these minorities with the end result being the equal representation of minorities within each position. Recruiting, training, and counseling provide support to this end.

Co. Personnel Involved: Each personnel department and all managers and supervisors with authority to hire.

Measure of Success: A majority of the company's facilities have made substantial progress in recruiting, selecting, hiring, training and promoting minorities.

ENTRY LEVEL PROGRAM

COMMERCIAL CREDIT CO.
300 St. Paul Place
Baltimore, Md. 21202

Business: Holding Company, Business Credit
  Institution
Sales: 512mm
CEO: Donald S. Jones   Employees: 4,540

Contact: James L. Roberts
Address: same as above
Telephone: (301) 685-1400, ext. 459
Program Reaches: 87 in the program
When Started: 1969
Budget: No specific money is set aside for this. Only
  money involved is salaries of new employees.

Program Outline:

The purpose of the program is to provide employment
opportunities for the unemployed and underemployed.
In addition, it is hoped that those trained in the program
can be retained by the company for permanent employment.

Under the National Alliance of Businessmen's JOBS
Program, Commercial Credit hires for its Entry Level
Program, individuals who are certified as being "disadvantaged" and provides training. These individuals are hired
as clerk typists and receive training in such areas as filing,
forms typing, dictaphone, answering telephones, etc. The
training period is not less than 8 weeks and not more
than 45 weeks, depending on the skill level of the
occupation. For clerk typists, the training was 710 hours.
The program also provides various supportive services
which are designed to better prepare and help these new
employees. Such services are: orientation, special counseling, job-related education, medical and dental services,
transportation and child care assistance. The mandatory
supportive services are on-the-job training and special
counseling. The cost of any of these services is paid by
the Department of Labor, unless they are obtained free
of charge from other agencies.

Co. Personnel Involved: Personnel Managers and Supervisors

Measure of Success: The turnover rate for those in this
program has been relatively low and many have advanced
to higher paying positions.

MINORITY PROGRAM

COMMERCIAL CREDIT CO.
300 St. Paul Place
Baltimore, Md. 21202

Business: Holding Company, Business Credit Institution
Sales: 3,400mm in assets
CEO: Donald S. Jones   Employees: 8,920

Contact: James L. Roberts
Address: same as above
Telephone: (301) 685-1400, ext. 459
Program Reaches: 1000s
When Started: 1968
Budget: $35,000 plus additional $30,000 for social com-
  mitment (scholarships, contributions to minority pro-
  grams)

Program Outline:

The following projects have been designed to help increase Commercial Credit's image in the minority community, and to keep the management appraised of problems of employment and unrest in the minority community:
  1. Cluster Program
  2. Project Go Luncheon and Visitations to Local
Junior and Senior High Schools
  3. National Urban League (NUL) and NAACP Conferences

  4. Central Intercollegiate Athletic Association (CIAA)
Luncheon
  5. Community-Management Seminars

By working closely with local predominately Black colleges through the Cluster Program, along with local junior
and senior high schools, Commercial Credit is able not
only to inform them of career opportunities in business,
but also to stress the importance of obtaining an education.

Participation in the NUL, NAACP Conferences, CIAA
Tournament and Community-Management Seminars
enables Commercial Credit to talk about career opportunities with the company, qualifications needed and
other information relative to Commercial Credit.

Commercial Credit feels that these activities educate the
community about Commercial Credit and in turn educate
the management about various minority activities and/or
problems.

Co. Personnel Involved: Personnel Managers and Supervisors

Measure of Success: Commercial Credit has been able to
attract hundreds of minorities for possible employment
opportunites and gain a better working relationship with
the minority community.

CAMPTON OPERATIONS

CONTROL DATA CORP.
8100 34th Avenue S.
P. O. Box 0
Minneapolis, Minn. 55440

Business: Manufacturing Digital Computing Systems and
  Electronic Components
Sales: 571mm
CEO: William C. Norris   Employees: 37,163

Contact: Gary H. Lohn
Address: P.O. Box O, HZN12U
  Minneapolis, Minn. 55440
Telephone: (612) 853-4642
Program Reaches: 180
When Started: 1969
Budget: n/a

Program Outline:

In order to bring employment to minority, inner city and other disadvantaged citizens, Control Data established an electronic sub-assembly plant in the rural poor area of Campton, Kentucky, located in the central eastern part of the state, in the Appalachian area. The plant produces the electronic sub-assemblies for the company's line of medium and high speed printers, used in Control Data Computer systems.

Co. Personnel Involved: n/a

Measure of Success: The company plans to continue introducing increasingly complex work into this plant. The adaptablility, productivity, efficiency and above all, the attitude of the Campton employees is as good as one can expect from Control Data's employees anywhere in the company. Their desire to work and their loyalty toward their plant, reflected in low turnover and low absenteeism, is described as outstanding.

CAPITOL OPERATIONS

CONTROL DATA CORP.
8100 34th Avenue S.
P. O. Box 0
Minneapolis, Minn. 55440

Business: Manufacturing Digital Computing Systems and
  Electronic Components
Sales: 571mm
CEO: William C. Norris   Employees: 37,163

Contact: Gary H. Lohn
Address: P. O. Box 0, HQNI2U
  Minneapolis, Minn. 55440
Telephone: (612) 853-4642
Program Reaches: 100
When Started: 1968
Budget: n/a

Program Outline:

In order to bring employment to minority, inner-city and other disadvantaged citizens, Control Data established a manufacturing plant in a ghetto area of Washington, D.C.

This operation, called the Capitol Plant, presently is housed in 32,000 square feet of leased facilities at 1228 First Street, N.E. Over 90% of the employees are minority individuals, including the plant manager. This plant produces electronic card readers and card punch units in Control Data computer systems. In addition, there is a printing operation which handles internal requirements in the Washington area as well as external customers.

Co. Personnel Involved: n/a

Measure of Success: Capitol will be the focal point of Control Data's work on the Washington Metropolitan Transit Authority contract.

NORTHSIDE OPERATIONS

CONTROL DATA CORP.
8100 34th Avenue, S.
P. O. Box 0
Minneapolis, Minn. 55440

Business: Manufacturing Digital Computing Systems and
   Electronic Components
Sales: 571mm
CEO: William C. Norris   Employees: 37,163

Contact: Gary H. Lohn
Address: P. O. Box 0-HQNI2U
   Minneapolis, Minn. 55440
Telephone: (612) 853-4642
Program Reaches: 350
When Started: 1967
Budget: n/a

Program Outline:

In order to bring employment to minority, inner city and other disadvantaged citizens in areas of highly concentrated employment, Control Data Corporation established a manufacturing plant in a temporary 17,000 square foot building located in a very low-income area on the near Northside of Minneapolis. The company remained there until it could acquire some land a few blocks away, also in the same area, and build a 90,000 square foot manufacturing plant, which was completed in 1968. Hiring preference has been given to the hard-core unemployed residents of the near Northside of the city, including minority persons, both Black and American Indian. Employment in the plant represents about the same ethnic mix as the Northside community itself. Electronic assembly, sheet metal fabrication and electronic test functions are performed. The plant produces peripheral controllers and various chassis and sub-assemblies. Northside is the focal point for the 1700 computer system product line.

Co. Personnel Involved: n/a

Measure of Success: Northside has come to be relied upon as the sole supplier of many products and sub-assemblies necessary to complete a computer system. The plant has absorbed the 1700 product line, and is starting to become profitable.

SELBY OPERATIONS

CONTROL DATA CORP.
8100 34th Avenue S.
P. O. Box 0
Minneapolis, Minn 55440

Business: Manufacturing Digital Computing Systems and
   Electronic Components
Sales: 571mm
CEO: William C. Norris   Employees: 37,163

Contact: Gary H. Lohn
Address: P. O. Box 0, HQN12U
   Minneapolis, Minn. 55440
Telephone: (612) 853-4642
Program Reaches: 80 employees
When Started: 1971
Budget: n/a

Program Outline:

Control Data provides part time employment to disadvantaged people who are residents of a ghetto area of St. Paul. Mothers, female heads of households with school age children and high school students who must assist in supplementing family income are part of the program. The real objective is to provide employment to individuals who cannot be employed any other way. The only selection criteria in hiring is a desire to work and stick with it. The work includes collating, drilling, and binding of technical documentation, as well as handling of all corporate mailings, including metering and mailing.

Co. Personnel Involved: n/a

Measure of Success: At this facility, 20 part-time employees have left over the past year to take full time jobs elsewhere, including employment at several Control Data operations in the Twin Cities. Selby is becoming consistently profitable on work performed for external customers.

COMMUNITY IMPROVEMENT OF ROCK ISLAND COUNTY

DEERE & CO.
John Deere Road
Moline, Ill. 61265

Business: Farm and Industrial Equipment and Consumer Products
Sales: 1,188mm
CEO: Ellwood F. Curtis   Employees: 41,700

Contact: Charles W. Toney
Address: same as above
Telephone: (309) 792-4540
Program Reaches: 175 youth each summer
When Started: 1968
Budget: about $50,000/year (Deere & Company support, $30,000)

Program Outline:

The purpose of the program is to provide summer work experience for underprivileged youth in Rock Island County between the ages of 14 and 16.

Business firms in Rock Island contribute funds. A part time director is hired. Youths 14-16 are hired by schools, cities, colleges, park boards and other local agencies with the money raised by business. They mow grass, paint city property, cut weeds, etc. In addition to earning money, they gain work experience to help them in later years. One day each week, their work consists of going to class. On this training day, the youths are counseled on education opportunities, drug dangers, handling money, etc.

Co. Personnel Involved: n/a

Measure of Success: n/a

MINORITY EMPLOYMENT

THE FIRST PENNSYLVANIA BANKING & TRUST CO.
15th and Chestnut Streets
Philadelphia, Pa. 19102

Business: Banking   Sales: not applicable
Deposits: Dec. 31, 1971, 2,900mm
CEO: John R. Bunting   Employees: 4,323

Contact: Rudolph H. Weber
Address: same as above
Telephone: (215) 786-9010
Program Reaches: Roughly 600 of the Bank's employees are members of minority groups
When Started: 1966
Budget: n/a

Program Outline:

The purpose of the program is to increase minority employment not only at the entry level but in management positions throughout the Bank. By making available both jobs and training, this program is designed to assist the entire minority community.

The Bank's commitment to this program involves the recruitment and professional development of minority group employees. Recruiting among minority schools, establishing workable management trainee programs, strengthening ties with agencies that stressed placement of minority applicants, and increasing credible communication with minority community are all important aspects of this program.

Co. Personnel Involved: The minority employment program involves all the employees directly concerned (approximately 600) and members of the personnel department (approximately 3). In addition, each department head must submit a semiannual report regarding the numbers and positions of minority employees under his supervision. These figures are evaluated by the Bank's Urban Affairs Committee made up of executive management. The committee may set guidelines as required.

Measure of Success: In 1966, the first year of this project, approximately 2.9% of the Bank's employees were minority group members. This included only 1 banking officer. By the end of 1971, minority group members made up approximately 13% of the Bank's work force, including 6 officers.

MINORITY EMPLOYMENT AND TRAINING

GENERAL DYNAMICS
QUINCY SHIPBUILDING DIVISION
Pierre Laclede Center
St. Louis, Mo. 63105

Business: Manufacturing Aircraft and Parts, Missiles, Navy and Commercial Vessels and Submarine Communications Equipment and Building Materials, Coal and Asbestos
Sales: 2,000mm
CEO: Hilliard W. Paige   Employees: 80,000

Contact: H. J. Kay
Address: 97 E. Howard Street
   Quincy, Mass. 02169
Telephone: (617) 471-4200
Program Reaches: several 1000
When Started: 1966
Budget: none formal—partially government sponsored

Program Outline:

The purpose of the program is to provide employment for the disadvantaged members of the greater Boston Community. The search for skilled manpower is coupled with the aim of the fulfillment of objectives of improving the ratio of minority members of the work force.

Procedure in recruitment provides for the following activities:

1. advertising in local media reaching the minority urban centers with high unemployment rates;

2. participation in special job marts conducted by such organizations as the NAACP, Urban League and private employment agencies specializing in minority placement;

3. visiting colleges with a high ratio of Black students, particularly in the southern states;

4. maintenance of close contact with veterans organizations and state employment centers;

5. using the JOB bank to announce openings;

6. attending meetings as participants in various urban organizations such as OIC, Positive Program for Boston, NAACP, Regional Manpower Conference, Award Banquets, Chamber of Commerce Meetings and Personnel Directors Associations;

7. news coverage on in-yard activities to inform the public about opportunities.

Co. Personnel Involved: varies; all supervision plus training staff numbering as high as 60 at times

Measure of Success: steady input of trainees for skilled trades

MINORITY EMPLOYMENT PROGRAM

MARCOR
(MONTGOMERY WARD & CO., INC.)
P.O. Box 8339
Chicago, Ill. 60690

Business: General Merchandising
Sales: 3,500mm
CEO: Leo H. Schoenhofen   Employees: 126,000

Contact: Melvin C. Hopson
Address: same as above
Telephone: (312) 467-3074
Program Reaches: unknown
When Started: 1967
Budget: Undetermined, since the program is incorporated into regular functions.

Program Outline:

The purpose of this program is to insure that all employees and prospective employees receive equal consideration and opportunity without regard to race, sex, creed or national origin.

Each Wards unit must evaluate formally its employment posture with respect to the community it serves to identify weaknesses. Specific goals and timetables to alleviate those weaknesses are then assigned by the unit manager and reviewed by the corporate office to insure completeness. Quarterly reports are submitted to measure attainment of goals.

Special emphasis is given to the input and upgrading of minority and female employees into management ranks through in-house communications and through recruiting at colleges with large minority enrollments.

Co. Personnel Involved: All employees who have responsibility for hiring and promotion are involved. One person has full time responsibility for policy recommendation and monitoring.

Measure of Success: One measure is the total number of minority employees. Minority employment has risen from 9.25% in 1967 to 12.3% in 1971. The number of minorities classified as officials and managers has risen from 1.2% to 3.2% in 4 years.

LAWNDALE MINISTERS' CIVIC LEAGUE

MOTOROLA, INC.
9401 W. Grand Avenue
Franklin Park, Ill. 60131

Business: Electronics   Sales: 926mm
CEO: William J. Weisz   Employees: 36,000

Contact: Rev. C. S. Hampton
Address: 1227 S. Independence Boulevard
   Chicago, Ill. 60623
Telephone: (312) 522-9304
Program Reaches: 5,000
When Started: 1967
Budget: Average $25,000/year raised through annual
   fund raising efforts.

Program Outline:

The purpose of this program is to assist unemployed job applicants, mostly of minority groups, in finding employment.

The Lawndale Ministers' Civic League, composed of approximately 100 ministers, on Chicago's West Side refer unemployed or underemployed minority applicants to a group of Chicago area employers to fill existing job openings. Applicants are counseled and instructed on proper presentations to be made during job interviews. Ministers follow up with applicants to determine successful placement and adjustment to the work environment. As needed, counseling is provided to help the applicant develop good work habits and to remain on the job and prepare for promotional opportunities through skill training or further education in night school classes.

No fees are charged to applicants or to employers for this service which supplements job finding efforts by other state and local agencies.

Co. Personnel Involved: From 6 to 12 staff people from Motorola are involved in part time efforts which supplement 2 full time staff members employed by the League.

Measure of Success: Best evidence of success is the percentage of applicants placed who have been processed through the LMCL Free Employment Service. The last statistics revealed a 42% placement ratio of all applicants processed.

BILL DELIVERY PROGRAM

THE PEOPLES GAS, LIGHT & COKE CO.
122 S. Michigan Avenue
Chicago, Ill. 60603

Business: Gas Utility   Sales: 593.4mm
CEO: Robert M. Drevs   Employees: 6,627

Contact: W. Chrisler
Address: same as above
Telephone: (312) 431-4592
Program Reaches: 28
When Started: April, 1969
Budget: student salaries

Program Outline:

The purpose of this program is to provide job opportunities for minority high school youths in their sophomore through senior years.

The program entails 28 minority high school students delivering gas bills to customers. During the summer months, the students work full time.

This program offers work experience to students in addition to giving them an opportunity to earn money. When the student graduates from high school, if he does not choose to enter college, full time employment with the company is offered. The program originally started with 14 students.

Co. Personnel Involved: Program is overseen by 4 supervisors—1 for each 7 students, and 1 superintendent.

Measure of Success: Only 1 graduating student chose full time employment; other students who have participated in the program have entered college or sought full time employment elsewhere.

SUMMER INTERNSHIP PROGRAM

THE PEOPLES GAS, LIGHT & COKE CO.
122 S. Michigan Avenue
Chicago, Ill. 60603

Business: Gas Utility　　　Sales: 593.4mm
CEO: Robert M. Drevs　　　Employees: 6,627

Contact: A. Logan, Mgr.
Address: same as above
Telephone: (312) 431-4656
Program Reaches: 17
When Started: May, 1970
Budget: student salaries and administrative costs

Program Outline:

The program enables minority college students to gain practical experience in their field of interest, in addition to earning money to continue their college career.

Students selected have completed their first, second, or third year of college. They are assigned to various departments in the company on the basis of their background and interests. Salaries are determined by the number of years of college completed.

The program opened with a special orientation program (including a trip to the Chicago Museum of Science and Industry) for the interns and 4 additional college students who were working in technical fields for the Gas Company during the summer.

Five of 1970's summer intern program students returned for summer employment in 1971.

Co. Personnel Involved: Program is coordinated by Peoples Gas Employment Department in conjunction with department where summer intern is placed.

Measure of Success: Four participants from 1970's program have been hired by Peoples Gas Company after graduating from college and placed in the management training program.

AFFIRMATIVE ACTION PROGRAMS

PHILLIPS PETROLEUM CO.
Bartlesville, Okla. 74004

Business: Petroleum and Petrochemicals
Sales: 2,400mm
CEO: John M. Houchin　　　Employees: 32,200

Contact: W. R. Thomas
Address: 112B Frank Phillips Bldg.
　　Bartlesville, Okla. 74004
Telephone: (918) 661-6067
Program Reaches: n/a
When Started: n/a
Budget: n/a

Program Outline:

The employment of minority individuals may involve far more than just providing jobs. Phillips has directed its equal opportunity employment efforts both towards furnishing jobs and towards providing special assistance. Each major Phillips facility has developed an individualized Affirmative Action Program designed to meet the needs of the local minority labor force. These programs represent commitments to work with local agencies involved in minority training and placement, provision of on-the-job training and counseling, and the presentation of opportunities for career advancement. For example, in the Atlanta office, extra efforts include holding job interviews at nights and during weekends. Also, "awareness" sessions are held regularly to help supervisors obtain an increased understanding of minority employment problems. In Kansas City, efforts are made to help persons working in "hiring line" jobs advance to semi-skilled and skilled positions. The programs at each Phillips facility are varied to meet the local needs.

Co. Personnel Involved: varies

Measure of Success: n/a

JOB PREPARATION SEMINAR

ROHM & HAAS CO.
Independence Mall West
Philadelphia, Pa. 19105

Business: Manufacturing Chemicals, Plastics, Fibers, Health Products
Sales: 507mm
CEO: Vincent L. Gregory   Employees: 13,805

Contact: John M. Geisel
Address: same as above
Telephone: (215) 592-3863
Program Reaches: approximately 75-100 high school seniors
When Started: March, 1972
Budget: approximately $3,000

Program Outline:

The purpose of this program is to help prepare work-bound high school seniors to seek employment as effectively as possible. The seminar provides information on hiring processes (interview techniques, content of application forms and tests, etc.) to help prepare students in locating possible job opportunities, to help them successfully pass the screening process, and to give them some insight into what to expect from employers once they have secured employment.

Co. Personnel Involved: 15 volunteer coaches conduct 1-hour seminars and workshops for 12 weeks.

Measure of Success: too early to tell

IN-SCHOOL EMPLOYMENT PROGRAM

TRAVELERS INSURANCE CO.
One Tower Square
Hartford, Conn. 06115

Business: Insurance   Sales: 3,000mm
CEO: Morrison H. Beach   Employees: 30,000

Contact: Wayne D. Casey
Address: Public Affairs Dept.
    same as above
Telephone: (203) 277-2764
Program Reaches: 12/each 6-week session
When Started: 1971
Budget: $150 in 1971 and 1972; $300 total

Program Outline:

The program provides school-jobs for non-employable 7th and 8th grade students. The Travelers served as fund raiser among local businesses for the $1,000 necessary to implement the program. A matching foundation grant ensured continuation of the program through the 1971-1972 school year.

The school "hires" their students to perform jobs at school for which they are paid $5/week, providing a much-needed source of income for daily necessities as well as practical exposure to the value of work and work opportunities. Every 6 weeks a new group of students are hired. The jobs are work with some meaning and learning: e.g. office aide, reading office, library, etc. Employment applications are filled out by students to simulate the adult experience.

Co. Personnel Involved: 1 as Travelers' contact with the school and as principal fund raiser among local businesses

Measure of Success: The program was developed in an effort to correct the petty pilfering, etc., that the school was experiencing. The incidence of stealing as well as the number of police visits to the school has dropped significantly since the program began. The school's evaluation of the program is most positive from both the guidance and educational viewpoints. The students' reaction is "one of the best deals we've ever had."

PROJECT BOOSTER

XEROX CORP.
Stamford, Conn. 06904

Business: Diversified Office Machines
Sales: 1,719
CEO: C. Peter McColough   Employees: 38,339

Contact: J. Westbrook McPherson
Address: Xerox Corp., Xerox Square
   Rochester, N.Y. 14603
Telephone: (716) 546-4500, ext. 4205
Program Reaches: n/a
When Started: 1968
Budget: n/a

Program Outline:

The purpose of PROJECT BOOSTER is to increase the number of minority employees at the level of technical representatives, salesmen, and clerical workers. Ready skills are required to qualify. Booster is not a massive hiring effort, but is working to meet a minority hiring target sufficient to integrate all major occupational groupings of field sales and service organizations in 1 year.

Booster's format is that of a partnership between Xerox staff members and the community leaders. Asking the help of opinion leaders resulted in a leap from 2% in a labor market in which minority members are only 6½% of the work force. This was over a period of 5 months. Booster does not mean a lowering of Xerox's hiring standards for sales, technical and clerical people. The standards have been changed, but only so hiring managers apply more realistic standards in determining qualifications.

Since July 1, 1968, the beginning of Booster nationwide, McPherson and his men have brought the managers and contacts together in 27 cities. The determination to find Negroes, but only Negroes who are qualified has resulted in some obvious problems. There is suspicion and cynicism in some quarters, and efforts to clarify the purpose of the program have not always been successful.

Co. Personnel Involved: n/a

Measure of Success: In Atlanta, the target of 1 salesman, 2 tech reps, and 1 clerk was exceeded by 1 tech rep and 1 clerk. In Chicago, the year's target was 3 salesmen, 4 tech reps, and 1 clerk. It got 7, 8 and 6. But, Washington is falling behind after 9 months of Booster. If Washington's frustrations are greater, they are of the same kind as those faced in Atlanta and Chicago: good prospects for sales, technical, and clerical jobs are hard to find in any color.

job training

CLERICAL TRAINING PROGRAM

THE AEROSPACE CORP.
P.O. Box 95085
Los Angeles, Cal. 90045

Business: General Systems Engineering for Military
   Research
Sales: 75mm
CEO: I. A. Getting   Employees: 3,285

Contact: William Drake, V.P. and Treas.
Address: same as above
Telephone: (213) 648-5000
Program Reaches: 222 graduated to date
When Started: 1965
Budget: n/a

Program Outline:

In 1965 Aerospace inaugurated the first on-the-job clerical training program in the Southern California industrial community intended exclusively for the training of minority and disadvantaged women. The cost of the training program is primarily borne by the company, but a contract with the Los Angeles Urban League provides partial reimbursement from Federal Funds for a share of the costs of classroom instruction.

Co. Personnel Involved: n/a

Measure of Success: The concept of the program that previously unemployable and unskilled individuals can meet acceptable secretarial qualifications after 5 months of intensive on-the-job training has attracted nationwide interest in the program. To date, 222 young women have graduated from the program and 95% of them have gone immediately into permanent jobs throughout the community.

WORK-STUDY PROGRAM

THE AEROSPACE CORP.
P.O. Box 95085
Los Angeles, Cal. 90045

Business: General Systems Engineering for Military
   Research
Sales: 75mm
CEO: I. A. Getting   Employees: 3,285

Contact: William Drake
Address: same as above
Telephone: (213) 648-5000
Program Reaches: 10 persons/year
When Started: 1970
Budget: n/a

Program Outline:

The project purpose is to provide part time employment for minority college students.

For the past 3 years the company has brought 10 minority college students per year into the work force as part time employees. This program is operated in cooperation with Southwest College, a 2-year Los Angeles community college which is located in a predominantly Negro section of the city. Participants are young men and women who are training for engineering and technical careers. They are assigned according to their occupational goals throughout the company in work situations ranging from computer operation to laboratory technicians.

Co. Personnel Involved: n/a

Measure of Success: n/a

CHURCH ACADEMY PROGRAM

AETNA INSURANCE CO.
55 Elm Street
Hartford, Conn. 06115

Business: Property and Casualty Insurance
Sales: 370mm
CEO: Frederick D. Watkins   Employees: 4,000

Contact: Beth Rawles
Address: Central Baptist Church
   457 Main Street
   Hartford, Conn.
Telephone: (203) 527-1698
Program Reaches: Hartford community
When Started: July, 1969
Budget: contract control by Urban League as agent;
   approx. $82,000 for 18 months contract

Program Outline:

The purpose of the program is to train and offer employment to the individual who does not have the education or skills to enter the business world. The program is under a government MDTA program to train primarily minority people in order to bring their skills to a level where they can function satisfactorily or better in the business world, and leave the welfare scene. All applicants are hired by a company before training starts and are promised a position upon completion of the 12 week schooling. Day Care for pre-school children is also available.

Co. Personnel Involved: 2 people: 1 active member of the Advisory Board of Directors and 1 alternate member

Measure of Success: 60% retention in the working world.

AIRCO WELDING TRAINING CENTERS

AIRCO, INC.
150 E. 42nd Street
New York, N.Y. 10017

Business: Alloys, Gases and Welding, Carbon
   and Medical Products
Sales: approx. 440mm
CEO: George S. Dillon   Employees: 14,200

Contact: Martin A. Hanfling
Address: same as above
Telephone: (212) 682-6700
Program Reaches: 400-800/year
When Started: 1968
Budget: $1.5 million; approx. 80% federally sponsored

Program Outline:

The purpose of the program is to train the unemployed and underemployed (emphasis is placed on veterans) in skills of welding and shipfitting, along with the supportive services of basic mathematics, English, counseling, etc. An integral part of the project is to place these people in well-paying jobs in this industry.

Airco, on a cost-sharing basis with the Federal Government, currently operates 2 training centers—1 in Brooklyn, N.Y., the other in Cleveland, Ohio. These centers operate in conjunction with community-based organizations which provide recruiting, screening and supportive services to the program. The skill training is modular in nature and thus enables a trainee to graduate with as little as 4 weeks training, or as much as the full 17-week course. The majority, however, have completed the entire program, and qualify not for merely entry-level jobs, but for mechanics-level positions.

Co. Personnel Involved: Training Centers are staffed entirely with Airco personnel. Three corporate persons are involved full time, in addition to several others participating on a project basis.

Measure of Success: There are waiting lists at both Brooklyn and Cleveland Centers. Because of Airco's industrial contacts and the high level of training available, the company has had virtually 100% job placement. In addition, the known job retention rate is 72%, and it is estimated to be about 85%. Training dropout rate averages 12%.

CRAFTS EXPERIENCE EXPLORER POST NO. 614

ALLEN-BRADLEY CO.
1201 S. Second Street
Milwaukee, Wis. 53204

Business: Electrical Motor Controls and
    Electronic Components
Sales: 169mm
CEO: I. Andrew Rader   Employees: 6,720

Contact: John W. Matheus, V.P. Per. Rel.
Address: same as above
Telephone: (414) 671-2000
Program Reaches: Post membership—45
When Started: September, 1971
Budget: none

Program Outline:

The purpose of the program is to introduce young adults (14-20 years of age) to selected industrial skills, i.e. carpentry, painting, drafting, model making, and tool and die making, and to help them decide through observation and participation if this is the type of occupation they would wish to pursue as a lifetime career. The project is geared primarily to boys and girls of Spanish/Mexican ancestry, living in the area adjacent to Allen-Bradley. Its goal is to provide an opportunity to learn, through direct exposure, about apprenticeable trades in industry.

The initial 4 sessions of the program involve learning/ listening-type exposure as skilled craftsmen (journeymen in their field) give classroom-type explanations of their trades. Work samples, slides, etc. are used in their presentations. After each session, the young adults are taken on a tour of the skill area at Allen-Bradley. With this definition of skill background, they are able to choose the specific trade they wish to explore. The balance of the program involves direct exposure to the trade. They choose a meaningful project, and are taught to operate the machines and hand tools necessary to build the project.

Co. Personnel Involved: Eight—5 trade instructors, 1 post advisor, 1 committee chairman and 1 safety officer and interpretor

Measure of Success: Success to date is best measured by the enthusiasm of the young adults in the program. Attendance average is 30 per meeting.

MIDDLETOWN JOB OPPORTUNITY COMMITTEE, INC.

ARMCO STEEL CORP.
P.O. Box 600
Middletown, Oh. 45042

Business: Basic Steelmaking
Sales: 1,700mm
CEO: Calvin William Verity, Jr.
Employees: 51,236

Contact: D. C. Osborne, V.P., Staff Operations
Address: same as above
Telephone: (513) 425-2889
Program Reaches: 230 young people in 1971; 150 young
    people in 1970
When Started: 1970
Budget: n/a

Program Outline:

Because past experience shows that retail, commercial and industry jobs for 16-17 year olds fall far short of meeting community needs, the committee supplements existing work opportunities by raising funds to pay for "made" jobs. This work is limited to non-profit organizations and provides a service for which funds would not otherwise be available. Young people are paid $1.45 an hour, 5 hours/day and 5 days/week. Thus it costs $36.25/week or about $375 to provide a job for 1 needy individual for the summer. The organization also places young people in summer jobs.

Co. Personnel Involved: One hundred fifty employees contributed money to the program; others provided leadership and counseling. Company provided free physical exams to several people who could not afford them.

Measure of Success: Last year 230 people were helped through this nonprofit volunteer community effort. Eighty-five were paid by Job Opportunity, Inc.; others were paid by companies who hired the youths.

COOPERATIVE WORK-STUDY PROGRAM

BAMBERGER'S DIVISION, R. H. MACY, INC.
131 Market Street
Newark, N.J. 07101

Business: Retail Department Store
Sales: n/a
CEO: n/a   Employees: n/a

Contact: Marilyn G. Brown
Address: same as above
Telephone: (201) 565-5243
Program Reaches: approx. 44/school year
When Started: 1965
Budget: n/a

Program Outline:

In order to provide on-the-job training for Newark's youth, to supplement their income and to help them develop the skills, attitudes and values necessary to become productive members of today's society, this program is offered to high school seniors from disadvantaged areas who are involved in work-study or distributive education programs.

The program at Bamberger's is separated into 2 distinct groups: Group A attends school in the morning and works in the store from 1 to 6 daily. They are provided with a weekly retail workshop to give them a broad view of a retail operation, and to build specific skills in the areas of salesmanship and customer relations. Group B is a pilot program with Barringer High School in Newark, employing 20 students 28/hours a week who attend a daily 1 hour class in distributive education with a teacher provided for the store by the Board of Education.

Co. Personnel Involved: coordinator/counselor, sales managers to whom students are immediately responsible and various managers used for weekly classes

Measure of Success: Twenty-three students from 1970-71 are permanently employed in the store: 1 sales manager, 5 assistant managers, 4 stock, 4 clerical and 9 sales.

DATA PROCESSING TRAINING CENTER

BANK OF AMERICA
P.O. Box 37000
San Francisco, Cal. 94137

Business: Banking   Sales: not applicable
CEO: A. W. Clausen   Employees: 31,700

Contact: Stanley F. Den Adel, V.P.
Address: Data Processing Center 4092
   555 S. Flower Street
   Los Angeles, Cal. 90071
Telephone: (213) 683-2159
Program Reaches: over 500
When Started: September, 1968
Budget: n/a

Program Outline:

The Bank of America Foundation makes available the use of a building, formerly a bank data processing center, as the training center site for disadvantaged residents to train them for employment and also pays maintenance and operating expenses. IBM provides the center with equipment, study materials and 4 instructors and the Urban League selects the candidates for training, provides counseling and administrative services and assists graduates in locating jobs. The training program is designed to qualify these persons for employment in a rapidly growing area of opportunity. It includes classes in computer operations, basic programming and keypunch techniques.

Co. Personnel Involved: Den Adel serves as advisor.

Measure of Success: By the end of 1971, 507 persons had graduated from the program. Of 430 available for employment, 398 were working as of December 31, 1971. Over 100 companies have hired these graduates and report 90% retention. The center also recently graduated its first clerical skills class of 10 women.

JOBS '70

BOISE CASCADE CORP.
One Jefferson Square
Boise, Idaho 83701

Business: Timber, Wood, Mobile and
Manufactured Housing
Sales: 1,717mm
CEO: Robert V. Hansberger   Employees: 47,889

Contact: John M. McCullen
Address: P.O. Box 200, Boise, Idaho 83701
Telephone: (208) 384-8440
Program Reaches: plus 500/year
When Started: January, 1971
Budget: n/a

Program Outline:

The purpose of the program is to provide meaningful employment for unemployed and underemployed persons.

The training consists of 4 major components:

1. Orientation—this includes an introduction to the industry, to the corporate policies and procedures, to the plant rules and regulations, and to the plant personnel.

2. Special Counseling—both group and individual counseling techniques are used as part of the classroom training.

3. Job Related Education—this component consists of classroom training in job duties and manufacturing procedures using training manuals and sound/slides. Basic education is provided for individual trainees on a needs basis.

4. On-the-Job Training—this component provides for application of the classroom training to the job itself under the guidance of plant supervisors.

Co. Personnel Involved: A corporate staff of 8 people is maintained, and the assistance of line operations is required on each program.

Measure of Success: Evaluation of the program is currently being conducted. No figures are available at the present time.

BUSINESS EXPERIENCE TRAINING PROGRAM (BET)

THE CHASE MANHATTAN BANK
1 Chase Manhattan Plaza
New York, N.Y. 10015

Business: Banking   Sales: not applicable
Total Assets: 25,000mm
CEO: Herbert Patterson   Employees: 18,900

Contact: Robert Walters
Address: 80 Pine Street, New York, N.Y.
Telephone: (212) 676-7003
Program Reaches: 277 students as of the end of 1971
When Started: 1964
Budget: n/a

Program Outline:

Chase Manhattan's BET Program is a work-study training project for high school students, particularly those from minority groups. The program's objective is to provide these youngsters with an exposure to the business world through a planned training program, with a view toward helping them qualify for employment responsibilities.

Chosen from schools with a high drop-out rate, the youngsters are recommended by the New York City Board of Education and screened by the Bank's Human Resources Department. They are employed at the Bank from 2 to 5 p.m., 5 days a week. Their morning hours are spent attending regular high school classes. At the Bank they received on-the-job training, supplemented by group orientation sessions and field trips conducted by representatives of the various areas of the Bank. BET trainees are not required to make an employment commitment to the Bank, nor does the Bank guarantee employment. However, they are offered permanent assignments after completing the program if they are able to meet Chase Manhattan's standards. Most trainees have planned for furthering their education and many are presently attending night school with the aid of the Bank's tuition refund plan.

Co. Personnel Involved: The program is coordinated by a full time member of Chase Manhattan's training staff. In addition, each student is supervised by appropriate personnel in the area of his assignment.

Measure of Success: Through 1971, 277 trainees have joined BET, of whom 195 finished high school and 57 went on to college. Another 101 became full time Chase Manhattan staff members.

ONE STOP COMMUNITY DAY CARE CENTER

THE CHASE MANHATTAN BANK
1 Chase Manhattan Plaza
New York, N.Y. 10015

Business: Banking
Total Assets: 25,000mm
CEO: Herbert Patterson

Sales: not applicable

Employees: 18,900

Contact: Rev. Charles Lott
Address: 20 Sutter Avenue, Brooklyn, N.Y.
Telephone: (212) 773-3041
Program Reaches: 100 children and their mothers
When Started: Fall, 1970
Budget: $335,000 loan

Program Outline:

This 2-pronged, community-based program, designed to help female heads of households without business training find a way out of welfare, was developed to provide the women with both skills to support their families and a stimulating and secure environment for their children during working hours. The 2-story day care center building, purchased last year and renovated from the frame was financed by the Chase Manhattan Bank. Five teachers and 10 assistant teachers have developed a curriculum for the children. Pre-schoolers spend the entire day there and elementary school youngsters are cared for between 3 and 6 P.M.

Just a block away is the One Stop Community Center School where mothers of the Day Care Center children are learning Data Processing skills. The training equipment (key punchers, progress cards for the computers, accounting machines, electric typewriters, sorters and verifiers) was furnished by IBM. The Day Care Center is free to those mothers in the training program and once on the job, they will pay a fee based on a sliding earnings scale.

Co. Personnel Involved: 4 with 2 sharing the primary responsibility

Measure of Success: Since the learning center opened in the fall of 1970, more than 425 people have received training and have earned more than $220,000 in jobs utilizing the skills acquired at the school.

SATELLITE ACADEMY PROGRAM

THE CHASE MANHATTAN BANK
1 Chase Manhattan Plaza
New York, N.Y. 10015

Business: Banking
Total Assets: 25,000mm
CEO: Herbert Patterson

Sales: not applicable

Employees: 18,900

Contact: Arthur J. Humphrey
Address: same as above
Telephone: (212) 552-2222
Program Reaches: To date, Chase has 100 of a total of 400 students in its program.
When Started: October, 1971
Budget: n/a

Program Outline:

The Satellite Academy Program, undertaken as a cooperative effort by the City of New York, The Chase Manhattan Bank and other private firms, is an attempt to implement innovative alternatives in secondary education for a cross-section of high school juniors and seniors. The program combines vocational and scholastic sides of the students' experience in a work-study program aimed at keeping them in school to earn a diploma. Chase is providing jobs for 100 students in 1 of 3 Satellite Academies in New York City. The Academy offers a high school program in units small enough to allow for individualized attention in a program which alternates a week of classes and a week at a paying job.

Co. Personnel Involved: One full time officer directs the program and 2 coordinators help monitor the students' work and development. In addition, participating students are supervised by Bank personnel in their job assignments.

Measure of Success: The Satellite Academy is very new, but an early sign of success is its 90% attendance rate which compares to a 60% rate in New York City's public high schools.

FOREMEN TRAINING PROGRAM

CHRYSLER CORP.
P.O. Box 1919
Detroit, Mich. 48231

Business: Automotive Manufacuring
Sales: 7,000mm
CEO: John J. Riccardo   Employees: 228,000

Contact: Albert J. Dunmore
Address: same as above
Telephone: (313) 956-2566
Program Reaches: n/a
When Started: 1969
Budget: n/a

Program Outline:

The purpose of the program is to train employees having entry level jobs to become foremen, without regard to academic or technical skills.

The trainees go for 8 days classroom training sessions to Chrysler Center Line Training Center covering management concepts, practices and procedures. The key to the innovative approach is provided at the corporation's Hoover Road Training Center. Here, in small groups, the trainees are exposed to new training methods during a concentrated 7-day session. Unknown to the trainees, on-the-job confrontations are staged. Afterwards, they are discussed and the trainees watch themselves and their reactions to the unexpected episode on video-tape. This continues all week, with discussions on the problems they will face in their new job. After these sessions, the trainees spend a total of 872 hours of on-the-job training. Once they become foremen they are provided with follow-up advice and counseling on a regular basis by 3 full-time advisors during a 25-week period.

Co. Personnel Involved: n/a

Measure of Success: Under the current foreman training program, 90% of the men and women who enter the program stay on to become foremen. Of the first 200 who completed the program, 60% are Black and 40% are White.

MANAGEMENT TRAINING PROGRAM

CHRYSLER CORP.
P.O. Box 1919
Detroit, Mich. 48231

Business: Automotive Manufacturing
Sales: 7,000mm
CEO: John J. Riccardo   Employees: 228,000

Contact: Albert J. Dunmore
Address: same as above
Telephone: (313) 956-2566
Program Reaches: n/a
When Started: 1971
Budget: n/a

Program Outline:

The purpose of this program is to provide an opportunity for managers to broaden their knowledge of managing people, resolving people's problems, and achieving a better understanding of the everyday supervisory actions related to the management of people in an industrial or business environment.

The program for plant management at the general foreman level or above is given on company time in 5 sessions each lasting 4 hours. It is conducted by specially-trained Chrysler employees from the Chrysler Institute and Automotive Manufacturing Group and blends psychological films, psychological instruments and group discussions to provide the manager with a wide assortment of management tools to help him be more effective in his job.

The course presentation includes: Concept of On-the-Job Conflict, Nature of the Human Being, The High Achievement Motive, Interpersonal Relationships, Motivational Theory, The Development of the Manager, The Art of Delegation, Styles of Management—A Tool for Self-Analysis, and Theory of Force-Field Analysis.

Co. Personnel Involved: n/a

Measure of Success: The program, in addition to improving the quality of management in a great many instances, has also become a valuable tool for better understanding of minority group employee progress at various levels.

PRE-APPRENTICE TRAINING PROGRAM

CHRYSLER CORP.
P.O. Box 1919
Detroit, Mich. 48231

Business: Automotive Manufacturing
Sales: 7,000mm
CEO: John J. Riccardo   Employees: 228,000

Contact: Albert J. Dunmore
Address: same as above
Telephone: (313) 956-2566
Program Reaches: n/a
When Started: n/a
Budget: n/a

Program Outline:

The purpose of this program is to increase minority representation in Chrysler's apprentice programs.

Trainees are sought out regularly on a cooperative basis by the pre-apprentice training office, by UAW representatives, and by management personnel in Chrysler's plants. Those who want to enroll in the program first take a 1 college credit hour seminar, lasting 11 weeks, which is designed to familiarize them with apprenticeship requirements and what lies ahead if they pursue the training. The seminar is broken down as follows: 3 sessions to instill pride in the trainee for his work, his company, and his union, and to indicate to him what apprenticeship qualifications he must meet; 3 sessions devoted to defining the trades, establishing a goal, and determining how to meet it; 1 session on correct study habits and test techniques; 4 sessions to create motivational and attitudinal interest and drive needed to carry the trainee through the first weeks of training. Then each trainee is assigned specific academic courses based on his need and ability: basic math, reading comprehension, spatial visualization, and tool familiarization.

Co. Personnel Involved: n/a

Measure of Success: During the 1970 sessions counselors advised 681 Chrysler employees on pre-apprentice training and enrolled 511 of them in the program. In that group are 120 men who have now been accepted for apprentice training after previously failing the test.

SEMI-SKILLED UPGRADER PROGRAM

CHRYSLER CORP.
P.O. Box 1919
Detroit, Mich. 48231

Business: Automotive Manufacturing
Sales: 7,000mm
CEO: John J. Riccardo   Employees: 228,000

Contact: Albert J. Dunmore
Address: same as above
Telephone: (313) 956-2566
Program Reaches: 440 scheduled to participate in the program
When Started: n/a
Budget: n/a

Program Outline:

The purpose of the program is to provide the necessary skills for semi-skilled jobs and to train Chrysler employees, particularly minority group employees currently holding entry-level jobs, for jobs that pay more and are preferred to the jobs in which they have remained since they joined Chrysler.

Largely funded by the federal government, this semi-skilled upgrader program is conducted at the Hoover Road Training Center. The program draws trainees from Detroit area car assembly and stamping plants, and includes both orientation and job skill instruction. The trainees are provided from 40 to 80 hours of job related training in 1 of 4 semi-skilled jobs: arc welding, gas welding, metal finishing, and torch soldering.

While at Hoover Road, the trainees receive the same hourly rate of pay that they received in their regular jobs. When they return to their plant, and are promoted, they receive an hourly rate equivalent to the mid-pay scale of their new job and continue in an on-the-job training program. Trainees picked for the program (1) must have been employed by Chrysler for a minimum 6-months in entry-level or near entry-level jobs and (2) be promotable in accordance with Chrysler-UAW "Production and Maintenance Agreement" or any applicable local plant agreement.

Co. Personnel Involved: n/a

Measure of Success: The current program will train 140 arc welders, 100 gas welders, 140 metal finishers, and 60 torch solderers. Some of the trainees had spent from 10 to 20 years in their present jobs prior to joining the program.

HARD CORE TRAINING PROGRAM

DANA CORP. (TRANSMISSION DIVISION)
4100 Bennett Road
Toledo, Ohio 43601

Business: Heavy Duty Truck Transmission
   Manufacturing
Sales: 750mm (corporation)
CEO: R. C. McPherson   Employees: 2,100

Contact: Walter Bancer
Address: Dev. and Training Ctr., 1928 N. Detroit
   Avenue, Toledo, Ohio 43606
Telephone: (419) 242-3531
Program Reaches: to date, 235 minority residents of
   model cities area trained
When Started: August 1, 1968
Budget: Dana, 1968—$5,000, 1969—$35,000,
   1970-71—$25,000; Dept. of Labor, 1968—$140,000,
   1969—$130,000 estimate

Program Outline:

The purpose of the program is to train unemployables in
becoming production machine operators in the company's Transmission Division plant in Toledo, Ohio. The
company hires so-called hard-core unemployables for its
small training facility located in a predominantly Black
area of the city. The company provides instruction in the
basic 3 R's plus specialized training in shop math,
blueprint reading, micrometer reading and machining
processes. Along with the training, medical assistance and
counseling services are offered. At present, the trainees
get $2.50/hour during training and $3.75 plus/hour after
employment at the company's main plant. The training
center is operated in cooperation with the National
Alliance of Businessmen's "JOBS" program under a
Department of Labor contract. Minor changes in teaching
techniques are expected to be made while the overall
program will remain the same.

Co. Personnel Involved: In the plant, over 150 first line
supervisors and all 1,500 employees are directly and
indirectly involved in working with trainees.

Measure of Success: Before the economic recession of
early 1971, the retention rate was well over 70%. Because
of lay-offs, this figure was sharply reduced. However, the
company is beginning to recall many trainees on an
almost daily basis.

OPPORTUNITIES INDUSTRIALIZATION CENTER, INC.

DUPONT CO.
1007 Market Street
Wilmington, Del. 19898

Business: Diversified Manufacturing
Sales: 3,800mm
CEO: Charles B. McCoy   Employees: 110,865

Contact: John Burchenal
Address: same as above
Telephone: (302) 774-2036
Program Reaches: n/a
When Started: n/a
Budget: n/a

Program Outline:

OIC, Inc. is an organization dedicated to providing
needed job skills to unemployed or underemployed
ghetto residents, so that they can seek employment in
industry with some degree of skill and confidence. Du-
Pont contributes in a number of ways: money (more than
$100,000 in the last 2 years), leadership, instructors (who
are released by DuPont both full time and part time), and
as a source of employment for graduates.

DuPont expects to contribute financial support based on
annual evaluation.

Co. Personnel Involved: Two DuPont employees serve on
the Board. Various others serve in advisory and counseling capacities.

Measure of Success: OIC's continued record of training
and placement.

WORLD OF WORK

EASTMAN KODAK CO.
343 State Street
Rochester, N.Y. 14650

Business: Manufacturing Photographic Equipment
Sales: 2,976mm
CEO: Walter A. Fallon   Employees: 110,700

Contact: Don Ginsberg,
     Director of Operation Young Adults
Address: Rochester Jobs, Inc.
     Sibley Tower Building
     Rochester, N.Y. 14604
Telephone: (716) 232-2600
Program Reaches: 350 involved in the 26-month program
When Started: January, 1970
Budget: n/a

Program Outline:

The purpose of this program is to give young men an opportunity to further their high school education, while learning marketable skills and building self-confidence, by rehabilitating urban housing in Rochester, N.Y. Their work experience compliments classroom education that is tailored to their work needs and is relevant to potential careers.

Eastman Kodak conceived the idea for the program and initially provided funding for a pilot trial. It is now administered by Rochester Jobs, Inc. and is 1 of 3 components of Operation Young Adults, a work-study program. It operates with a grant from the U.S. Labor Department. Metropolitan Rochester Foundation, a non-profit community housing agency, buys run-down property with capital established by a $75,000 no-interest loan from Kodak. After work is completed, the houses are sold to lower-income families.

Most work-study students attend class every other day where they are taught academic subjects in small, informal classes with emphasis on material relating to work experience. On alternate days, the young men work from 8 a.m. to 5 p.m. rehabilitating houses for $1.85 an hour. They are not paid for going to class, but must attend in order to have the opportunity to work.

In the months ahead, the plan is to develop an even better core curriculum that presents academic subjects in a way that is more relevant to the real world of work.

Co. Personnel Involved: several staff persons on leave of absence

Measure of Success: In the first 18 months of the program, trainees have completed 15 homes. So far, 25 trainees have graduated from the program and 18 have found full-time employment in a tight job market, including 6 who joined the World of Work staff.

JOB TRAINING PROGRAMS

EASTMAN KODAK CO.
343 State Street
Rochester, N.Y. 14650

Business: Manufacturing Photographic Equipment
Sales: 2,976mm
CEO: Walter A. Fallon   Employees: 110,700

Contact: Kenneth D. Howard
Address: same as above
Telephone: (716) 724-4620
Program Reaches: 1,000 plus
When Started: 1966
Budget: not separately budgeted

Program Outline:

The program provides employment and job training for persons, including minority group members, who would ordinarily be unlikely candidates for employment. It is designed to provide what such persons need most: regular work, a chance to succeed, and an opportunity to prove their worth.

The basic principle in Kodak's training program is simple: the individual is hired as a regular, wage-earning employee from the first day of his training. At Kodak Park, trainees are hired to prepare for skilled trades, for work in research labs, and for jobs in production departments. They are receiving on-the-job training with a strong helping hand. At the Kodak Apparatus Division, new low-skilled employees receive direct personal on-the-job training in manufacturing operations. Training programs range up to a year in duration and stress normal job-holding requirements for attendance, punctuality and teamwork.

Kodak also prepares people with limited education for clerical jobs through a program in cooperation with the Rochester Urban League. Kodak helped establish the Advancement through Clerical Training (ACT) program. In a work-study program, trainees attend school half-day and learn job skills at Kodak during the other half-day.

Co. Personnel Involved: Numerous—program is handled through plant training departments.

Measure of Success: excellent results; good retention rate

MENTALLY RETARDED TRAINING PROGRAM

ECONOMICS LABORATORY, INC.
4 Corporate Park Drive
White Plains, N.Y. 10604

Business: Manufacturing Consumer Dishwasher
    Detergents and Industrial and
    Institutional Cleaners
Sales: 129.6mm
CEO: Edward B. Osborn   Employees: 3,400

Contact: John T. Thielke
Address: same as above
Telephone: (914) 694-8626
Program Reaches: attempts to reach all trainable MRs
When Started: 1968
Budget: n/a

Program Outline:

The purpose of the program is to assist state agencies and associations in setting up a continuing program to select, train and find jobs for trainable mentally retarded people.

The program consists of schooling the educable mentally retarded in restaurant and institutional food service duties such as dishwashing, sanitation procedures, and machine operation.

Co. Personnel Involved: 3—1 full time; 2 part time

Measure of Success: 300-400 MRs now working full time earning a minimum or better wage—without job they cost society $3500/year, now they earn $3500/year; net gain $7000/year x 300 = $210,000

IN-HOUSE EDUCATION, JOB PLACEMENT AND CAREER ADVANCEMENT

FIRST NATIONAL CITY BANK
399 Park Avenue
New York, N.Y. 10022

Business: Banking   Sales: not applicable
CEO: William I. Spencer   Employees: 31,700

Contact: Dr. Norman Willard, V.P.
Address: same as above
Telephone: (212) 559-0459
Program Reaches: NYC work force, 18,000
When Started: 1968
Budget: staff time

Program Outline:

The purpose of the program is to offer all segments of the New York work force the broadest opportunity for employment at FNCB; and to offer all employees the broadest opportunity for education, training and advancement.

Since 1968, the Bank has had a training program for "hardcore" unemployed to prepare for entry-level jobs in the Bank. Over 2,000 persons have entered this program lasting about 20 weeks and including basic business skills, remedial instruction in basic academic skills and personal counseling.

In addition, the Bank is committed to assuring that all employees are given the opportunity to improve themselves and their skills. There is a tuition refund program for employees attending school after hours, a Bank-managed training facility which provides both skills and supervisory and management training programs, and a program for the remediation of basic education deficiencies (including courses in English as a second language, a high school equivalency course, and experimental courses in reading and math).

Co. Personnel Involved: variable, upward of 15 for "hard-core" program

Measure of Success: The retention rate is comparable to that of other groups of new hires.

BEEP & STEP

FIRST PENNSYLVANIA BANKING AND TRUST CO.
BANKING & TRUST CO.
555 City Line Ave.
Bala Cynwyd, Pa. 19004

Business: Banking   Sales: not applicable
Deposits: Dec. 31, 1971—$2.9 billion
CEO: John R. Bunting   Employees: 4,323

Contact: Kathryn C. McDermott
Address: 15th & Chestnut Streets, Philadelphia, Pa.
Telephone: (215) 786-8004
Program Reaches: to date approx. 120
When Started: 1967
Budget: n/a

Program Outline:

The purpose of this program is to acquaint inner city high school students with the business world and to encourage their striving for careers in banking.

In both the BEEP and STEP programs, the students attend regular high school classes in the mornings and work in the bank 5 afternoons a week for a period of 8 months. Along with the job training, the students receive training in written communications and inter-personal relations. This application of educational training to work experience tends to reduce school drop-out rates.

Co. Personnel Involved: Two people directly involved. All employees working in the areas where students are placed are indirectly involved.

Measure of Success: Upon completion of high school, nearly all of the program's students become full-time bank employees.

JOB TRAINING

GENERAL DYNAMICS
Pierre Laclede Center
St. Louis, Mo. 63105

Business: Manufacturing Aircraft and Parts, Missiles, Navy
Vessels and Submarines, Communication Equipment
and Building Materials, Coal and Asbestos
Sales: 2,000mm
CEO: Hilliard W. Paige   Employees: 80,000

Contact: Lewis A. Corwin
Address: same as above
Telephone: (314) 862-2440
Program Reaches: undetermined number
When Started: 1967
Budget: no single budget

Program Outline:

The purpose of several programs sponsored by General
Dynamics is to provide job training for the hard-core
unemployed and other disadvantaged citizens under the
JOBS program sponsored by the National Alliance of
Businessmen, following the typical NAB pattern of a
period of vestibule training, succeeded by on-the-job
activity. The programs include: (1) a GD plant built and
largely staffed by the Navajo Tribe opened November,
1967, in Window Rock, Arizona. This $800,000 plant
provides employment for 100 American Indians engaged
in the production of electronic assemblies; (2) GD began
operations in San Antonio, Texas under the Federal Job
Development Test Program. The facility, located in the
depressed area of the city, provides employment for 30
members of minority groups; (3) in San Diego the
company is operating a retraining program for unemployed aerospace engineers and technicians to qualify
them for new jobs as test technicians in the nuclear
power industry.

Co. Personnel Involved: Variable; all supervisors are
directly involved in these programs at one time or
another.

Measure of Success: (1) good productivity; (2) fulfillment of need for overflow production; (3) undetermined at this time

---

ON SITE TRAINING FOR INMATES
OF PENAL INSTITUTIONS

GENERAL DYNAMICS
Pierre Laclede Center
St. Louis, Mo. 63105

Business: Manufacturing Aircraft and Parts, Missiles, Navy
Vessels and Submarines, Communication Equipment
and Building Materials, Coal and Asbestos
Sales: 2,000mm
CEO: Hilliard W. Paige   Employees: 80,000

Contact: Lewis A. Corwin
Address: same as above
Telephone: (314) 862-2440
Program Reaches: 25 San Diego County Honor Camp
inmates, including 2 women
When Started: initial program 1971
Budget: not budgeted separately; partially government
sponsored

Program Outline:

The purpose of this program is to provide on-site training
and work utilization for persons still under sentence in a
penal institution. These trainees all have less than 4
months to serve and this program enables them to obtain
skills necessary for employment after their release.

General Dynamics participates in penal rehabilitation
programs at its Convair Aerospace facility. Twenty-five
inmates were among 600 trainees employed during a
4-month period and given 2-5 weeks of classroom training
and 13 weeks of on-the-job training as aircraft assemblers
on the DC-10 program. No distinction was made between
the inmates and other trainees after they were employed.
These inmates had been selected for employment and the
training program after being interviewed at the Work
Furlough Center by members of the employment section
of industrial relations. One-half of their training cost was
provided through federal funds administered by the
Mayor's Committee for Jobs, Inc. Individuals selected for
training/employment were brought to the facility, released on their own recognizance during work hours (no
guards) and picked up at the end of the shift by penal
authorities.

Co. Personnel Involved: n/a

Measure of Success: primarily the absence of unusual
problems

APPRENTICE TRAINING

GENERAL MOTORS CORP.
3044 W. Grand Boulevard
General Motors Bldg.
Detroit, Mich. 48202

Business: Automotive Industry
Sales: 28,264mm (1971)
CEO: Edward N. Cole   Employees: 696,000

Contact: G. R. Stauffacher
Address: same as above
Telephone: (313) 556-2849
Program Reaches: n/a
When Started: n/a
Budget: n/a

Program Outline:

The purpose of the program is to assist minority group members to advance to journeymen skilled trades positions.

Traditionally among the highest paid hourly rated employees in General Motors, skilled tradesmen are frequently selected for promotion to management. Negotiated contracts with unions require that journeymen status be granted employees only after they have served a formal apprenticeship consisting of several years of formal classroom studies and in-plant training, or have spent a commensurately longer time of in-plant training with no classroom study. Many GM plants have implemented programs designed to increase the prospective apprentice's formal educational skills. Administered in conjunction with local school systems, these pre-apprentice training courses emphasize the study of math.

Co. Personnel Involved: numerous at various plants

Measure of Success: Excellent results have been obtained in increasing the number of Blacks who enter the formal Apprentice Program as a result of the added schooling.

OPPORTUNITIES INDUSTRIALIZATION CENTERS OF AMERICA

THE B.F. GOODRICH CO.
500 S. Main Street
Akron, Ohio 44318

Business: Rubber   Sales: 1,236.7mm
CEO: H. B. Warner   Employees: 47,900

Contact: Gary J. Rine
Address: P.R. Dept. same as above
Telephone: (216) 379-3411
Program Reaches: n/a
When Started: 1969
Budget: n/a

Program Outline:

The purpose of the program is to develop more minority group managers for BFG retail stores and to assist Opportunities Industrialization Centers of America in the training of Blacks and other minority group members to take their rightful places in the economic system.

BFG first became involved with Rev. Leon Sullivan's OIC organization in 1969 when a special program was designed to develop more minority group managers for company stores. Since then, involvement has grown to include considerable financial support and to make available considerable managerial talent to assist in the overall operation of the OIC organization. In 1971, for example, an OIC office was established in the BFG World Headquarters Building in Akron to help conduct a pilot fund raising drive for OIC.

Co. Personnel Involved: Scores of BFG people have been and/or are involved in the BFG OIC program, including BFG President, Harry B. Warner, who is a member of OIC's National Industrial Advisory Council.

Measure of Success: The OIC approach to job training is widely acclaimed as one of the most effective of its type. Cost per person is far less and placement and retention rates far better for people trained through OIC than for those trained in other programs.

PROJECT TRANSITION

THE B.F. GOODRICH CO.
500 S. Main Street
Akron, Ohio 44318

Business: Rubber   Sales: 1,236.7mm
CEO: H. B. Warner   Employees: 47,900

Contact: Gary J. Rine
Address: P.R. Dept., same as above
Telephone: (216) 379-3411
Program Reaches: 221 (through '71)
When Started: 1969
Budget: n/a

Program Outline:

The purpose of the program is to give young men nearing
the end of active military service a "running start"
toward a promising civilian occupation.

The program, conducted at Fort Bragg, N.C. in cooperation with the U.S. Army, consists of training soldiers
for jobs as salesmen or servicemen in BFG tire retail
stores. Participating GI's receive 6 weeks of training, part
in the classroom and part OJT at a BFG retail store. In
addition to the full-scale program at Fort Bragg, BFG has
"working agreements" at selected other military bases.
There is no obligation on the part of the participating GI
to join B.F. Goodrich upon discharge from the service.

Co. Personnel Involved: People from several BFG departments in Akron are involved in providing materials
and assistance in conducting classes and in preparing
subject matter for the classes.

Measure of Success: In the 1½ years BFG has been
involved in the project, approximately 35% of the soldiers who have participated have taken jobs with BFG.

SUMMER PROGRAM FOR NEEDY YOUTH

LEEDS & NORTHRUP CO.
Sumneytown Pike
North Wales, Pa. 19454
(Suburban Philadelphia)

Business: Electronic Instruments and
    Process Control Systems
Sales: approx. 100mm
CEO: George E. Beggs, Jr.   Employees: 4,270

Contact: M. Ceaser, Mgr., Org. Dev.
Address: same as above
Telephone: (215) 643-2000, ext. 610
Program Reaches: 26 trainees each summer
When Started: 1968
Budget: approx $27,000 for direct salaries for trainees
    and coordinator

Program Outline:

The purpose of the program is to provide needy youth
(who have achieved at least 10th grade in high school,
and either were potential drop-outs, actual drop-outs, or
graduates unable to obtain employment) with a summer
work experience which would give them certain basic
skills and an understanding of the work habits, attitudes
and motivation needed if an underprivileged young man
is to become a responsible, productive citizen.

With the assistance of a Black coordinator experienced in
DPA case work, school and recreation supervision, specially hired for this project, the program was operational

for a 10-week period with 4 hours daily spent on
indoctrination and training (handling of personal
finances, how to apply for a job, math review, blueprint
reading, soldering, use of hand tools, assembly, wiring
and inspection techniques, etc.) and 4 hours in light
maintenance work around plant and grounds.

The union cooperated and was permitted to give an
indoctrination session on union philosophy and practice.
Pay was at "going rates," with provision for modest
increases if merited. Preparation included careful indoctrination of regular line supervision in company areas
affected, with sensitivity-training on ghetto-induced
problems and attitudes.

In order to implement this program, children of regular
employees had to forego summer jobs previously available to them.

The program was repeated in substantially the same form
during the following 2 summers and is expected to be
essentially the same for subsequent summers.

Co. Personnel Involved: coordinator, employed specially
for program, as well as 2 full time regular supervisory
staff and 9 supervisory staff who participated as needed

Measure of Success: Only 2 trainees resigned voluntarily;
they planned to return to high school. Four more
resigned on request. Remaining 20 stuck to program, or
were placed in permanent jobs before end of schedule.
Trainees learned that training and skills help determine
ability to get and hold a job.

JOB TRAINING FOR HANDICAPPED

LOCKHEED AIRCRAFT CORP.
P.O. Box 551
Burbank, Cal. 91503

Business: Aerospace Sales: 2,500mm
CEO: A. Carl Kotchian Employees: 72,000

Contact: Howard C. Lockwood, Corp. Dir. Pers.
Address: same as above
Telephone: (213) 847-6548
Program Reaches: 34
When Started: 1968
Budget: no special budget—part of company employee
  training program

Program Outline:

The purpose of the program is to train and employ handicapped individuals (deaf mutes and paraplegics).

In 1968 the Lockheed-Georgia Company employed 15 deaf mutes who had completed pre-employment training for the assembly of sophisticated electronic equipment. In 1969, 2 paraplegics were employed.

Co. Personnel Involved: 2 instructors

Measure of Success: Original program was successful enough to lead to second training class of 17 deaf mutes who were trained and subsequently employed by Lockheed-Georgia in 1969. Work habits and attitudes of employees were judged excellent.

TRAINING HARD-CORE UNEMPLOYED WITH ARREST RECORDS

LOCKHEED AIRCRAFT CORP.
P.O. Box 551
Burbank, Cal. 91503

Business: Aerospace Sales: 2,500mm
CEO: A. Carl Kotchian Employees: 72,000

Contact: Howard C. Lockwood, Corp. Dir. Pers.
Address: same as above
Telephone: (213) 564-5747
Program Reaches: 147
When Started: 1968
Budget: Program is part of a special hard-core training
  program funded approx. 80% by Department of
  Labor—total cost is approx. $1,200/trainee.

Program Outline:

The purpose of the program is to train and employ individuals who have past arrest records.
In a 1968 Lockheed-Georgia Company training program for the hard-core unemployed, 46% or 147 of 320 trainees had arrest records, 5 of these having 7-15 arrests. Rather than categorically denying employment to persons with police records, the company has developed a policy that states conditions under which such persons may be hired, within the bounds of government security requirements.

Co. Personnel Involved: Six people, including program supervision, handled this program.

Measure of Success: The 147 trainees hired were successful on the job without any repeat of criminal activity.

VOCATIONAL IMPROVEMENT PROGRAM (JOBS '70 PROGRAM)

MARCOR (MONTGOMERY WARD & CO.)
P.O. Box 8339
Chicago, Ill. 60680

Business: General Merchandising
Sales: 2,805mm
CEO: Leo H. Schoenhofen   Employees: 126,000

Contact: R. W. Berry
Address: same as above
Telephone: (312) 467-3846
Program Reaches: over 800
When Started: August, 1970 (prior 9-68 to 7-70)
Budget: approx. $1 million

Program Outline:

The purpose of the program is to hire, train and retain the unemployable or underemployed and to provide on-the-job, as well as, job-related education for retail and auto service occupations.

The functions of the program are to:(1) secure actual job commitments from each of the company's hiring locations in preparation for writing a government contract; (2) prepare and submit proposals to the government for approval; (3) prepare, evaluate and administrate training materials and curricula; (4) provide close on-the-job supervision, as well as personal counseling; (5) recruit job applicants from the community and other referral agencies for interview and subsequent hire; (6) provide monetary assistance for other supportive services, such as babysitting, medical and transportation costs; (7) provide the VIP hirees with the overall atmosphere which will enable them to become active, full time Wards Employees.

Marcor also plans to provide more training and assistance to veteran employees so that they can be upgraded into higher existing jobs.

Co. Personnel Involved: a VIP staff of 50 full time employees—up to 50% involvement by all 4 regional personnel directors, their staff, departmental supervisors and other employees

Measure of Success: Company has compiled a complete teaching program with audio-visual training materials and is now in the process of hiring and training over 200 VIP hirees in various locations. Recently in the Oakland, California area, a class of auto mechanics was graduated and members are now employed as regular auto service personnel.

YOUTH OPPORTUNITY IN BANKING

MARINE MIDLAND BANK
237 Main Street
Buffalo, N.Y. 14203

Business: Banking   Sales: not applicable
CEO: John L. Hettrick   Employees: 2,250

Contact: Sylvia Maye
Address: same as above
Telephone: (716) 843-4197
Program Reaches: 90
When Started: 1968
Budget: n/a

Program Outline:

The purpose of this program is to provide opportunity and motivation for potential high school drop-outs in the banking industry, with part time training and employment while they continue their studies. The program encompasses students in the Buffalo school system who are potential drop-outs. To qualify for the program and to continue on-the-job training, the students are required to maintain passing grades, show improvement in their work performance and to maintain a good attendance record at both school and work.

Co. Personnel Involved: The Bank's Personnel Department is responsible for administering the program.

Measure of Success: Many of those in the YOB program have remained in full time positions at the Bank after graduating from high school.

SUMMER TRAINING EMPLOYMENT PROGRAM (STEP)

MCDONNELL DOUGLAS CORP.
P.O. Box 516
St. Louis, Mo. 63166

Business: Aerospace
CEO: Sanford N. McDonnell

Sales: 2,088mm
Employees: 92,552

Contact: T. H. Allison
Address: same as above
Telephone: (314) 232-7438
Program Reaches: 50-100/year
When Started: 1968
Budget: $1,275/trainee

Program Outline:

The purpose of the program is to provide disadvantaged youth with the opportunity to develop personal and work habits required to obtain and maintain employment.

Summer employment is provided to high school youth of low-income families, introducing them to a satisfactory work experience. The students participate in a work environment simulating production with its responsibilities and regulations and observe the upward mobility available to skilled craftsmen. The program is rounded with a generous share of training devoted to showing direct relationships between responsible citizenship, success in personal management and a rewarding career.

Co. Personnel Involved: During the program, 8 employees full time and 10-12 part time.

Measure of Success: A high percentage completing the program continue their schooling and enter college.

YOUTH SCREEN PRINTING, INC.

THE MEAD CORP.
Talbott Tower
Dayton, Ohio 45402

Business: Diversified
CEO: J. W. McSwiney

Sales: 1,000mm
Employees: 36,900

Contact: Melvin Hanton, Dir.
Address: 12 Ventura Street, Dayton, Ohio 45407
Telephone: (513) 268-6826
Program Reaches: n/a
When Started: June, 1970
Budget: estimated $50,000/year

Program Outline:

The purpose of the program is to provide business training, experience, and eventually advanced vocational training for disadvantaged young people of high school age, primarily Black.

The program involves all aspects of the silk screen operation including graphic design, screen preparation, production, marketing, accounting, etc. The idea is to give some work experience to disadvantaged young people. As the program is fully implemented, Youth Screen Printing, Inc. has an opportunity to serve as a training operation for the screen printing trade. The Midwest Screen Printing Association has provided support in terms of technical advice, used equipment, etc. with this goal in mind. The program possibly will be expanded to include a scholarship program, classes, field trips, etc.

Co. Personnel Involved: Four—a member of the P.R. department has served as an advisory board member since the organization started and has provided some technical help in writing proposals and obtaining publicity for the program. Financial planning personnel have helped suggest budgets, capital needs, etc. Office services supervisor helped with office layout, systems, etc.

Measure of Success: Demonstrated ability to produce in excess of $4,000 sales per month. Ultimately an important measure would be the number of youth that move into the screen printing business elsewhere.

JOBS '70—TRAFFIC READINESS TRAINING

NEW JERSEY BELL TELEPHONE CO.
540 Broad Street
Newark, N.J. 07101

Business: Communications   Sales: 691mm
CEO: Robt. W. Kleinert   Employees: 30,800

Contact: D. W. Heckman
Address: 682 Park Avenue, East Orange, N.J.
Telephone: (201) 677-9921
Program Reaches: 110
When Started: February, 1971
Budget: total, $181,800; government subsidy $136,000

Program Outline:

The purpose of this program is to train women hired in central city environments to be technically skillful Directory Assistance Operators with a good attitude toward their jobs so they will be well accepted by customers, their supervisors and fellow operators.

The program includes 5 weeks of classroom training followed by 7 weeks of on-the-job experience with close supervisory attention. An outline of the content of the 12 weeks follows:

Orientation—40 hours: attendance, punctuality, money management, safety, health, promotional opportunities.

Skill Training and On-The-Job Training—350 hours: includes extensive role plays and discussions on how to deal with customers and supervisors.

Basic Education—90 hours: alphabetizing, geography, pronunciation, spelling, listening skills.

Counseling—22 hours: help set career and personal goals, work and home problems.

The present format reflects extensive changes. All basic education is now taught as a means to improve job skills. Games have been introduced as teaching tools and the students help with the teaching.

Co. Personnel Involved: 4 full time people at the training center plus 36 days of non-management trainer time for each 5-week class—trainees also get close supervision on the job

Measure of Success: Early results show that graduates make far fewer mistakes during the first months on the job while handling more calls. The rate of resignations and dismissals has not changed. However, losses occur much sooner. This saves money in supervision and, in poor work cases, more quickly removes a source of customer irritation.

JOBS '70 PLANT READINESS TRAINING

NEW JERSEY BELL TELEPHONE CO.
540 Broad Street
Newark, N.J. 07101

Business: Communications   Sales: 691mm
CEO: Robt. W. Kleinert   Employees: 30,800

Contact: W. R. Mott, Training Mgr.
Address: 650 Park Ave., East Orange, N.J.
Telephone: (201) 672-3040
Program Reaches: 48
When Started: planned for 1/31/72
Budget: total $391,000; government subsidy $170,500

Program Outline:

This trail program is designed to train underqualified hires to succeed as telephone installers. It will provide jobs in the Newark area for men who should adapt well to the Newark working environment. The company also hopes graduates will improve quality of work, productivity and loss rates compared with normally trained men.

The program is comprised of 12 weeks of classroom training followed by 25 weeks of on-the-job experience with close supervisory attention. An outline of the content of the 37 weeks follows:

Orientation—40 hours: attendance, punctuality, money management, safety, health, dress, the union, promotions, work habits, customer sensitivity, interpersonal relations.

Skill Training and On-the-Job Training—1270 hours.

Basic Education—160 hours: reading, writing and math taught in terms of job activities, reading manuals and orders, talking with customers.

Counseling—6 hours: help with personal and work-related problems.

If students' reactions and teachers' suggestions show opportunities for improvements, changes in format will be made.

Co. Personnel Involved: Three instructors spend full time on the project. A.T.&T. is providing several man/months of effort to set up an evaluation study. Trainees will also get close supervision on the job.

Measure of Success: Company will measure graduates' production load, quality rating, workmen-caused trouble reports, customer complaints, sales and safety performance and force loss. Graduates' performances will be compared with that of qualified hires trained by normal means.

NARTRANS
(NORTH AMERICAN ROCKWELL TRAINING AND SERVICES)

NORTH AMERICAN ROCKWELL CORP.
1700 E. Imperial Highway
El Segundo, Cal. 90245

Business: Manufacturing Aerospace, Electronics,
  Automotive and Industrial Products
Sales: 2,200mm
CEO: R. Anderson   Employees: 81,400

Contact: N. H. Casson, Pres.
Address: 531 Mateo Street, Los Angeles, Cal. 90013
Telephone: (213) 627-8061
Program Reaches: 670 people have participated full time
When Started: June 17, 1968
Budget: NR has invested approx. $1 million with
  NARTRANS. The planned budget for 1972 is approx.
  $2 million.

Program Outline:

The purpose of the program is to provide, through continuous and productive work programs, an opportunity for so-called "hard-core unemployed" to develop vocational skills and work attitudes which would enable them to obtain and keep jobs in the mainstream of American industry.

As originally conceived, NARTRANS provided goods and services to Los Angeles Aerospace divisions. However, the steep decline in Aerospace business reduced the requirements for goods and graduates drastically. In December, 1969, the function was redirected to a plan that would establish NARTRANS as a viable enterprise to be divested to a minority group. The subsidiary produces electrical assemblies and plastic goods. SBA contracts have been awarded for both shops. In addition, cassette albums are produced for the commercial market. NARTRANS is now approaching viability in the production of electrical assemblies and developing the production know-how to attain a balanced cost/price position on plastic products.

Co. Personnel Involved: Two people as officers of the subsidiary devote approximately ¼ of their time to the project. Eleven others have assignments as officers or as board directors. They are involved in weekly or monthly meetings as required. Numerous others are involved in special assignments or liason between divisions and NARTRANS.

Measure of Success: With minority managers in 7 of the 9 key positions, NARTRANS has made the transition from dependency on sales to NR divisions to government contracts and commercial products. Present backlog: government, $694,000; commercial, $30,000; and NR, $2,700—101 F-100 AIMS Electronic kits delivered on or ahead of schedule from an order for 140 kits for $249,433. Approximately 100 workers have been placed in productive work as graduates of NARTRANS.

CONSTRUCTION TRADES TRAINING FOR LEGAL OFFENDERS, LORTON, VIRGINIA

NORTHERN SYSTEMS CO.
4701 Lydell Drive
Cheverly, Md. 20785

Business: Modification of Human Behavior
Sales: n/a
CEO: Sam Segnar   Employees: n/a

Contact: Robert DeWolfe
Address: Minimum Security Center
  Lorton, Va.
Telephone: (703) 768-9200, ext. 510
Program Reaches: 60/year
When Started: July, 1970
Budget: $24,000

Program Outline:

This program offers guaranteed training and placement for 60 felons in the trades. Increased freedom as trainee progresses through program.

Job skills are broken out in small modules involving simple, compound and complex uses of tools and tasks. Time and error perimeters are placed on each skill. Reading and math are tied into the skill unit. Social skills seminars provide training in handling job stress. Reinforcement is provided for positive training related activities. Alternative reward systems are discouraged. Program has a monitoring function built into it. All trainees are placed.

Co. Personnel Involved: 1 instructor and 1 quality assurance specialist

Measure of Success: In the first year of operation the intake was 58; graduates, 54; placements, 54, employed after 1 year, 43.

PRECONSTRUCTION TRADES TRAINING
FOR JUVENILE BOYS

NORTHERN SYSTEMS CO.
4701 Lydell Drive
Cheverly, Md. 20785

Business: Modification of Human Behavior
Sales: n/a
CEO: Sam Segnar   Employees: n/a

Contact: Earl Mello, Prin.
Address: Northern Systems Co.
   Cheltenham, Md. 20785
Telephone: (301) 782-4223
Program Reaches: n/a
When Started: September, 1971
Budget: $17,000

Program Outline:

The purpose of the program is to provide training in construction trades to 24 juvenile boys aged 14-15. Upon leaving the facility, they return to school.

Job skills are broken down into small modules involving simple, compound and complex uses of tools and tasks. Time and error perimeters are placed on each skill. Reading and math are tied into the skill unit. Social skills seminars provide training in handling job stress. Reinforcement is provided for positive training related activities. Alternative reward systems are discouraged. Program has a monitoring function built into it. All trainees are placed.

Co. Personnel Involved: 1 part time instructor and 1 quality assurance specialist

Measure of Success: 100% success of the first 10 boys who graduated from the program. They returned to school. None are presently in trouble.

A PILOT TRAINING PROJECT
FOR COMMERCIAL SKILLS

THE NORTHWESTERN MUTUAL LIFE
INSURANCE CO.
720 E. Wisconsin Avenue
Milwaukee, Wis. 53202

Business: Life Insurance   Sales: 2,000mm
CEO: Francis E. Ferguson   Employees: 2,150

Contact: William Cary
Address: same as above
Telephone: (414) 271-1444
Program Reaches: 30 junior high school inner city
   students/year
When Started: 1967
Budget: n/a

Program Outline:

The purpose of this program is to teach students commercial skills and to relate what they are learning in the classroom to possible uses in business.

Classes of 10 junior high school students each—boys and girls—took typing courses at each of the 3 church centers in the inner city for 8 weeks. During the period, they made field trips to 4 different companies, including NML, to see how the skills they were learning could be used. The tour of a company was followed by a question and answer period.

Co. Personnel Involved: n/a

Measure of Success: n/a

THE COOPERATIVE TRAINING PROGRAM

THE NORTHWESTERN MUTUAL
LIFE INSURANCE CO.
720 E. Wisconsin Avenue
Milwaukee, Wis. 53202

Business: Life Insurance   Sales: 2,000mm
CEO: Francis E. Ferguson   Employees: 2,150

Contact: William Cary
Address: same as above
Telephone: (414) 271-1444
Program Reaches: n/a
When Started: 1964
Budget: n/a

Program Outline:

High school seniors from Milwaukee work part time (from 1:10 to 4:10 P.M.) at regular hourly wages for beginners. They work in Underwriting Policy, Actuarial Change Calculation, Actuarial Policy Loan, Accounting, Secretarial Files and Controls, Benefit Planning, and other areas.

A majority of young people who have come to NML under this program have stayed on.

Co. Personnel Involved: n/a

Measure of Success: The company has been pleased with the performance of the young people. Last spring, the trainees working at the 24 cooperating companies in Milwaukee spontaneously arranged and paid for an appreciation luncheon for their employers.

NATIONAL ALLIANCE OF BUSINESSMEN'S JOBS PROGRAM

OSCAR MAYER & CO.
910 Mayer Avenue
Madison, Wis. 53701

Business: Meat Processing   Sales: 651mm (1971)
CEO: P. Goff Beach   Employees: 11,800

Contact: Harold Polzer
Address: same as above
Telephone: (608) 241-3311
Program Reaches: n/a
When Started: 1969
Budget: n/a

Program Outline:

The purpose of the program is to assist low-income, disadvantaged persons in getting and keeping jobs.

Madison NAB, affiliated with the national NAB, attempts to get local businessmen to pledge jobs for low-income, disadvantaged persons. These are entry-level, permanent jobs that have some possibility of later advancement. Madison NAB, working with the Wisconsin State Employment Service, attempts to fill these job slots with unemployed individuals. The employer is urged to hire, train and retain the disadvantaged person. The board chairman, Oscar G. Mayer, served as Madison Metro chairman for NAB in 1969. During 1970, the company president, P. Goff Beach, served as Madison Metro NAB chairman and its personnel director, Harold Polzer, was Metro director. In addition, the Madison plant of Oscar Mayer & Co., as well as its other plants throughout the country, has been active in hiring and training low-income disadvantaged persons through this program.

Co. Personnel Involved: n/a

Measure of Success: Some of the persons hired in this program are then trained under federal programs.

COOPERATIVE OFFICE EDUCATION AND NEW JERSEY PART TIME PROGRAMS

PENN MUTUAL LIFE INSURANCE CO.
Independence Square
Philadelphia, Pa. 19105

Business: Life Insurance
CEO: Frank K. Tarbox

Sales: 354mm
Employees: 1,860

Contact: Daniel E. Dawley
Address: same as above
Telephone: (215) 925-7300
Program Reaches: n/a
When Started: 1946
Budget: n/a

Program Outline:

Instead of waiting until June graduation to seek out jobs, 30-50 top commercial students from area high schools begin working part time at Penn Mutual in late January or early February.

Depending on their skills in commercial classes, students are placed throughout the company as stenographers, typists, file clerks, office machine operators or general clerks. The work experience becomes part of their course load, and at the end of the term their performance is rated by their Penn Mutual supervisors. Although the Cooperative Education and New Jersey Part Time programs are similar in many ways, procedural details do differ somewhat.

Co-ops alternately spend a week at work, maintaining the same hours as regular employees, and a week at school. So that the job is covered at all times, 2 pupils fill each position. The part timers work daily from 1:30 p.m. to 4:30 p.m. Their mornings are spent in high school commercial classes.

Co. Personnel Involved: n/a

Measure of Success: About 80% of the student employees are made permanent in June.

JOBS '70

PENN MUTUAL LIFE INSURANCE CO.
Independence Square
Philadelphia, Pa. 19105

Business: Life Insurance
CEO: Frank K. Tarbox

Sales: 354mm
Employees: 1,860

Contact: Carolyn Ellison
Address: same as above
Telephone: (215) 925-7300
Program Reaches: n/a
When Started: June, 1970
Budget: government contract

Program Outline:

The purpose of this program is to train persons with limited employment opportunities.

The JOBS '70 employees enter a 5-week training program including 195 hours of pre-job orientation, counseling and job related education at an OIC training center. On-the-job training at Penn Mutual is given on a part time basis during the last 2 weeks of the OIC program and continues after the new employees are in the home office full time.

Penn Mutual has also contracted with OIC to provide counseling in the home office for supervisors who will be working with JOBS '70 employees and other participants in affirmative action employment programs.

Following placement of the trainees in company jobs, they and their supervisors are interviewed by members of the Personnel Department to discuss job satisfaction, performance and adaption to the business world. Once the employee becomes an integral part of the work force, he is encouraged to expand his opportunities for advancement by enrolling in company education programs, such as LOMA and Tuition Aid, and in skill training programs such as typing and shorthand classes which are being developed.

Co. Personnel Involved: n/a

ACADEMY OF APPLIED ELECTRICAL SCIENCE

PHILADELPHIA ELECTRIC CO.
2301 Market Street
Philadelphia, Pa. 19101

Business: Electric Utility   Sales: 504mm
CEO: James L. Everett   Employees: 10,500

Contact: Hendrik B. Koning
Address: same as above
Telephone: (215) 841-4000
Program Reaches: n/a
When Started: n/a
Budget: n/a

Program Outline:

The purpose of this program is to offer practical instruction to students emphasizing individual needs as related to future employment.

The company, the School District of Philadelphia, and the Urban Coalition are engaged in a joint venture at Edison High School offering practical instruction in electronics and electricity, combined with mathematics and English courses tailored to complement laboratory work. There is also a summer employment program that offers young people the opportunity to earn money while they learn. During the school year, the company offers part time employment which is designed to further motivate and stimulate students' technical skills.

Co. Personnel Involved: Mr. Koning, a senior engineer in Philadelphia Electric Company's mechanical engineering division is assigned full time to this project.

Measure of Success: n/a

PREP (PROGRAM RESULTING IN EMPLOYMENT POSSIBILITIES)

PHILADELPHIA ELECTRIC CO.
2301 Market Street
Philadelphia, Pa. 19101

Business: Electric Utility   Sales: 504mm
CEO: James L. Everett   Employees: 10,500

Contact: Joseph F. Van Hart, Mgr., P.R. Dept.
Address: 2301 Market Street
    Philadelphia, Pa. 19101
Telephone: (215) 841-4000
Program Reaches: high school seniors in the school district of Philadelphia
When Started: 1969
Budget: n/a

Program Outline:

The long-range purpose of PREP is to provide high school youths with the skills needed to gain meaningful employment after graduation.

PREP offers paid supervised work experience in conjunction with education. It also provides counseling, training, and supplementary tutoring. The program runs concurrent with the school year—30 weeks, September through June. A typical week consists of 4 afternoons of work at a company location. The 5th afternoon is devoted to skills stimulation in mathematics and communications, and sessions dealing with group concern and the world in which we live. A review and lessons in mathematics and word problems, grammar, spelling, reading and oral communications as well as opportunities for PREPers to express themselves in writing are offered. Reading improvement, as well as personal development courses designed to give positive attitudes towards one's self, the job and the public are also included. Periodic sessions are offered to the students which are devoted to company orientation and presentation of the utility's history, as well as seminars on career development.

Co. Personnel Involved: n/a

Measure of Success: n/a

CAREER DEVELOPMENT PROGRAM

THE PHILADELPHIA SAVING FUND SOCIETY
1212 Market Street
Philadelphia, Pa. 19107

Business: Savings Bank   Sales: not applicable
CEO: M. Todd Cooke   Employees: 828

Contact: Donald L. Geiger, Asst. V.P.
Address: same as above
Telephone: (215) 629-2402
Program Reaches: 111 to date
When Started: May, 1968
Budget: $76,641; MA 6 Job 70 Contract with U.S. Dept
   of Labor, Manpower Admin.

Program Outline:

The program's purpose is to provide opportunities for
minority group individuals for the development of careers
in the banking industry. It is designed to provide a
challenging mix of classroom instruction and on-the-job
training for culturally and economically disadvantaged
young people, predominantly Black.

Small groups of men and women, about 15 to 20 in
number, discuss such subjects as grooming, fashion, mathematics and communications skills. These sessions are
guided by other PSFS employees, many of whom have
themselves benefitted from similar courses earlier in their
careers. Concurrently, these students also receive on-the-
job training as tellers, clerks or secretaries throughout
PSFS, before "graduating" into permanent assignments.

Co. Personnel Involved: The personnel department is
responsible for the program. Training is supplied by key
personnel from several Bank departments.

Measure of Success: Thus far, 7 groups, totalling 111
people, have received training under the Career Development Program with a retention rate of 80%. This figure is
considered well above the average retention rate for
employees who begin working at the normal entry level.

INDIAN EMPLOYMENT OFFICES

PHILLIPS PETROLEUM CO.
Bartlesville, Okla. 74004

Business: Petroleum and Petrochemicals
Sales: 2400mm
CEO: John M. Houchin   Employees: 32,200

Contact: Marvin L. Franklin
Address: 257 Adams Building
   Bartlesville, Okla. 74004
Telephone: (918) 661-4384
Program Reaches: cannot estimate
When Started: 1970
Budget: n/a

Program Outline:

To enable Indians from rural backgrounds to locate
employment and overcome the "cultural shock" of the
city, Phillips has helped 4 Indian tribes set up employment assistance centers in Kansas City and Topeka,
Kansas. Both cities have experienced large influxes of
Indian families in recent years.

Established under contract with the Bureau of Indian
Affairs, the centers are operated by Indian Enterprises,
Inc. The 9 staff members in the Kansas City office and
the 2 employees in the Topeka office are all of Indian
heritage. Through contacts with local businesses, the
centers place applicants in jobs as auto mechanics, iron
workers, telephone operators, clerk-typists and many
more vocations. Applicants who need vocational training
to qualify for employment are enrolled in local trade
schools where their course fees and other expenses are
paid through the Bureau. The staff gives primary consideration to helping applicants find housing, locate
public transportation facilities and manage personal
finances.

Co. Personnel Involved: varies

Measure of Success: n/a

PHILLIPS PRODUCTS CO.

PHILLIPS PETROLEUM CO.
Bartlesville, Okla. 74004

Business: Petroleum and Petrochemicals
Sales: 2,400mm
CEO: John M. Houchin   Employees: 32,000

Contact: Marvin L. Franklin
Address: 257 Adams Building
   Bartlesville, Okla. 74004
Program Reaches: 50-70 employees, depending on season
When Started: 1966
Budget: n/a

Program Outline:

A Phillips subsidiary, this enterprise demonstrates how private industry can make a significant contribution toward enhancing the living standards of minority or disadvantaged persons. Phillips Products Co., Inc., along with a number of other new industries, has created a wide variety of jobs for local residents. The Phillips plant provides approximately 50-70 jobs, depending upon seasonal requirements. Since few of the plant's original employees were experienced in pipe manufacturing, the company set up an on-the-job training program in cooperation with the Bureau of Indian Affairs. This program continues to provide training for new employees and to help veteran employees achieve higher job classifications. The Bureau of Indian Affairs assists the company in screening job applicants and in paying for training costs. Among the employees who have completed the entire 52 weeks of the 3-stage training program, are the plant's leading operators. During their shifts, these 4 men have the responsibility for keeping production running smoothly, for handling equipment problems and for maintaining quality control.

Co. Personnel Involved: varies

Measure of Success: At the time the plant was constructed in 1966, Pryor and the surrounding small towns comprised an economically depressed area. Despite the existence of a sizable work force, composed primarily of Indians, the lack of job opportunities has resulted in extremely high unemployment. Today the situation has changed. An Indian was recently promoted to plant supervisor.

CHURCH ACADEMY

PHOENIX MUTUAL LIFE INSURANCE CO.
One American Row
Hartford, Conn. 06115

Business: Life Insurance   Sales: 1,249mm
CEO: R.T. Jackson   Employees: 2,000

Contact: C. Russell Noyes, V.P., P.R.
Address: same as above
Telephone: (203) 278-1212
Program Reaches: n/a
When Started: n/a
Budget: n/a

Program Outline:

The purpose of this office skills program is to equip young mothers, many of whom are on welfare, for responsible jobs. The Phoenix Company spearheaded the formation of the Church Academy, a work training school, which teaches typing, spelling, vocabulary, reading and grammar.

Special interest subjects include personal grooming, foods and nutrition, consumer economics, telephone techniques and child psychology. A child day care center cares for the children of the mothers participating in the program while they are attending the school and, later on, during working hours.

Co. Personnel Involved: n/a

Measure of Success: This has now become a federal project funded through the U.S. Department of Labor and the NAB. Through the success of this program, many more individuals have been employed by the 8 Hartford business firms participating than would have been ordinarily.

PRE-JOB ORIENTATION PROGRAM

A. H. ROBINS CO.
1407 Cummings Drive
Richmond, Va. 23220

Business: Pharmaceuticals   Sales: 150mm
CEO: W. L. Zimmer III   Employees: 4,000

Contact: John T. Terry
Address: same as above
Telephone: (703) 257-2309
Program Reaches: 12
When Started: 1968
Budget: $10,000

Program Outline:

The program is aimed primarily at minority high school seniors with limited resources who do not possess the advantages generally available to middle and upper socio-economic groups.

Individuals are assigned to unskilled "aide" jobs performing assignments while working under the guidance and direction of department supervisors and other personnel who are qualified to instruct in guided work experience. The program is approximately 10 weeks long and consists of 2 methods for providing learning experiences—actual on-the-job experience, and a series of classroom orientation meetings which are designed to emphasize personal development.

Co. Personnel Involved: 13—direct supervision and counseling

Measure of Success: The company has employed 3 graduates of past programs, and as far as can be determined, all of the enrollees have completed their requirements for graduation from high school.

LABORATORY ASSISTANT TRAINING

ROHM & HAAS CO.
Independence Mall West
Philadelphia, Pa. 19105

Business: Manufacturing Chemicals, Plastics, Fibers, and Health Products
Sales: 507mm (1971)
CEO: Vincent L. Gregory   Employees: 13,805

Contact: John M. Geisel
Address: same as above
Telephone: (215) 592-2863
Program Reaches: approx. 40
When Started: 1968
Budget: approx. $14,000/year

Program Outline:

The purpose of the program is to train unemployed, underqualified but trainable high school graduates from disadvantaged families for entry-level work as chemical laboratory assistants.

The program provides basic training in chemistry, mathematics, and laboratory procedures enabling students to perform the duties of laboratory assistant. (Public school teachers are hired as instructors.)

Program was temporarily discontinued in 1971 because of economic conditions and lack of employment opportunities.

Co. Personnel Involved: coordinator, personnel departments (for placement) and laboratory supervisors (curriculum development)

Measure of Success: Twenty-six individuals successfully completed the course and have been placed in laboratory positions with good advancement possibilities. Several have been placed in non-laboratory positions.

WORK/STUDY PROGRAM

ROHM & HAAS CO.
Independence Mall West
Philadelphia, Pa. 19105

Business: Manufacturing Chemicals, Plastics, Fibers,
and Health Products
Sales: 507mm
CEO: Vincent L. Gregory   Employees: 13,805

Contact: John M. Geisel
Address: same as above
Telephone: (215) 592-2863
Program Reaches: approx 30
When Started: 1968
Budget: n/a

Program Outline:

The purpose of the program is to prevent high school students from dropping out of school and to give them work experience.

Cooperative education style enables students to spend part of the school day at company offices on clerical and other office jobs to learn techniques, habits, etc. required. Students work full time during summer and half days during school year. If the student does not attend morning session at school, he is not permitted to work in the afternoon.

Co. Personnel Involved: department heads, supervisors, fellow employees for training and supervision; members of Personnel Department for orientation and guidance

Measure of Success: Reports of supervisors indicate adequate to excellent performance on job. Some students joined permanent work force after graduation.

JOB PREP CENTER

SAFEWAY STORES, INC.
P.O. Box 660
Fourth & Jackson Streets
Oakland, Cal. 94604

Business: Chain Food Stores   Sales: 4,868mm
CEO: Quentin Reynolds   Employees: 96,000

Contact: R. Zachary
Address: 6700 Columbia Park Road
Washington, D.C.
Telephone: (202) 772-6900
Program Reaches: n/a
When Started: 1970
Budget: $175,000

Program Outline:
The program is designed to school culturally disadvantaged individuals in the skills needed to be retail food clerks. It was set up with the National Alliance of Businessmen. Safeway obtained most of its trainees through referrals from social service agencies set up to assist the disadvantaged in finding jobs. Up to 12 trainees can be handled at one time. The students are paid the entry level wages for the jobs for which they are training. Initial training at the center lasts for 1 month, which is spent in classes and occasionally in an adjoining Safeway Store. Following this is 5 months of on-the-job training. Any person completing the course automatically has a job with Safeway.

Co. Personnel Involved: n/a

Measure of Success: To date, there are about 10 individuals who have passed the entire course of training and are employed by Safeway. Another 15 are now in the second phase of training.

LORTON PROGRAM

SAFEWAY STORES, INC.
P.O. Box 660
Fourth & Jackson Streets
Oakland, Cal. 94604

Business: Chain Food Stores   Sales: 4,868mm
CEO: Quentin Reynolds   Employees: 96,000

Contact: R. Zachary
Address: 6700 Columbia Park Road
    Washington, D. C.
Telephone: (202) 772-6900
Program Reaches: n/a
When Started: 1971
Budget: $5,000

Program Outline:

This program was created as a spin-off of Safeway's "Job Prep Center." It is the second training program in cooperation with the Lorton Reformatory. The prison itself runs the program; Safeway supplies the physical equipment and the training for the 2 instructors. The instructors themselves are long-term inmates who were released to the Washington, D. C. City Jail during their 4-week stint at the Job Prep Center. They received practical job experience before being transferred to Safeway's regular training school, assisting its instructor in giving new employees a 1-week orientation program. The prison course, now training some dozen or so inmates, is set up to offer instruction for 4 hours a day for an approximate 2-month period. The program attempts to be flexible to adapt to the individual needs of inmates who are about to be released from prison and are looking for jobs.

Co. Personnel Involved: n/a

Measure of Success: The program is too new to evaluate.

AUTOMOTIVE PROFESSIONAL TRAINING

SHELL OIL CO.
P.O. Box 2463
One Shell Plaza
Houston, Tx. 77001

Business: Petroleum Products   Sales: 4,331mm
CEO: H. Bridges   Employees: 36,700

Contact: Lou Glist
Address: same as above
Telephone: (713) 220-5002
Program Reaches: n/a
When Started: 1968
Budget: Basic equipment and material is $5,000/school
    year; upkeep is $200 for replacement materials.

Program Outline:

This program aims to teach automotive work skills and service station sales and service methods to interested, potential high school drop-outs, inmates of San Quentin Prison, Log Cabin Ranch (a modern reform school in La Honda, California), and other correctional institutions. This program was first adopted in Brandeis High School in the core area of Manhattan from a training course based upon Shell Oil Company's Dealer Management Development Program. Today it is being used in 44 high schools and 4 correctional institutions.

Students learn automotive repair skills using the latest electronic testing devices and training aids, most of which are provided by Shell. Additionally, service station sales and service are taught to aid students in obtaining future employment. APT is a high school elective and one of the requirements for completing the course is that the students maintain a perfect record of attendance and passing grades in all their other academic classes.

The students are very interested in automobiles and this program channels this interest productively and in a way that encourages the desire for continuing education, as well as the skills useful in later employment. The San Quentin Prison Program and the Log Cabin correctional institution programs are similar with some changes in format.

Co. Personnel Involved: It is part of 5 managers' responsibilities, with available district office maintaining the needed liaison. The time allocation is minimal after the initial installation.

Measure of Success: Sixty percent of APT boys at Brandeis have gone to college while the average for the school is only 30%. Due to the overall success of the program, additional schools will include APT in their curriculum as funding and capabilities to serve this need are provided. Budgeting for 1973 is already planned.

INDUSTRIAL TRAINING CENTER

SIGNODE CORP.
2600 N. Western Avenue
Chicago, Ill. 60647

Business: Manufacturing Steel and Plastic Strapping with
  Necessary Equipment To Apply It
Sales: approx. 200mm
CEO: J. Milton Moon   Employees: 5,084

Contact: J. J. Palen
Address: same as above
Telephone: (312) 276-8500
Program Reaches: approx. 25 trainees thus far
When Started: April 1, 1970
Budget: approx. $45,500

Program Outline:

The purpose of the program is to hire hard-core unemployed persons who would probably not be hired through normal channels and to train them to become self-supporting and valuable employees.

The program is a small "vestibule" type in which disadvantaged persons are given the opportunity to train to become effective workers. Signode products are manufactured in the training area and so the trainees have the satisfaction of knowing that they are doing useful work. The trainees are required to follow the same rules which apply to other employees but these rules are more liberally enforced than would be true in an actual plant or office situation. The trainees are kept in the program until they are considered to be ready for fully competitive employment in another department. At that time they are transferred as soon as a suitable job can be found.

Co. Personnel Involved: The program is run by an orientation counselor under the supervision of the Coordinator of Community Affairs.

Measure of Success: Nine of the trainees are still with Signode and 1 remained with the company until his death. Several have left Signode for better paying jobs. The remainder left during the training program or shortly after for various reasons. Of those who left, most have contacted Signode subsequently seeking reinstatement in the program.

NPAED (NATIONAL PROGRESS ASSOCIATION FOR ECONOMIC DEVELOPMENT)

THE SPERRY & HUTCHINSON CO.
3330 Madison Avenue
New York, N.Y. 10017

Business: Trading Stamps and Holding Company
Sales: 570mm
CEO: Frederick A. Collins, Jr.   Employees: 8,000

Contact: Edward A. Hynes
Address: same as above
Telephone: (212) 983-7912
Program Reaches: n/a
When Started: 1969
Budget: n/a

Program Outline:

In trying to set up Black-operated shopping centers in every community where OIC operates, the NPAED was to plan, construct and manage these centers as a brother corporation to OIC. However, NPAED needed trained analysts to plan and follow through on all the marketing research needed for the planning of such centers.

In January, 1969, the first of several groups of NPAED management trainees arrived at S&H to begin an intensive course in all phases of marketing research with emphasis on retail site selection. Beside "classroom" instruction, the trainees were taken on field trips to see how retail site problems can be solved. After completing the course, the trainees became a cadre of instructors training others in marketing research techniques.

Co. Personnel Involved: 3 men worked full time on the program

Measure of Success: The training project was completed in 1969. Construction is about to begin on a $30 million urban renewal project in Cincinnati's Black community. Ground has been cleared for others. Graduates of the training program S&H launched are playing key roles in each project. Other graduates are operating retail stores, started with Black capital. And still others are managing OIC job training centers.

PRE-EMPLOYMENT SECRETARIAL TRAINING

SUN OIL CO.
1608 Walnut Street
Philadelphia, Pa. 19107

Business: Diversified Oil Refining
Sales: 1,942mm
CEO: H. R. Sharbaugh   Employees: 28,400

Contact: Robert Matteson
Address: 240 Radnor-Chester Road
    St. Davids, Pa. 19087
Telephone: (215) 985-1600, ext. 220

Program Reaches: 6/year
When Started: 1970
Budget: n/a

Program Outline:

The purpose of the program is to enhance employment level for individuals with minimum training and limited job experience or opportunity.

A 16-week pre-employment secretarial training and development program is held for people with limited job experience or opportunity. The program will enable successful participants to join the work force above the employment level for which they qualified before training. The plan provides for individually charted training to insure that each individual can perform effectively.

Co. Personnel Involved: approx. 8 part time

Measure of Success: The participants work effectively.

MINORITY JOB TRAINING AND PLACEMENT

SYNTEX CORP.
Stanford Industrial Park
Palo Alto, Cal. 94304

Business: Pharmaceutical, Veterinary and Health Care
    Products
Sales: 100mm
CEO: George Rosenkranz   Employees: n/a

Contact: Frank Koch, Dir. of Corp. P.R.
Address: same as above
Telephone: (415) 855-6111
Program Reaches: minority persons in the area
When Started: n/a
Budget: n/a

Program Outline:

The purpose of this program is to stimulate and aid job-training and placement of minority persons in the area.

The company provides financial and executive support on a continuing basis to 2 minority job training and placement centers: OICW (Organization Industrial Centers West) located in East Palo Alto and East Menlo Park; OIC (Organization Industrial Centers) in San Jose. A grant was also made to the Santa Clara Valley Skills Center which conducts training and placement activities for about 200 people each year, principally with funds from the Office of Economic Opportunity. The company also gave support to Bayshore Employment Service, Inc. which provides a unique screening and placement service at no cost to minority applicants or employers. In addition, Syntex makes an annual contribution and also designed the BES brochure which was printed for Bayshore Employment by Hewlett-Packard.

Co. Personnel Involved: n/a

Measure of Success: n/a

SUMMER JOB PROGRAM

TECHNICON INSTRUMENTS CORP.
511 Benedict Avenue
Tarrytown, N.Y. 10591

Business: Manufacturing Medical and Instrumental Test
   Equipment
Sales: 102mm
CEO: William Smyth   Employees: 2,900

Contact: Barry Katz, Employment Mgr.
Address: same as above
Telephone: (914) 631-8000
Program Reaches: varies each year
When Started: 1969
Budget: varies

Program Outline:

The purpose of the program is to provide summer employment and funds for disadvantaged youths who would not otherwise be financially able to further their education.

Technicon has for the past several years participated in the NAB's Summer Jobs Program in which at least 20 disadvantaged youths have secured summer employment with the company.

In addition, the company matches the employees' summer earnings in the form of a scholarship fund for the individuals to use for advanced training and/or schooling.

Co. Personnel Involved: Personnel Department and respective supervisors

Measure of Success: participants continuing education; personal letters of appreciation

APPRENTICE SCHOOL
(NEWPORT NEWS SHIPBUILDING)

TENNECO, INC.
(Newport News Shipbuilding Division)
4101 Washington Avenue
Newport News, Va. 23607

Business: Construction, Modification and Repair
   of Ships
Sales: Tenneco, Inc.: 2,883mm
CEO: N. V. Freeman   Employees: 60,000

Contact: Conrad H. Collier, P.R. Dir., NNS
Address: same as above
Telephone: (703) 247-4792
Program Reaches: 4,000 graduates
When Started: 1919
Budget: n/a

Program Outline:

The purpose of the program is to provide skilled craftsmen for Tenneco's shipyard located at Newport News, Virginia, and to provide job opportunities for residents of surrounding area. Shipyard has employment total of over 24,000.

This company-owned and operated school, with its own buildings and staff of 65, offers a full 4-year program of academic instruction and vocational training to an enrollment of approx. 800 students at a time. Students learn many types of technological skills and are paid for both their apprenticeship labor and time spent in school. Most remain in company's employ and many have become top level supervisors and executives. The school also has full program of extra-curricular activities, including varsity sports.

Co. Personnel Involved: School has administrative and teaching staff of 65 people.

Measure of Success: Highly successful in providing corps of skilled craftsmen for complex manpower needs of shipyard, ranging from welders to technicians in nuclear propulsion and computer controlled machinery. Of approximately 3,000 graduates presently under 65 years of age, 60% are currently employed at the shipyard and 1/3 of these are in supervisory positions.

3M FACTORY TRAINING CENTER

3M COMPANY
3M Center
St. Paul, Minn. 55101

Business: General Manufacturing
Sales: 1,690mm
CEO: Raymond H. Herzog   Employees: 66,000

Contact: Abram H. Weaver
Address: 1197 University Avenue
   St. Paul, Minn. 55104
Telephone: (612) 646-7356
Program Reaches: presently 54
When Started: May 1, 1968
Budget: MA-6 Contract

Program Outline:

The purpose of the program is to locate, hire and train employees from the ranks of the disadvantaged and to develop productive citizens in St. Paul as part of 3M's role of corporate citizenship. Applicants are certified hard-core unemployed by the "Minnesota Department of Manpower Service."

The Center offers job training, counseling, remedial education, and supportive services to allow for complete development of necessary skills, work habits, and proper attitudes required by business and industry. Auxiliary programs conducted in social education include: Consumer Education, Income Management, Industrial Training, Medical and Dental Care, Health Relations, Safety, Job Attitude and Family Planning.

"On-the-Job Training" consists of actual production jobs similar to those operations performed in 3M main plants. Adult basic education comprises classroom assignments, basic, intermediate, or advanced, and assistance with achieving high school equivalency diplomas. This is done on a voluntary classroom enrollment basis. The response has been quite favorable.

Co. Personnel Involved: 13 F.T.C. staff members and a 3M management steering committee, consisting of 9 members

Measure of Success: Since the inception of the program 80 of 156 job placements are still employed with 3M, representing a 51% retention rate. Twenty-eight trainees were placed with outside companies. Eight are still on the job and 5 were placed on layoff. The tight economy has made it difficult.

MODERN OFFICE SKILLS TRAINING (MOST)

TRAVELERS INSURANCE CO.
One Tower Square
Hartford, Conn. 06115

Business: Insurance   Sales: 1,603mm
CEO: Morrison H. Beach   Employees: 30,000

Contact: Adrienne E. Reeves
Address: MOST 1GS, same as above
Telephone: (203) 277-4771
Program Reaches: 180 thus far
When Started: August, 1967
Budget: n/a

Program Outline:

The purpose of this program is to provide clerical training for adult women who are at an educational and cultural disadvantage in the labor market with the intent of hiring them at the end of training. MOST trains women in clerical skills such as typing, filing, adding machine operation, flexowriting and keypunch. There are 3 components: (1) 4-week basic education in language, math, typing, spelling and vocabulary; (2) 6-week skill training,

e.g. 2 hours typing, filing, office practice, language, spelling and vocabulary, math, communication skills; (3) 6-week on-the-job training with work in the mornings and program participation for 2 hours in the afternoon.

The trainees receive individual and group counseling, attitudinal training and services which will acclimate them to their new environment. The class includes 12 persons, ages 19-52 and the 15th class is now being trained. The program began on an 8-week basis, then 10, and is now 16.

Co. Personnel Involved: Eight people are directly involved with substantial amounts of responsibility and about 5 peripherally.

Measure of Success: After 3 years, some of the women from the first and second classes are still employed. About 87% of the women who begin the training complete it and are hired. If the graduate can stay employed for the first 6 months, her chances of being on the job at 18 or 24 months are quite high. MOST graduates are praised by their supervisors as being good workers. Several have received substantial promotions; all have received salary raises after the first 6 months and at regular intervals thereafter. Also, it is becoming easier and easier to place a MOST graduate in a department.

MINORITY JOB TRAINING

UNITED CALIFORNIA BANK
600 S. Spring Street
Los Angeles, Cal. 90054

Business: Banking   Sales: not applicable
CEO: Norman Barker, Jr.   Employees: 10,000

Contact: Dr. Larry Wilson, V.P.
Address: same as above
Telephone: (213) 624-0111, ext. 2813
Program Reaches: 2, so far
When Started: 1969
Budget: n/a

Program Outline:

To assist members of minority groups in banking employment opportunities, the Bank, in cooperation with ABA and NBA, trained a young Black in middle management for the local Bank of Finance in 1969-70, and he is now serving as Assistant Manager for the Bank. In 1971, the Bank trained another young man of a minority group (Mexican-American) for the Pan American Bank located in the Southeast section of Los Angeles. NBA selected the candidates upon the recommendations of the minority bank.

Co. Personnel Involved: UCB's management training team worked with these individuals for 10-12 months.

Measure of Success: The 2 trainees have been very successful to date.

WASHINGTON HIGH SCHOOL GRANT

UNITED STATES NATIONAL BANK OF OREGON
321 S.W. Sixth Avenue
P.O. Box 4421
Portland, Oregon 97208

Business: Banking   Sales: not applicable
CEO: E. L. Dresler   Employees: 3,998

Contact: John D. Mills, V.P. Urban Affairs
Address: same as above
Telephone: (503) 225-6111
Program Reaches: n/a
When Started: n/a
Budget: n/a

Program Outline:

The purpose of the program is to provide experience to a group of high school students from Washington High School, an opportunity to work within the free enterprise system, and to provide jobs for the summer.

The Bank enabled a group of high school students to take a grant of $10,000 with no strings attached and set up the Malcolm X Corporation, a wholly owned subsidiary of the Bank that was non-profit in nature.

Co. Personnel Involved: n/a

Measure of Success: The company operated and built pallets for construction work. It hired up to 22 people.

"EARN - LEARN" PROGRAM

XEROX CORP.
Stamford, Conn. 06904

Business: Diversified Office Machines
Sales: 1,719mm
CEO: C. Peter McColough   Employees: 38,339

Contact: H. Daniel Altmere, Program Mgr.
Address: Xerox Corp., Xerox Square
   Rochester, N.Y.
Telephone: (716) 546-4500
Program Reaches: high school students from the Webster
   area, Henrietta and Xerox Square
When Started: July, 1968
Budget: n/a

Program Outline:

An earn-learn program for more than 200 inner city high school students is underway at the Xerox Corporation. The project allows the student to spend about 25% of the 40-hour week in off-the-job discussion and instruction. The program began with these objectives: to allow needy students the opportunity to earn money (each makes $1.80/hour); to introduce them to their first work experience in industry, (their ages are from 16 up, and most have never held a real job); to allow time for counseling and discussions which, Xerox officials hope, will motivate them to continue their education at least through high school and hopefully through college.

About 100 students are at work in the Webster plant, another 20 in Henrietta and about 90 at Xerox Square downtown. They are working in what are described as "non-hazardous" jobs, such as clerks, secretaries, maintenance and draftsmen. About 2/3 of those hired are Negroes. Three-fourths of the total number hired are males. The students spend 2 hours each Monday through Thursday afternoon in group (about 20 in each) activities. Each Friday afternoon, all the groups get together for lectures and discussions. Those students who work in the Webster and Henrietta plants are picked up by Xerox buses at their high schools and taken to work each day. Reading material, with particular emphasis on Black history and consumer education, is available for the students. In recent discussion groups, they have also been discussing the Xerox sponsored CBS-TV news series "Of Black America." If the students do well, Xerox will offer them a job—but not directly out of the program. They must return and at least finish high school. The company hopes to be able to offer summer jobs for those who go on to college, as a major part of the follow-through effort.

Co. Personnel Involved: n/a

Measure of Success: n/a

NEW YORK ASSOCIATION FOR RETARDED CHILDREN (ARC) WORKSHOP

XEROX CORP.
Stamford, Conn. 06904

Business: Diversified Office Equipment
Sales: 1,719mm
CEO: C. Peter McColough   Employees: 38,339

Contact: George Guryan
Address: Xerox Corp., Xerox Square
   Rochester, N.Y.
Telephone: (716) 545-4500
Program Reaches: over 75
When Started: 1966
Budget: n/a

Program Outline:

The Monroe County chapter of the New York Association for Retarded Children has more than 75 handicapped people in a day training program that seeks to employ youngsters in useful tasks to give them profit and the chance to grow in normal adult skills that bring self-confidence.

Impressed by the variety of jobs the youngsters can handle in their workshop, Xerox and other Rochester companies regularly farm out routine jobs to ARC. Some of the work done for Xerox includes envelope stuffing for purchasing and credit, and billing and simple packaging and subassembly operations for departments in Webster. The workshop also handles many kinds of Xerox mailings on a year 'round basis. These include mostly customer meter cards, equipment release forms requested by branches and replenishment of small parts inventories in the field.

People in the workshop range in age from 16 to 45, though most are between 17 and 21. Day training sessions are held in a facility established about 2 years ago. ARC tries to provide retarded persons with 30 hours of experience each week in situations where relationships are intended to influence them toward greater maturity and stability.

Co. Personnel Involved: A Xerox general credit manager is a member of the board and the department responsible for awarding contracts.

Measure of Success: n/a

minority enterprise

GOOD NEIGHBOR PROGRAM

THE AEROSPACE CORP.
P.O. Box 95085
Los Angeles, Cal. 90045

Business: General Systems Engineering for Military
   Research
Sales: 75mm
CEO: I. A. Getting   Employees: 3,285

Contact: William Drake
Address: same as above
Telephone: (213) 648-5000
Program Reaches: general community
When Started: May, 1969
Budget: $100,000 in deposits

Program Outline:

The goal of the program is to replenish the local money supply by asking the Los Angeles business community to deposit a portion of its reserve in banks and savings and loan associations specializing in services to the Negro community.

Aerospace Corporation established time deposit accounts in banking and lending institutions determined to be appropriate to the fulfillment of the Good Neighbor Program. Since that date, the Company has made deposits in a total of 7 banks and savings and loan associations in the greater Los Angeles area serving predominantly minority communities.

Co. Personnel Involved: n/a

Measure of Success: Currently, time deposit accounts totaling $100,000 remain active in 5 of the 7 institutions.

AID TO MINORITY ENTERPRISES

ALUMINUM COMPANY OF AMERICA
Alcoa Building
Pittsburgh, Pa. 15219

Business: Aluminum Producing
Sales: approx. 1,500mm
CEO: John D. Harper   Employees: 46,500

Contact: M. J. Ryan
Address: 1501 Alcoa Building
Telephone: (412) 553-4308
Program Reaches: unlimited
When Started: July, 1970
Budget: none—charged to cost of doing business

Program Outline:

The purpose of this program is to aid minority enterprises which Alcoa has defined as non-sectarian businesses employing less than 500 economically disadvantaged American Black, Mexican, Puerto Rican and/or Indian workers who, by virtue of this business, are striving to attain more than a minimum economic and social stature.

The program coordinates the activity of Alcoa's purchasing in aiding minority enterprises. A purchasing committee, formed to coordinate this activity, prepared Alcoa's definition of a minority enterprise and communicates with purchasing agents and district purchasing agents regarding the goals of the projects. The committee has prepared a list of minority enterprises which is kept updated. Alcoa purchasing people are periodically encouraged to do business with minority enterprises, and to report activity. Minority enterprises are contacted for information about themselves. The committee also acts as an information and advisory clearing house for Alcoa's purchasing staff.

Co. Personnel Involved: Approximately 140 Alcoa purchasing men are involved. A committee of 4 gives direction to the efforts.

Measure of Success: Alcoa has set up a simplified purchasing procedure for Wylie Centre Industries. Business direction has been given to All-Pro Enterprises and in the first half of 1971, $317,000 worth of goods and services were purchased from minority enterprises.

ARCATA INVESTMENT COMPANY

ARCATA NATIONAL CORP.
2750 Sand Hill Road
Menlo Park, Cal. 94025

Business: Diversified Communications, Printing,
   Lumber
Sales: 200mm
CEO: Robert O. Dehlendorf II
Employees: 11,000

Contact: company is being dissolved
Program Reaches: 300
When Started: June, 1968
Budget: approx. $500,000 for 3-year period

Program Outline:

The purpose of the program is to provide financial assistance to minority group entrepreneurs either through loans or small equity positions.

The company makes seed capital accessible to minority businessmen to facilitate the establishment of a broad spectrum of minority-owned businesses within the urban community. It also provides technical and management assistance to the businessmen through sister company, Arcata Management. Arcata Investment Company served as the pilot model in the MESBIC Program to help determine the special considerations and needs of minority enterprise. It reached a capital impaired position in mid-1971 and is precluded from making further investments.

Co. Personnel Involved: Three top executive officers of Arcata National are members of the Board of Directors of Arcata Investment. Various other executives have provided consulting assistance to the portfolio businesses over the years.

Measure of Success: Remaining 24 portfolio businesses employ approximately 300 people and have annual payroll of $1.5 million. Arcata Investment sparked interest of both financial community and government in minority enterprise. Corrective legislation is being supported to help insure success of future MESBIC programs.

MESBIC
(EQUAL OPPORTUNITY FINANCE, INC.)

ASHLAND OIL, INC.
P.O. Box 391
Ashland, Ky. 41101

Business: Petroleum Producing, Refining, Transportation
   and Marketing; Chemical Manufacturing and Sales;
   Road Building and Construction Materials
Sales: 1,600mm
CEO: Orin E. Atkins   Employees: 21,500

Contact: Frank P. Justice
Address: 1202 S. Third Street
   Louisville, Ky. 40203
Telephone: (502) 637-8761
Program Reaches: disadvantaged persons in Ky., W. Va.,
   Ohio, and Ind.
When Started: September 24, 1970
Budget: $44,000 at present

Program Outline:

The purpose of this program is to provide a vehicle to enable the private business community to become involved in a sound, private enterprise—government partnership to effectively assist disadvantaged entrepreneurs. A "MESBIC" is a Minority Enterprise Small Business Investment Corporation. The MESBIC is privately owned and operated; however, it is licensed and regulated, and in part financed, by the Small Business Administration. The MESBIC agrees to operate solely for the purpose of providing assistance, both financial and technical, which will contribute to a well-balanced national economy by facilitating the acquisition or maintenance of ownership of small business concerns by individuals whose participation in the free enterprise system is hampered because of social or economic disadvantage.

Co. Personnel Involved: The "MESBIC" has a staff of 3, however, numerous corporate officers and other employees of Ashland Oil, Inc. are actively involved on a day-to-day basis.

Measure of Success: The Ashland Oil MESBIC has financed and provided assistance to 21 companies to date. Total loan funds have exceeded $244,000. Company has also leveraged additional funds in excess of $1,300,000. Technical assistance is also being provided for those who have any operational weaknesses which they themselves cannot overcome.

BUSINESS OPPORTUNITIES

BUSINESS OPPORTUNITIES, INC.
Howard Bldg.
Providence, R.I. 02903

Business: Banking and Business Development
Sales: not applicable
CEO: Clifton A. Moore   Employees: n/a

Contact: Paul G. Collins
Address: Industrial National Bank
    111 Westminster Street, Providence, R.I. 02903
Telephone: (401) 278-6241
Program Reaches: n/a
When Started: 1968
Budget: approx. $35,000/year

Program Outline:

The purpose of the program is to seek out potential borrowers among minority businessmen, provide them with expert managerial assistance, and loan them money for development of new enterprises. In addition, the development of financial relationships and general up-grading of the minority economic community are objectives.

This minority development organization called Business Opportunities, Inc., was formed by the Business Development Co. in conjunction with Citizen's Trust and Citizen's Savings Bank and Industrial National Bank as a subsidiary of BDC, thus creating a distinct and separate program for Blacks. In operation, a full time Black president is responsible for liaison between the community and with banks. Loan applications are screened by a committee of Blacks and Whites.

The organization is involved in providing working capital lines of credit for materials and labor to some minority contractors.

Co. Personnel Involved: n/a

Measure of Success: BOI has financed the development of 18 new enterprises in approximately 3 years. These represent an investment of $325,000. More importantly they represent an addition of nearly 100 people to the employment rolls. To date 5 companies have failed. Total loss is approximately $22,000. Three companies have fully paid their loan and 10 are still operating.

SUPPORT OF MINORITY BUSINESS

CARSON PIRIE SCOTT & CO.
1 S. State Street
Chicago, Ill. 60603

Business: Retail   Sales: 250mm
CEO: Norbert F. Armour   Employees: 12,100

Contact: J. Gordon Gilkey, Jr.
Address: same as above
Telephone: (312) 744-2152
Program Reaches: 10
When Started: 1968
Budget: none—except time of Carson's people

Program Outline:

The purpose of this program is to provide support for minority individuals seeking to establish business. In addition to depositing corporate funds in minority banks, Carson assists minority businessmen not only by purchase of services and merchandise (very small amounts), but by providing "counselling and coaching" of minority businessmen in fields of Carson's competence.

Thus far, the project has set up a fast food restaurant, purchased a retail shoe store, established a women's dress shop, men's and boys' store and a children's shop.

Co. Personnel Involved: 7

Measure of Success: fair

ECONOMIC DEVELOPMENT DIVISION

THE CHASE MANHATTAN BANK
1 Chase Manhattan Plaza
New York, N.Y. 10015

Business: Banking   Sales: not applicable
Total Assets: 25,000mm
CEO: Herbert Patterson   Employees: 18,900

Contact: Ralph H. Teepe, V.P.
Address: same as above
Telephone: (212) 552-2222
Program Reaches: over 250 small businesses as of early
   1972
When Started: 1969
Budget: $10 million

Program Outline:

This program aims to help minority owned business development. In discovering that the key to successful small business development is strong managerial and specialized consultant support, Chase offers both funds and technical assistance from the Economic Development Division to small businesses to develop their ideas to a profitable end.

EDD finances those businesses it thinks have potential for success, but it especially considers applicants who would not normally qualify for a bank loan. The division looks particularly to help businesses which can benefit a disadvantaged community by creating more jobs, expanding community ownership and increasing the flow of funds within the neighborhood.

The Chase analyst, a lending officer and EDD officer are able to maintain a close relationship with the borrower, and they constantly monitor his progress.

Co. Personnel Involved: Under the direction of the V.P. in charge, the EDD Program has a full time staff of 7. In effect, however, most lending officers in the Bank are members of the program. Loans are most often generated through Chase's network of branches.

Measure of Success: The diverse portfolio of small businesses included restaurants, long distance trucking, bus companies, designers, etc.

WYLIE CENTRE INDUSTRIES, INC. (NAIL MANUFACTURING)

ALUMINUM CO. OF AMERICA
Alcoa Building
Pittsburgh, Pa. 15219

Business: Aluminum Producing
Sales: approx. 1,500mm
CEO: John D. Harper   Employees: 46,500

Contact: Louis Rowe
Address: 3228 Penn Avenue
   Pittsburgh, Pa. 15201
Telephone: (412) 471-6933
Program Reaches: n/a
When Started: 1970
Budget: $250,000 (capitalization)

Program Outline:

The purpose of this program is to assist a Pittsburgh minority group to establish a manufacturing and marketing organization for aluminum nails. To assist in forming this concern, Wylie Centre Industries, Inc., Alcoa will train employees in both production and management and provide engineering, purchasing and accounting services. Such assistance is expected to end in about 2 years when successful operation of the new venture should permit Alcoa to phase out its role and send the concern on its way under experienced Black ownership, management and production personnel.

Co. Personnel Involved: about 6 directly—approximately 50 in various other ways

Measure of Success: The business is operating and is expected to make a profit about 18 months ahead of schedule.

MINORITY BANK DEPOSIT PROGRAM

COMMERCIAL CREDIT COMPANY
300 St. Paul Place
Baltimore, Md. 21202

Business: Financing, Factoring, Leasing
   Insurance and Lending
Sales: 512mm   Assets: 3,400mm
CEO: Donald S. Jones   Employees: 8,290

Contact: Ackneil M. Muldrow
Address: same as above
Telephone: (301) 685-1400
Program Reaches: n/a
When Started: November, 1968
Budget: This is included in the Treasurer's Department
   budget.

Program Outline:

The purpose of this program is to develop a financial
relationship with minority owned banks. Additionally,
ideas can be exchanged on manpower and total economic
development of the minority community while assisting
in increasing the financial base of the minority owned
institution, through the deposit program.

Most financial institutions such as Commercial Credit
Company use bank loans as one of their sources of funds
for their daily operations. The relation to the bank is
commonly called a line of credit or an account relationship. The bank has certain legal or policy limitations as to
how much it can or will lend to any one customer. Once
this is mutually agreed upon by the bank and Commercial
Credit, 10% is then deposited to remain on account as
long as the line is available. It is on this basis that deposits
have been made in minority banks. This 10% balance can
be in the form of an active account (field office uses for
its day-to-day activity) or a dormant (inactive) account.
Most banks, of course, prefer the active accounts. There
are representatives from the various regions that make
courtesy calls on some 500 plus banks with whom
Commercial has account relationships which also include
the minority banks. The Commercial Credit Business
Services Group is exploring the possibility of joint economic development programs with the minority-owned
banks and other banks.

Co. Personnel Involved: approximately 15 persons who
make courtesy calls on the banks and handle operating
accounts as well as the field office personnel that visit
these banks

Measure of Success: the increased number of minority
owned banks that have extended credit lines to Commercial Credit Company

CHRISTIAN BROTHERS INDUSTRIES

DANA CORP.—TRANSMISSION DIVISION
4100 Bennett Road
Toledo, Oh. 43001

Business: Manufacturing Heavy Duty Truck
   Transmissions
Sales: 750mm (corporate)
CEO: R. C. McPherson   Employees: 2,100

Contact: Walter Bancer
Address: Dana Corp., Dev. & Training Center
   1928 N. Detroit Avenue
   Toledo, Ohio 43006
Telephone: (419) 242-3531
Program Reaches: less than 100 at present time
When Started: August, 1971
Budget: no set budget established

Program Outline:

The purpose of the program is to help develop a minority
enterprise known as The Christian Brothers Industries, a
division of Christian Brothers Development Corp. Fred
Culp, now General Manager of Christian Brothers Industries, was hired in June, 1971. Mr. Culp was trained at
Dana Development and Training Center for 3 months.
After September 1, 1971, he started the Christian Brothers manufacturing facility with technical assistance and
start-up equipment from the Dana Corp. Transmission
Division, Development and Training Center.

Co. Personnel Involved: at present, about 10 people

Measure of Success: sales volume increasing

ROCHESTER BUSINESS OPPORTUNITIES CORPORATION

EASTMAN KODAK CO.
343 State Street
Rochester, N.Y. 14650

Business: Manufacturing Photographic Equipment
Sales: 2,976mm
CEO: Walter A. Fallon   Employees: 110,700

Contact: William Priesto
Address: Rochester Business Opportunities Corp.
  55 St. Paul Street
  Rochester, N.Y. 14604
Telephone: (716) 546-3695
Program Reaches: at least 85 independent businesses in
  the area
When Started: 1968
Budget: n/a

Program Outline:

To aid in establishing independently owned and operated businesses in Rochester's inner city, Kodak conceived the original idea for RBOC and the city's business community joined together to make it work. RBOC seeks out business opportunities and finds persons who can benefit from them. Kodak, assisting in the original plan, continues to give financial aid to RBOC and is represented on its Board of Directors. Kodak also considers itself a potential customer for all those products and services of the new businesses that it can use and provides training and consultation in areas of production and marketing to RBOC firms in need of such assistance.

Co. Personnel Involved: n/a

Measure of Success: In 2½ years, RBOC assisted in the formation of more than 75 businesses with a total investment of $2.5 million.

METROPOLITAN ECONOMIC DEVELOPMENT ASSOCIATION

FIRST NATIONAL BANK OF MINNEAPOLIS
120 S. Sixth Street
Minneapolis, Minn. 55402

Business: Banking   Sales: not applicable
CEO: George H. Dixon   Employees: 1,500

Contact: Hugh Harrison
Address: P.O. Box 307, Wayzata, Minn.
Telephone: (612) 473-2577
Program Reaches: n/a
When Started: 1971
Budget: $1,250,000 over a 5-year period

Program Outline:

The purpose of this program is to provide capital for Black-managed business, existing or newly organized. It will help Minneapolis-St. Paul minority persons get established in business by giving them counseling on business accounting and management and helping them obtain financing. Some financial assistance may be given in conjunction with commercial lenders.

Co. Personnel Involved: 2, as organizers

Measure of Success: no experience yet

MINORITY ECONOMIC ASSISTANCE

FIRST NATIONAL CITY BANK
399 Park Avenue
New York, N.Y. 10022

Business: Banking   Sales: not applicable
CEO: William I. Spencer   Employees: 31,700

Contact: Robert J. McKeon
Address: same as above
Telephone: (212) 559-3167
Program Reaches: to date, approximately 300
When Started: early 1968
Budget: management time

Program Outline:

The purpose of this program is to establish and assist minority owned businesses within the New York City area, by building a stronger, more broadly based business area. In order to do this, as well as support new ventures, it is sometimes necessary to have a degree of flexibility beyond everyday lending criteria. It is this which, among other things, the Economic Development Center provides, reviewing and financing a constant flow of loan and investment requests.

Co. Personnel Involved: almost all of the time of 1 lending official, 50% of the time of a Senior Analyst, and 10% of the time of some 7 other officials

Measure of Success: Approximately 70% of loans and investments made appear to be succeeding.

URBAN MORTGAGE LENDING

FIRST PENNSYLVANIA BANKING & TRUST CO.
555 City Line Avenue
Bala Cynwyd, Pa.

Business: Banking   Sales: not applicable
    Deposits: 12/31/71 2,900mm
CEO: John R. Bunting   Employees: 4,323

Contact: William A. Patterson
Address: 15th and Chestnut Streets
    Philadelphia, Pa. 19102
Telephone: (215) 786-8430
Program Reaches: n/a
When Started: 1971
Budget: initially $4 million; future amount to be determined

Program Outline:

The purpose of the program is to provide specialized attention to low-income group members attempting to secure mortgage loans, for residential or commercial properties. The Bank's Urban Affairs Committee, made up of members of senior and executive management, has earmarked an initial $1 million fund for commercial and non-profit properties.

Co. Personnel Involved: Three members of the Bank's staff have major responsibility for the management of these funds. The real estate staff and the Bank's management team are involved in a supportive manner.

Measure of Success: In only 6 months time, over $1.1 million of the earmarked funds have been used.

CITY OF COMMERCE INVESTMENT CO.

FLUOR CORP.
2500 S. Atlantic Boulevard
Los Angeles, Cal. 90040

Business: Engineering, Construction for Chemical
   Processing Industries
Sales: 513mm (1970)
CEO: Melvin A. Ellsworth   Employees: 10,230

Contact: Manuel Aragon, General Manager
Address: 1117 S. Goodrich Blvd.
   Los Angeles, Cal. 90022
Telephone: (213) 724-6141
Program Reaches: n/a
When Started: 1970
Budget: $75,340 annually—initial funding was
   $200,000

Program Outline:

The purpose of the program is to provide financial aid through a loan and equity participation to minority business and to provide management counseling to clients. City of Commerce Investment Co. is a MESBIC Co. whose function is to give financial assistance in the form of a straight debt instrument, convertible or revolving line of credit to minority or economically disadvantaged businessmen. Also, staff or volunteer management consultants are provided to help the minority businessman solve problems he might encounter. Appropriate business and financial monitoring is performed by CCIC in attempting to provide an information system for its clients. The goal is that the businessman become self dependent. During his learning process the latter functions (monitoring) are to hopefully minimize the cost of learning.

Co. Personnel Involved: 5—Board of Directors, 3—Finance Committee, 3—staff, includes General Manager, secretary and management counselor

Measure of Success: a list of 16 clients with a loss ratio of 1

MANTUA INDUSTRIAL DEVELOPMENT CORP.

GENERAL ELECTRIC
RE-ENTRY & ENVIRONMENTAL
SYSTEMS DIVISION
3198 Chestnut Street
Philadelphia, Pa. 19101

Business: Aerospace and Environmental Systems
Sales: n/a
CEO: Otto Klima, Jr., V.P. and Div. Gen. Mgr., RESD
Employees: 4,000

Contact: Wilbur Pierce
   Mantua Industrial Dev. Corp.
   56th and Lancaster Avenue
   Philadelphia, Pa. 19139
Telephone: (215) 879-2750
Program Reaches: n/a
When Started: 1968
Budget: n/a

Program Outline:

The purpose of the program is to set up and support an ongoing Black-owned industrial complex through the pooling of Black and White small businesses.

MIDC is the first predominantly Black-owned business complex in the United States. It was organized as a special purpose corporation SBA Local Development Company. Wilbur Pierce brought together predominantly Black businessmen and their independent enterprises to form the corporation and to purchase a building in which to incubate and nurture the business complex. A common marketing umbrella for these firms was utilized through national sales representatives attracting the purchasing power of major corporations. The complex provides integrated services between member companies, employment, skills, etc. for minority personnel, intercompany manufacture, and increases the economic viability of the inner city community, stressing the possibility of Black and White "mixed" capitalism in what could be called the first industrial shopping center.

Co. Personnel Involved: General Electric RESD was intimately involved in the initial formation of MIDC, starting with the daily details of support of the Public Affairs division, to presently being a customer in 10 different divisions on the East Coast. RESD also sells products to MIDC, extends capital financing, and contributes equipment.

Measure of Success: After 4 years MIDC has a 190,000 sq. foot physical facility and has begun to do major contract work with customers, such as Philco-Ford, Fischer-Porter, General Motors, IBM, RCA, Western Electric, Xerox, etc.

MINORITY BUSINESS DAY
PACE COLLEGE, WESTCHESTER

GENERAL FOODS CORP.
250 North Street
White Plains, N.Y. 10602

Business: Consumer Goods Manufacturing
   (Primarily Food)
Sales: 2,200mm
CEO: Tex Cook   Employees: 44,000

Contact: Sandy MacFarlane
Address: same as above
Telephone: (914) 694-2443
Program Reaches: about 100 participated
When Started: September 24, 1970 (1-time event)
Budget: n/a

Program Outline:

The event was planned to expand economic opportunities for the small businessman, including important minority enterprises, and the concurrent need by large suburban companies for a wide variety of goods and services. The end result: to bring together key purchasing officials of major companies and small businessmen. In this way, General Foods hoped to help the small minority entrepreneur who has a service or product to offer large firms in the Westchester and southern Connecticut area.

The morning was devoted to classroom discussions and workshops led by technical advisors in such areas as small business financing, sales and marketing, requirements for business success, how to expand a business and when not to do so. The afternoon program consisted of an open dialogue among minority entrepreneurs and purchasing agents of participating firms. In addition, booths were available for suppliers to display products and services.

Co. Personnel Involved: 6-8 staff people in Personnel, Purchasing and Public Relations

Measure of Success: Because of the number and diversity of companies involved in this project, as well as the length of time needed to satisfactorily contract with vendors, General Foods has no conclusive report on the success of the program. The company did learn, however, that the ability of small business to meet the volume requirements of major corporations was a serious problem, although certain service businesses such as painting, landscaping and cleaning were able to contract with large enterprises.

MESBIC

GENERAL FOODS CORP.
250 North Street
White Plains, N.Y. 10602

Business: Consumer Goods Manufacturing
   (Primarily Food)
Sales: 2,200mm
CEO: Tex Cook   Employees: 44,000

Contact: Fred Jackson
Address: same as above
Telephone: (914) 694-4251
Program Reaches: n/a
When Started: 1971
Budget: $150,000

Program Outline:

The purpose of this program is to assist the establishment of minority business enterprises. In this way, General Foods hopes to help minority businessmen and their employees. The company loans funds and supplies volunteer management assistance to, chiefly, Black businessmen endeavoring to start private businesses.

Co. Personnel Involved: indeterminate

Measure of Success: n/a

MINORITY ENTERPRISE

GENERAL MOTORS CORP.
3044 W. Grand Boulevard
General Motors Building
Detroit, Mich. 48202

Business: Automotive Industry
Sales: 28,264mm (1971)
CEO: Edward N. Cole   Employees: 696,000

Contact: R. B. Harris, Marketing Staff,
   Sales Section
Address: same as above
Telephone: (313) 556-2933
Program Reaches: n/a
When Started: n/a
Budget: n/a

Program Outline:

The purpose of the program is to aid and seek out minority persons, across the country, to be GM dealers and employees. Since few members of minority groups have the necessary management experience and capital required to acquire a GM franchise, GM has developed and implemented a training program designed to prepare minority persons to be GM dealers. GM also assists with capital investments where necessary. A training program is planned for June, 1972 to qualify 25 people for car and truck dealerships.

Co. Personnel Involved: corporate policy for all employees to help and recommend candidates

Measure of Success: GM presently has 76 minority-owned car-and-truck dealerships, 17 of which are owned by Blacks; 17 minority Frigidaire franchise holders, of whom 10 are Black; 297 minority parts jobbers representing AC Spark Plug Division, 69 of whom are Black; and 55 Black parts jobbers for the United Delco Division. In addition, many minority businessmen sell and service GM products throughout the U.S.

MOTOR ENTERPRISES, INC.

GENERAL MOTORS CORP.
3044 W. Grand Boulevard
General Motors Building
Detroit, Mich. 48202

Business: Automotive Industry
Sales: 28,264mm (1971)
CEO: Edward N. Cole   Employees: 696,000

Contact: H. F. Lorenz
Address: Motor Enterprises, Inc., General Motors
   Bldg., Detroit, Mich. 48202
Telephone: (313) 556-4273
Program Reaches: n/a
When Started: February, 1970
Budget: GM has committed up to $1 million to the
   project

Program Outline:

The purpose of this program is to aid minority enterprises through financial loans. Under the auspices of the Small Business Administration Act, GM has established Motor Enterprises, Inc., a Minority Enterprise Small Business Investment Company (MESBIC). GM's commitment, in conjunction with financial institutions and the Small Business Administration guaranteed loans, can provide up to $15 million in funds for loans to minority enterprises. GM also provides employees to work with the entrepreneurs. Skilled in operations analysis, budget control, marketing and other necessary business skills, the GM employees furnish guidance and counseling to fledgling businesses.

Co. Personnel Involved: 3 full time personnel organizing and reviewing loan requests; numerous contact persons in the various cities acting as advisors

Measure of Success: In less than 26 months, GM's Motor Enterprises, Inc. has financed 62 minority-owned businesses in 28 cities located in 13 different states.

AID TO MINORITY ENTERPRISE

HONEYWELL, INC.
2701 4th Avenue South
Minneapolis, Minn. 55408

Business: Manufacturing Control Systems
Sales: 1,920mm
CEO: Stephen F. Keating   Employees: 95,000

Contact: J. E. Remington, Dir.
   Corporate Material Services
Address: same as above
Telephone: (612) 332-5200
Program Reaches: n/a
When Started: pledge made February, 1972
Budget: $4 million

Program Outline:

The purpose of this program is to offer concrete help to minority suppliers.

In order to implement a program promoting economic, social and educational equality for all citizens, Honeywell established a corporate pledge to spend 1% of its money for domestic procurement with minority suppliers. This same percentage goal was assigned to the responsible manager of each operating unit of the company. The company further identified a minority procurement representative in each of its domestic locations and assigned him the responsibility of accomplishing the end result. Thus he became the interface with the company's management in each location as well as with minority suppliers. Accomplishments are monitored each month and reported to the company's president. In addition, the company recognizes the possibilities of the need to supply management assistance to certain minority entrepreneurs in order to make the program effective.

Co. Personnel Involved: n/a

Measure of Success: too early to tell

MINORITY ECONOMIC DEVELOPMENT PROGRAMS

MARCOR (Montgomery Ward & Co., Inc.)
Box 8339
Chicago, Ill. 60680

Business: General Merchandising
Sales: 3,500mm
CEO: Leo H. Schoenhofen   Employees: 126,000

Contact: Fred Veach
Address: same as above
Telephone: (312) 467-2520
Program Reaches: n/a
When Started: 1968
Budget: None—however, each sponsor of CBOF guarantees $2,500 for unreimbursed expenses.

Program Outline:

The purpose of this program is to use Ward's resources and expertise to promote economic development and business initiative in the disadvantaged by helping minority entrepreneurs. Ward co-sponsors and partici-pates in the Chicago Business Opportunity Fair which provides contacts between minority suppliers and buyers from large corporations. The company participates in similar programs in Oakland, Los Angeles and New York and actively promotes the program in other cities.

In 1970, Ward franchised the first inner city catalog agency to a Black businessman. To date, there are 5 of these agencies providing opportunities for individual minority ownership: 2 in Chicago, and 1 each in Baltimore, Kansas City and Oakland. In addition, Ward places deposits in Black banks. Through a series of meetings, memos from top executives and review by committee, Ward encourages its buyers to expand purchases from minority suppliers.

Co. Personnel Involved: Over 500 as part of their normal activities. In addition, a minority relations committee composed of 5 top executives continually monitors and stresses this program.

Measure of Success: The 1970 CBOF in Chicago generated over $4 million in sales by minority businessmen. Over $½ million is now on deposit at 13 minority banks across the country.

COMMUNITY DEVELOPMENT DIVISION

MARINE MIDLAND BANK—WESTERN
237 Main Street
Buffalo, N.Y. 14203

Business: Banking
CEO: John L. Hettrick

Sales: not applicable
Employees: 2,250

Contact: William L. Martin
Address: P.R. Div., same as above
Telephone: (716) 843-4197
Program Reaches: Bank customers
When Started: 1968
Budget: n/a

Program Outline:

The purpose of this division is to provide financial and technical assistance to existing or just starting minority businesses. Through the Community Development some 200 members of minority groups have been given loan assistance, but the stress has been on follow-up advice including managerial guidance. After the loan has been made, the Community Development Division assigns members of its staff to counsel and work with some companies. It also helped form Reckful Consultants, Inc., an organization of community service-minded men with special talents.

Co. Personnel Involved: Personnel Department and Community Development Division

Measure of Success: 200 minority persons have had loan assistance and managerial guidance.

MINORITY BUSINESS LOAN PROGRAM

NORTH CAROLINA NATIONAL BANK
200 S. Tryon
Charlotte, N.C. 28201

Business: Banking
CEO: Thomas I. Storrs

Sales: n/a
Employees: 3,200

Contact: D. Smith Patterson
Address: P.O. Box 120, Charlotte, N.C. 28201
Telephone: (704) 374-5533
Program Reaches: North Carolina residents
When Started: 1972
Budget: no separate budget—incorporated into existing structure

Program Outline:

This program is designed to satisfy the special credit needs of minority-owned business through an aggressive loan program designed around "relaxed" credit standards and direct managerial assistance. It will increase minority involvement in the economic mainstream of the community; thereby raising the overall standard of living in these areas.

The program aims to provide assistance to both existing and potential minority businesses. Initially, the program will operate as a part of the Bank's statewide loan structure. Applicants will be considered for loans on the basis of character, willingness to accept management assistance, past experience and definite success chances of the business. NCNB will assist in preparing projections for S.B.A. loans and in providing pre-loan management training—in addition to the necessary post loan assistance. Possible basic business courses, which might be taken at local colleges, will be suggested, as well as assistance from local agencies. "Relaxed" conditions will be applied for applicants not having the required collateral. Evaluation of this program will take place after 6 months in operation and, if necessary, modifications will follow.

Co. Personnel Involved: One person currently coordinates the state-wide program through the regional offices and local city loan officers. NCNB anticipates establishing a section to assist loan personnel and provide assistance to businessmen.

Measure of Success: It is too early in the program to make a judgement on the degree of success, but all indications are that the Black businesses welcome the honest approach of the program. Outside agencies are willing to cooperate in providing managerial assistance and counseling and the participating loan officers have accepted the concept of promoting Black loans as a necessary measure.

AID TO BLACK BANKS PROGRAM

OLIN CORP.
120 Long Ridge Road
Stamford, Ct. 06904

Business: Diversified Manufacturing
Sales: 1,145mm
CEO: Gordon Grand   Employees: 3,200

Contact: Joseph G. McIntyre, Jr.
Address: same as above
Telephone: (203) 356-3239
Program Reaches: probably 100s
When Started: 1969
Budget: Total cash passing through banks is in excess of
   $7 million annually

Program Outline:

The purpose of this program is to strengthen the lending power of Black owned or managed institutions so as to help increase the critically short supply of short- and long-term low interest venture capital in poverty areas.

Funds made available to the ghettos through this program reach borrowers through established Black banks who are in a good position to evaluate the Black businessman's problems and capabilities.

Olin deposits monthly Federal withholding taxes to six banks which have use of the funds short-term until the U.S. Treasury withdraws them. Olin also makes time deposits of its own working capital to six other banks at interest rates lower than could be obtained elsewhere, enabling the banks to lend the funds to ghetto entrepreneurs at lower cost. For every dollar Olin adds to banks' lending resources, the banks can lend several more, so the program has a "seed money" multiplier effect on the banks' lending power. All participating banks are in states where the company has manufacturing operations or tax-handling offices.

Co. Personnel Involved: 2 part time

Measure of Success: Enthusiastic reports from these banks have assured Olin that its purposes are being realized.

MINORITY BANKS

OSCAR MAYER & CO.
910 Mayer Avenue
Madison, Wis. 53701

Business: Meat Processing   Sales: 651mm
CEO: P. Goff Beach   Employees: 11,800

Contact: L. D. Sheldahl
Address: same as above
Telephone: (608) 241-3311
Program Reaches: n/a
When Started: 1971
Budget: n/a

Program Outline:

To help strengthen minority-owned business throughout the country, the company deposited some of its funds in minority banks. By having such funds, the banks are then able to lend the money to minority businessmen and give their ventures a chance for success. At present, Oscar Mayer & Co. has deposits in 5 banks: 2 in Chicago, 2 in Los Angeles, and 1 in Milwaukee.

The major thrust of the Bank Deposit Program is to establish an effective business relationship between the major corporations and minority banks, based on mutual needs. For example: an oil company makes a deposit in a local bank, and the bank locates entrepreneurs and finances local service stations; a construction company makes a deposit, and the bank finances a new home. Doing business with the minority banks offers corporations professional banking services, an approach to a major market, and a significant role in community development.

Co. Personnel Involved: n/a

Measure of Success: n/a

SMALL BUSINESS LOAN DEPARTMENT

THE PHILADELPHIA NATIONAL BANK
Broad and Chestnut Streets
Philadelphia, Pa. 19101

Business: Banking   Sales: not applicable
Earning Assets: 2,000mm
CEO: G. Morris Dorrance, Jr.   Employees: 2,788

Contact: Wilson E. DeWold
Address: same as above
Telephone: (215) 629-3504
Program Reaches: 40 accounts
When Started: 1968
Budget: n/a

Program Outline:

The purpose of the program is to aid minority economic development in the Philadelphia area (commercial-retail).

The program provides high-risk loans and intensive financial counseling to thinly-capitalized minority-owned businesses, with little or no net worth. Financial counseling, including legal and accounting assistance, is part of the follow-up procedure once a loan is made. Department has close contact with customers, making field calls at least once a month.

Co. Personnel Involved: 2 loan officers and 1 secretary full time

Measure of Success: The loan portfolio has tripled during 1971. Delinquencies have dropped by two-thirds in dollar value.

INDIAN ECONOMIC ASSISTANCE

PHILLIPS PETROLEUM CO.
Bartlesville, Okla. 74004

Business: Petroleum and Petrochemicals
Sales: 2,400mm
CEO: John M. Houchin   Employees: 32,200

Contact: Marvin L. Franklin
Address: 257 Adams Building
    Bartlesville, Okla. 74004
Telephone: (918) 661-4384
Program Reaches: hard to estimate
When Started: 1966
Budget: n/a

Program Outline:

Through the efforts of the Federal Bureau of Indian Affairs, tribal governments and various businesses, people of Indian heritage are attaining economic self-sufficiency and are assuming their rightful place in the national economy.

Phillips' involvement in Indian economic assistance began when a special cooperative products division was formed to help develop Indian-owned and operated enterprises. Since then, the company has assisted with evaluation, planning and financing numerous Indian industrial enterprises, and has furnished continuing management and training assistance where appropriate. Whenever possible, these enterprises have been developed in areas where there are existing concentrations of Indians, not only to avoid the problems of dislocating Indian workers from their native environment, but also to bring new income sources into generally poor communities. Some of the enterprises aided by the company are: the Cherokee Nations Industries for electronic assembly, upholstery work, carpet fitting and welding; Navajo Chemicals, Inc., which handles the packaging, distribution and sale of blasting materials and fertilizers; White Eagle Industries, a mattress manufacturer.

As a way of encouraging employee safety in Indian-owned and operated plants, Phillips recently helped organize the American Indian Safety Council which will survey plants and provide educational programs and materials.

Co. Personnel Involved: varies, depending upon the project, stage of the project, etc.

Measure of Success: n/a

PHILLIPS INDUSTRIAL FINANCE CORP.

PHILLIPS PETROLEUM CO.
Bartlesville, Okla. 74004

Business: Petroleum and Petrochemicals
Sales: 2,400mm
CEO: John M. Houchin   Employees: 32,200

Contact: Marvin L. Franklin
Address: 257 Adams Building
　　Bartlesville, Okla. 74004
Telephone: (918) 661-4384
Program Reaches: hard to estimate
When Started: 1970
Budget: n/a

Program Outline:

A cooperative effort between the federal government and private industry, the program enables a large corporation such as Phillips to set up a subsidiary called a Minority Enterprise Small Business Investment Company (MESBIC) which invests money in minority enterprise.

The Phillips MESBIC subsidiary, Phillips Industrial Finance Corp., seeks out and evaluates minority small business enterprises from all over the country. It can supply needed funds to a worthwhile venture either through purchasing stock in the company or by granting it a loan. A MESBIC loan qualifies the minority businessman for a supplemental loan from the federal Small Business Administration, and additional financing from private banks, if necessary. MESBIC money may be used either to start a new business or expand an existing one. Management and technical aid is also an important part of the program. This assistance is designed to help minority businessmen overcome the major problems that cause business failures—inadequate planning and market research, unsound management policies, unfamiliarity with complex tax laws and government regulations, and the lack of skilled employees and insufficient training resources.

To help minority businessmen overcome difficulties in such fields as personnel management, taxation, accounting and market research, Phillips lends company experts in these areas. These individuals work directly with the minority businessman and his employees, examining such problems as how to improve accounting procedures, increase production efficiency or develop markets for the firm's products. Two minority enterprises currently receiving financial aid and management assistance from Phillips Industrial Finance Corp. are Papago Explosives of Casa Grand, Arizona, and LeeFac, Inc. of Boley, Oklahoma. The company is also participating in the MESBIC program through part-ownership of Aleyeska Investment Co. of Anchorage, Alaska.

Co. Personnel Involved: varies at different times

PETROLEUM RETAIL OWNERSHIP PROGRAM

PHILLIPS PETROLEUM CO.
Bartlesville, Okla. 74004

Business: Petroleum and Petrochemicals
Sales: 2,400mm
CEO: John M. Houchin   Employees: 32,200

Contact: D. E. Braden
Address: 358 Adams Building
　　Bartlesville, Okla. 74004
Telephone: (918) 661-4126
Program Reaches: n/a
When Started: n/a
Budget: n/a

Program Outline:

Nearly 90% of the service stations which sell Phillips products are independently operated. However, insufficient financing and inadequate management expertise have discouraged minority individuals from becoming service station dealers. This program was begun to involve more Negroes, Indians, Spanish Americans and other minority persons in the operation and management of service stations.

Known as Operation PRO, the program is a joint effort between 10 oil companies marketing in Oklahoma and several state and federal agencies. The program provides the prospective dealer with training in station management, merchandising, cost accounting, inventories, long range planning and public relations. The program can also help the minority individual obtain initial financing for his new venture.

Phillips has constructed a service station at Tahlequah, Oklahoma to serve as a training center for minority persons wishing to learn the fundamentals of station operations and management. To aid the recruitment of minority dealers in urban areas, the company sales department has retained a consultant in minority affairs who specializes in seeking out marketing opportunities and prospective dealers in Black communities.

Co. Personnel Involved: varies

Measure of Success: n/a

SAVINGS AND LOAN ASSOCIATIONS

PHOENIX MUTUAL LIFE INSURANCE CO.
One American Row
Hartford Conn. 06115

Business: Life Insurance   Sales: 1,249mm (assets)
CEO: R. T. Jackson   Employees: 2,000

Contact: C. Russell Noyes, V.P., P.R.
Address: same as above
Telephone: (203) 278-1212
Program Reaches: n/a
When Started: 1969
Budget: n/a

Program Outline:

The purpose of this program is to help create a Black savings and loan association in Hartford. Key employees of the Phoenix Company helped to set up this organization, which is the first of its kind in New England. The Phoenix employees, working with other civic leaders, established the association and it now serves as a Black-oriented financial focal point for the local community. The Phoenix was the first to deposit funds in the association and also made company facilities and equipment available.

Co. Personnel Involved: n/a

Measure of Success: n/a

MINORITY BUSINESS LENDING

PITTSBURGH NATIONAL BANK
1 Oliver Plaza
Pittsburgh, Pa. 15230

Business: Banking   Sales: not applicable
CEO: Robert C. Milsom   Employees: 2,311

Contact: Wallace Abel, Dir. P.R.
    and Urban Affairs
Address: same as above
Telephone: (412) 355-2000
Program Reaches: n/a
When Started: August, 1968
Budget: n/a

Program Outline:

The purpose of the program is to help minority members of the community establish or expand businesses, primarily located in Homewood and the Hill District.

Since August, 1968, Pittsburgh National Bank has distributed approximately $1,600,000 in loans. Of the 126 loans 6 were made for manufacturing purposes, 1 to a wholesaler, 68 to service businesses, and 51 to retailers. These were made under the auspices of the Allegheny Conference on Community Development and the Small Business Administration. After the loan is made, the bank officer in charge follows up with the customer to determine the current status of the project and to provide continuing financial service and counseling.

Co. Personnel Involved: n/a

Measure of Success: n/a

HUNTERS POINT COOPERATIVE SUPERMARKET

SAFEWAY STORES, INC.
P.O. Box 660
Fourth & Jackson Streets
Oakland, Cal. 94604

Business: Chain Food Stores   Sales: 4,868mm
CEO: Quentin Reynolds   Employees: 96,000

Contact: Quentin Reynolds
Address: same as above
Telephone: (415) 444-4711
Program Reaches: n/a
When Started: 1968
Budget: $120,000

Program Outline:

To revive a cooperative supermarket which was on the edge of bankruptcy, a task force ran a computerized analysis of the entire operation from management to stock. Safeway provided management consultant services covering all phases of food retailing except pricing, where they did not interfere. A clean-up squad of Safeway employees was put together and spent 3 days cleaning up the store. They received, opened, priced and marked 4,000 cases of food and goods in 3 days. Replacements for Safeway's team were hired from the community. For all of the consultant and management services, Safeway charged the co-op $1.00.

Co Personnel Involved: n/a

Measure of Success: good

STANDOFF SUPERETTE

SAFEWAY STORES, INC.
P.O. Box 660
Fourth & Jackson Streets
Oakland, Cal. 94604

Business: Chain Food Stores   Sales: 4,868mm
CEO: Quentin Reynolds   Employees: 96,000

Contact: A. G. Ancelmo, Mgr.
  Canada Safeway Prairie Division
Address: contact general offices
Telephone: (415) 444-4711
Program Reaches: n/a
When Started: n/a
Budget: $20,000

Program Outline:

The purpose of this project is to bring needed merchandise to and increase needed income of the Blood Indian tribe in Southern Alberta, Canada. With a small grant from the tribe, plus their labor, plus contributed time and effort by Safeway people, an abandoned dilapidated grocery store at Standoff, one of the reservation's small communities, was completely remodeled, refixtured, stocked, promoted, and opened for business. People from the tribe were trained as meat cutters, checkers, meat wrappers, clerks, and a store manager. Safeway provided a manager to train people in store management, and provided also good used equipment at no cost to the tribe.

Co. Personnel Involved: n/a

Measure of Success: Seven Blood Indians were manning the store at Standoff on opening day. Most recent reports point to continued good business at the new store.

MINORITY BANK DEPOSITS

SHELL OIL CO.
P.O. Box 2463
One Shell Plaza
Houston, Tx. 77001

Business: Petroleum Products   Sales: 4,331mm
CEO: H. Bridges   Employees: 36,700

Contact: H. T. Richards
Address: Shell Oil Co., 50 W. 50th Street
  New York, N.Y. 10020
Telephone: (212) 262-8478
Program Reaches: minority banks and their clients
When Started: 1968
Budget: $2 million

Program Outline:

In order to increase the availability of investment funds for the formation and operation of minority-owned businesses, Shell's Financial Organization has deposited more than $1.6 million in minority-owned and operated banks, for the purposes of freeing more capital for the minority community.

Co. Personnel Involved: Approximately 50 members of the Financial Management and affected local managers maintain contact with each bank in which the company has deposits.

Measure of Success: success and growth of minority banks concerned and their increasing involvement in funding minority businesses

MINORITY DEALER DEVELOPMENT PROGRAM

SHELL OIL CO.
P. O. Box 2463
One Shell Plaza
Houston, Tx. 77001

Business: Petroleum Products   Sales: 4,331mm
CEO: H. Bridges   Employees: 36,700

Contact: Lou Glist
Address: same as above
Telephone: (713) 220-5002
Program Reaches: currently 1,000 minority dealers
When Started: n/a
Budget: Special recruitment programs for minority busi-
  nessmen have required additional budgets of $50,000
  and upward/year

Program Outline:

To secure increasing numbers of minority businessmen and provide them with growth opportunity as independent Shell dealers, the company has undertaken this long-range project to increase its percentage of minority dealers to the point where it approximates the nation's minority profile. Minority dealers presently make up 10.1% of the company's dealer complement.

Co. Personnel Involved: Hundreds of Shell personnel are involved at all levels of the company in the nationwide Marketing Organization, including all 45 marketing divisions.

Measure of Success: There has been a steady upward trend of minority Shell service station dealers from 6.7% in 1969 to the present 10.1%.

TRENTON PACKAGING COMPANY

SHELL OIL CO.
P.O. Box 2463
One Shell Plaza
Houston, Tx. 77001

Business: Petroleum Products   Sales: 4,331
CEO: H. Bridges   Employees: 36,700

Contact: Lester F. Allen
Address: 100 Bush Street
   San Francisco, Cal. 94106
Telephone: (415) 392-5400
When Started: operations began February, 1969
Budget: $200,000

Program Outline:

The idea for the Trenton Packaging operation came from a National Alliance of Businessmen report that stated only 1% of the Black community is involved in business ownership. To involve the Black community in business ownership and management, and to provide jobs and future ownership possibilities for minority group members, Shell decided to set up a Black capitalism project close to the Princeton Chemical plant to package Shell No-Pest Strips in Trenton, New Jersey. The initial plan was to set up the business, and later when it proves to have a fair chance of surviving, to train a Black manager and still later, the business will be turned over to the Black community. The project is carried on completely without government funds and has, so far, contributed greatly to the community. It has given people in a depressed employment area jobs, and has taught them employment responsibility which will prepare them for even better job possibilities.

Shell hopes to divest itself of ownership to qualified minority entrepreneurs when the plant is sufficiently viable.

Co. Personnel Involved: Two Shell employees who are on loan to the plant full time, serving in administrative capacities, plus members of Shell Chemical management who are involved in long-range planning for the plant are involved.

Measure of Success: The plant is now operating on about a break-even basis. However, a major share of the plant's activities involves No-Pest Strips, and the continuation of this business for an extended period is questionable. Hence, long-range viability is by now means assured.

ALLIANCE ENTERPRISE CORP.

SUN OIL CO.
1608 Walnut Street
Philadelphia, Pa. 19103

Business: Diversified Oil Refining
Sales: 1,942mm
CEO: H. Robert Sharbaugh   Employees: 28,400

Contact: Kenneth Hill
Address: Suite 802, 1616 Walnut St.
   Philadelphia, Pa. 19103
Telephone: (215) 985-1600, ext. 3566
Program Reaches: n/a
When Started: October, 1971
Budget: operating budget from Sun approx. $88,000;
   $150,000 investment capital

Program Outline:

As a Minority Enterprise Small Business Investment Company (MESBIC), Alliance is designed to make investment loans to small minority businesses.

The Corporation makes investment loans, usually in the form of front or seed capital to minority manufacturing, retail and wholesale enterprises. Sun provides employees with technical and administrative expertise to allow this type of consultation to the minority entrepreneur. Alliance Enterprise will identify within Sun Oil those employees who can be most valuable to these businesses as counselors on a volunteer basis. Working within a team concept, a group of these experts is assigned to each client with the team leader making personal calls on the client, monitoring progress and providing whatever management or technical assistance is needed.

Co. Personnel Involved: Three full time—out of the first request for the volunteer consultants, there were 38 responses, 20 of which will be used as team members

Measure of Success: too early to tell

MINORITY BANKING PROGRAM

SUN OIL CO.
1608 Walnut Street
Philadelphia, Pa. 19103

Business: Diversified Oil Refining
Sales: 1,942
CEO: H. Robert Sharbaugh   Employees: 28,400

Contact: Robert A. Matteson
Address: 240 Radnor-Chester Road
   St. Davids, Pa. 19087
Telephone: (215) 985-1600, ext. 220
Program Reaches: n/a
When Started: 1972
Budget: $250,000

Program Outline:

A sum of $250,000 has been allocated for implementation of a program to open company accounts with minority-controlled banks within Sun's operating territory. Sun personnel responsible for execution of the problem will actively search out banks within the company's, or a subsidiary's, operating territory. Selection guidelines provide that the banks must meet the minimum corporate requirements of having their deposits insured by FDIC, and will be chosen on a competive basis within their own geographic area with emphasis on available potential service.

The company is prepared to accept fewer services as necessary to accomplish the goals of the program. Services which the banks could provide the company include interest funds, marketing deposit accounts, dealer financing and deposit accounts.

Co. Personnel Involved: several

Measure of Success: too early to tell

MINORITY BUSINESS FINANCING

SUN OIL CO.
1608 Walnut Street
Philadelphia, Pa. 19103

Business: Diversified Oil Refining
Sales 1,942mm
CEO: H. Robert Sharbaugh   Employees: 28,400

Contact: Robert A. Matteson
Address: 240 Radnor-Chester Road
   St. Davids, Pa. 19087
Telephone: (215) 985-1600, ext. 220
Program Reaches: n/a
When Started: April, 1972
Budget: n/a

Program Outline:

The purpose of this program is to effect a significant transaction with a minority-owned financial institution as part of the company's action to increase business with such minority operations. Sun has directed reassignment of more than $25 million in group life insurance to Black-owned North Carolina Mutual Life Insurance Co. The sum is a segment of the more than $500 million in group life insurance or approximately 22,700 U.S. Sun employees presently underwritten by John Hancock Mutual Life Insurance Company.

Co. Personnel Involved: n/a

Measure of Success: n/a

MINORITY DEALERSHIP FINANCIAL DEVELOPMENT PROGRAM

SUN OIL CO.
1608 Walnut Street
Philadelphia, Pa. 19103

Business: Diversified Oil Refining
Sales: 1,942mm
CEO: H. Robert Sharbaugh   Employees: 28,400

Contact: Robert A. Matteson
Address: 240 Radnor-Chester Road, St. Davids, Pa. 19087
Telephone: (215) 985-1600, ext. 220
Program Reaches: n/a
When Started: February, 1972
Budget: n/a

Program Outline:

The purpose of this program is to provide additional business opportunities for members of minority communities. The 2-pronged program provides for guaranteeing a significant portion of each bank loan made to minority individuals who will be Sunoco or DX service station dealers, using minority- controlled banks as the source of the loans to dealers in the program whenever practiced.

The Marketing Financial Administration will provide the financial and accounting guidance and support for the program and will implement and control the credit and collection function necessary for the successful impact of the program. Retail Sales will perform the identification, development and training, and placement of individuals for successful service station dealer operations. Corporate Credit will monitor and evaluate the overall program, the Cash Management Department in Philadelphia will identify minority-controlled banks.

Co. Personnel Involved: n/a

Measure of Success: n/a

MINORITY VENDOR PURCHASING PROGRAM

SUN OIL CO.
1608 Walnut Street
Philadelphia, Pa. 19103

Business: Diversified Oil Refining
Sales: 1,942mm
CEO: H. Robert Sharbaugh   Employees: 28,400

Contact: Harry C. Melton
Address: 240 Radnor-Chester Road, St. Davids, Pa. 19087
Telephone: (215) 985-1600, ext. 460
Program Reaches: n/a
When Started: October, 1971
Budget: n/a

Program Outline:

To increase purchasing of goods and services from minority vendors, Sun plans to stimulate the economic growth of minority enterprises which strengthen the business community by providing additional suppliers and new jobs in the minority community. Since this program includes minority vendors who may not be fully competitive, one or more of the usual purchasing criteria may have to be relaxed within the range of company specifications. It is not the intent of this program to injure any of the existing vendors which have served the company well.

Co. Personnel Involved: many as part of their job; 1 full time

Measure of Success: Sun has increased the number of minority vendors identified and has increased the volume of business done with these vendors.

ALL-PRO ENTERPRISES, Inc.

THE TRAVELERS INSURANCE CO.
One Tower Square
Hartford, Conn. 06ll5

Business: Insurance	Sales: 3,000mm
CEO: Morrison H. Beach	Employees: 30,000

Contact: James R. Miller, II
Address: same as above
Telephone: (203) 277-2906
Program Reaches: n/a
When Started: 1970
Budget: The company has invested $500,000 in this concern

Program Outline:

The purpose of this program, co-sponsored by Aetna Life and Casualty, Berkshire Life, Connecticut Mutual and the Travelers Corp., is to provide opportunities for Blacks to own and operate their own businesses. It does this by operating as franchisor to a chain of fast food stores located in the inner city areas of several large metropolitan cities.

In addition to implementing the main purpose of the program, the company provides employment opportunities for persons in the inner city areas.

Co. Personnel Involved: n/a

Measure of Success: n/a

URBAN NATIONAL, INC.

THE TRAVELERS INSURANCE CO.
One Tower Square
Hartford, Conn. 06115

Business: Insurance	Sales: 3,000mm
CEO: Morrison H. Beach	Employees: 30,000

Contact: James R. Miller, II
Address: same as above
Telephone: (203) 277-2906
Program Reaches: n/a
When Started: 1971
Budget: n/a

Program Outline:

Urban National, Inc. is a company whose objective is to make venture capital loans and provide technical assistance to minority-owned businesses. The Travelers has invested $500,000 in this project.

Urban National will focus initially on the need for economic development of ghettos: (1) the need for capital; (2) the need for trained manpower; and (3) the need for community leadership and control. Without capital there can be no basis of economic development. Without adequate training the poor cannot achieve significant social or economic mobility or self sufficiency. Most importantly, without community leadership and control, a base for future development cannot be created and current frustration cannot be alleviated. To solve these problems, Urban National will work with indigenous community leadership to develop a base for capital formation.

Co. Personnel Involved: 3 man-months

Measure of Success: unknown as of now

BLACK OWNED SALES AND SERVICE CENTERS

UNIROYAL, INC.
1230 Avenue of the Americas
New York, N.Y. 10020

Business: Manufacturing Rubber Products, Plastics, Chemicals, etc.
Sales: 1,678mm
CEO: George R. Vila   Employees: 64,168

Contact: H. D. Smith, V.P., Publ. Affairs
Address: same as above
Telephone: (212) 247-5000
Program Reaches: n/a
When Started: n/a
Budget: n/a

Program Outline:

Uniroyal has supported Black-owned tire sales and service centers. Each was started in collaboration with the Federal Small Business Administration. Uniroyal joined with the government to establish these tire centers, franchised to sell the company's passenger, truck, farm and industrial tires to retail commercial and wholesale buyers. The company provided management counsel and training assistance in site location and building design, guidance in advertising and sales training for all employees.

Co. Personnel Involved: n/a

Measure of Success: n/a

"ENTERPRISE"

UNITED BANK OF DENVER
1740 Broadway
Denver, Colo. 80217

Business: Banking   Sales: not applicable
CEO: John D. Hershner   Employees: 966

Contact: C. Bennett Lewis, V. P.
Address: same as above
Telephone: (303) 244-8811, ext. 271
Program Reaches: approx. 100
When Started: department started in May, 1971
Budget: approx. $5 million

Program Outline:

Through the "enterprise" department of the Bank, various services will be performed, designed to assist small businesses in starting up and realizing their full potential.

This department offers assistance through counseling to small businesses and through evaluation and coordination of community resources for technical and management resources in the start-up and maintenance of a small business enterprise. As a part of the service, the Bank has printed and distributed a "How to Apply for A Small Business Loan" guide. This describes some of the small enterprises the Bank has helped finance, and in very concise layman's language, it provides information on how to prepare a small business loan request. The booklet includes simple worksheets that are easy to read and understand. The booklet is designed to make the process of requesting and receiving a loan as simple as possible and at the same time make the loan recipient fully aware of responsibilities that the loan entails.

Co. Personnel Involved: 5

Measure of Success: approx. 50 successful businesses

JOB DEVELOPMENT CORPORATIONS

UNITED CALIFORNIA BANK
600 S. Spring Street
Los Angeles, Cal. 90054

Business: Banking
CEO: Norman Barker, Jr.

Sales: not applicable
Employees: 10,000

Contact: Dr. Larry Wilson, V.P.
Address: same as above
Telephone: (213) 624-0111, ext. 2813
Program Reaches: n/a
When Started: see below
Budget: April 1, 1970

Program Outline:

The purpose of these programs started by UCB was to found companies that could make loans to minority entrepreneurs who cannot qualify for direct bank loans.

In cooperation with 6 other banks in the San Francisco Bay area, UCB formed Opportunity Through Ownership in March, 1969 and helped fund the corporation (OPTO) with $1.05 million, later doubled to $2.1 million. Collaborating with 7 other banks in the Los Angeles Clearinghouse Association, the Bank helped form a similar corporation in Southern California in May, 1970 providing $282,200 of the initial $2 million funding. This company is known as Los Angeles Job Development Corporation.

Co. Personnel Involved: John Greenwood, a UCB vice president, was loaned to LAJDC for 1 year and has served as its first president. Elmer L. Stone, Senior V.P., represents UCB on the Board of Directors.

Measure of Success: Since beginning operations April 1, 1970 through March 1, 1971, LAJDC has had 164 loan contracts for a requested dollar amount in excess of $5 million. It has approved 21 loans for $470,650. There are 12 proposals under consideration by the staff and 27 have been withdrawn. Fifty-one proposals representing a dollar amount in excess of $2 million are presently inactive.

MINORITY BUSINESS DEVELOPMENT

UNITED CALIFORNIA BANK
600 S. Spring Street
Los Angeles, Cal. 90054

Business: Banking
CEO: Norman Barker, Jr.

Sales: not applicable
Employees: 10,000

Contact: Dr. Larry Wilson, V.P.
Address: same as above
Telephone: (213) 624-0111
When Started: see below
Budget: see below

Program Outline:

The purpose of these programs is to aid minority businessmen in forming their own operations through loans and management assistance.

In 1970, the Bank received 28 SBA loan requests and of these 13 were approved for $526,800; an additional 4 loans were approved for $351,000 in 1971. Two of the loans are noteworthy in that they permitted the opening of nursery schools in the Watts area for working mothers. Several others were made to minority businessmen to enable them to expand their operations and capability.

Additionally, UCB made a number of loans (not needing SBA guarantees) to Magnificent Hair Products for $200,000, a $300,000 line of credit to the Schlitz Brewing Company distributorship run by Willie Davis, former defensive star for the Green Bay Packers, and over $50,000 to Negroes to enable them to secure Kentucky Fried Chicken outlets.

Co. Personnel Involved: all lending officers

Measure of Success: 1971, 260 conventional minority business loans—$5,252,124.19; 33 SBA guaranteed loans to minority business—$2,000,000

**BANCAP CORPORATION
(MESBIC)**

UNITED STATES TRUST CO. OF NEW YORK
45 Wall Street
New York, N.Y. 10005

Business: Trust Banking
Sales: not applicable
CEO: Charles W. Buck   Employees: 1,500

Contact: Robert Lane
Address: same as above
Telephone: (212) 425-4500
Program Reaches: n/a
When Started: 1971
Budget: originally capitalized at $1 million

Program Outline:

The purpose of the program is to provide equity financing for minority enterprises.

BANCAP Corp. provides financing for qualified minority owned or operated businesses in the New York Metropolitan area. It is a vehicle to provide venture capital and equity investments to develop new and existing minority business.

Co. Personnel Involved: 1—member of board of directors

Measure of Success: A number of loans have been made.

HOUGH MANUFACTURING CO.

WARNER & SWASEY CO.
11000 Cedar Avenue
Cleveland, Ohio 44106

Business: Manufacturing Machine Tools, Construction Equipment and Textile Equipment
Sales: 120mm
CEO: Joseph T. Bailey   Employees: 4,338

Contact: J. H. Tinsley, Dir. Pub. Affairs
Address: same as above
Telephone: (216) 431-6015
Program Reaches: people of the inner city
When Started: n/a
Budget: n/a

Program Outline:

The purpose of the establishing of Hough Manufacturing Company was to provide the beginnings of minority enterprise in an inner city ghetto community.

The company was established to promote minority enterprise and to provide employment for the citizens of the community. The company has two divisions: a machine shop and a fiberglass shop, capable of laying up large fiberglass parts.

Co. Personnel Involved: n/a

Measure of Success: The original goal of Warner & Swasey was to eventually produce a wholly independent, employee and community-owned company. When the company elected to go for total Black management, it sacrificed experience. Therefore, Hough Manufacturing Company has been plagued by high turn-over, absenteeism and poor-quality production. These, plus inaccurate cost estimating and poor pricing, bidding too low in order to get jobs, forced a change of plans. Warner and Swasey attempted to merge this company into a larger, better managed one but did not succeed. Warner & Swasey therefore, concluded that the best solution for Hough Manufacturing Company was to sell its shares to the little company and retire from the field, which has recently been done.

FINANCIAL ASSISTANCE TO MINORITY ENTREPRENEURS (FAME)

VALLEY NATIONAL BANK
141 N. Central Avenue
Phoenix, Ariz. 85001

Business: Banking   Sales: not applicable
CEO: Earl L. Bimson   Employees: 4,270

Contact: William Best, Jr., Dir. Corp. Rel.
Address: same as above
Telephone: (602) 261-2063
Program Reaches: Some 60 such businesses have been started
When Started: February, 1969
Budget: n/a

Program Outline:

The purpose of the program is to expand the opportunity for minority ownership and operation of a successful business enterprise.

Through special attention and consideration in depth to minority individuals, the Bank offers assistance in the form of capital, as well as structural, organizational, and management advice. The Bank also provides, free of charge, professional counseling from advisors in the business community, i.e. attorneys, CPA's, and retailers.

Co. Personnel Involved: n/a

Measure of Success: Of the 60 minority businesses that were given this consideration, 58 of them have succeeded.

SPECIAL EDUCATION PROGRAM

WEYERHAEUSER CO.
2525 S. 336th Street
Federal Way
Tacoma, Wash. 98401

Business: Sawmills Manufacturing, Hardwood, Plywood Containers
Sales: 1,233mm
CEO: George H. Weyerhaeuser   Employees: 42,721

Contact: Benjamin Burton
Address: P. O. Box 1060
    Hot Springs, Ark. 71901
Telephone: (501) 623-9762
Program Reaches: 350
When Started: 1970
Budget: n/a

Program Outline:

The purpose of the program is to hire and train disadvantaged individuals for jobs, and help them adjust to the basic orientation of working in the facilities in Arkansas.

In 1970, Weyerhaeuser bought Dierks Forest, Inc., a company with about 1,800,000 acres of forest. Capital investments went into development of new mills, facilities, etc. With these new facilities came the need for new employees. The Special Education Programs were designed specifically to help the citizens of the community around which Weyerhaeuser built. They were tied in with a strong Human Relations Program and a group basic-orientation for all new employees. The company attempted to convey a sense of individuality and importance to all entry level employees. An employee would be shown around the plant and given a chance to see the area and the people with whom he would be working. Then he would be given an opportunity to decide if he wanted to work there.

Co. Personnel Involved: n/a

Measure of Success: The Program of basic orientation for all disadvantaged employees was expanded to include all entry-level employees. The start-up operation was considered one of the smoothest operations that the company has ever had.

FIGHTON

XEROX CORP.
Stamford, Conn. 06904

Business: Diversified Office Machines
Sales: 1,719mm
CEO: C. Peter McColough   Employees: 38,339

Contact: DeLeon McEwen, Jr. or Ron Jones
Address: Xerox Corp., Xerox Square
   Rochester, N.Y. 14603
Telephone: (716) 436-9880
Program Reaches: n/a
When Started: 1969
Budget: $800,000—The funds to launch the Fighton came largely from a $450,000 U.S. Labor Dept. manpower training grant.

Program Outline:

The purpose of this program is to set up a peoples' manufacturing enterprise to be called FIGHTON, that will employ inner city residents. It is owned and operated by a militant Black community group called FIGHT (Freedom, Integration, God, Honor—Today) and was established with the help of Xerox Corporation. The aim is to satisfy a mounting clamor for " Black capitalism."

The company (FIGHTON) produces metal stampings and electrical transformers, and Xerox has guaranteed to buy $1.2 million of the firm's output over a 2-year period. In addition, Xerox assists in training management and production workers of FIGHTON, and it provides technical and managerial support and counseling, through the loan of 2 key management advisors. Also, Xerox opened the doors to bank financing.

Almost all the company's workers, with the exception of managerial personnel, were once hard-core unemployables. Because few new employees have had any experience in the metalworking trades, training can be a more difficult task than in most plants. Training is both formal and informal, with the latter consisting largely of one-to-one instruction in which a department supervisor or a veteran employee teaches the new worker right on the job. The curriculum at FIGHTON includes everything from teaching basic work habits on up through blueprint reading, various shop procedures, math, principles of electricity, etc. Classroom work, which takes place in the plant, also included courses designed to improve the knowledge and upgrade experienced workers. FIGHTON is a place where the disadvantaged can get a new start at a decent wage (about $2.10 to start), learn a respectable trade, and feel a sense of participation in a new, growing industry.

Co. Personnel Involved: n/a

Measure of Success: FIGHTON employs 75 persons, 80% of whom were hard-core unemployed when hired, and showed a profit for the first time last year. Though subsidies have maintained the company to date, it is hoped that by 1973 FIGHTON will be self-supporting. During its first 9 months of operation, FIGHTON lost 23 of its original employees, 20 of them to other jobs. This created problems in maintaining smooth operation, but was in line with what FIGHTON's originators had hoped for. Those who quit went to higher paying jobs for which they weren't qualified before FIGHTON.

health

MOBILE DENTAL CARE UNIT

CITIZENS AND SOUTHERN NATIONAL BANK
99 Annex
Atlanta, Ga. 30399

Business: Banking   Sales: not applicable
Total Assets: $2,065,374,460
CEO: Mills B. Lane, Jr.   Employees: 3,550

Contact: William J. VanLandingham
Address: same as above
Telephone: (404) 588-2774
Program Reaches: 11,000 children
When Started: April, 1971—started raising money; October, 1971—began treating patients
Budget: $25,000/year; Public Affairs Dept. raised $100,000 to get the project started.

Program Outline:

The Mobile Dental Unit was established to bring children of less advantaged families accustomed to little or no dental care, the care they need. A complete mobile unit was built into a large bus, including 3 dentist's offices, complete with all necessary equipment. Approximately 75% of the local dentists volunteered a day of their time. The bus travels an established route, visiting schools, where children are allowed complete necessary dental work.

Total cost of the mobile unit was approximately $50,000 of which 40% was raised by local school children selling tubes of toothpaste at $1.00 a tube. The bank and several other interested participants made up the remainder of the cost.

Co. Personnel Involved: One hundred people were actively involved in the initial thrust of the program.

Measure of Success: Since the Dental Unit started treating patients on October 22, 1971, records show 2500 children have been treated for fillings, extractions, etc. There have also been 650 X-ray examinations.

NATIONAL CYSTIC FIBROSIS RESEARCH FOUNDATION

COMPTON ADVERTISING, INC.
625 Madison Avenue
New York, N.Y. 10022

Business: Advertising   Sales: 130mm
CEO: Milton Gossett   Employees: 486

Contact: Robert B. McCreery, Pres.
Address: 3379 Peachtree Road, N.E., Atlanta, Ga. 30326
Telephone: (404) 262-1100
Program Reaches: hard to estimate
When Started: Compton has been handling advertising for 3 years
Budget: approx. $2 million

Program Outline:

The purpose of the program is to get more public and government support for research, etc.

As part of this program Compton assists the National Cystic Fibrosis Research Foundation in fund raising. It also serves to educate the public about the number of children (about 5 million) who are suffering from serious lung diseases.

Co. Personnel Involved: Three: art director and writer create all advertising material for each year's drive, agency president acts in advisory capacity.

Measure of Success: More funds have been raised, more volunteers recruited, new chapters are opening and more children are being treated. There has been an upsurge of interest in genetic diseases which has resulted in a Federal appropriation to a Genetic Task Force. Whether this was due entirely to advertising is difficult to say.

MENTALLY RETARDED TRAINING PROGRAM

ECONOMICS LABORATORY, INC.
Park Drive
White Plains, N.Y. 10604

Business: Manufacturing Consumer Dishwasher
    Detergents and Industrial and
    Institutional Cleaners
Sales: 129.6mm
CEO: Edward B. Osborn   Employees: 3,400

Contact: John T. Thielke
Address: same as above
Telephone: (914) 694-8626
Program Reaches: attempts to reach all trainable MRs
When Started: 1968
Budget: n/a

Program Outline:

The purpose of the program is to assist state agencies and associations in setting up a continuing program to select, train and find jobs for trainable mentally retarded people.

The program consists of schooling the educable mentally retarded in restaurant and institutional food service duties such as dishwashing, sanitation procedures, and machine operation.

Co. Personnel Involved: 3—1 full time; 2 part time

Measure of Success: 300-400 MRs now working full time earning a minimum or better wage—without job they cost society $3500/year, now they earn $3500/year; net gain $7000/year x 300 = $210,000

MANTUA COMMUNITY VECTOR CONTROL UNIT

GENERAL ELECTRIC
RE-ENTRY AND ENVIRONMENTAL
SYSTEMS DIVISION
3198 Chestnut Street
Philadelphia, Pa. 19101

Business: Aerospace and Environmental Systems
Sales: n/a
CEO: Otto Klima, Jr., V.P. & Div. Gen. Mgr., RESD
Employees: 4,000

Contact: Hezekiah "Doc" Thomas
Address: 3326 Melon St., Philadelphia, Pa. 19104
Telephone: (215) 222-3741 or 382-5611
Program Reaches: 22,000 in target area
When Started: 1968
Budget: $20,000

Program Outline:

The MCVCU has a double purpose: to exterminate and to educate. The unit works in Mantua, an 81-block Philadelphia community where rats, mice, roaches and flies are a constant health problem. Generally, the cost of an exterminator in Mantua is $25, a price few residents can afford. However, with G.E.'s help, the MCVCU can charge only $3/visit. Since this low charge doesn't cover the basic costs, the Employee Community Service Fund of General Electric helps MCVCU purchase pesticides and meet operational costs. Education of the residents about the causes of pests and how to get rid of them is the second task of the unit. On each service call, residents are taught to identify all kinds of pests and to understand the diseases each carries and spreads. Where possible, actual samples of the pests are used as object lessons. GE RESD assists through the preparation of easy-to-follow brochures.

Co. Personnel Involved: Five, at various stages plus employee contribution; involvement has been supportive but not intimate, though regular contact is kept.

Measure of Success: Modest profits from the unit help to support "Mantua Mobilization," an effort to bring school and church groups into the ghetto to work with the people. Numerous families have had their residences freed of rodents through the work of the unit and fewer rat bites of children have been experienced.

4—H NUTRITION PROGRAM

GENERAL FOODS CORP.
250 North Street
White Plains, N.Y. 10602

Business: Major Consumer Goods Manufacturing
  (particularly food)
Sales: 2,200mm
CEO: Tex Cook   Employees: 44,000

Contact: Elena Smith
Address: mail code N2-3, same as above
Telephone: (914) 694-2420
Program Reaches: 700,000
When Started: approx. 1960
Budget: n/a

Program Outline:

The purpose of the program is to improve understanding of nutrition in American youth. In its effort to help 4-H members and young people in general, the program asks young members to complete simple food projects. Advanced members study nutrition, plan balanced family meals and menus, shop for food, cook it and then serve it on a properly set table.

Co. Personnel Involved: indeterminate

Measure of Success: impossible to calculate

NUTRITION AWARENESS PROGRAM

THE GRAND UNION CO.
100 Broadway
East Paterson, N.J. 07407

Business: Retail Food and General Merchandise Chain
Sales: 1,300mm
CEO: Charles G. Rodman   Employees: 26,000

Contact: Jean F. Judge
Address: same as above
Telephone: (201) 796-4800
Program Reaches: estimated 3 million
When Started: September, 1971
Budget: n/a

Program Outline:

The purpose of this program is to increase the consumer's knowledge about good nutrition; what it means and how to achieve it. Good nutrition, and how to shop for it, was featured in institutional newspaper advertising inserts, on radio and through extensive in-store signs. Nutritionally-balanced menus were distributed to customers in 225 supermarkets in the chain's New York Region. In Connecticut, nutrition information centers were established on a pilot basis for several weeks in 6 supermarkets and were staffed with personnel from the Connecticut Extension Service who were available to answer questions from customers. The program operated on an experimental basis for 6 weeks and ended in November, 1971. During 1972, Grand Union plans to utilize some of the more successful ideas from the program.

Co. Personnel Involved: n/a

Measure of Success: No formal study was conducted to measure the program's success, but informal reactions from customers and consumer educators indicate the program was exceptionally well-received.

RECYCLING CENTER

HEWLETT-PACKARD CO.
1501 Page Mill Road
Palo Alto, Cal. 94304

Business: Electronic, Medical, Analytical and Computing
  Instrumentation
Sales: 375mm
CEO: William R. Hewlett   Employees: 16,000

Contact: Matt Schmutz
Address: same as above
Telephone: (415) 493-1501
Program Reaches: all HP employees at divisions and
  offices where a cycling center has been established
When Started: 1970
Budget: n/a

Program Outline:

A program for recycling waste computer paper printout
and cards has been started by the corporate Bay Area
Electronic Data Processing Center of HP. It is estimated
that more than 140 tons in printout and IBM cards can
be recycled during the coming year. One source reported
that each 115 pounds that is recycled will save 1 tree.
Most other HP divisions have their own recycling centers.
Recycling of company-generated waste paper materials in
many cases has resulted from the private initiative of
interested employees. One outgrowth of the recycling
project has been the use of used computer cards in the
Palo Alto's Association for the Retarded.

The donated used cards have both monetary and thera-
peutic value. Sale of the recyclable paper and cards has
brought in more than $1,000 a month to the association,
but the highlight of the program is the enthusiasm with
which retarded youngsters and adults take to the job of
sorting the cards by color. This activity increases the
recycle value of the cards significantly, and the money
the participants earn represents for many of them the
first success they've had in life. The twice monthly
payday is a big event.

Contact for the Card Donation Program:
  George Lewis, Personnel Manager
  HP Automatic Measurement Division
  Palo Alto Office
  (415) 326-1755

Co. Personnel Involved: almost all who are involved with
the use of recyclable computer printout paper and cards

Measure of Success: financially, the more than
$1,000/month earned by Palo Alto's Association for the
Retarded; on a more human level, the enthusiasm and
feeling of success experienced by the retarded children
and adults who participate

LOW COST COOKERY

HUNT-WESSON FOODS, INC.
1645 Valencia Drive
Fullerton, Cal. 92634

Business: Manufacturing Foods and Matches
Sales: 400mm
CEO: Edward Gelsthorpe   Employees: 6,800

Contact: Kenneth J. Ward, Dir. Corp. Rel.
Address: same as above
Telephone: (714) 871-2100
Program Reaches: n/a
When Started: 1968
Budget: About 2.5mm was spent in advertising and
  material preparations.

Program Outline:

This program is a campaign to show women how they
could shop and prepare more nutritious meals for less
money. It could help anyone who cooks meals for
themselves or their families. The program involved a
series of newspaper ads over a period of 9 months. The
campaign told how to select various cuts of meat,
poultry, fish, etc. and gave preparation tips, recipes and
meal planning ideas. It also published the USDA Plentiful
Foods for that month and offered a special low cost
cookery cookbook published by Hunt-Wesson.

Additionally, the company did a special campaign on the
Low Cost Cookery idea which was expanded into Black
media such as EBONY and Black newspapers in selected
cities. This campaign was entitled "The Little Cookbooks" and featured Esther Coley, one of the company's
home economists.

Co. Personnel Involved: n/a

Measure of Success: Because of the excellent results
experienced with the Lost Cost Cookery program, the
company knew it wanted to build a similar program for
the next year. They wanted one that could do an even
better job in helping the American consumer understand
that he could buy food inexpensively, and more important, that inexpensive food could be both nutritious
and interesting. As a result, Hunt-Wesson's Computer
Menu Program was created.

NUTRITION ASSISTANCE PROGRAM FOR THE NEEDY

HUNT-WESSON FOODS, INC.
1645 W. Valencia Drive
Fullerton, Cal. 92634

Business: Manufacturing Foods and Matches
Sales: 400mm
CEO: Edward Gelsthorpe   Employees: 6,800

Contact: Kenneth J. Ward, Dir. Corp. Rel.
Address: same as above
Telephone: (714) 871-2100
Program Reaches: n/a
When Started: 1970
Budget: n/a

Program Outline:

With the knowledge that other programs Hunt-Wesson has had have failed to communicate with that 20% of the population who have low incomes, low educational levels and are least apt to be reached by conventional media, and the fact that these are the people who need and can benefit from such a program the most, the Nutrition Assistance Program for the Needy was initiated.

With the cooperation of Ralph's Grocery Co. in Los Angeles, Hunt-Wesson began a pilot program in 3 of the stores located in the Watts section of L.A. A local home economist was first recruited, then 3-5 women in the neighborhood around each store, and a 3-week course in nutrition, meal planning, food shopping and purchasing was conducted. In short, the objective was to provide all the information that would help the ghetto-dweller get the most value for her dollar.

The main concept of the plan was to establish one-to-one communication. The shoppers' guides, as they were called, were stationed in the stores during peak shopping periods and met shoppers in the aisles. Their objective was to point out ways to get more balanced diets on a set budget through wise planning, spending and meal preparation. Pamphlets on the subject were distributed by the guides. The guides are paid by Hunt-Wesson, but do not attempt to influence brand purchase attitudes. No mention was made of Hunt-Wesson, nor did the pamphlets carry the Hunt-Wesson name.

Co. Personnel Involved: 12-15 total, home economists plus administrative personnel

Measure of Success: The program has been in operation for just over a year. It has worked and Hunt-Wesson plans to continue it indefinitely. The company is in the process of now working with others in the food and supermarket industry to expand the program. It is planned to share the company's information, experiences and personnel and whatever else is necessary with others to ensure its successful implementation in other areas of need.

SNACK PACK

HUNT-WESSON FOODS, INC.
1645 W. Valencia Drive
Fullerton, Cal. 92634

Business: Manufacturing Foods and Matches
Sales: 400mm
CEO: Edward Gelsthorpe   Employees: 6,800

Contact: Kenneth J. Ward
Address: same as above
Telephone: (714) 871-2100
Program Reaches: hard to estimate
When Started: Fall, 1971
Budget: combined—$500,000

Program Outline:

This brand has been involved in 2 service campaigns. In the first, Snack Pack participated in a national UNICEF Drive. The second had to do with an education program the company felt obliged to undertake in relation to the new, easy-open Snack Pack cans.

(1) In the UNICEF drive, through the contribution of labels, needy children can be immunized against whooping cough, diptheria and tetanus. The company estimates this program will result in several thousand vaccinations for needy children throughout the world.

(2) It seemed, because the container was new and was oriented toward children, that a problem with cuts due to mishandling was experienced. The company ran a letter to parents in a national women's magazine, plus did a special television commercial aimed at children, as well as adults, to educate them on opening the container.

Co. Personnel Involved: 5 people, primarily marketing and advertising as well as sales promotion

Measure of Success: $135,569 was donated to UNICEF as a result of this program

"WE'LL HELP YOU MAKE IT"
COMPUTERIZED MENU PLAN PROGRAM

HUNT-WESSON FOODS, INC.
1645 W. Valencia Drive
Fullerton, Cal. 92634

Business: Manufacturing Food and Matches
Sales: 400mm
CEO: Edward Gelsthorpe   Employees: 6,800

Contact: Kenneth J. Ward, Dir. Corp. Rel.
Address: same as above
Telephone: (714) 871-2100
Program Reaches: so far, 1,300,000
When Started: 1970
Budget: Over 1 million was spent on the preparation of
  the plan and its distribution.

Program Outline:

The program's purpose is to provide women with specialized menu planning in accordance with their family's needs and budget. Women are asked to give Hunt-Wesson the number of people in their family in certain age groups along with their weekly food budget. In return, they receive a personalized computer menu plan covering a menu for breakfast, lunch and dinner for 30 days. All the meals are designed to feed the particular family size within the specified weekly food budget.

In total, the company prepared and offered 3 separate menu plans and as of January 1972, 1,300,000 requests have been received and filled. Each day's menu is nutritionally balanced, as well.

Co. Personnel Involved: 15-20 people ranging from home economists, marketing personnel, management people, etc.

Measure of Success: This plan was endorsed by the U.S. Department of Agriculture and has been commended by consumers and the grocery trade alike. The program received Congressional Commendation and was read into the Congressional Record.

1ST DAY OF YOUR PERSONAL COMPUTERIZED MENU PLAN

BREAKFAST	DINNER
GRAPEFRUIT SECTIONS	HOME-STYLE ROSEMARY
GRIDDLE CAKES WITH SYRUP	FRIED CHICKEN
BACON STRIPS	PARSLEY BOILED POTATOES
BEVERAGE	BUTTERED GREEN BEANS
	LETTUCE WEDGES WITH
LUNCH	CHILI SAUCE MAYONNAISE
SLOPPY JOES	
POTATO STICKS/PICKLES	
CARROT SLAW	
BROWNIES	
BEVERAGE	

TIP: FOR EXTRA VALUE AND ASSURED QUALITY, SELECT
A CHICKEN WEARING A WING TAG: "EXTRA TENDER".

3RD DAY OF YOUR PERSONAL COMPUTERIZED MENU PLAN

BREAKFAST	DINNER
PINEAPPLE JUICE	CONSOMME
READY-TO-EAT CEREAL	HOT SALMON MOUSSE
TOASTED ENGLISH MUFFINS	GREEN PEAS FLUFFY TURNIPS
GRAPE JELLY	PAN FRIED POTATOES
BEVERAGE	ICE CREAM
	BEVERAGE
LUNCH	
EASY LASAGNE	
TOSSED MIXED SALAD	
FRESH FRUIT PLATTER	
CHEESE WEDGES	
BEVERAGE	

2ND DAY OF YOUR PERSONAL COMPUTERIZED MENU PLAN

BREAKFAST	DINNER
ORANGE JUICE	CREAMED HAM
SCRAMBLED EGGS WITH HAM CUBES	FRENCH FRIED POTATOES
TOAST MARMALADE	CRISP ONION RINGS
BEVERAGE	LETTUCE WEDGES WITH
	THOUSAND ISLAND DRESSING
LUNCH	CHERRY PIE
CHICKEN SOUP	BEVERAGE
ROMANO PIZZA	
TOSSED GREEN SALAD	
BEVERAGE	

4TH DAY OF YOUR PERSONAL COMPUTERIZED MENU PLAN

BREAKFAST	DINNER
FRESH FRUIT	SAVORY VEAL STEW
READY-TO-EAT CEREAL	WHIPPED POTATOES
TOAST STRAWBERRY JAM	TOSSED GREEN SALAD
BEVERAGE	BOSTON CREAM PIE
	BEVERAGE
LUNCH	
JIFFY LUNCH SKILLET	
COLE SLAW	
BUTTERSCOTCH PUDDING	
BEVERAGE	

HOME STYLE ROSEMARY FRIED CHICKEN
1 FRYING CHICKEN, 2 1/2 TO 3 LBS.
3/4 CUP FLOUR
1 TEASPOON SALT
1/8 TEASPOON PEPPER
1 TEASPOON ROSEMARY
1 CUP WESSON OIL FOR FRYING

WASH AND DRY CHICKEN PIECES WELL. PUT FLOUR,
SALT, PEPPER AND ROSEMARY IN PAPER BAG. PLACE CHICK.
IN BAG; SHAKE TO COAT. HEAT WESSON OIL IN SKILLED
MEDIUM HEAT FOR 3 MIN. PLACE CHICKEN IN OIL. FRY
TURNING FREQUENTLY UNTIL BROWN. REMOVE AND DRAIN ON
ABSORBENT PAPER. PLACE ON HOT PLATTER; KEEP WARM UNTIL
SERVING TIME.

BISCUITS
2 CUPS SIFTED ALL PURPOSE FLOUR
1 TABLESPOON BAKING POWDER
1 TEASPOON SALT
1/3 CUP SNOWDRIFT
3/4 CUP MILK

SIFT FLOUR, BAKING POWDER AND SALT. CUT IN SNOWDRIFT
TO CONSISTENCY OF CORN MEAL. STIR IN MILK. TURN OUT
ON LIGHTLY FLOURED SURFACE; KNEAD LIGHTLY 6 TO 8 TIMES.
ROLL 1/2 TO 3/4 INCH THICK. CUT WITH FLOURED BISCUIT
CUTTER, PLACE ON UNGREASED BAKING SHEET. BAKE AT 450
FOR 12 RO 14 MINUTES. MAKES 12-16.

GLAZED PORK ROAST
1 PORK SHOULDER ROAST (4 TO 4 1/2 LBS.)
SALT AND PEPPER
1/2 CUP HUNT'S KETCHUP
1 TABLESPOON BROWN SUGAR
1 TEASPOON DRY MUSTARD
1 CAN (15 OUNCES) HUNT'S PEACH HALVES - DRAINED

PLACE ROAST, FAT SIDE UP ON RACK IN SHALLOW BAKING PAN;
SPRINKLE WITH SALT AND PEPPER. INSERT MEAT THERMOMETER,
IF DESIRED. ROAST AT 350 FOR 2 HRS. MEANWHILE, COMBINE
HUNT'S KETCHUP, BROWN SUGAR AND DRY MUSTARD, SPOON OVER
ROAST AND COOK 15 MINUTES MORE. ARRANGE PEACHES AROUND
ROAST. COOK 15 MINUTES MORE. MAKES 6 SERVINGS

SAUCEPAN BROWNIES

1/3 CUP SNOWDRIFT	1/8 TEASPOON BAKING
2 SQUARES UNSWEETENED CHOCOLATE	POWDER.
1 CUP SUGAR	1/8 TEASPOON SALT
2 EGGS	1/2 CUP CHOPPED NUT
1/2 CUPS SIFTED ALL PURPOSE FLOUR	1 TEASPOON VANILLA

IN SAUCEPAN MELT SNOWDRIFT AND CHOCOLATE OVER VERY LOW
HEAT; COOL TO LUKEWARM. BEAT IN SUGAR, THEN EGGS, 1 AT A
TIME. SIFT FLOUR, BAKING POWDER AND SALT; BLEND INTO
CHOCOLATE MIXTURE. STIR IN NUTS AND VANILLA. POUR INTO
GREASED 8 INCH SQUARE PAN. BAKE AT 350 FOR 25 TO 30 MIN.
CUT INTO SQUARES. MAKES 16 BROWNIES.

KAISER BAUXITE'S COMMUNITY PROGRAMS

KAISER ALUMINUM & CHEMICAL CORP. (KACC)
Kaiser Center
300 Lakeside Drive
Oakland, Cal. 94604

Business: Aluminum, Chemicals, Specialty Metals
    and Refractories Products, and
    Diversified Operations
Sales: 904.5mm
CEO: Thomas J. Ready, Jr.   Employees: 26,000

Contact: R. L. Spees, Corp. Dir. of Pub. Affairs
Address: same as above
Telephone: (415) 271-3967
Program Reaches: over 1,000
When Started: 1953
Budget: unable to accurately estimate

Program Outline:

Kaiser Bauxite, a subsidiary of KACC, in mining bauxite on the North Coast of Jamaica, has pursued and is continuing a comprehensive community involvement program so that the people of the area, mostly small land farmers, can understand the mining operation and the company behind it.

As part of this program Kaiser Bauxite donated a good portion of the money that has built a new hospital wing at St. Ann's Bay. This hospital serves the Jamaicans of the area and, in addition, Kaiser Bauxite's own health clinic is open for public use and training purposes for medical professionals on the island. In the area of community services, the company has been a leader in the development of beaches and restoring artificats and historical parks.

Co. Personnel Involved: Company involvement in the whole community involvement program includes: 5 management personnel; liason and support from the parent company in Oakland is supplied by 4 senior management personnel. This does not include the 150 Kaiser Bauxite salaried people working directly and indirectly with the various Jamaican communities.

Measure of Success: 90% of the supervisory personnel employed by the company are Jamaicans indicating acceptance by the local people of the company presence.

LIFE CYCLE CENTER

KIMBERLY-CLARK CORP.
N. Lake Street
Neenah, Wis. 54956

Business: Manufacturing Paper and Cellulose Products
Sales: 938mm
CEO: Darwin E. Smith   Employees: 29,051

Contact: Mary Louise Lennon
Address: Life Cycle Center, Kimberly-Clark Corp.
Telephone: (414) 729-1212, ext. 6429
Program Reaches: hard to estimate
When Started: 1967
Budget: n/a

Program Outline:

The Life Cycle Center is a clearinghouse for information on the various phases of womanhood from the pre-teen through the mature years. It is an outgrowth of Kimberly-Clark's original basic education program on menstrual hygiene that the company started 50 years ago. Originally in 1922 the first booklet on menstruation was published, HEALTH FACTS ON MENSTRUATION. During WW II, THAT DAY IS HERE AGAIN was distributed to industries throughout the country and was credited with playing a substantial role in reducing absenteeism among working women. Through Walt Disney Productions, the film, THE STORY OF MENSTRUATION was produced along with supplementary booklets and has been done in many languages. Over 88 million girls and women in the United States have seen it. It also has been shown in other countries throughout the world. The company produced booklets in Braille and information for parents and teachers of retarded girls.

The Life Cycle Center program is now a multi-media approach to the teaching of feminine growth and development and sexuality, available to individuals, schools and community organizations. The Center's materials consist of 6 booklets designed for different age levels, 2 transparency series, a film and a filmstrip and introductory kits.

Co. Personnel Involved: n/a

Measure of Success: The company gets at least 1,000 letters a week asking for help and information. Kimberly-Clark's efforts have helped to dispel fears, taboos and misconceptions of the menstrual process.

JOB TRAINING FOR HANDICAPPED

LOCKHEED AIRCRAFT CORP.
P.O. Box 551
Burbank, Cal. 91503

Business: Aerospace   Sales: 2,500mm
CEO: A. Carl Kotchian   Employees: 72,000

Contact: Howard C. Lockwood, Corp. Dir. Pers.
Address: same as above
Telephone: (213) 564-5747
Program Reaches: 34
When Started: 1968
Budget: no special budget—part of company employee
    training program

Program Outline:

The purpose of the program is to train and employ handicapped individuals (deaf mutes and paraplegics).

In 1968 the Lockheed-Georgia Company employed 15 deaf mutes who had completed pre-employment training for the assembly of sophisticated electronic equipment. In 1969 2 paraplegics were employed.

Co. Personnel Involved: 2 instructors

Measure of Success: Original program was successful enough to lead to second training class of 17 deaf mutes who were trained and subsequently employed by Lockheed-Georgia in 1969. Work habits and attitudes of employees were judged excellent.

HEALTH AND WELFARE DIVISION
PUBLIC HEALTH EDUCATION

METROPOLITAN LIFE INSURANCE CO.
One Madison Avenue
New York, N.Y. 10010

Business: Insurance   Sales: 5,209mm
CEO: Richard R. Shinn   Employees: 57,000

Contact: Claude M. Eberhart, M.D.
Address: same as above
Telephone: (212) 578-5235
Program Reaches: majority of population
When Started: 1909
Budget: approx. $1 million

Program Outline:

The purpose of this program is to improve health maintenance and disease prevention through education. The Division develops and distributes publications and films in family health and safety, school health, and occupational health. Consultation, studies, correspondence in response to inquiries and cooperation with professional and community groups and individuals all are part of the work of the Division.

The current program emphasizes drug abuse, venereal disease, health observations of school children, medical emergency programs, day care and child development, weight control and physical fitness, and improvement of medical care. The Division is now also engaged in studies of prenatal health education for inner city residents and on health care delivery through health maintenance organizations; exploring an environmental education program for schools; and participating in the work of the President's Committee on Health Education.

Co. Personnel Involved: 38 on staff of Health and Welfare Division, including professionals and clerical staff, plus many other divisions of the company to a lesser degree

Measure of Success: high esteem for the program and enthusiastic reports of users concerning the quality and usefulness of the services; 90,000 inquiries annually including requests for films, publications, consultation and assistance in program-planning—many from professional and community leaders who use the services repeatedly

OPERATION GREAT CONCERN

PFIZER, INC.
235 E. 42nd Street
New York, N.Y. 10017

Business: Pharmaceuticals, Fine Chemicals,
    Cosmetics and Toiletries
Sales: 870mm
CEO: Edmund T. Pratt   Employees: 5,000

Contact: William J. Fournier
Address: same as above
Telephone: (212) 573-3664
Program Reaches: n/a
When Started: n/a
Budget: $300,000

Program Outline:

The purpose of this program is to bring about public awareness of the current V.D. epidemic—its signs and symptoms—through the cooperation of public health agencies, volunteer groups and private practicing physicians.

Physician education includes a film on V.D. treatment, programmed instruction courses on diagnosis and treatment of gonorrhea, a V.D. treatment newspaper, a yearly national symposium on V.D. and provision of support for a nationwide speaker program for local symposia including a complete slide program.

In order to facilitate public awareness of V.D., grants are available to local public health and volunteer groups. A television special, "V.D., A Plague on Our House," is available for broadcast and is also available in a special film version for small-group showing. In addition, educational brochures, posters and public education program kits have been made available.

Co. Personnel Involved: 4 full time, 150 part time

Measure of Success: countless requests for educational materials (50/day) from public service/health groups and educational institutions plus 100s of thank you letters

CREO

SYNTEX CORP.
Stanford Industrial Park
Palo Alto, Cal. 94304

Business: Pharmaceutical, Veterinary and Health Care
    Products
Sales: 100mm
CEO: George Rosenkranz   Employees: n/a

Contact: Frank Koch, Dir. of Corp. P.R.
Address: same as above
Telephone: (415) 855-6111
Program Reaches: Indian population—several thousand
When Started: 1965
Budget: n/a

Program Outline:

CREO is a non-profit medical and self-help program organized with the help of the Junior Chamber of Commerce groups in Palo Alto, California and San Cristobal, Mexico and several companies.

Volunteer doctors, nurses, student engineers, teachers and students from Stanford University spend part of their summer vacations providing medical care and constructing community health and sanitary facilities for the Indian population. Volunteer engineers last year provided permanent water supplies for the Indians who previously had no source of clean water.

The CREO group directed the building of homes by the Indians themselves in a village called Mexiquito. Syntex has supported this project for several years—once by purchasing a truck, another time by encouraging companies to donate pharmaceutical products to the project, and most recently by printing its annual report which is used for fund raising.

Co. Personnel Involved: n/a

Measure of Succes: annual reports

LOCAL HEALTH CARE SERVICES

SYNTEX CORP.
Stanford Industrial Park
Palo Alto, Cal. 94304

Business: Pharmaceutical, Veterinary and Health Care
    Products
Sales: 100mm
CEO: George Rosenkranz   Employees: n/a

Contact: Frank Koch, Dir. of Corp. P.R.
Address: same as above
Telephone: (415) 855-6111
Program Reaches: n/a
When Started: n/a
Budget: n/a

Program Outline:

Syntex has provided financial support to a number of institutions in the area including the Children's Health Council (also designed a brochure for them), the Children's Hospital at Stanford, the Community Association for the retarded. In addition, the company has contributed a quantity of its drugs to the People's Medical Center in Redwood City, Cal., an experiment in attempting to provide health care services to minorities and poor people.

Co. Personnel Involved: n/a

Measure of Success: n/a

VOICES IN SOCIETY: "TIME TO TALK"

TRAVELERS INSURANCE CO.
One Tower Square
Hartford, Conn. 06115

Business: Insurance   Sales: not applicable
Assets: 3,000mm
CEO: Morrison H. Beach   Employees: 30,000

Contact: Francis K. Holland
Address: (203) 277-4079
Telephone: (203) 277-4079
Program Reaches: 100 million plus potential
When Started: 1971
Budget: $11,000

Program Outline:

To contribute to the fight against venereal disease and suggest appropriate alleviating steps, the company made a 1-minute film that was sent to 500 T.V. stations across the country.

Using the voice-over technique, the film shows a teenage boy rushing away from his home as his parents dramatically discuss what their son has just told them—that he has contracted VD.

The camera follows the boy as he wanders, worrying, through a park where lovers walk holding hands, and later, shows him watching youngsters in a playground. The spot closes with a third voice-over which points out that VD is a disease, not a crime and that "if we discuss it openly—we can cure it."

Co. Personnel Involved: 8 in brainstorming sessions before scripting and filming, thereafter, 1 man, responsible for the project

Measure of Success: "Time to talk" was released on October 10, 1971. As of January 21, 1972, it had been broadcast 2,666 times by 108 stations in 96 cities and 40 states. It is estimated that more than 225,000,000 viewers saw the film in the total broadcast time of 44.43 hours.

MINORITY HEALTH AND MEDICAL FACILITIES

UNITED CALIFORNIA BANK
600 S. Spring Street
Los Angeles, Cal. 90054

Business: Banking
CEO: Norman Barker, Jr.

Sales: not applicable
Employees: 10,000

Contact: Dr. Larry Wilson, V.P.
Address: same as above
Telephone: (213) 624-0111, ext. 2813
Program Reaches: n/a
When Started: 1969
Budget: see below

Program Outline:

The purpose of the various projects that UCB participates in is to aid in the construction of health and medical facilities by minority groups and individuals. These projects are conducted in several areas of California and on many different levels:

(1) In collaboration with the local Black Bank of Finance and 7 other banks, UCB constructed a $4 million health center in Southeast Los Angeles known as the Central Community Mental Health Center ($216,646).

(2) Bank provided financing and management assistance for a 34-bed convalescent hospital in the Watts area of Los Angeles ($207,800).

(3) In Northern California the Bank aided in the East Palo Alto Health Center in a predominantly Black neighborhood.

(4) Bank provided interim construction financing for a medical center in San Diego by a group of Black doctors and dentists ($800,000).

(5) In Fresno, an interim construction loan to 6 Black medical doctors for the John Henry Hale Medical Center ($425,000 with an additional $60,000 to the individual doctors) was made.

(6) Also, a loan to a minority partnership to construct Fresno Westview Convalescent Hospital ($45,000 and an additional $50,000 to the hospital) was negotiated.

Co. Personnel Involved: n/a

Measure of Success: n/a

NUTRITION COUNSELING PROGRAM

WASHINGTON GAS LIGHT CO.
1100 H Street, N.W.
Washington, D. C. 20002

Business: Natural Gas Utility
CEO: Paul E. Reichardt

Sales: 135mm
Employees: 3,000

Contact: Charles C. Krautler
Address: same as above
Telephone: (202) 624-6467
Program Reaches: Since 1971, 11,713 people have been reached in 305 of Mrs. Hill's demonstrations
When Started: 1968
Budget: Mrs. Hill's salary plus expenses

Program Outline:

This program was established to teach families with low incomes how to prepare low-cost, nutritious, attractive and tasty meals in a variety of ways. In order to communicate effectively with the poorer residents of inner city Washington, the company hired Mrs. Fannie Hill as Nutrition Counselor—a person who could identify with the problems of Black people and who could offer empathy, not sympathy.

A native of Mississippi, Mrs. Hill has been cooking since she was 12 years old. She also had experienced unemployment and having to survive on a monthly welfare check. In demonstrations, she tells her audiences how to plan balanced meals and how to purchase foods economically. She prepares the meal as her audience watches, explains how food items, both supplemental and other, can be used best. Following the demonstration, the group samples the meal which has just been prepared, and informal discussions are held.

Each week, Washington Gas publishes a new recipe sheet known as "Fannie's Foods Ideas." Recently, the company began distributing them in Spanish. Mrs. Hill also gives demonstrations, with the help of an interpreter, to Spanish-speaking audiences. Her weekly recipes are designed to feed a family of 6 for $2.00, an entire meal, excluding staples.

Co. Personnel Involved: Mrs. Hill is an employee of Washington Gas Light Co.

Measure of Success: Hundreds of letters and personal calls have been received from persons of varying backgrounds, and are indicative of the warm reception Mrs. Hill receives everywhere. As a result of her popularity, she has appeared on several television shows. She was also selected by the mayor of Washington to serve on the City's Commission on Food, Nutrition and Health, and on this group's Subcommittee on Children's Food and School Lunches.

urban development

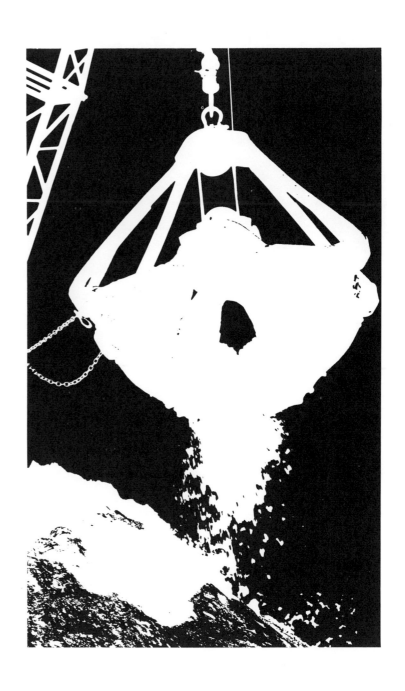

CINDERELLA NO. 2

BROOKLYN UNION GAS CO.
195 Montague Street
Brooklyn, N.Y. 11201

Business: Public Utility   Sales: 143mm
CEO: Gordon C. Griswold   Employees: 3,150

Contact: Frederic H. J. Rider
Address: same as above
Telephone: (212) 643-3881
Program Reaches: n/a
When Started: n/a
Budget: a 5-year period averaged about $500,000/year, exclusive of staff time

Program Outline:

Brooklyn Gas encourages the renaissance of Brooklyn. Not only have its officers participated virgorously in businessman's organizations especially set up for this purpose, but the company has participated in 2 home renovation projects which are having noticeable effects.

The first of these is the renovation of a dilapidated brownstone house at 211 Berkely place which attracted national attention. Thousands toured the house by appointment and there was a general revival of the whole neighborhood.

At the suggestion of a local community group, Brooklyn Union then undertook a second project, the renovation of a whole block not far from the original project. Here the company tried to pursuade builders and bankers that the abandoned houses on the periphery of a redeemable neighborhood represent a good business opportunity.

Co. Personnel Involved: n/a

Measure of Success: All the participants in this program believe that other similar neighborhoods can be brought back from decay if the company continues to take the leadership to bring the right parties together and provide the promotional muscle.

COMMUNITY DEVELOPMENT CORP.

CITIZENS & SOUTHERN NATIONAL BANK
99 Annex
Atlanta, Ga. 30399

Business: Banking   Sales: not applicable
Total Assets: $2,065,374,460
CEO: Mills B. Lane, Jr.   Employees: 3,550

Contact: William J. Van Landingham
Address: same as above
Telephone: (404) 588-2774
Program Reaches: all major Georgia cities
When Started: 1968
Budget: Currently CDC has a $3 million capital base.

Program Outline:

Community Development Corp. is a wholly-owned subsidiary of Citizens and Southern National Bank, founded for the purpose of providing minority business loans and low-income business loans, home mortgages for low-income families and low-income housing.

Business loans are made to those individuals who qualify, taking into consideration character, ability, and potentially profitable business projections. Home mortgages are provided to families who have never owned a home. Down payment financing is provided through second mortgages; first mortgages are placed in C&S National Bank or with other lenders. Five low-income housing projects have been built or renovated throughout Georgia. The businesses are provided managerial assistance by a young bank officer or management trainee on a continuing basis. Families purchasing their homes are given budgetry counseling. The housing projects have all been approached with the concept that environmental change and upgrading can substantially improve a family's present status and outlook.

The lending function of CDC is now being administered by the Bank's Term Loan Department to enable a broader managerial and technical assistance. However, all business loans are still being made by CDC.

Co. Personnel Involved: approximately 20 people on a statewide basis involved with CDC

Measure of Success: To date, 210 businesses have been financed with a total investment of $2.3 million. Over 300 home mortgages have been provided with over $800,000 currently outstanding. The 5 housing projects have produced over 200 living units.

EL MODENA IMPROVEMENT PROJECT

FIRST NATIONAL BANK OF ORANGE COUNTY
101 E. Chapman Avenue
Orange, Cal. 92669

Business: Banking   Sales: not applicable
CEO: C. E. Schroeder   Employees: 140

Contact: James Beam, V.P.
Address: same as above
Telephone: (714) 639-5000
Program Reaches: n/a
When Started: April, 1969
Budget: total cost $167,913.62

Program Outline:

The purpose of the program is to improve the physical environment of the El Modena section of the community of Orange, Calif. with the Bank providing special financial arrangements.

In its efforts to assist the Mexican-American people living in the El Modena section, First National Bank of Orange County made arrangements for special low-cost unsecured loans to property owners to go toward improving the physical condition of the area. Agreements were made between the city and the property owner and in April, 1970, the project was completed and the area of El Modena had new street lights, along with curbs, gutters, sidewalks and new streets.

Co. Personnel Involved: n/a

Measure of Success: Within the area of El Modena there is a new confidence and a determination to make things better. The people of this particular barrio are now willing and capable of doing more for themselves and for their community.

LOCAL COMMUNITY SUPPORT

FIRST NATIONAL CITY BANK
399 Park Avenue
New York, N.Y. 10022

Business: Banking   Sales: not applicable
CEO: William I. Spencer   Employees: 31,700

Contact: William G. Herbster, S.V.P.
Address: same as above
Telephone: (212) 559-4211
Program Reaches: indeterminate
When Started: primarily since 1967
Budget: urban contributions and management time

Program Outline:

The purpose of the program is to support various community organizations in New York and thus help enable them to bring about improvements in living conditions in some of the more disadvantaged areas of the City.

The Bank has traditionally been a principal supporter of the Greater New York Fund and, more recently, has been one of the leading supporters of community-oriented organizations such as the New York Urban Coalition, the Bedford-Stuyvesant Restoration Corporation and similar organizations. This is supplemented by volunteer activities of a large number of staff coordinated by a professional volunteer coordinator. In addition, experts from the Bank have provided significant managerial and technical assistance to a number of these organizations. Furthermore, this past summer the Bank undertook a Summer Intern Program which placed in excess of 130 youngsters from low-income families into community action projects which were managed by local organizations.

First National is actively involved in "joint venture" activities with the Coalition in housing and with both the Economic Development Council and the Coalition in specific high schools in hard-pressed neighborhoods.

The Bank has already designated an officer who will be working full time in South Jamaica to make Bank assistance more easily available in response to the multitude of needs of that community.

Co. Personnel Involved: 2 people full time and another 6-8 part time

Measure of Success: The Bedford-Stuyvesant Corporation, of which FNCB is one of the largest non-government supporters, is a strong viable organization with significant beneficial impact on its community. Other community organizations which are supported are also showing substantial progress.

DOWNTOWN DETROIT RIVERFRONT DEVELOPMENT

FORD MOTOR LAND DEVELOPMENT CORP.
The American Road
Dearborn, Mich. 48121

Business: Land Development   Sales: n/a
CEO: W. S. Doran   Employees: n/a

Contact: W. S. Doran, President
Address: same as above
Telephone: (313) 322-3711
Program Reaches: not determinable
When Started: third quarter 1971
Budget: ultimate value on the order of $5 million

Program Outline:

The purpose of the program is to encourage renewed interest and economic activity in the city of Detroit through an extended base of economic participants.

The program encourages business, residential, retail and convention activity through construction of an economically viable complex consisting of a major hotel of 1,500 rooms, approximately 5 million square feet of office space, 1 million square feet of retail space and 1,000 housing units. All components are to be integrated as a complex via a deck system serving parking, pedestrian traffic and service functions.

Co. Personnel Involved: Wide range of participation within FMLDC and staffs of the Ford Motor Company.

Measure of Success: Wide range of expressions of acceptance and enthusiasm by City Government, general public, potential participants and local and national news media.

OPPORTUNITY PARK URBAN RENEWAL PROJECT

THE B.F. GOODRICH CO.
500 S. Main Street
Akron, Ohio 44318

Business: Rubber   Sales: 1,205mm
CEO: H. B. Warner   Employees: 47,900

Contact: Gary J. Rine
Address: P.R. Dept., same as above
Telephone: (216) 379-3411
Program Reaches: several 1,000
When Started: 1964
Budget: $3.8 million

Program Outline:

The purpose of this program is to revitalize a badly deteriorated 404-acre area surrounding B.F. Goodrich at the south edge of the business district of Akron, Ohio.

BFG gave City of Akron $300,000 in 1964 for feasibility study, then an additional $3.5 million in 1965 to serve as the city's cash share of the project. Most of the remaining funds are coming from the federal government. This is believed to be the first time that private and public funds have meshed to pay for a renewal project. The "old" has now been removed from the area and the "new" is steadily growing. One of the first new buildings in the area was BFG's World Headquarters Building, which opened in 1970. Numerous other projects within the area are now in various stages of completion.

The program is administered by the City of Akron and individual programs within the overall project are constantly being evaluated and modified in the best interests of the community.

Co. Personnel Involved: Many people from BFG, including several of its top executives, have been and/or are involved in the project.

Measure of Success: An area infested with shabby stores, abandoned hotels and boarding houses, and dilapidated houses is fast taking on the look of a new community with a blending of industry, housing and recreational facilities.

GREATER HARTFORD COMMUNITY DEV. CORP. (DEVCO)

GREATER HARTFORD CORP.
Offices of Greater Hartford Chamber of Commerce
Constitution Plaza
Hartford, Conn. 06101

Business: Nonprofit company, supported by 27 area corporations to fund social and physical renewal development
Sales: n/a
CEO: Arthur Lunsden   Employees: n/a

Contact: Arthur Lunsden, Pres. GHC
  Peter Libassi, Pres. GHP
Address: same as above
Telephone: (203) 243-8811
Program Reaches: n/a
When Started: 1969
Budget: $10 million estimated overall corporate contributions spent or committed

Program Outline:

The purpose of Greater Hartford Process is to act as a nonprofit public service planning corporation engaged in the basic examination of the region and in the social, economic, and physical planning of the community development models. Devco's purpose is to summon capital, acquire land, engage developers, and otherwise implement physical aspects of Greater Hartford Process's plans.

This program is an effort to undertake a massive renewal and redesign of an entire city, with the help and coordinative support of 27 Hartford area businesses. It is described by the sponsors and planners in terms of not only building things and providing services, but of designing an entirely new process of community life and growth for Hartford and its region. This nonprofit corporation is a major group effort among the area's corporations and businesses to support the development of the means to design and implement new and workable designs for the rapidly growing area. Greater Hartford Process, Inc. attempts to develop and coordinate the life-support systems of this large urban center. Greater Hartford Process, Inc. brings in the experts in the applicable social fields of education, transportation, health services, etc. for the formulation of new directions and ideas in these areas to make the urban environment viable.

This corporation is an ongoing development entity. Changes, both in the nonprofit corporations and the involvement and commitment of supporting companies can be expected as Process matures.

Co. Personnel Involved: Henry R. Roberts, Chairman of Greater Hartford Process, Inc. is president of Connecticut General Life Insurance Company. Roger Wilkins, Chairman of Devco, is Chairman of Travelers Insurance Company. Other leading community executives and lower echelon management talent also contribute time to Process and Devco.

Measure of Success: too early to tell

PROJECT PRIDE

NATIONAL BANK OF DETROIT
611 Woodward Avenue
Detroit, Mich. 48232

Business: Banking   Sales: not applicable
CEO: Robert M. Surdam   Employees: 5,213

Contact: James E. Glynn, A.V.P.
Address: same as above
Telephone: (313) 965-6000
Program Reaches: 23,000 residents
When Started: May, 1970
Budget: $10,000

Program Outline:

The purpose of the program is to clean up a 55-block ghetto area of Detroit's East side.

Under the sponsorship of National Bank of Detroit, with the help of some 60 inner city organizations, citizen volunteer groups, in a single day, carried away 500 tons of refuse and distributed 1,000 trash cans, hundreds of pounds of grass and flower seeds, fertilizer and instructions for planting, fencing and lawn care. In addition, over 150 junk cars were removed and a rat extermination program carried out. To help with requests for additional campaigns in other sections, the Bank prepared a documentary report and 16mm film explaining the project.

Co. Personnel Involved: n/a

Measure of Success: Program has stimulated requests for additional clean-up campaigns in other sections of Detroit. NBD worked closely with the Greater Detroit Chamber of Commerce on a city-wide clean-up campaign known as "Pride 71" and plans are being laid for a "Pride 72" program.

PLACE DU SABLE REDEVELOPMENT PROJECT

MADISON BANK AND TRUST CO.
400 W. Madison Street
Chicago, Ill. 60606

Business: Banking   Sales: not applicable
CEO: A. Andrew Boemi   Employees: 112

Contact: Yolanda M. Deen, Dir. P.R.
Address: same as above
Telephone: (312) 332-4600
Program Reaches: impossible to estimate
When Started: conceived in '58, implemented in '68, and
    scheduled for completion in '76
Budget: Overall cost of the project is $350 million.

Program Outline:

The purpose of the program is to eliminate the area of
Chicago known as Skid Row, and to redevelop the area as
an extension of Chicago's downtown commercial and
residential section.

As the prime mover in this redevelopment concept,
Madison Bank included in its campaign not only focusing
on the area as one of great potential for the city of
Chicago, but also an action program encompassing feasibility studies, recommendations and alternatives for redevelopment as well as a new concept in the urban
renewal process. This was, namely, redevelopment on a
"no write-down" basis eliminating the use of federal,
state and municipal funds. A number of sub-objectives
had to be reached: (1) to build private and public
awareness as to the area's potential, (2) to study the area
and determine feasibility for redevelopment, and (3) to
propose alternatives for actual implementation of the
redevelopment. Also, the help of the Department of
Urban Renewal and the City of Chicago had to be
enlisted for implementation of the project.

In 1958, A. Andrew Boemi, Madison Bank's president,
organized the Gateway Committee which began to study
and research the area in order to gain a solid base of
information for the project. Due to other projects the
city felt were more pressing, no real action could be
taken until 1965 when Boemi introduced his "no write-
down" plan he had developed and the idea was finally
accepted and could be put into action.

In August, 1967, following a 2-year period of formal plan
development and orientation to gain the attention of the
business community, the Urban Renewal Department
officially declared the 6-block area as "slum and
blighted." The development plan of the accepted bidder
called for a 90-story office building of 1,215 feet, a
28-story office and apartment building and smaller retail
and community facilities. There would be a total of 5
million square feet of office space, 1,300 apartments and
3,000 automobile parking places in a 2-level subterranean
structure.

Co. Personnel Involved: Project was conceived by A.
Andrew Boemi, President of Madison Bank and Trust
Company.

Measure of Success: Place du Sable is yet to happen, but
still the project has had a definite impact on the City of
Chicago. The development of the 16-acre Place du Sable
can provide a unified and enlarged downtown as one
whole central business district while ridding the city of an
unsightly and unproductive situation. Chicago can have a
purposeful and well-planned city core, one which the
corporate world will find extremely suitable from employment and convenience standpoints.

It is expected that the areas north and south of the
project will be developed more intensively by their
owners. An influx of new businesses and new individuals
is anticipated. Now that final steps for Place du Sable are
being taken, the day moves closer to the actual completion of the auctioneer's modified lines, "Skid Row—
going, going, gone."

LASALLE PARK PROJECT

RALSTON PURINA CO.
Checkerboard Square Plaza
St. Louis, Mo. 63188

Business: Manufacturing Food and Feed
Sales: 1,700mm
CEO: Albert J. O'Brien   Employees: 24,000

Contact: John Fox
Address: same as above
Telephone: (312) 982-2765
Program Reaches: undetermined
When Started: 1968
Budget: estimate total new investment in the area to be
   $37 million

Program Outline:

The purpose of the program is to redevelop 140 urban acres in St. Louis inner city and thus provide improved housing, and locations for commercial and light industrial development.

The program calls for 500-600 housing units for low- and moderate-income families. It also envisions a mix of commercial and light industrial development. Ralston Purina Company hopes to be named Developer of the project by the local Land Clearance for Redevelopment Authority. The company has agreed to commit up to $2 million which represents the City of St. Louis's share of redevelopment costs.

Co. Personnel Involved: 25 people to varying degrees; 1 management person full time

Measure of Success: The Department of Housing and Urban Development has approved the plan and reserved $4 million for initial development work. The project has also been approved by the necessary local authorities.

CITIZENS FOR ACTING NOW, INC. (C.A.N.)

SCOTT PAPER CO.
Scott Plaza
Philadelphia, Pa. 19113

Business: Manufacturing Sanitary Paper Products
Sales: 756mm
CEO: Charles D. Dickey, Jr.
Employees: 21,700

Contact: Sam Ross
Address: 2108 Third Street
   Chester, Pa. 19013
Telephone: (215) 497-1747
Program Reaches: 4,000
When Started: July, 1970
Budget: $150,000 (1972)

Program Outline:

The purpose of this program is to upgrade persons of Census Tract 57 in Chester in 5 areas: education, housing, employment, health, and recreation.

The program has a Community Board that sets policy. It is set up to get specific directions from the community and to move in the 5 general areas listed above. Presently, the program has in operation the following: day care center, tutorial program, counseling and referral program, and a youth recreational program.

Co. Personnel Involved: One person is involved directly; a great number of company supporters are indirectly involved.

ALLEGHENY WEST COMMUNITY DEVELOPMENT PROJECT

TASTY BAKING CO.
2801 Hunting Park Avenue
Philadelphia, Pa. 19129

Business: Bakery, Cookies, Cane Sugar Refinery,
   Graphic Arts, Toys
Sales: 91mm
CEO: Paul R. Kaiser   Employees: 2,200

Contact: Philip Price, Jr.
Address: same as above
Telephone: (215) 228-4200, ext. 423
Program Reaches: 23,000
When Started: November, 1968
Budget: $80,000 in 1971; $117,000 in 1972

Program Outline:

The purpose of the program is to strengthen the community, to improve quality of life and to halt urban decay in the area bounded by Westmoreland Street, 22nd Street, Lehigh Avenue and Ridge Avenue in Philadelphia.

After meetings with community leaders, a partnership was formed: industry (supplying know-how), the city (supplying services) and the residents (supplying leadership). Tasty Baking hired 2 full time staff persons to work with the community. A 2-year trial period was agreed upon. Tasty Baking planned to ask other neighboring companies to help if the approach worked. Two nonprofit civic associations were incorporated, 5 neighborhood improvement organizations have sprung up and more than 50 block organizations have been formed to give "grass roots" direction to the renewal project. A wide variety of programs were started to improve opportunities for better education, health, jobs, recreation, housing and land use. For example, there are now 325 boys participating in 23 separate neighborhood cub packs and scout troops under a unique block scouting program pioneered at Allegheny West.

Co. Personnel Involved: 3 full time employees of The Greater Philadelphia Foundation, the nonprofit affiliate of the Greater Philadelphia Chamber of Commerce, which administers the project

Measure of Success: The residents' response has been good. By providing a way for leadership to emerge, the program has made it possible for many persons to come forward to work for the area's improvement. The groups formed still function for the betterment of the community.

Tasty Baking has met with many other companies who have made a commitment to the project, both within the area and outside.

STAMFORD AREA COMMERCE & INDUSTRY ASSOC.

CLAIROL, INC.
345 Park Avenue
New York, N.Y.

Business: Hair Color, Hair Care, Toiletries,
   Beauty Appliances
Sales: n/a
CEO: Bruce S. Gelb   Employees: 2,500

Contact: W. L. Tyson, Mgr. Com. Rels.
Address: One Blachley Road, Stamford, Conn. 06902
Program Reaches: ultimately 250,000
When Started: formally in 1970
Budget: SACIA's budget is $250,000/year.

Program Outline:

In its effort to assist in solving the urban problems of the Stamford area, to marshal the resources of the private sector, and to deal with urban problems with area companies, Clairol effected the merger of 3 business-oriented organizations: Stamford Chamber of Commerce, Management Council of Southwestern Connecticut, and Citizens Action Council, into Stamford Area Commerce & Industry Association. SACIA has 15 Action Councils including Environmental Quality, Public Safety & Justice, Educational Quality, Human Resources Development, Housing & Urban Development.

Co. Personnel Involved: Twenty-five people are assigned to Action Councils, company president serves on SACIA Board, 1 executive is chairman of Housing & Urban Development Action Council.

Measure of Success: Concerted action on environment is developing. A citizens' effort is being launched to modernize local government. SACIA has become an action center for housing and is spearheading a citizens' program for cooperation with law enforcement.

consumer safety

CHAMPION HIGHWAY SAFETY PROGRAM

CHAMPION SPARK PLUG CO.
P. O. Box 910
Toledo, Ohio 43601

Business: Manufacturing   Sales: 290mm
CEO: Robert A. Stranahan, Jr.   Employees: 11,000

Contact: R. J. Mougey, Jr.
Address: same as above
Telephone: (419) 536-3711
Program Reaches: 768,000 students/year
When Started: 1955
Budget: n/a

Program Outline:

The purpose of the program is to acquaint secondary schools and young military audiences with the responsibilities and proper attitudes in safe driving. By using sports figures, i.e. professional race drivers, the company attempts to approach the subject of highway safety from a different direction. These sports figures are uniquely able to discuss the hazards of speed, reaction time and attitudes, and to relate them to highway situations.

Co. Personnel Involved: 8 full time driver/lecturers, 1 director and assistant

Measure of Success: letters from students, parents, educators and law enforcement officials; newspaper clippings, radio and television exposure

DRIVER EDUCATION CAR LOAN PROGRAM

FORD MOTOR CO.
The American Road
Dearborn, Mich. 48121

Business: Automotive Manufacturing
Sales: 15,000
CEO: Lee A. Iacocca   Employees: 431,000

Contact: F. N. Platt
Address: same as above
Telephone: (313) 322-9171
Program Reaches: minimum of 360,000 students/year
When Started: Company support of dealer car loans began early in the 1930s; Company financial support began in mid-1950s.
Budget: $5.5 million (1971)

Program Outline:

The purpose of this program is to lend cars (through participating dealers) to state-approved private, public and parochial non-profit secondary schools for use in driver education programs. Ford encourages its dealers to support the driver education loan program throughout the U.S.

The company pays its dealers an allowance of up to $400 per vehicle placed in an approved program. Ford and Lincoln-Mercury dealers are contacted directly by school representatives requiring driver education cars.

Co. Personnel Involved: One man from each of 2 car divisions (Ford Division and Lincoln-Mercury Division), a Corporate Coordinator and secretarial assistance are involved.

Measure of Success: American Driver and Traffic Saftey Education Association (department of National Education Association) reports this program to be one of the most important contributions to driver education in high schools.

DRIVER EDUCATION FILMSTRIP PROGRAM

FORD MOTOR CO.
The American Road
Dearborn, Mich. 48121

Business: Automotive Manufacturing
Sales: 15,000mm
CEO: Lee A. Iacocca   Employees: 431,000

Contact: F. N. Platt
Address: same as above
Telephone: (313) 322-9171
Program Reaches: made available to nearly all of the
  29,000 secondary schools in the U.S.
When Started: 1959
Budget: n/a

Program Outline:

The purpose of this program is to improve traffic safety by improving driver skills through the distribution of a series of 35mm filmstrips.

Tailor-made audio-visual materials are made available to new and experienced drivers through high school driver education programs, passenger car and fleet operators, traffic courts, state driver improvement programs and driver licensing and law enforcement agencies. The driver education filmstrip packets are provided free to schools through the company's Dealer Community Affairs Committees and Corporate Community Relations Committees. The materials are also made available at no cost to the public and new materials are produced each year. Plans are to put more emphasis on the development of materials for commercial truck and passenger car fleets.

Co. Personnel Involved: department manager part time, supervisor full time plus outside film producer services

Measure of Success: Filmstrip packets are used in virtually every secondary school in the U.S. Sales of the filmstrip packets have risen steadily over the past several years. These materials are approved by the American Driver and Traffic Safety Education Association, a department of the National Education Association.

EXPERIMENTAL SAFETY CAR PROGRAM

FORD MOTOR CO.
The American Road
Dearborn, Mich. 48121

Business: Automotive Manufacturing
Sales: 15,000mm
CEO: Lee A. Iacocca   Employees: 431,000

Contact: J. D. Collins, Chief Res. Eng.
Address: Prod. Dev. Group, 21175 Oakwood Blvd.
  Dearborn, Mich. 48121
Telephone: (313) 322-9475
Program Reaches: undetermined
When Started: Spring, 1970
Budget: approx. $4,000,000

Program Outline:

The purpose of this program is to develop an experimental safety car to retain crashworthiness for barrier and pole impact speeds up to 50 mph.

The major functions of the program are: (1) to identify and analyze new technical problems; (2) to develop design ideas which could provide significant improvement in automotive safety performance and crash survivability; (3) to determine the extent to which these potential advances could be accomplished within proven manufacturing technology with practical materials; (4) to evaluate testing methods and procedures to determine the effectiveness of safety improvements.

Co. Personnel Involved: An average of 60 people are involved throughout the duration of the program. Involvement is mainly in design, build and test activities of the advanced engineering and research office of the company.

Measure of Success: increased level of understanding of the special problems of automotive safety and of practical approaches to their solutions

SNACK PACK

HUNT-WESSON FOODS, INC.
1645 West Valencia Drive
Fullerton, Cal. 92634

Business: Manufacturing Foods and Matches
Sales: 400mm
CEO: Edward Gelsthorpe   Employees: 6,800

Contact: Kenneth J. Ward, Dir. Corp. Rel.
Address: same as above
Telephone: (714) 871-2100
Program Reaches: hard to estimate
When Started: Fall, 1971
Budget: $500,000 combined

Program Outline:

Two service campaigns have been conducted by the company under this brand. The first was an educational program the company felt obliged to undertake in relation to the new easy-open Snack Pack cans. It seemed that because the container was new and was oriented toward children, a problem with cuts due to mishandling was experienced. The company ran a letter to parents in a national women's magazine and did a special television commercial aimed at children, as well as adults, to educate them on opening the container. The second involved participation in a national UNICEF drive, in which needy children, through the contributions of labels, could be immunized against whooping cough, diptheria and tetanus. It is estimated that the program will result in several thousand vaccinations throughout the world.

Co. Personnel Involved: 5 people, primarily marketing and advertising personnel as well as sales promotion

Measure of Success: $135,569 was donated to UNICEF as a result of the program

---

OPERATION: BOOBY TRAP

THE HOME INSURANCE CO.
59 Maiden Lane
New York, N.Y. 10038

Business: Insurance   Sales: 624mm
CEO: John H. Washburn   Employees: 6,270

Contact: Richard Doyle
Address: same as above
Telephone: (212) 530-7051
Program Reaches: millions
When Started: January, 1971
Budget: $50,000

Program Outline:

This program is designed to clean up the roads and highways of booby traps such as inadequate guard rails that guide out-of-control cars into unyielding signpoles, light standards and obstructions that have been placed on the highway side of the guard rail. This can usually be done without any loss of effectiveness. If terrain conditions require or dictate that necessary sign standards must be placed on the highway side, then these should be of the "breakaway" type.

Bridge abutments, especially where the bridge is narrow or where it is approached by a curving road, have caused many deaths and injuries. "Gore" areas, triangular patches between the main highway and the turn-off roads, are loaded with "booby traps" such as concrete curbs, unburied guard rail ends and above-the-ground concrete bases for fixtures and signs. Trees and large rocks kept as landscaping features and water culverts are also hazardous "booby traps" this program helps to eliminate.

Co. Personnel Involved: 100s to one degree or another

Measure of Success: correction of booby traps by highway officials

The following two pages illustrate this program.

HIGHWAY HAZARD REPORT

1. GUARD RAILS

_____ A unburied ends
_____ B lead vehicles into obstruction
_____ C improperly constructed (material)
_____ D hazard placed outside guard rail

2. INADEQUATE OR MISSING GUARDING AT

_____ A bridge abutments
_____ B drop-offs at side of road
_____ C trees
_____ D sign posts or utility posts
_____ E culverts

3. UTILITY POSTS AND SIGN SUPPORTS

_____ A non-breakaway type
_____ B exposed concrete foundation

4. SIGNS

_____ A non-standard
_____ B improperly placed
_____ C obstructed or obscured
_____ D missing

5. LIGHTING

_____ A inadequate
_____ B lack of reflector or warning devices

6. GORE AREA OBSTRUCTIONS

_____ A sign supports
_____ B curbing

7. ROAD DESIGN AND CONDITIONS

_____ A slippery road surfaces (poor drainage)
_____ B bumps or dips in road surface
_____ C rough roadway (pot holes, uneven pavement slabs)
_____ D highway striping (improper or worn)

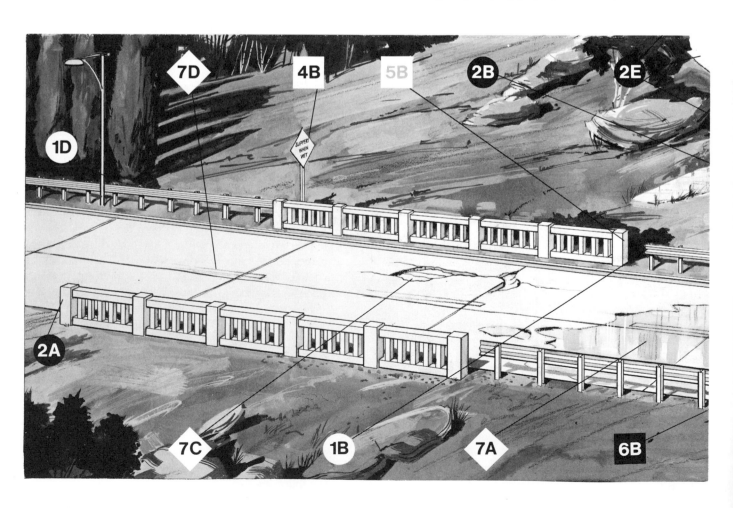

LOCATION

Street or highway No. _____

Intersecting street or
highway No. _____

City _____ County _____

Note: (If not identifiable from above, cite mileage from nearest
intersection, mileage marker, or landmark.)

_____

_____

_____

_____

_____

_____

(CLAIM DEPT. USE ONLY)
Brief Description of Accident as related to
hazard indicated

Date Observed _____

Time _____ AM _____ PM _____

Observer _____

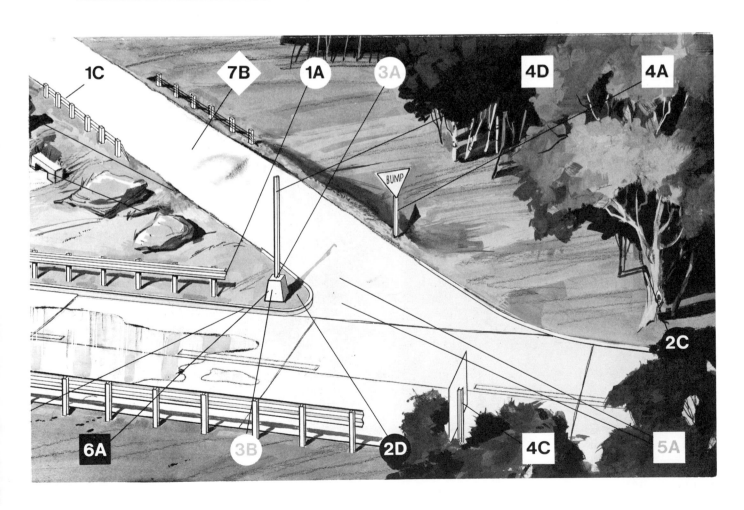

CONSUMER SAFETY SERVICE
(VOICES IN SOCIETY PROGRAM)

THE TRAVELERS CORP.
One Tower Square
Hartford, Conn. 06115

Business: Insurance
CEO: Morrison H. Beach

Sales: 3,000mm
Employees: 30,000

Contact: Francis K. Holland
Address: same as above
Telephone: (203) 277-4079
Program Reaches: unknown
When Started: November, 1971
Budget: $51,000 initially

Program Outline:

The purpose of this program is to make available, at a low cost, a variety of safety devices for motorists, especially auto drivers.

The test program kit will include safe car seats for infants and children, first aid kits for automobiles and flashing safety lights for roadside emergency use. Possible changes in the format of the program will be made after testing in Buffalo, N.Y.

Co. Personnel Involved: 6 part time

Measure of Success: too early to tell

HURRICANE CHART

THE TRAVELERS CORP.
One Tower Square
Hartford, Conn. 06115

Business: Insurance
CEO: Morrison H. Beach

Sales: 3,000mm
Employees: 30,000

Contact: Francis K. Holland
Address: same as above
Telephone: (203) 277-4079
Program Reaches: 2,000,000 plus
When Started: 1956
Budget: $25,000

Program Outline:

The purpose of this program is to offer information and suggestions designed to permit persons in hurricane areas to minimize injury and damage to themselves and their property.

Following distribution by the company's agents, the Hurricane Chart is made available to all radio and television stations on the East and Gulf coasts of the United States. The respective media publicize the availability of the material before and during the hurricane season.

Co. Personnel Involved: an artist, a writer, a researcher plus printing staff— all part time

Measure of Success: the annual total distribution of 2 million copies of the material and the regular, annual requests of radio and television stations for early delivery of the publication

OCCUPATIONAL SAFETY AND HEALTH ACT OF 1970

TRAVELERS INSURANCE CO.
One Tower Square
Hartford, Conn. 06115

Business: Insurance
CEO: Morrison H. Beach

Sales: 3,000mm
Employees: 30,000

Contact: David E. Nash
Address: same as above
Telephone: (203) 277-3359
Program Reaches: n/a
When Started: n/a
Budget: $120,000

Program Outline:

The purpose of this program is to act as a source of information and to provide reference material on the Occupational Safety and Health Act of 1970 to all Travelers customers and the general public.

The program functions on several levels: (1) the company distributes kits of OSHA material; (2) develops, prints and distributes a reference guide including a list of 356 publications containing OSHA standards; (3) participates in training sessions to explain the Act; (4) makes mock compliance officer-type team inspections at typical customer locations; (5) assists the state of Iowa in establishing a state program to meet federal OSHA requirements; (6) provides Arthur D. Little Co., consultants, with a list of accident causes and reccomendations for long range research to eliminate and reduce unsafe conditions and hazardous acts which cause accidents; (7) develops and distributes a chart listing Workmen's Compensation First Reports of Injury form numbers, by state, to avoid duplicate accident record-keeping.

Co. Personnel Involved: Approximately 500 field engineers and 20 home office engineers are involved on a part time basis.

Measure of Success: compliance with recommendations, customer satisfaction and reduction in losses to customers

PRODUCT LIABILITY

TRAVELERS INSURANCE CO.
One Tower Square
Hartford, Conn. 06115

Business: Personal and Casualty—Property Insurance
Sales: 3,000mm
CEO: Morrison H. Beach   Employees: 30,000

Contact: David E. Nash
Address: same as above
Telephone: (203) 277-3359
Program Reaches: n/a
When Started: n/a
Budget: $124,000

Program Outline:

The purpose of this program is to reduce, as much as possible, hazards for the intended and forseeable unintended usage of the wide range of products, chemicals, pharmaceuticals, food stuffs and consumer appliances being manufactured for industries and general public alike.

The basic philosophy is attuned to early anticipation of potential hazards, positive elimination of the underlying peril wherever possible and clear identification of the potential hazard via adequate warnings when the peril is inherent.

In the manufacturing environment, this is effectively accomplished by building in safety at the design level and then by policing product/design integrity by an effective quality assurance program during the manufacturing cycle.

At the user level, product safety is controlled by adequate labeling, warnings and instructional information.

The above is accomplished by partnership with industry to foster a full awareness of safety at the industrial scene coupled with stimulation of industry to adopt attitudes and thought processes.

Co. Personnel Involved: 60 staff engineers at home office, approximately 500 field engineers and specialists 1% of the time

Measure of Success: Compliance with recommendations, customer satisfaction and reduction of losses to customers. The day by day, report by report, awareness that more effective safety and quality practices are being implemented with attendant reductions in product failures and public liability.

A SAFE START

UNIROYAL, INC.
1230 Avenue of the Americas
New York, N.Y. 10020

Business: Manufacturing Rubber Products, Plastics, Chemicals, etc.
Sales: 1,678mm
CEO: George R. Vila   Employees: 64,168

Contact: H. D. Smith, V.P., Pub. Affairs
Address: same as above
Telephone: (212) 247-5000
Program Reaches: thousands of driver education students in the U.S.
When Started: n/a
Budget: n/a

Program Outline:

Thousands of driver education students across the country are participating in a project known as "A Safe Start," a programmed learning supplement to driver training courses. The course, presented by Uniroyal as a public service, consists of 5 hours of programmed instruction for classroom or home study. The student learns about driving hazards so they can be handled if they occur. Key topics include such points as "defensive driving," handling the car in hazardous road conditions and sudden emergencies. Uniroyal tire dealers are distributing these materials in their local market areas.

Materials distributed in connection with the Safe Start program include information directed at making the student driver a more responsible citizen. Subjects such as anti-littering and the dangers of drinking and driving are among those treated.

The Safe Start program will be used in driver training in Central and South American countries, through arrangements allowing the Pan American Health Organization to reprint, without charge, the material in Spanish.

Co. Personnel Involved: n/a

Measure of Success: n/a

COLOR ME SAFE COLORING BOOK

WHIRLPOOL CORP.
Benton Harbor, Mich. 49022

Business: Appliance Manufacturing
Sales: 1,200mm
CEO: John H. Platts   Employees: 28,280

Contact: William L. Kucera
Address: Whirlpool Safety Ed.
   Benton, Mich. 49022
Telephone: (616) 925-0651, ext. 7120
Program Reaches: over 100,000
When Started: 1971
Budget: $60,000 to $70,000

Program Outline:

To teach children safety in the home through a medium which is both fun and instructive, Whirlpool Corporation has made available a coloring book designed to teach children household safety rules. The book is entitled "Color Me Safe Coloring Book" and is aimed primarily at children between the ages of 5 and 10. It contains 16 pages of safety measures both in word and picture form which children can color and discuss with their parents. The book is available in 3 languages: English, Chinese and Spanish, and recommended for use in schools, day care centers and other similar agencies. It is available free through Whirlpool's Safety Education Division.

Co. Personnel Involved: Most of the manpower is involved in handling requests and it varies between 20 to 30% of 1 man's time.

Measure of Success: Over 100,000 English copies have been circulated and the company has since had the book translated into French, Spanish and Japanese. Whirlpool is also considering conducting a national "Color Me Safe" contest in which the company will solicit safety suggestions from general consumers. A prize will be awarded to the best safety suggestions.

volunteerism

CELANESE VOLUNTEER POOL

CELANESE CORP.
522 Fifth Ave.
New York, N.Y. 10036

Business: Chemical & Textile Manufacturing
Sales: 1,300mm
CEO: John W. Brooks   Employees: 36,000

Contact: David A. Gardner
Address: same as above
Telephone: (212) 867-2000
Program Reaches: n/a
When Started: 1971
Budget: no direct cost

Program Outline:

The purpose of this program is to provide volunteers from within Celanese to specific community-social agencies. Through a clearinghouse procedure developed by the company's Special Projects Director, the volunteer pool matches individual talents, such as budget or administration expertise, to be of short-term help to community social agencies. Volunteer talents are determined in advance through a short questionnaire available to company employees through the Special Projects office.

Co. Personnel Involved: 120 to varying degrees; 1 full time administrator

Measure of Success: definitive rapid solution of short-term problems within agencies

CHASE VOLUNTEERS FOR COMMUNITY ACTION (CVCA)

THE CHASE MANHATTAN BANK
1 Chase Manhattan Plaza
New York, N.Y. 10015

Business: Banking   Sales: not applicable
Total Assets: 25,000mm
CEO: Herbert Patterson   Employees: 18,900

Contact: Charles H. Ballard, Jr.
Address: same as above
Telephone: (212) 552-3986
Program Reaches: n/a
When Started: 1968
Budget: n/a

Program Outline:

The purpose of the Chase Volunteers for Community Action is threefold: (1) to support those who are already engaged in voluntary work; (2) to find constructive outlets for those who would like to help solve community problems; and (3) to create opportunities for volunteers to exchange ideas and benefit from each other's experience.

The Bank acts as a clearinghouse between various private and public community agencies seeking volunteer help and willing employees who express interest in donating their spare time, energy, ingenuity and initiative to urban ills. The volunteer program involves some 300 staff members who set aside 1 evening a week or part of the weekend to work in various communities as tutors, athletic coaches, hospital workers, etc. To help volunteers get better acquainted with the types of agencies and activities that need help, Bank staff representatives prepared a 22-page opportunities booklet listing a cross section of the volunteer needs.

Co. Personnel Involved: The 300 volunteers are counseled and supervised by the Urban Affairs staff representative.

Measure of Success: In 4 years, the program has grown to 3 times its initial size. Volunteers and assisted agencies report frequently on their enthusiasm for the program.

PANEL TO EXPLORE VOLUNTEER OPPORTUNITIES

ELI LILLY & CO.
307 E. McCarty Street
Indianapolis, Ind. 46206

Business: Pharmaceutical Manufacturing
Sales: 600mm
CEO: B. E. Beck   Employees: 23,450

Contact: John S. Thomas
Address: same as above
Telephone: (317) 261-3181
Program Reaches: n/a
When Started: panel was held in 1969
Budget: n/a

Program Outline:

Panel discussions were held for employees interested in learning about opportunities for volunteer work in Indianapolis community activities. Panel members discussed public service organizations and their need for volunteers, volunteer work in the VAC program, and other means of involvement in community affairs. Some of the types of services discussed were visiting, driving, tutoring, recreation, office work, music, arts, crafts, casework aid, woodworking and assisting in clinics.

Co. Personnel Involved: n/a

Measure of Success: more employee involvement in community affairs and volunteer services

EMPLOYEE URBAN INVOLVEMENT

FIRST NATIONAL CITY BANK
399 Park Avenue
New York, N. Y. 10022

Business: Banking   Sales: not applicable
CEO: William I. Spencer   Employees: 31,700

Contact: Jac Friedgut, V.P.
Address: same as above
Telephone: (212) 559-2722
Program Reaches: indeterminate
When Started: 1970
Budget: management and employee time

Program Outline:

The purpose of this program is to encourage and facilitate the involvement of the Bank's employees at all levels in problems of the environment in which we live and work.

Traditionally, Bank personnel have been encouraged to take part in the activities of local community organizations. A large number have participated on their own time at every level of such organizations. Recently, to assure that employees were given further opportunities to find the most meaningful activity, the bank set up a volunteer coordinator function which matches people with programs.

In addition, the Bank publishes a monthly report which keeps employees informed of the organization's activities, runs a series of forums in which outside experts lead informal discussions concerning such problems as education, narcotics addiction, etc. and has created an advisory group composed of a broad spectrum of employees which acts as a channel of communication to senior management and provides recommendations on new directions for the Bank as a corporate citizen.

Co. Personnel Involved: one full time and 12 part time

Measure of Success The number of participants in the volunteer program now stands at 200. Approximately 250 employees, on average, attended each of 5 forums in 1971. The Advisory Group has already made impact on Bank thinking with regard to pollution, narcotics and internal communication.

COMMUNITY SERVICE AWARDS

FORD MOTOR CO.
The American Road
Dearborn, Mich. 48121

Business: Automotive Manufacturing
Sales: 15,000mm
CEO: Lee A. Iacocca   Employees: 431,000

Contact: Richard Powers, Mgr. Comm. Affairs
Address: same as above
Program Reaches: over 200,000 employees
When Started: 1956
Budget: n/a

Program Outline:

The purpose of this program is to stimulate voluntary community service among employees and encourage others to contribute similar services.

The program locates employees or spouses who have voluntarily contributed noteworthy service to their fellow men and recognizes this service through the presentation of awards.

Co. Personnel Involved: approximately 1,000 management employees who are members of Ford's 74 community relations committees across the country, plus staff people who administer the program

Measure of Success: Recognition from community leaders, national awards and widespread news coverage; since the program's inception, over 15,000 Ford employees and their spouses have received awards.

SCHOOL VOLUNTEERS PROGRAM

MUTUAL LIFE INSURANCE CO. OF NEW YORK
1740 Broadway
New York, N.Y. 10019

Business: Life Insurance   Sales: n/a
CEO: J. McCall Hughes   Employees: 10,000

Contact: D.A. Pfeiffer, Dir.Per.
Address: same as above
Telephone: (212) 586-4000
Program Reaches: 125 plus
When Started: October, 1971
Budget: approx. $25,000 in employee salaries

Program Outline:

This program functions as part of the company's overall corporate affairs program whose purpose is to assist the urban poor and disadvantaged in one of the prime areas in which MONY conducts business.

Through the Public Education Association, a volunteer group started in New York City in 1956, the School Volunteers Program offers 6 hours a week of tutoring help to school children at all levels in public schools, from kindergarten through high school. Tutoring is on a one-to-one basis and includes primarily reading and writing, English as a second language and arithmetic. Although help is offered in other subjects, reading presents the biggest single need among students in New York City. One thousand three hundred volunteers participate throughout the 5 boroughs of the city in this program.

Co. Personnel Involved: Forty employees take 3 hours from work 1 morning each week.

Measure of Success: The program has been so successful that in the late '60s it was incorporated into the New York City Board of Education. This is the first large group from one company offering assistance to the program on company time or on a release-time basis.

VOLUNTEERS FOR INTERNATIONAL TECHNICAL ASSISTANCE

SHELL OIL CO.
P.O. Box 2463
One Shell Plaza
Houston, Tx. 77001

Business: Petroleum Products   Sales: 4,331mm
CEO: H. Bridges   Employees: 36,700

Contact: C. E. Bishop
Address: same as above
Telephone: (713) 220-5044
Program Reaches: n/a
When Started: n/a
Budget: n/a

Program Outline:

In order to match personal skills with community needs, 35 Shell employees have volunteered their professional talents to be used by VITA, a non-profit organization which seeks to place minority people in contact with professionals who can advise them on improving their economic status. In a sense, VITA is a broker of talents. Minority businessmen come to VITA with ideas to start businesses. VITA puts them in touch with poverty agencies or with professionals who can advise them as to whether or not the idea can be successfully implemented. Volunteers, such as those at Shell, place their talents in VITA's "skill bank" and are called upon when need for their services arises. For further information on VITA contact VITA-Houston, 4702 Jackson Street, Houston, Texas, 77004.

Co. Personnel Involved: The 35 employees that are presently part of the VITA skill bank.

Measure of Success: There is a growing interest and involvement with VITA on the part of Shell volunteers.

ESSO COMMUNITY ACTION VOLUNTEERS

STANDARD OIL CO. OF N.J.
1251 Avenue of the Americas
New York, N.Y. 10020

Business: Petroleum   Sales: 21,000mm
CEO Milo M. Brisco   Employees: 145,000

Contact: C. Vinton Hoey, Jr., P.R. Dept.
Address: same as above
Telephone: (212) 974-3735
Program Reaches: about 600 directly
When Started: late 1970
Budget: $20,000

Program Outline:

The purpose of the Volunteers Program is to help solve community problems through employee volunteers, and to supplement employee development and job satisfaction.

The program assists people through about 40 community agencies in the New York metropolitan area where the volunteers serve. Basically, the program serves as an informal clearinghouse to match employee skills (academic, clerical, athletic, and managerial) to the needs of community agencies. It also supports employee family members and those employees who were already engaged in volunteer efforts. Employees are granted release time from work for a few of the volunteer projects.

The program includes follow-up and back-up support for employee volunteers and creates opportunities for volunteers and community agency representatives to exchange ideas collectively.

Co. Personnel Involved: approx. 200 employee volunteers

Measure of Success: There has been significant growth in the number of community agency requests for volunteers, in requests for additional volunteers from agencies where employees are presently serving, and in the development of additional innovative ways to serve these agencies. There has also been an increase in the number of companies interested in launching similar programs.

INVOLVEMENT CORPS TASK FORCE

UNITED BANK OF DENVER
1740 Broadway
Denver, Colo. 80217

Business: Banking   Sales: not applicable
CEO: John D. Hershner   Employees: 966

Contact: Tom Gordon, Task Force Pres.
Address: same as above
Telephone: (303) 244-8811
Program Reaches: 300-500 juveniles
When Started: September, 1971
Budget: $500/month raised by individual members' contributions

Program Outline:

The Task Force is a voluntary association which matches the resources of its members with the needs of a chosen community project.

United Bank of Denver's group of employees is working with the Partners Program, a self-funded organization attempting to take problem children out of the overloaded juvenile court system by pairing them with adults who give them contact with a broader and more stable environment.

Co. Personnel Involved: Employee Task Force has 75 members

Measure of Success: (1) a growing task force; (2) increased in-depth involvement with Partners through activities, partnerships between juveniles and adults and more financial support; (3) involvement has helped publicize Partners more widely in the Metropolitan area.

UNITED STATES TRUST CO.
URBAN VOLUNTEERS

U. S. TRUST CO. OF N. Y.
45 Wall Street
New York, N.Y. 10005

Business: Trust Banking   Sales: not applicable
CEO: Charles W. Buck   Employees: 1,600

Contact: Edward A. Maurer
Address: same as above
Telephone: (212) 425-4500
Program Reaches: cannot measure
When Started: October, 1971
Budget: minimal—as required

Program Outline:

This program endeavors to provide a channel for company employees to volunteer their services to social service organizations in the New York metropolitan area. Its principal purpose is to bring together employees' interests and community needs.

Through the program, interested employees are referred to various community organizations who seek volunteer assistance in a wide variety of areas including hospitals, youth organizations, homes for children and aged and after-school tutoring programs.

Co. Personnel Involved: 1 coordinator, 30 volunteers

Measure of Success: At this time, 30 volunteers have been placed with various groups.

SOCIAL SERVICE LEAVE PROGRAM

XEROX CORP.
Xerox International Headquarters
Stamford, Conn. 06904

Business: Diversified Office Machines
Sales: 1,719mm
CEO: C. Peter McColough   Employees: 38,339

Contact: Thomas C. Abbot
Address: same as above
Telephone: (203) 329-8711
        or
Contact: Alfred R. Zipser
Address: 280 Park Avenue
   New York, N.Y. 10017
Telephone: (212) 972-1600
Program Reaches: 1971
Budget: n/a

Program Outline:

The purpose of this program is to enable Xerox employees who are involved in the problems of society on a part time basis to delve into a problem full time. Also, they get a chance to do this during the prime of their working careers and won't have to wait until they retire.

Under the Social Service Leave Program a Xerox employee can get a leave of absence for up to a year—at full pay, with full benefits—to go out and make his contribution to a better society. The employees keep union seniority, provided they return to Xerox as soon as the leave is over. They get the same job back and if for any reason the old job is not available, the employee is guaranteed an equal job: one that offers the same pay, responsibility, status, and opportunity for advancement. There are just a few limits to the kind of social service an employee can propose:

(1) It must be a program or activity sponsored or conducted by an existing, functioning, legitimate organization of some kind;

(2) The employee must have written acceptance from the organization of participation he proposes;

(3) What the employee does must be legal;

(4) No partisan politics for any candidate or party, no profit-making sponsoring organizations, no personal schooling is allowed;

(5) The employee pays his own way to and from wherever his mission takes him.

The only other requirement is that the applicants must have completed 3 years of employment with Xerox when they apply.

Co. Personnel Involved: 7 members of the Evaluation Committee who review and decide those who will be granted leave (they serve for 2 years)

Measure of Success: Twenty-one Xerox employees have been chosen from nearly 200 applicants, to participate in the experimental Social Service Leave Program. These 18 men and 3 women granted leaves come from many different Xerox departments and represent a wide range of occupations from factory employee to corporate executive. The youngest is 26 and the oldest, 60.

XEROX SOCIAL SERVICE LEAVE APPLICATION

To be returned to:

Evaluation Board,
Social Service Leave Program
Xerox Corporation
Stamford, Connecticut 06904

My name: _____
        (print)   first   middle   last

Home address: _____

Phone: _____
                    home   Xerox

Xerox Group/Division: _____ Location: _____

Present Position: _____ Employee Number: _____ Date Hired: _____

don't write here | Application No :

- -

don't write here | Application No :

In one sentence, what I want to do is: _____

_____

Time desired: _____ Dates desired: _____

This is the organization I'll work with: _____

name

_____

address   department   name & function of person I would report to

Phone: _____ Acceptance Letter attached ☐   Salary, if any, I'll receive from the organization: _____

These are the details of the program I want to work on: (goals, history, scope, program, people affected, other workers involved, nature of activities, budget — *very specific description, please,* that will help us understand the project; attach any literature or reports or clippings that will help)

_____

_____

_____

_____

_____

My specific work will be: (what skill, what function, what tasks, what aims — or programmed results, if these can be stated in advance)

_____

_____

_____

_____

_____

_____

I am specially qualified to do this by: (cite specific experience, training, skills, prior involvement, personal history — or just gnawing desire)

_____

_____

This is why I want to work on this project and this is what I hope to accomplish:

_____

_____

_____

_____

_____

My present monthly salary is: $ _____

Circle Highest Grade Completed:

High School	College	Graduate
9 - 10 - 11 - 12	13 - 14 - 15 - 16	17 - 18 - 19 - 20 - 21 - 22

College or University Attended	Degree Awarded	Major Subject
_____	_____	_____
_____	_____	_____
_____	_____	_____
_____	_____	_____

Please use as many extra sheets as you need to answer the questions fully.

youth

OPERATION IMPACT

AEROJET LIQUID ROCKET CO.
P.O. Box 13222
Sacramento, Cal. 95813

Business: Energy Management   Sales: $33 million
CEO: R. C. Stiff, Jr.   Employees: n/a

Contact: Francis Orlaski, Dep. Scout Exec.
Address: Boy Scouts of America
   Golden Empire Council
   P.O. Box 4946
   Sacramento, Cal. 95825
Telephone: (916) 481-4111
Program Reaches: n/a
When Started: March, 1972
Budget: n/a

Program Outline:

The problem faced by Scouting all over America is to recruit qualified personnel that will find acceptance in inner city neighborhoods and to raise the money to support this activity. Even where funding is assured, finding qualified leadership is difficult because the demand for minority personnel in industry is so competitive. The Aerojet Liquid Rocket Company is providing that leadership. Scouting served approximately 1 out of every 5 boys in the inner Sacramento neighborhoods. The new goal is to increase this ratio to at least 1 out of 3 boys.

Specific responsibilities assigned to the Impact executive include:
   1. Develop overall "grass roots" neighborhood and area-wide support;
   2. Recruit and provide desperately needed personalized training for inner city adult leadership;
   3. Extend boy recruiting efforts in the inner city area;
   4. Sell the summer camping program to youths in the "impact" neighborhoods;
   5. Build support with industry and other community organizations for this program;
   6. Organize, promote and conduct special community events in support of unit activities.

Co. Personnel Involved: 1 "Impact Executive" full time

Measure of Success: n/a

YOUTH OPPORTUNITIES FOUNDATION

AEROSPACE CORP.
P.O. Box 95085
Los Angeles, Cal. 90045

Business: General Systems Engineering for Military
   Research
Sales: 75mm
CEO: I. A. Getting   Employees: 3,285

Contact: William Drake
Address: same as above
Telephone: (213) 648-5000
Program Reaches: n/a
When Started: 1963
Budget: n/a

Program Outline:

In 1963 a Spanish-surnamed member of the Aerospace Technical Staff organized an endeavor in the Mexican-American community named the Youth Opportunities Foundation, which was intended to improve educational opportunities for minority youth. The company provided this individual's services on a full time basis for 3 years, together with secretarial and administrative support, to organize the Foundation until it could acquire a broader base of support from community and government agencies. When the Foundation was firmly established in 1968, the employee left the company to become Executive Director of the Foundation and has since continued to receive financial support from the company.

Co. Personnel Involved: n/a

Measure of Success: n/a

MIDDLETOWN JOB OPPORTUNITY COMMITTEE, INC.

ARMCO STEEL CORP.
P.O. Box 600
Middletown, Oh. 45042

Business: Basic Steelmaking
Sales: 1,700mm
CEO: Calvin William Verity, Jr.
Employees: 51,236

Contact: D. C. Osborne, V.P., Staff Operations
Address: same as above
Telephone: (513) 425-2889
Program Reaches: 230 young people in 1971; 150 young
    people in 1970
When Started: 1970
Budget: n/a

Program Outline:

Because past experience shows that retail, commercial and industry jobs for 16-17 year olds fall far short of meeting community needs, the committee supplements existing work opportunities by raising funds to pay for "made" jobs. This work is limited to non-profit organizations and provides a service for which funds would not otherwise be available. Young people are paid $1.45 an hour, 5 hours per day and 5 days per week. Thus it costs $36.25 per week or about $375 to provide a job for 1 needy individual for the summer. The organization also places young people in summer jobs.

Co. Personnel Involved: One hundred fifty employees contributed money to the program; others provided leadership and counseling. Company provided free physical exams to several people who could not afford them.

Measure of Success: Last year 230 people were helped through this nonprofit volunteer community effort. Eighty-five were paid by Job Opportunity, Inc.; others were paid by companies who hired the youths.

COOPERATIVE WORK-STUDY PROGRAM

BAMBERGER'S
131 Market Street
Newark, N.J. 07101

Business: Retail Department Store
Sales: n/a
CEO: n/a   Employees: n/a

Contact: Marilyn G. Brown
Address: same as above
Telephone: (201) 565-5243
Program Reaches: approx. 44/school year
When Started: 1965
Budget: n/a

Program Outline:

In order to provide on-the-job training for Newark's youth, to supplement their income and to help them develop the skills, attitudes and values necessary to become productive members of today's society, this program is offered to high school seniors from disadvantaged areas who are involved in work-study or distributive education programs.

The program at Bambergers is separated into 2 distinct groups: Group A attends school in the morning and works in the store from 1 to 6 daily. They are provided with a weekly retail workshop to give them a broad view of a retail operation, and to build specific skills in the areas of salesmanship and customer relations. Group B is a pilot program with Barringer High School in Newark, employing 20 students 28/hours a week who attend a daily 1 hour class in distributive education with a teacher provided for the store by the Board of Education.

Co. Personnel Involved: coordinator/counselor, sales managers to whom students are immediately responsible and various managers used for weekly classes

Measure of Success: Twenty-three students from 1970-71 are permanently employed in the store: 1 sales manager, 5 assistant managers, 4 stock, 4 clerical and 9 sales.

SAY (SOCIAL ADVOCATES FOR YOUTH CENTERS)

BANK OF AMERICA
P. O. Box 37000
San Francisco, Cal. 94137

Business: Banking
CEO: A. W. Clausen

Sales: not applicable
Employees: 31,700

Contact: C. J. Bocchieri, Asst. V.P.
Address: Contributions 3246, same as above
Telephone: (415) 622-4690
Program Reaches: about 450/year
When Started: October, 1971
Budget: $46,000

Program Outline:

Aimed at the 8-15 year old age group, the program's primary goal is the reduction of delinquent behavior and proneness. The basic philosophy is to teach by doing, with volunteers becoming the regular companion of the child. Activities include tutoring, counseling, camping, attending recreational events or otherwise sharing and developing special interests of the child. SAY stresses preventative measures to help those who have not yet committed crimes. There are 3 centers operating at present in San Francisco, Santa Rosa and San Diego.

Co. Personnel Involved: several as adult volunteers, several in administrative or fund raising posts

Measure of Success: Each of the 3 centers will reach about 150 children a year. If the current rate of success continues, the program will be expanded statewide, but with a continued emphasis on the one-to-one approach.

COOPERATIVE WORK-STUDY

BELL TELEPHONE CO. OF PENNSYLVANIA
201 Stanwix Street
Pittsburgh, Pa. 15222

Business: Communications
CEO: William S. Cashel

Sales: 698mm
Employees: 34,300

Contact: Richard E. Thorn
Address: 8th fl., same as above
Telephone: (412) 633-3670
Program Reaches: about 50% of all seniors and juniors in Fifth Avenue High School
When Started: 1970
Budget: n/a

Program Outline:

The program is designed to give juniors and seniors at Fifth Avenue High School, Pittsburgh, Pennsylvania, exposure to the world of work.

Students are assigned meaningful jobs and are expected to make some contribution to the work group. High school juniors work 2 hours/day, 5 days/week for 6 weeks. Seniors work a full half-day tour the entire school term. Both juniors and seniors are paid basic starting salaries for whatever job they are doing.

Each student is assigned to a supervisor who provides continuing counseling service, supervision and required job training. Supervisors are required to complete an evaluation of students on completion of the program. During the 6-week period, students are given the opportunity to take Bell's employment exam. If the students are interested, and the employment situation permits, the scores they make on the test can be considered if they apply for full time employment after graduation.

Co. Personnel Involved: One management person coordinates this and other activities at the school. Other employees are involved to the extent that they have work-study students working for them.

Measure of Success: According to the school counselor, students who have participated in the work-study program are more readily placed following graduation from high school.

EMPLOYMENT READINESS TRAINING

BELL OF PENNSYLVANIA
201 Stanwix Street
Pittsburgh, Pa. 15222

Business: Communications
CEO: William S. Cashel

Sales: 698mm
Employees: 34,300

Contact: Richard E. Thorn
Address: 8th fl., same as above
Telephone: (412) 633-3670
Program Reaches: entire senior class of Pittsburgh's Fifth
   Avenue High School each year
When Started: 1969
Budget: n/a

Program Outline:

The purpose of this program is to inform the students of
qualifications and information needed to apply for a job.

Students come to the Telephone Company building in
groups of 20 for 2 half-day sessions of job readiness
training. During the 6-hour session, the students fill out
applications and counselors discuss in detail each item on
the application. Problems that most new employees face
are discussed. The goals of the program are to develop job
qualifications, encourage students to present themselves
well, encourage initiative, develop an awareness of a company's need for qualified employees, impart knowledge
required for job application and employment interviews,
and discuss employee responsibilities.

Co. Personnel Involved: Three people conduct the program and are involved 1 or 2 days each year. A coordinator spends additional time organizing the program so
that it meshes with school schedules.

Measure of Success: Feedback from students indicates
they felt better prepared during job interviews.

LEADERSHIP SEMINAR

BELL OF PENNSYLVANIA
201 Stanwix Street
Pittsburgh, Pa. 15222

Business: Communications
CEO: William S. Cashel

Sales: 698mm
Employees: 34,300

Contact: Richard E. Thorn
Address: 8th fl., same as above
Telephone: (412) 633-3670
Program Reaches: n/a
When Started: 1969
Budget: under $500

Program Outline:

The purpose of this program is to develop leadership
among the students of the Fifth Avenue High School,
Pittsburgh, Pennsylvania.

Bell Telephone and school administrators conduct an
annual leadership seminar for students and/or teachers.
Items such as public speaking, how to conduct meetings,
administrative details and procedures, self-critique and
motivational sessions are conducted during a weekend
seminar held on a camp location somewhat removed from
the school surroundings.

Each year this program changes slightly to meet the
present needs of the students or teachers, but the format
itself will not be changed.

Co. Personnel Involved: 3-6 people including the company administrator for the school project

Measure of Success: The student council has been somewhat more active and effective following this type seminar.

TUTORING PROGRAM

BELL OF PENNSYLVANIA
201 Stanwix Street
Pittsburgh, Pa. 15222

Business: Communications
CEO: William S. Cashel

Sales: 698mm
Employees: 34,300

Contact: Richard E. Thorn
Address: 8th fl., same as above
Telephone: (412) 633-3670
Program Reaches: 75-100 students/year
When Started: 1969
Budget: no out-of-pocket expense

Program Outline:

The tutoring program assists individual students in various subjects and is the program that launched Bell Tel's various activities at Fifth Avenue High School, Pittsburgh, Pennsylvania.

In its effort to help students who are not progressing as well as they should, tutors have been made available in a variety of different courses of study. Student participation is strictly voluntary and is available to all students requesting it. The tutors, volunteers, are local Bell employees who offer their services (2 wives of Bell employees are also participating).

Co. Personnel Involved: The coordinator who administers other projects in the school for Bell also administers this program. Generally, about 10 company tutors are involved on released time.

Measure of Success: The success of the tutoring program has been shown in the fact that at least 50 of the students showed improvement, some as much as 4 grade levels. More important has been the development of a 2-way street of understanding, insight and respect between the tutors and students.

LIVING WITNESSES

BETHLEHEM STEEL CORP.
Corporate Headquarters
Bethlehem, Pa. 18106

Business: Steelmaking and Related Activities
Sales: 3,000mm
CEO: Lewis W. Foy

Employees: 130,000

Contact: J.V. Robertson, Mgr. Com. Affairs
Address: same as above
Telephone: (215) 694-3131
Program Reaches: several thousand to date
When Started: 1968
Budget: no budgeted amount

Program Outline:

The company has set up the Living Witnesses Program to convince young people from 13-16 years of age, primarily those from disadvantaged homes, of the need for completing at least a high school education. The Living Witnesses are, for the most part, young minority group Bethlehem employees who, by virtue of their education, were employed by Bethlehem and are now progressing in their employment. The Living Witnesses travel to schools to present a program to students that will counter the belief that due to race, national origin, or sex, it is a waste of time for them to pursue their education.

Co. Personnel Involved:, about 75, part time

Measure of Success: There is no way of determining the number of students who remain in school solely because of the program.

CRISPUS ATTUCKS YOUTH CENTER

BORG-WARNER CORP.
(YORK DIVISION)
P.O. Box 1592
York, Pa. 17405

Business: Manufacturing Air Conditioning, Heating, Refrigerating Equipment, Automatic Ice Makers, Oxygen Chambers, and Air Purifiers
CEO: James F. Bere   Employees: 41,500

Contact: Ralph G. Meisenhelder
Address: same as above
Telephone: (717) 843-0731
Program Reaches: 2,300
When Started: 1969
Budget: $1,300,000

Program Outline:

This program's purpose is to lend assistance in the forms of money, equipment and personnel to the community-wide task of relocating and revitalizing the Crispus Attucks Center in York, Pa. The facility would provide constructive and recreational opportunities for the Black Youth of the City in an effort to alleviate racial tensions in the City.

Careful consideration of several worthwhile community projects led to the conclusion that the purpose could be best served by supporting the Crispus Attucks redevelopment project. The Center was originally conceived in 1931 and by 1969, when the City of York was torn by racial dissent and strife, was sorely in need of revitalization. In fact, post-strife investigations indicated that the racial conflict was due, in part at least, to the fact that young people had no recreational and constructive opportunities. York initiated its involvement by seeking the support of Borg-Warner's Foundation and by taking a leadership role in a city-wide fund-raising effort to build a new community center.

Co. Personnel Involved: 14 York Division of Borg-Warner Corporation employees were involved in this project. Initially, a group of 5 key employees evaluated the merits of the Crispus Attucks project and other community efforts. Subsequently other employees joined the effort filling various volunteer roles.

Measure of Success: n/a

COMMUNITY RELATIONS/UNIVERSITY STUDENTS

CASTLE & COOKE, INC.
Drawer 2990
Honolulu, Hi. 96802

Business: Food Products, Land Development, Manufacturing and Merchandising
Sales: 507mm
CEO: Malcolm MacNaughton   Employees: 15,000

Contact: Emil A. Schneider, P.R. Dir.
Address: same as above
Telephone: (808) 548-6611
Program Reaches: about 60 outside company
When Started: n/a
Budget: $500/year

Program Outline:

The program aims, through informal meetings with business students, to give them a better idea of how a major company operates and to let the company learn about the student viewpoints. Face-to-face meetings of this kind are the most valuable means of reaching a better understanding between business and college students who think that business is composed of nothing but robber barons.

Three to 4 sessions are held per school year with groups of 12-15 students per meeting, along with 1 or 2 professors; all from the business college. The program involves a half-hour slide presentation depicting the company's varying operations followed by a question and answer session. This is followed by a tour and lunch with question and answer sessions with 2 or 3 of the company's top executives. The purpose of these sessions is not recruiting. They provide not only an opportunity for the students to learn more about business, but for our business executives to learn more about the student viewpoint and why that viewpoint exists.

Co. Personnel Involved: 12-15 people, 3-6 hours/year/person on average

Measure of Success: Desired expansion is a result of favorable reaction on all sides.

DRUG EDUCATION

CASTLE & COOKE, INC.
Drawer 2990
Honolulu, Hi. 96802

Business: Food Products, Land Development,
   Manufacturing and Merchandising
Sales: 507mm
CEO: Malcolm MacNaughton   Employees: 15,000

Contact: Emil A. Schneider, P.R. Dir.
Address: same as above
Telephone: (808) 548-6611
Program Reaches: 3-5,000
When Started: 1971
Budget: $2,000 to date

Program Outline:

The purpose of this program is to make available a series of films on drug education designed for use with students from about the 6th through 10th grades—an age range considered to cover those who have not yet turned on to drugs but may be wondering about it all.

Each film is 15 minutes in length and usage is accompanied by trained instructors who develop dialogue among the students. Each film treats a different subject: marijuana, LSD, amphetamines, barbituates, heroin and glue sniffing. All films are offered to the school system (public and private) for use in their drug education programs.

Co. Personnel Involved: 1 person—handles reservations and requests for films

Measure of Success: These are the only drug films of this type in Castle and Cooke's community. They receive heavy usage and have been highly praised by the instructors using them.

STEP PROGRAM

CELANESE CORP.
522 Fifth Avenue
New York, N.Y. 10036

Business: Chemicals, Films, Coatings,
   Manufacturing
Sales: 1,300mm
CEO: John W. Brooks   Employees: 36,000

Contact: S. J. Brockman
Address: same as above
Telephone: (212) 867-2000, ext. 3155
Program Reaches: 12-16/year
When Started: 1967
Budget: $18,000

Program Outline:

Celanese sponsors each summer at Hampton Institute a program to train selected female minority high school graduates to be efficient and resourceful office workers at various Celanese plants and facilities. The students receive an 8-week scholarship to Hampton.

Co. Personnel Involved: primarily 1, for about 8% of his time in summer months.

Measure of Success: The program will run again in 1972 for the 6th consecutive summer. The retention rate for 5 years has been about 60%.

ONE-TO-ONE PROGRAM

CENTRAL PENN NATIONAL BANK
5 Penn Center
Philadelphia, Pa. 19101

Business: Banking
CEO: Harold F. Still, Jr.

Sales: not applicable
Employees: 1,115

Contact: Cecil W. Bond, Jr., Asst. Cashier
Address: 4th Fl., same as above
Telephone: (215) 854-3137
Program Reaches: 20
When Started: September, 1970
Budget: no planned budget

Program Outline:

The purpose of the program is to improve reading levels and arithmetic skills of children in city's inner schools, specifically, Bartlett Junior High School, 11th and Catherine Streets, Philadelphia.

The program gives these children, many of whom come from fatherless families, individual attention which usually is lacking at home or in the classroom. In addition, it exposes them to situations which they would not ordinarily encounter in the inner city, in the form of field trips to the seashore, to the Art Museum, Central Penn's executive offices and other points of interest in the Philadelphia area.

Central Penn plans to increase the number of tutors participating in the program and thus increase the number of children reached.

Co. Personnel Involved: Ten employees serve as tutors with 13 more serving as alternates.

Measure of Success: The children have come to rely on the tutors and look forward to the individual attention they are receiving and to sharing experiences with the tutors. In addition, the tutors enjoy the sessions with the children and feel they are "becoming involved."

BUSINESS EXPERIENCE TRAINING PROGRAM (BET)

THE CHASE MANHATTAN BANK
1 Chase Manhattan Plaza
New York, N.Y. 10015

Business: Banking
Total Assets: 25,000mm
CEO: Herbert Patterson

Sales: not applicable

Employees: 18,900

Contact: Robert Walters
Address: 80 Pine Street, New York, N.Y. 10005
Telephone: (212) 676-7003
Program Reaches: 277 students as of the end of 1971
When Started: 1964
Budget: n/a

Program Outline:

Chase Manhattan's BET Program is a work-study training project for high school students, particularly those from minority groups. The program's objective is to provide these youngsters with an exposure to the business world through a planned training program, with a view toward helping them qualify for employment responsibilities.

Chosen from schools with a high drop-out rate, the youngsters are recommended by the New York City Board of Education and screened by the Bank's Human Resources Department. They are employed at the Bank from 2 to 5 P.M., 5 days a week. Their morning hours are spent attending regular high school classes. At the Bank they received on-the-job training, supplemented by group orientation sessions and field trips conducted by representatives of the various areas of the Bank. BET trainees are not required to make an employment commitment to the Bank, nor does the Bank guarantee employment. However, they are offered permanent assignments after completing the program if they are able to meet Chase Manhattan's standards. Most trainees have planned for furthering their education and many are presently attending night school with the aid of the Bank's tuition refund plan.

Co. Personnel Involved: The program is coordinated by a full time member of Chase Manhattan's training staff. In addition, each student is supervised by appropriate personnel in the area of his assignment.

Measure of Success: Through 1971, 277 trainees have joined BET, of whom 195 finished high school and 57 went on to college. Another 101 became full time Chase Manhattan staff members.

SATELLITE ACADEMY PROGRAM

THE CHASE MANHATTAN BANK
1 Chase Manhattan Plaza
New York, N.Y. 10015

Business: Banking   Sales: not applicable
Total Assets: 25,000mm
Ceo: Herbert Patterson   Employees: 18,900

Contact: Arthur J. Humphrey
Address: same as above
Telephone: (212) 552-2222
Program Reaches: To date, Chase has 100 of a total of
   400 students in its program.
When Started: October, 1971
Budget: n/a

Program Outline:

The Satellite Academy Program, undertaken as a cooperative effort by the City of New York, The Chase Manhattan Bank and other private firms, is an attempt to implement innovative alternatives in secondary education for a cross-section of high school juniors and seniors. The program combines vocational and scholastic sides of the students' experience in a work-study program aimed at keeping them in school to earn a diploma. Chase is providing jobs for 100 students in 1 of 3 Satellite Academies in New York City. The Academy offers a high school program in units small enough to allow for individualized attention in a program which alternates a week of classes and a week at a paying job.

Co. Personnel Involved: One full time officer directs the program and 2 coordinators help monitor the students' work and development. In addition, participating students are supervised by Bank personnel in their job assignments.

Measure of Success: The Satellite Academy is very new, but an early sign of success is its 90% attendance rate which compares to a 60% rate in New York City's public high schools.

NEIGHBORHOOD LIBRARY PROGRAM

CITIZENS AND SOUTHERN NATIONAL BANK
99 Annex
Atlanta, Ga. 30399

Business: Banking   Sales: not applicable
CEO: Mills B. Lane, Jr.   Employees: 3,550

Contact: William J. Van Landingham
Address: same as above
Telephone: (404) 588-2774
Program Reaches: Albany minority community
When Started: 1971
Budget: $23,000

Program Outline:

The purpose of the program is to stimulate and encourage reading by children in low-income areas of Albany, Georgia. The Neighborhood Library program, established in Albany, provides 3 new libraries which are housed in mobile home units. The books are all paperbacks and cards have been issued to over 1,000 individuals as library members. Follow-up is not rigidly kept up since the scope of the program was to get as many books into as many neighborhood homes as possible.

Additional community assistance has provided such adjuncts as movies, story telling sessions, remedial reading programs and volunteer staff members. A remedial reading program for first graders has also been initiated in Albany. Over 200 children enrolled in classes which met for 6 weeks with students identified by local educators as in need of reading help.

Co. Personnel Involved: 65 or 70

Measure of Success: Over 2500 people in the disadvantaged neighborhoods have registered for library membership since last spring. Over 1,200 books are being checked out each month by the area's residents.

TAMARAC CENTER

DAYTON HUDSON CORP.
700 Nicollet Mall
Minneapolis, Minn. 55402

Business: Retail Stores   Sales: 1,000mm
CEO: Kenneth N. Dayton   Employees: 2,700

Contact: Tommy Thompson, Minn. City Coordinator
Address: 301 City Hall
    Minneapolis, Minn. 55415
Telephone: (612) 330-2032
Program Reaches: 1,300 for 1 year
When Started: The project was conceived and organized
    in 1970.
Budget: $210,391, about ½ raised privately

Program Outline:

Tamarac Center is a summer camp for job training, human resources development, modern conservation education and social interaction.

Students from Minneapolis junior and senior high schools participate. Most of the campers are from the inner city schools and 75% are disadvantaged.

The Center is operated by a consortium: the City, the Minneapolis Public Schools and the YMCA. The Minneapolis Schools staff and direct the educational programs. The camp operates for 10 weeks in 5 2-week periods. About 5 hours a day 6 days a week, are spent in classes with the balance of the day available for recreational activities in which the use of the natural environment is emphasized.

Dormitory counselors, many of whom are college graduates, live with and help the campers. In each of the sessions some 200 youngsters learn how to build fiberglass canoes, rebuild fireplaces at refuge picnic sites, learn photography, auto mechanics and other skills. Other courses offered include field ecology, Indian culture, carpentry, metal work, recreational careers, remedial reading and math.

The recreational program enables the teens to interact and form friendships in a coed multi-racial community as well as affording them the opportunity to develop social, physical and individual sports skills. For many, this is their first wilderness experience.

The project was conceived and organized by the Dayton Hudson Corporation Environmental Development Department and funds were provided by the Dayton Hudson Foundation. Even though Dayton Hudson initiated the project and is the major principal funder, about a dozen other companies also contribute to the Center.

Co. Personnel Involved: Members of the company are involved on the Board of Directors and as fund raisers.

Measure of Success: Class attendance in the 1971 session was better than 95% and only 20 of the total enrollees dropped out, mostly due to discipline problems or homesickness. Parent evaluations were very supportive, campers cited a significant number of learning and personal growth experiences and were enthusiastically looking forward to the 1971 season.

COMMUNITY IMPROVEMENT OF
ROCK ISLAND COUNTY

DEERE & CO.
John Deere Road
Moline, Ill. 61265

Business: Farm and Industrial Equipment and Consumer
    Products
Sales: 1,188mm
CEO: Ellwood F. Curtis   Employees: 41,700

Contact: Charles W. Toney
Address: same as above
Telephone: (309) 792-4540
Program Reaches: 175 youth each summer
When Started: 1968
Budget: about $50,000/year (Deere & Company support,
    $30,000)

Program Outline:

The purpose of the program is to provide summer work experience for underprivileged youth in Rock Island County between the ages of 14 and 16.

Business firms in Rock Island contribute funds. A part time director is hired. Youths 14-16 are hired by schools, cities, colleges, park boards and other local agencies with the money raised by business. They mow grass, paint city property, cut weeds, etc. In addition to earning money, they gain work experience to help them in later years. One day each week, their work consists of going to class. On this training day, the youths are counseled on education opportunities, drug dangers, handling money, etc.

Co. Personnel Involved: n/a

Measure of Success: n/a

UPWARD BOUND

DUPONT CO.
1007 Market Street
Wilmington, Del. 19898

Business: Diversified Manufacturing
Sales: 3,800
CEO: Charles B. McCoy   Employees: 110,865

Contact: John Burchenal
Address: same as above
Telephone: (302) 774-2036
Program Reaches: n/a
When Started: 1967
Budget: $41,000 in 1971; $140,800 since 1967

Program Outline:

DuPont was one of the nation's pioneer sponsors of the Upward Bound Program designed to bring underachieving, deserving high school students into college, students who would ordinarily not get to college. For example, in the high school class of 1966, 50 high school students were selected, some of whom had no intention or chance to go to college. These rising seniors spent the summer before their senior year on the campus of the University of Delaware, getting accustomed to campus life, attending special classes and receiving intensive guidance. In addition, DuPont assumed responsibility for providing and finding summer employment for those youngsters who needed the money. Other companies are now being asked to participate.

Co. Personnel Involved: about 4-6 involved in planning, funding, handling procurement of summer jobs

Measure of Success: Of the 50 seniors selected from the class of 1966, 46 were accepted by and entered college. Today 33 are still in college, 8 different colleges. In subsequent years, 45 out of 50 entered college and 33 are still enrolled. This year, out of 40 seniors and 16 high school graduates, making a total of 56, 55 were admitted to 10 different colleges last fall.

UNITED STATES YOUTH GAMES

EASTERN AIR LINES, INC.
l0 Rockefeller Plaza
New York, N.Y. 10020

Business: Transportation, Hotels, Distribution
    Services
Sales: 971mm
CEO: Samuel L. Higginbottom   Employees: 31,500

Contact: Howard L. Levine, Sr. Staff Assoc.
Address: same as above
Telephone: (212) 956-4026
Program Reaches: 1000's of inner city young people
When Started: 1965
Budget: About $12,000

Program Outline:

The purpose of the program is to provide inner-city athletic competition for boys and girls, 10-15 during the summer.

Young people in some 12 U.S. cities compete throughout each summer for the right to represent their city in the annual U.S. Youth Games each August. Eastern contributes funds which enable them to fly to the games, arranges charter flights, writes newspaper stories, and provides for media coverage. As a result, underprivileged team members, who might otherwise find it very difficult to fly commerically, are given the opportunity to visit new cities. Eastern Air Lines, in turn, receives the benefit of positive image media coverage while helping disadvantaged youth.

Co. Personnel Involved: Two public relations executives supplemented by volunteer help in each city

Measure of Success: The numbers of youngsters reached is great and grows each year.

PROJECT BEACON

EASTMAN KODAK CO.
343 State Street
Rochester, N.Y. 14650

Business: Manufacturing Photographic Equipment
Sales: 2,976mm
CEO: Walter A. Fallon   Employees: 110,700

Contact: Kenneth Howard, Dir. Urban Affairs
Address: same as above
Telephone: (716) 724-4620
Program Reaches: n/a
When Started: n/a
Budget: n/a

Program Outline:

Project Beacon is a camera-in-the-classroom program developed in the Rochester schools under the guidance of Dr. Keith Whitmore, a Kodak research scientist on loan to the school system as a full time consultant. The project stresses self-expression, the organization of complex material, and the communication of it in an understandable way. This is accomplished through the use of film cameras by children in 5 Rochester inner city schools on the first grade level. The children participate in the filming and editing of movies, expressing themselves in pictures even when written and spoken words are difficult for them. Kodak loaned the cameras and contributed the film used in the program. Teachers were given short courses in filmmaking.

The basic concept behind this experiment is the fact that today's children are the first children to grow up with television and they understand visual communication intuitively. The over-all goals of the project are: building the child's self image, early success in language arts, cultural enrichment, development of new materials and presentation of programs on minority history and culture.

Co. Personnel Involved: In addition to Dr. Whitmore, several persons from Learning Systems Laboratory of Kodak Research Labs, as required by the project, are involved.

Measure of Success: Dr. Whitmore says that the average child in Project Beacon has advanced his skills level 1½ years. A by-product of the program is the way the films have drawn parents from the inner city neighborhoods into closer contact with the schools. For example, PTA meetings which otherwise might have drawn sparse attendance bring many parents to see the films which the children have made.

YOUTH PHOTOGRAPHY PROGRAM

EASTMAN KODAK CO.
343 State Street
Rochester, N.Y. 14650

Business: Manufacturing Photographic Equipment
Sales: 2,976mm
CEO: Walter A. Fallon   Employees: 110,700

Contact: Charles E. Fitzgibbon
Address: same as above
Telephone: (716) 724-4520
Program Reaches: 15,000 youngsters/year
When Started: Summer of 1968
Budget: n/a

Program Outline:

The purpose of the program is to teach communication, and to help youngsters who need and desire to learn how to communicate to understand the world around them. This is a national program sponsored in more than 50 U.S. cities with about 100 local individual projects.

The program is a joint effort of the National Association of Photographic Manufacturers, NAPM member companies, and local community sponsors. Photographic manufacturers contribute equipment and materials for use by young people. The young people snap and develop their own still pictures. For movies, they write the scenarios, shoot the film and edit it. They learn to tell a story through photography and are amazingly successful even though many of them have to struggle to read and write.

Co. Personnel Involved: Several are involved in the national program coordination, plus volunteers for Rochester projects and other communities.

Measure of Success: Evaluation of the past year's results across the country indicate that many youngsters who have been in the program communicate better in school and improved their scholastic performances.

BEEP & STEP

THE FIRST PENNSYLVANIA
BANKING & TRUST CO.
555 City Line Ave.
Bala Cynwyd, Pa. 19004

Business: Banking   Sales: not applicable
Deposits: Dec. 31, 1971—$2.9 billion
CEO: John R. Bunting   Employees: 4,323

Contact: Kathryn C. McDermott
Address: 15 & Chestnut Sts., Philadelphia, Pa.
Telephone: (215) 786-8004
Program Reaches: to date approx. 120
When Started: 1967
Budget: n/a

Program Outline:

The purpose of this program is to acquaint inner-city high school students with the business world and to encourage their striving for careers in banking.

In both the BEEP and STEP programs, the students attend regular high school classes in the mornings and work in the bank 5 afternoons a week for a period of 8 months. Along with the job training, the students receive training in written communications and inter-personal relations. This application of educational training to work experience tends to reduce school drop-out rates.

Co. Personnel Involved: Two people directly involved. All employees working in the areas where students are placed are indirectly involved.

Measure of Success: Upon completion of high school, nearly all of the program's students become full-time bank employees.

AEROSPACE AND AVIATION ACADEMY

GENERAL ELECTRIC
RE-ENTRY & ENVIRONMENTAL
SYSTEMS DIVISION
3198 Chestnut Street
Philadelphia, Pa. 19101

Business: Aerospace and Environmental Systems
Sales: n/a
CEO: Otto Klima, Jr., V.P. and Div. Gen. Mgr. RESD
Employees: 4,000

Contact: Hank Koenig
Address: Phila. Urban Coalition
    1512 Walnut Street, Phila., Pa. 19102
Telephone: (215) 841-5568
Program Reaches: n/a
When Started: January, 1970
Budget: RESD invested approx. $8,000

Program Outline:

The purpose of this program is to provide educational opportunity to high school students in Philadelphia's depressed areas to improve their career potential through skills in highly sophisticated aerospace and aviation industries.

RESD acted as a catalyst at the inception of the academy, bringing together representatives of aerospace and aviation to lay the groundwork to develop a curriculum that would ensure the readiness of students in facing job challenges in industry. Designed as a school within a school for non-college bound students, the academy was developed under the auspices of Philadelphia's Urban Coalition and held in cooperation with South Philadelphia and Benjamin Franklin (Malcolm X) high schools.

Co. Personnel Involved: about 5 persons—1 man full time for 5 months

Measure of Success: RESD trained 10 students. Upon graduation, at least 3 of the students were placed in G.E.'s Philadelphia Works.

FLEXIBLE CAMPUS PROGRAM

JOHN HANCOCK MUTUAL LIFE INSURANCE CO.
200 Berkeley Street
Boston, Mass. 02117

Business: Insurance   Sales: 1,760mm
CEO: Frank B. Maher   Employees: 22,554

Contact: Marion L. Nierintz
Address: same as above
Telephone: (617) 421-4267
Program Reaches: 1,000
When Started: planning—mid-1971; implementation—early 1972
Budget: n/a

Program Outline:

John Hancock, in cooperation with the city of Boston and other firms and community organizations, has combined educational and business resources to provide high school students off-campus credit courses and internships.

In this new dimension of high school curriculum involving initially 1,000 students, the company donates its facilities and personnel for teaching courses such as electronic data processing, job instruction, effective communications and business organization. At John Hancock, 8 students from the Burke School are attending a 10-week course in business machines and meet at the company 3 afternoons a week. The rest of their time is spent at the high school where they are completing required courses. Also, 4 11th grade students attend a class in job instruction training which is also attended by John Hancock employees. In addition, John Hancock offers a basic computer programming course. Two boys attend all day, every day, for 2 months, while most other students in the program do have to report to school at least a few hours a day or 1 per week.

This is a pilot program; it is too early to fully evaluate yet. Changes will be made only in conjunction with Boston Public School personnel.

Co. Personnel Involved: approx. 10 (predominantly in-company instructors from education and training and EDP)

Measure of Success: Initial indications show that students have been able to meaningfully participate in classes and have expressed a high degree of enthusiasm. Boston Public School coordinators have also been pleased with the program.

SNACK PACK

HUNT-WESSON FOODS, INC.
1645 West Valencia Drive
Fullerton, Cal. 92634

Business: Manufacturing Foods and Matches
Sales: 400mm
CEO: Edward Gelsthorpe   Employees: 6,800

Contact: Kenneth J. Ward, Dir. Corp. Rel.
Address: same as above
Telephone: (714) 871-2100
Program Reaches: hard to estimate
When Started: Fall, 1971
Budget: $500,000 combined

Program Outline:

Two service campaigns have been conducted by the company under this brand. The first was an educational program the company felt obliged to undertake in relation to the new easy-open Snack Pack cans. It seemed that because the container was new and was oriented toward children, a problem with cuts due to mishandling was experienced. The company ran a letter to parents in a national women's magazine and did a special television commercial aimed at children, as well as adults, to educate them on opening the container. The second involved participation in a national UNICEF drive, in which needy children, through the contributions of labels, could be immunized against whooping cough, diptheria and tetanus. It is estimated that the program will result in several thousand vaccinations throughout the world.

Co. Personnel Involved: 5 people, primarily marketing and advertising personnel as well as sales promotion

Measure of Success: $135,569 was donated to UNICEF as a result of the program

TUTORING PROGRAM

HEWLETT-PACKARD CO.
1501 Page Mill Road
Palo Alto, Cal. 94304

Business: Electronic, Medical, Analytical and Computing
    Instrumentation
Sales: 375mm
CEO: William R. Hewlett   Employees: 16,000

Contact: Ena Yale
Address: same as above
Telephone: (415) 493-1501
Program Reaches: no official count
When Started: 1968
Budget: n/a

Program Outline:

The purpose of this program is to allow HP persons to take time off with pay to serve as teaching assistants at local junior high schools in order to assist primarily minority students in East Palo Alto who need assistance in reading and other subjects.

Originally, the program was operated in conjunction with 3 junior high schools in East Palo Alto. Volunteers go 2 days per week to help tutor minority children who need help with reading problems. The tutoring project always has been an informal program which depends upon the individual efforts of HP persons rather than company involvement. Individuals pay their own expenses for travel, but HP does allow paid time off so they can participate and provides some supplies and use of duplicating and related equipment.

Although past participants feel it would be beneficial to initiate this program at the lower grades, no plans have been made for this at this time. It may be introduced at some future date.

Co. Personnel Involved: n/a

Measure of Success: There have been many individual successes, but the program as a whole has not worked satisfactorily. Of the 30-40 persons originally participating, the number has dwindled to only a few. The primary difficulty concerns the age level of the students being tutored. All participants agreed that it would have been much better to be with younger children (3rd and 4th graders for example). The most mentioned negative factors were lack of discipline and interest on the part of the 7th and 8th graders. Mrs. Ena Yale—most active of the tutors—now spends more time performing various support functions (preparing special assignments, etc.) than she spends in actual tutorial sessions. She feels there still is a need for this type of program at the junior high level, but that untrained persons such as those volunteers from HP could perform a more valuable service in the lower grades.

YOUTH OPPORTUNITY IN BANKING

MARINE MIDLAND BANK
237 Main Street
Buffalo, N.Y. 14203

Business: Banking   Sales: not applicable
CEO: John L. Hettrick   Employees: 2,250

Contact: Sylvia Maye
Address: same as above
Telephone: (716) 843-4197
Program Reaches: 90
When Started: 1968
Budget: n/a

Program Outline:

The purpose of this program is to provide opportunity and motivation for potential high school drop-outs in the banking industry, with part time training and employment while they continue their studies. The program encompasses students in the Buffalo school system who are potential drop-outs. To qualify for the program and to continue on-the-job training, the students are required to maintain passing grades, show improvement in their work performance and to maintain a good attendance record at both school and work.

Co. Personnel Involved: The Bank's Personnel Department is responsible for administering the program.

Measure of Success: Many of those in the YOB program have remained in full time positions at the Bank after graduating from high school.

SUMMER PROGRAM FOR NEEDY YOUTH

LEEDS & NORTHRUP CO.
Sumneytown Pike
North Wales, Pa. 19454
(Suburban Philadelphia)

Business: Electronic Instruments and
    Process Control Systems
Sales: approx. 100mm
CEO: George E. Beggs, Jr.   Employees: 4,270

Contact: M. Ceaser, Mgr., Org. Dev.
Address: same as above
Telephone: (215) 643-2000, ext. 610
Program Reaches: 26 trainees each summer
When Started: 1968
Budget: approx $27,000 for direct salaries for trainees and
    coordinator

Program Outline:

The purpose of the program is to provide needy youth (who have achieved at least 10th grade in high school, and either were potential drop-outs, actual drop-outs, or graduates unable to obtain employment) with a summer work experience which would give them certain basic skills and an understanding of the work habits, attitudes and motivation needed if an underprivileged young man is to become a responsible, productive citizen.

With the assistance of a Black coordinator experienced in DPA case work, school and recreation supervision, specially hired for this project, the program was operational for a 10-week period with 4 hours daily spent on indoctrination and training (handling of personal finances, how to apply for a job, math review, blueprint reading, soldering, use of hand tools, assembly, wiring and inspection techniques, etc.) and 4 hours in light maintenance work around plant and grounds.

Union local cooperated with Leeds & Northrup Company and was permitted to give an indoctrination session on union philosophy and practice. Pay was at "going rates," with provision for modest increases if merited. Preparation included careful indoctrination of regular line supervision in company areas affected, with sensitivity-training on ghetto-induced problems and attitudes.

Measure of Success: Only 2 trainees resigned voluntarily; they planned to return to high school. Four more resigned on request. Remaining 20 stuck to program, or were placed in permanent jobs before end of schedule. Trainees learned that training and skills help determine ability to get and hold a job. In order to implement this program, children of regular employees had to forego summer jobs previously available to them.

Program was repeated in substantially the same form during the following 2 summers and is expected to be essentially the same for subsequent summers.

Co. Personnel Involved: coordinator, employed specially for program, as well as 2 full time regular supervisory staff and 9 supervisory staff who participated as needed.

SUMMER TRAINING EMPLOYMENT PROGRAM (STEP)

MCDONNELL DOUGLAS CORP.
P.O. Box 516
St. Louis, Mo. 63166

Business: Aerospace   Sales: 2088mm
CEO: Sanford N. McDonnell   Employees: 92,552

Contact: T. H. Allison
Address: same as above
Telephone: (314) 232-7438
Program Reaches: 50-100/year
When Started: 1968
Budget: $1,275/trainee

Program Outline:

The purpose of the program is to provide disadvantaged youth with the opportunity to develop personal and work habits required to obtain and maintain employment.

Summer employment is provided to high school youth of low-income families, introducing them to a satisfactory work experience. The students participate in a work environment simulating production with its responsibilities and regulations and observe the upward mobility available to skilled craftsmen. The program is rounded with a generous share of training devoted to showing direct relationships between responsible citizenship, success in personal management and a rewarding career.

Co. Personnel Involved: During the program, 8 employees full time and 10-12 part time.

Measure of Success: A high percentage completing the program continue their schooling and enter college.

UNICEN, INC.

THE MEAD CORP.
Talbott Tower
Dayton, Ohio 45402

Business: Diversified
CEO: J. W. McSwiney

Sales: 1,000mm
Employees: 36,900

Contact: Percy Jones
Address: W. Third and Conover Streets
  Dayton, Ohio
Telephone: (513) 277-4291
Program Reaches: n/a
When Started: 1968
Budget: $150,000 estimated for full operation; prospects
  for 1972, $10-40,000

Program Outline:

The purpose of this program is to provide comprehensive services, including recreation, informal counseling, cultural enrichment and business experience.

UNICEN started as a teen club, then the idea was expanded. UNICEN is still struggling to get its program moving. It began with a $10,000 "seed money" grant from Mead Corporation in 1968. The first phase of the program to be started will be the recreation phase—providing a center where teenagers can get together for dances, games, recreation, conversation, etc. and where they will meet with counselors who will be, for the most part, young Black people who have "made it" in terms of economic and social situations.

In addition, UNICEN hopes to operate a series of small businesses which will not only provide work experience, but will eventually help carry the other parts of the program. A building has been acquired and remodeling has begun. The program will eventually include lectures, movies, field trips, etc.

Co. Personnel Involved: Approximately 12 have been involved in various stages—ranging from leadership on the Board of Trustees to extended planning leadership, to proposal writing. Mead management was influential in helping to obtain a $150,000 building for UNICEN.

Measure of Success: n/a

YOUTH SCREEN PRINTING, INC.

THE MEAD CORP.
Talbott Tower
Dayton, Ohio 45402

Business: Diversified
CEO: J. W. McSwiney

Sales: 1,000mm
Employees: 36,900

Contact: Melvin Hanton, Dir.
Address: 12 Ventura Street, Dayton, Ohio 45407
Telephone: (513) 268-6826
Program Reaches: n/a
When Started: June, 1970
Budget: estimated $50,000/year

Program Outline:

The purpose of the program is to provide business training, experience, and eventually advanced vocational training for disadvantaged young people of high school age, primarily Black.

The program involves all aspects of the silk screen operation including graphic design, screen preparation, production, marketing, accounting, etc. The idea is to give some work experience to disadvantaged young people. As the program is fully implemented, Youth Screen Printing, Inc. has an opportunity to serve as a training operation for the screen printing trade. The Midwest Screen Printing Association has provided support in terms of technical advice, used equipment, etc. with this goal in mind. The program possibly will be expanded to include a scholarship program, classes, field trips, etc.

Co. Personnel Involved: Four—a member of the P.R. department has served as an advisory board member since the organization started and has provided some technical help in writing proposals and obtaining publicity for the program. Financial planning personnel have helped suggest budgets, capital needs, etc. Office services supervisor helped with office layout, systems, etc.

Measure of Success: Demonstrated ability to produce in excess of $4,000 sales per month. Ultimately an important measure would be the number of youth that move into the screen printing business elsewhere.

COOPERATIVE STUDENT PLAN

METROPOLITAN LIFE INSURANCE CO.
One Madison Avenue
New York, N.Y. 10010

Business: Insurance   Sales: 5,555mm
CEO: Richard R. Shinn   Employees: 57,000

Contact: J. G. Reiners
Address: same as above
Telephone: (212) 578-3440
Program Reaches: 300-400/year
When Started: 1947
Budget: varies according to employee needs

Program Outline:

Each year, hundreds of high school seniors, including large numbers of Negro and Puerto Rican students, work in Metropolitan's Home Office. In addition to providing needed financial help while attending school, this work experience also motivates them to remain in school until graduation.

Under this program, students work alternate weeks in pairs. At the time of graduation, if they remain with the company, they are given credit for their work service in terms of starting salary, vacation allowance, job assignment, etc.

Co. Personnel Involved: Difficult to answer since program is used throughout the Home Office. The individual supervisors provide on-the-job training, orientation and encourage self-development.

Measure of Success: Almost all qualify for permanent employment and about 70-80% continue in full time regular employment following graduation.

HIGH SCHOOL SERVICE STATION TRAINING PROGRAM

MOBIL OIL CORP.
150 E. 42nd Street
New York, N.Y. 10017

Business: Petroleum Operations Sales: 7,261mm
CEO: William P. Tavoulares   Employees: 75,600

Contact: A. L. Roe
Address: same as above
Telephone: (212) 833-3372
Program Reaches: from 25 to 100 boys/year
When Started: September, 1970
Budget: varies, depending on facilities and equipment already available at the school

Program Outline:

The purpose of this program is to reduce the high school dropout rate at inner city high schools.

A pilot program was instituted by Mobil at a New York City high school in which junior year boys are given automotive and service training plus paid work experience as service station attendants, attending school 1 week and working the next week throughout the school year. Emphasis is on providing an interesting classroom experience relevant to the world of work, and developing a marketable skill. Mobil trained the school system instructors who teach the course. Mobil also helped develop the course outline; supplies service station equipment used in teaching; provides text materials and visual aids and arranges for field trips and jobs with Mobil dealers.

Co. Personnel Involved: several people from headquarters and from 2 to 6 field offices for each project

Measure of Success: Success in achieving and maintaining a high level of class attendance at New York City schools, plus evidence of increased interest in other courses, e.g. math and reading, have resulted in introducing the program to a Los Angeles school in January, 1972. Initial results there are good. Further expansion to 2 additional cities is planned for September, 1972.

EDUCATION PROGRAMS

MOTOROLA, INC.
9401 Grand Avenue
Franklin Park, Ill. 60131

Business: Electronics
CEO: Wm. J. Weisz

Sales: 900+mm
Employees: 36,000

Contact: Judy Ressler, P.R.
Address: same as above
Telephone: (312) 451-1000, ext. 3692
Program Reaches: n/a
When Started: n/a
Budget: n/a

Program Outline:

The purpose of this program is to encourage a greater quality of educational enterprise.

Program function: (1) SPD gives 2 graduate fellowships at $2,400 each to support an outstanding student in the public interest; (2) Motorola encourages its employees to serve on educational boards, committees and commissions; (3) Motorola takes an active interest in forming curricula of universities, colleges, institutes and high schools by meeting with deans and other educational persons, and serving on curricula review committees; (4) pays tuitions for education of its full time employees; (5) employees are encouraged to lecture at universities; (6) puts out "Motorola Volunteers in Civic Affairs" on a quarterly basis which encourages Motorola employees to become involved with educational institutions, among other groups; (7) donates 1,000s of dollars of electronics equipment to schools to give students a wider experience in their education; (8) offers in-plant courses (credit and non-credit) so employees may continue their education. Also encourages schools to offer a broader spectrum of courses to fulfill needs of industry's employees and the community; (9) donates a $10,000 unrestricted grant to Arizona State University each year; (10) sponsors or assists with research done by students or student groups (11) Motorola Chairman, Robert W. Galvin is one of 12 Fellows of the University of Notre Dame. Other officers and directors are trustees, etc. (12) There are a large number of other donations and cooperation between Motorola and educational institutions which are too numerous to include.

Co. Personnel Involved: all the training employees and countless number of persons who lecture or teach, become involved on school boards or committees and work on special projects with schools.

Measure of Success: A large percentage of Motorola employees receive degrees through the encouragement of the company. In Arizona State University's College of Engineering, about half of those receiving masters degrees are Motorola employees.

WELCOME TO THE POLLING BOOTH

NORTHERN ILLINOIS GAS CO.
P. O. Box 190
Aurora, Ill. 60507

Business: Distributing Natural Gas
Sales: approximate annual sales of 500 billion cubic feet of gas
CEO: C. J. Gauthier

Employees: 3,100

Contact: Chuck Schrader, Pub. Affairs
Address: same as above
Telephone: (312) 355-8000, ext. 215
Program Reaches: 200 employees and, through public summaries, an additional 3,000 employees and undetermined number of the public
When Started: 1971
Budget: n/a

Program Outline:

The purpose of the program is to interest and inform employees who are first-time voters in the American political system.

Northern Illinois Gas began this educational program because it believes strongly that achievement of the nation's goals requires a partnership between business and government. To inform young voters, to interest them in the American political system, and to help all of its employees and the general public understand the necessary partnership between business and government, NI-Gas held a program which featured Congressman Robert H. Steele (R-Conn) discussing the role of government with business and the responsibilities for young, first-time voters; Joseph F. Grimes, President of Brighams, Inc., speaking for business; and Ms. Anita Johnson, a Nader's Raider, who urged young voters to know the issues and speak out.

Co. Personnel Involved: Approximately 10 persons from the Public Affairs and Public Relations department were involved in the organization of the program. About 200 persons attended it.

Measure of Success: The enthusiastic response of those attending was reflected in controversial questions posed to the panelists. The success of the program was also reflected by inquiries from other business and media pick-up.

PRE-CONSTRUCTION TRADES TRAINING FOR JUVENILE BOYS

NORTHERN SYSTEMS CO.
4701 Lydell Drive
Cheverly, Md. 20785

Business: Modification of Human Behavior
Sales: n/a
CEO: Sam Segnar   Employees: n/a

Contact: Earl Mello, Principal
Address: Northern Systems Co.
    Cheltenham, Md. 20785
Telephone: (301) 782-4223
Program Reaches: n/a
When Started: September, 1971
Budget: $17,000

Program Outline:

The purpose of the program is to provide training in construction trades to 24 juvenile boys aged 14-15. Upon leaving the facility, they return to school.

Job skills are broken down into small modules involving simple, compound and complex uses of tools and tasks. Time and error perimeters are placed on each skill. Reading and math are tied into the skill unit. Social skills seminars provide training in handling job stress. Reinforcement is provided for positive training related activities. Alternative reward systems are discouraged. Program has a monitoring function built into it. All trainees are placed.

Co. Personnel Involved: 1 part time instructor and 1 quality assurance specialist

Measure of Success: 100% success of the first 10 boys who graduated from the program. They returned to school. None are presently in trouble.

THE COOPERATIVE TRAINING PROGRAM

THE NORTHWESTERN MUTUAL
LIFE INSURANCE CO.
720 E. Wisconsin Avenue
Milwaukee, Wis. 53202

Business: Life Insurance   Sales: 2,000mm
CEO: Francis E. Ferguson   Employees: 2,150

Contact: William Cary
Address: same as above
Telephone: (414) 271-1444
Program Reaches: n/a
When Started: 1964
Budget: n/a

Program Outline:

High school seniors from Milwaukee work part time (from 1:10 to 4:10 P.M.) at regular hourly wages for beginners. They work in Underwriting Policy, Actuarial Change Calculation, Actuarial Policy Loan, Accounting, Secretarial Files and Controls, Benefit Planning, and other areas.

A majority of young people who have come to NML under this program have stayed on.

Co. Personnel Involved: n/a

Measure of Success: The company has been pleased with the performance of the young people. Last spring, the trainees working at the 24 cooperating companies in Milwaukee spontaneously arranged and paid for an appreciation luncheon for their employers.

BETTER BREAK

PENN MUTUAL LIFE INSURANCE CO.
Independence Square
Philadelphia, Pa. 19105

Business: Life Insurance   Sales: 354mm
CEO: Frank K. Tarbox   Employees: 1,860

Contact: William Brooks,
    Coordinator of Special Events
Address: same as above
Telephone: (215) 925-7300
Program Reaches: 45/summer
When Started: Penn Mutual participated from 1968 until
    Summer, 1971.
Budget: $5,000/year

Program Outline:

The purpose of this program was to provide summer
employment for disadvantaged young people.

A dozen disadvantaged Philadelphia teenagers were off
the streets and on-the-job during the summer as a result
of the company's contribution to the city's Better Break
'70 program. The program, also known as the Mayor's
Youth Opportunities Program, will provide a wide variety
of employment, cultural and recreational programs to
Philadelphia youngsters throughout the summer.

Penn Mutual's contribution was earmarked for the "Jobs
for Hard to Reach Youth" phase of the program and
provided 8 weeks of employment for 12 boys and girls
ranging from age 14 to 18.

A total of 45 youths had jobs under the program working
with younger children at neighborhood recreation centers. The boys will organize and coach athletic activities
and the girls will supervise music, drama and handicraft
programs.

Co. Personnel Involved: n/a

Measure of Success: n/a

COOPERATIVE OFFICE EDUCATION AND
NEW JERSEY PART TIME PROGRAMS

PENN MUTUAL LIFE INSURANCE CO.
Independence Square
Philadelphia, Pa. 19105

Business: Life Insurance   Sales: 354mm
CEO: Frank K. Tarbox   Employees: 1,860

Contact: Daniel E. Dawley
Address: same as above
Telephone: (215) 925-7300
Program Reaches: n/a
When Started: 1946
Budget: n/a

Program Outline:

Instead of waiting until June graduation to seek out jobs,
30-50 top commercial students from area high schools
begin working part time at Penn Mutual in late January
or early February.

Depending on their skills in commercial classes, students
are placed throughout the company as stenographers,
typists, file clerks, office machine operators or general
clerks. The work experience becomes part of their course
load, and at the end of the term their performance is
rated by their Penn Mutual supervisors. Although the
Cooperative Education and New Jersey Part Time programs are similar in many ways, procedural details do
differ somewhat.

Co-ops alternately spend a week at work, maintaining the
same hours as regular employees, and a week at school.
So that the job is covered at all times, 2 pupils fill each
position. The part timers work daily from 1:30 p.m. to
4:30 p.m. Their mornings are spent in high school
commercial classes.

Co. Personnel Involved: n/a

Measure of Success: About 80% of the student employees are made permanent in June.

McCALL SCHOOL TUTORIAL PROJECT

PENN MUTUAL LIFE INSURANCE CO.
Independence Square
Philadelphia, Pa. 19105

Business: Life Insurance   Sales: 354mm
CEO: Frank K. Tarbox   Employees: 1,860

Contact: Suzanne Kaplan
Address: same as above
Telephone: (215) 925-7300
Program Reaches: n/a
When Started: 1971
Budget: n/a

Program Outline:

The purpose of this program is to provide tutorial assistance to pupils at the McCall Elementary School in Philadelphia, in a variety of subjects including non-academically oriented areas such as astronomy and photography.

Employee volunteers spend up to 2 hours/week at the school helping pupils with academic problems on a one-to-one basis or in a group on topics of general interest. Another group of volunteers work with students involved in educational programs held in the home office.

With the financial difficulties of the Philadelphia school system, a program of this kind is definitely needed. It enables the Penn Mutual employees to assist teachers by taking charge of the students and acting as positive influences on them. It also enables the classes to be somewhat smaller in size, increasing teacher contact with students.

Co. Personnel Involved: The Manpower Planning and Development Division is responsible for this project.

Measure of Success: n/a

BILL DELIVERY PROGRAM

THE PEOPLES GAS, LIGHT & COKE CO.
122 S. Michigan Avenue
Chicago, Ill. 60603

Business: Gas Utility   Sales: 593.4mm
CEO: Robert M. Drevs   Employees: 6,627

Contact: W. Chrisler
Address: same as above
Telephone: (312) 431-4592
Program Reaches: 28
When Started: April, 1969
Budget: student salaries

Program Outline:

The purpose of this program is to provide job opportunities for minority high school youths in their sophomore through senior years.

The program entails 28 minority high school students delivering gas bills to customers. During the summer months, the students work full time.

This program offers work experience to students in addition to giving them an opportunity to earn money. When the student graduates from high school, if he does not choose to enter college, full time employment with the company is offered. The program originally started with 14 students.

Co. Personnel Involved: Program is overseen by 4 supervisors—1 for each 7 students, and 1 superintendent.

Measure of Success: Only 1 graduating student chose full time employment; other students who have participated in the program have entered college or sought full time employment elsewhere.

ACADEMY OF APPLIED ELECTRICAL SCIENCE

PHILADELPHIA ELECTRIC CO.
2301 Market Street
Philadelphia, Pa. 19101

Business: Electric Utility
CEO: James L. Everett

Sales: 504mm
Employees: 10,500

Contact: Hendrik B. Koning
Address: same as above
Telephone: (215) 841-4000
Program Reaches: n/a
When Started: n/a
Budget: n/a

Program Outline:

The purpose of this program is to offer practical instruction to students emphasizing individual needs as related to future employment.

The company, the School District of Philadelphia, and the Urban Coalition are engaged in a joint venture at Edison High School offering practical instruction in electronics and electricity, combined with mathematics and English courses tailored to complement laboratory work. There is also a summer employment program that offers young people the opportunity to earn money while they learn. During the school year, the company offers part time employment which is designed to further motivate and stimulate students' technical skills.

Co. Personnel Involved: Mr. Koning, a senior engineer in Philadelphia Electric Company's mechanical engineering division is assigned full time to this project.

Measure of Success: n/a

PREP (PROGRAM RESULTING IN EMPLOYMENT POSSIBILITIES)

PHILADELPHIA ELECTRIC CO.
2301 Market Street
Philadelphia, Pa. 19101

Business: Electric Utility
CEO: James L. Everett

Sales: 504mm
Employees: 10,500

Contact: Joseph F. Van Hart, Mgr., P.R. Dept.
Address: 2301 Market Street
   Philadelphia, Pa. 19101
Telephone: (215) 841-4000
Program Reaches: high school seniors in the school district of Philadelphia
When Started: 1969
Budget: n/a

Program Outline:

The long-range purpose of PREP is to provide high school youths with the skills needed to gain meaningful employment after graduation.

PREP offers paid supervised work experience in conjunction with education. It also provides counseling, training, and supplementary tutoring. The program runs concurrent with the school year—30 weeks, September through June. A typical week consists of 4 afternoons of work at a company location. The 5th afternoon is devoted to skills stimulation in mathematics and communications, and sessions dealing with group concern and the world in which we live. A review and lessons in mathematics and word problems, grammar, spelling, reading and oral communications as well as opportunities for PREPers to express themselves in writing are offered. Reading improvement, as well as personal development courses designed to give positive attitudes towards one's self, the job and the public are also included. Periodic sessions are offered to the students which are devoted to company orientation and presentation of the utility's history, as well as seminars on career development.

Co. Personnel Involved: n/a

Measure of Success: n/a

OPERATION PREPARE

THE PHILADELPHIA NATIONAL BANK
Broad and Chestnut Streets
Philadelphia, Pa. 19101

Business: Banking   Sales: not applicable
Earnings Assets: 2,000mm
CEO: Morris Dorrance, Jr.   Employees: 2,788

Contact: Robert A. Evans, Asst. Pers. Officer
Address: same as above
Telephone: (215) 629-4707
Program Reaches: 35-45 students
When Started: 1968
Budget: n/a

Program Outline:

This is a cooperative work-study program that provides
business awareness and experience to young men and
women from inner city high schools. During the 1971-72
school year, 19 juniors and 19 seniors from 7 Philadelphia high schools go to school during the morning and
work afternoons in various PNB departments. This provides valuable job experience and school back-up which
emphasizes the learning of skills and good work habits.
Job assignments normally are for periods of 6 months or
a year to give depth of experience. During the summer,
the students work full time at their assignments.

Co. Personnel Involved: Three persons are involved in
program development and administration. Twenty-five
department heads and immediate supervisors work with
the student on the job.

Measure of Success: Of the 25 seniors in the 1970-71
program, 11 work for PNB full time, 9 went to college
and 5 are in military service, married and not working, or
unaccounted for.

SCHOOL VOLUNTEER PROGRAM

THE PHILADELPHIA SAVINGS FUND SOCIETY
1212 Market Street
Philadelphia, Pa. 19107

Business: Savings Bank   Sales: not applicable
CEO: M. Todd Cooke   Employees: 828

Contact: Anne Ruasch, Com. Affairs Coordinator
Address: same as above
Telephone: (215) 629-2132
Program Reaches: approx. 100
When Started: September, 1969
Budget: $1,000 plus and transportation costs for indivi-
    dual tutors involved

Program Outline:

The purpose of the program is to provide tutors as aids
for South Philadelphia's Meredith Elementary School
pupils in the elementary reading area. Through one-to-
one pupil ratio and in-class tutoring in the Volunteer
School Program, employees of the Bank work with
students of 1 local school, 2 hours, 1 morning per week,
for each of 20 tutors.

They work in class under the guidance of teachers, to
help pupils develop basic reading skills. Evaluation
meetings are held annually at the end of each tutoring
program to discuss satisfactoriness of efforts and develop
possible changes of direction or expansion of plans.

Co. Personnel Involved: A roster of 20 of the Bank's
employees participate each year, which represents a total
of 60 different employees involved over the 3-year period
of the program at the Bank. This represents over 700
man-hours.

Measure of Success: The volunteer tutors are enthusiastic
and have indicated good response to their efforts during
in-class sessions. The children are responding by exhi-
biting more interest in learning when a tutor concentrates
his or her efforts on the slow learner or pupil lacking
motivation.

PRE-JOB ORIENTATION PROGRAM

A. H. ROBINS CO.
1407 Cummings Drive
Richmond, Va. 23220

Business: Pharmaceuticals   Sales: 150mm
CEO: W. L. Zimmer III   Employees: 4,000

Contact: John T. Terry
Address: same as above
Telephone: (703) 257-2309
Program Reaches: 12
When Started: 1968
Budget: $10,000

Program Outline:

The program is aimed at predominantly minority high school rising seniors with limited resources who do not possess the advantages generally available to middle and upper socio-economic groups.

Individuals are assigned to unskilled "aide" jobs performing assignments while working under the guidance and direction of department supervisors and other personnel who are qualified to instruct in guided work experience. The program is approximately 10 weeks long and consists of 2 methods for providing learning experiences—actual on-the-job experience, and a series of classroom orientation meetings which are designed to emphasize personal development.

Co. Personnel Involved: 13—direct supervision and counseling

Measure of Success: The company has employed 3 graduates of past programs, and as far as can be determined, all of the enrollees have completed their requirements for graduation from high school.

JOB PREPARATION SEMINAR

ROHM & HAAS CO.
Independence Mall West
Philadelphia, Pa. 19105

Business: Manufacturing Chemicals, Plastics, Fibers, Health Products
Sales: 507mm
CEO: Vincent L. Gregory   Employees: 13,805

Contact: John M. Geisel
Address: same as above
Telephone: (215) 592-3863
Program Reaches: approximately 75-100 high school seniors
When Started: March, 1972
Budget: approximately $3,000

Program Outline:

The purpose of this program is to help prepare workbound high school seniors to seek employment as effectively as possible. The seminar provides information on hiring processes (interview techniques, content of application forms and tests, etc.) to help prepare students in locating possible job opportunities, to help them successfully pass the screening process, and to give them some insight into what to expect from employers once they have secured employment.

Co. Personnel Involved: 15 volunteer coaches conduct 1-hour seminars and workshops for 12 weeks.

Measure of Success: too early to tell

WORK/STUDY PROGRAM

ROHM & HAAS CO.
Independence Mall West
Philadelphia, Pa. 19105

Business: Manufacturing Chemicals, Plastics, Fibers,
    and Health Products
Sales: 507mm (1971)
CEO: Vincent L. Gregory   Employees: 13,805

Contact: John M. Geisel
Address: same as above
Telephone: (215) 592-2863
Program Reaches: approx 30
When Started: 1968
Budget: n/a

Program Outline:

The purpose of the program is to prevent high school students from dropping out of school and to give them work experience.

Cooperative education style enables students to spend part of the school day at company offices on clerical and other office jobs to learn techniques, habits, etc. required. Students work full time during summer and half days during school year. If the student does not attend morning session at school, he is not permitted to work in the afternoon.

Co. Personnel Involved: department heads, supervisors, fellow employees for training and supervision; members of Personnel Department for orientation and guidance

Measure of Success: Reports of supervisors indicate adequate to excellent performance on job. Some students joined permanent work force after graduation.

POTENTIALS

SMITH, KLINE & FRENCH LABORATORIES, INC.
1500 Spring Garden Street
Philadelphia, Pa. 19101

Business: Pharmaceuticals and Other Health Products
Sales: 347mm
CEO: Thomas M. Rauch   Employees: 10,000

Contact: Carver Portlock
Address: same as above
Telephone: (215) 564-2400
Program Reaches: n/a
When Started: 1968
Budget: n/a

Program Outline:

This is a program of employment, guidance and education for young people from the Spring Garden community. The program gives ambitious teenagers a chance to have working learning experiences that will prepare them for broader opportunities at the completion of high school. Classroom sessions and college and career counseling are included.

Co. Personnel Involved: 6, not full time

Measure of Success: Since the program was started in 1968, 200 young people have participated.

IN-SCHOOL EMPLOYMENT PROGRAM

TRAVELERS INSURANCE CO.
l Tower Square
Hartford, Conn. 06115

Business: Insurance   Sales: 3,000mm
CEO: Morrison H. Beach   Employees: 30,000

Contact: Wayne D. Casey
Address: Public Affairs Dept.
   same as above
Telephone: (203) 277-2764
Program Reaches: 12/each 6-week session
When Started: 1971
Budget: $150 in 1971 and 1972; $300 total

Program Outline:

The program provides school-jobs for non-employable
7th and 8th grade students. The Travelers served as fund
raiser among local businesses for the $1,000 necessary to
implement the program. A matching foundation grant
ensured continuation of the program through the
1971-1972 school year.

The school "hires" their students to perform jobs at
school for which they are paid $5/week, providing a
much-needed source of income for daily necessities as
well as practical exposure to the value of work and work
opportunities. Every 6 weeks a new group of students are
hired. The jobs are work with some meaning and learning: e.g. office aide, reading office, library, etc. Employment applications are filled out by students to simulate
the adult experience.

Co. Personnel Involved: 1 as Travelers' contact with the
school and as principal fund raiser among local businesses

Measure of Success: The program was developed in an
effort to correct the petty pilfering, etc., that the school
was experiencing. The incidence of stealing as well as the
number of police visits to the school has dropped significantly since the program began. The school's evaluation
of the program is most positive from both the guidance
and educational viewpoints. The students' reaction is
"one of the best deals we've ever had."

SUMMER JOB PROGRAM

TECHNICON INSTRUMENTS CORP.
511 Benedict Avenue
Tarrytown, N.Y. 10591

Business: Manufacturing Medical and Instrumental Test
   Equipment
Sales: 102mm
CEO: William Smyth   Employees: 2,900

Contact: Barry Katz, Employment Mgr.
Address: same as above
Telephone: (914) 631-8000
Program Reaches: varies each year
When Started: 1969
Budget: varies

Program Outline:

The purpose of the program is to provide summer
employment and funds for disadvantaged youths who
would not otherwise be financially able to further their
education.

Technicon has for the past several years participated in
the NAB's Summer Jobs Program in which at least 20
disadvantaged youths have secured summer employment
with the company.

In addition, the company matches the employees' summer earnings in the form of a scholarship fund for the
individuals to use for advanced training and/or schooling.

Co. Personnel Involved: Personnel Department and respective supervisors

Measure of Success: participants continuing education;
personal letters of appreciation

SUMMER FUN PROGRAM

UNION ELECTRIC CO.
P. O. Box 87
St. Louis, Mo. 63166

Business: Electric Production and Distribution
Sales: 317mm
CEO: Charles J. Dougherty   Employees: 6,063

Contact: Eugene Cerulo
Address: same as above
Telephone: (314) 621-3222
Program Reaches: 2,400 youngsters and parents annually
When Started: 1969
Budget: for Union Electric, about $1,000

Program Outline:

The program provides inner city youngsters, ages 9, 10 and 11 with an opportunity to spend a day in a "country" environment with their contemporaries.

The program is a joint effort of the company and the St. Louis Board of Education. Three days a week, 4 teachers bring about 120 children by bus to the Employee Club. They are at the club from 9 till 3 and are kept busy every minute. The program begins with the Pledge of Allegiance, and ends with an educational movie. In between, there is a nature walk identifying trees, a Reddy Kilowatt movie, an artcraft session and play table and field games.

Co. Personnel Involved: 2; 1 full time for about a month and the other part time

Measure of Success: Many youngsters show interest in repeating their visit.

JUNIOR ACHIEVEMENT PROGRAMS

UNIROYAL, INC.
1230 Avenue of the Americas
New York, N.Y. 10020

Business: Manufacturing Rubber Products, Plastics, Chemicals, etc.
Sales: 1,678mm
CEO: George R. Vila   Employees: 64,168

Contact: H. D. Smith, V.P., Public Affairs
Address: same as above
Telephone: (212) 247-5000
Program Reaches: n/a
When Started:: n/a
Budget: n/a

Program Outline:

Nearly every Uniroyal location in the United States actively supports a Junior Achievment Program in its community, offering young people a chance to learn the rewards and benefits of the competitive business system. In addition, the Uniroyal Foundation supports the national J-A effort. Uniroyal people volunteer their time beginning when a Junior Achievement "company" starts business in the fall, continuing until liquidation in the spring.

Co. Personnel Involved: n/a

Measure of Success: n/a

WASHINGTON HIGH SCHOOL GRANT

UNITED STATES NATIONAL BANK OF OREGON
321 S.W. Sixth Avenue
P.O. Box 4421
Portland, Oregon 97208

Business: Banking
CEO: E. L. Dresler

Sales: not applicable
Employees: 3,998

Contact: John D. Mills, V.P. Urban Affairs
Address: same as above
Telephone: (503) 225-6111
Program Reaches: n/a
When Started: n/a
Budget: n/a

Program Outline:

The purpose of the program is to provide experience to a group of high school students from Washington High School, an opportunity to work within the free enterprise system, and to provide jobs for the summer.

Bank enabled a group of high school students to take a grant of $10,000 with no strings attached and set up the Malcolm X corporation, a wholly owned subsidiary of the Bank that was non-profit in nature.

Co. Personnel Involved: n/a

Measure of Success: The company operated and built pallets for construction work. It hired up to 22 people.

YOUTH ENTERPRISE AWARDS

JIM WALTER CORP.
P. O. Box 22601
Tampa, Fla. 33622

Business: Building and Construction Materials Manufacturing, Home Builder
Sales: 700mm
CEO: F. J. Pizzitola

Employees: 20,000

Contact: Dayton Todd
Address: same as above
Telephone: (813) 872-3439
Program Reaches: 25 directly and an unknown number indirectly
When Started: December, 1971
Budget: $154,000

Program Outline:

This 1-year program was begun in recognition of the 25th anniversary of the Jim Walter Corporation. The purpose is to search the United States for 25 especially enterprising young adults (ages 18-25) who have been successful in a business initiated by them, or have shown outstanding ambition and drive in personal progress or in an activity to aid fellow man. The specific purpose is to call attention to the positive contribution youth is making to society, and to help the person in his or her own efforts with a $1,000 cash award and with the recognition they will receive.

Through publicity in newspapers and industrial trade journals, plus the help of organizations such as National Association of Manufacturers, Jaycees, Junior Achievement, Chamber of Commerce, etc., the company hopes to reach a large share of the U.S. population. Candidates will submit entry forms describing their achievements and a panel of judges, (prominent business and government people) will select the winners in December, 1972.

Co. Personnel Involved: 2 internal people, plus secretarial help and an agency individual part time

Measure of Success: There has been widespread use of the story that was filed through United Press International. The Company received confirmation from some major organizations in the country that they will cooperate in the search. For example, the National Association of Manufacturers, has told the company it will urge the 10,000 women's clubs with which they have contact to take on the search as a club project.

JUNIOR ACHIEVEMENT FOR BLACK YOUTH

WESTERN MASSACHUSETTS ELECTRIC CO.
174 Brush Hill Avenue
West Springfield, Mass. 01089

Business: Public Utility   Sales: 66.9mm
CEO: Robert E. Barrett, Jr.   Employees: 987

Contact: Mack W. Jacobs
Address: same as above
Telephone: (413) 785-5871, ext. 298
Program Reaches: 30
When Started: 1971-1972 period
Budget: $500

Program Outline:

Because of the apathy towards Junior Achievement exhibited by Black high school students, an all Black J.A. Company was established in the WMECO business office located in the Black Community. Its purpose is to help Black high school students learn the fundamentals of running a business.

The company abides by all the rules and regulations of National Junior Achievement, Inc. They call themselves the T.C.B. Company (Take Care of Business Company). Their products, all featuring a clenched fist, are: desk pen sets, lamps, book ends and so forth.

Co. Personnel Involved: 5 people involved as advisors and coordinators

Measure of Success: first year attendance very good

YOUTH MOTIVATION PROGRAM

WESTERN MASSACHUSETTS ELECTRIC CO.
174 Brush Hill Avenue
West Springfield, Mass. 01089

Business: Public Utility   Sales: 66.9mm
CEO: Robert E. Barret, Jr.   Employees: 987

Contact: Mack W. Jacobs
Address: same as above
Telephone: (413) 785-5871, ext. 298
Program Reaches: 300 plus
When Started: 1969
Budget: n/a

Program Outline:

The program's purpose is to convey to urban area 9th graders the importance of staying in school and earning at least a high school diploma and to warn them of the futility and pitfalls of being a drop-out. All urban area 9th graders are exposed to the program. It aids the participants in gaining self-confidence and the ability to relate to groups of people.

Teams of "living witnesses" visit the 9th grade inner-city classes to stress the relationship between education and earning power. They tell who they are, what they do and why at least a high school education is important for a success in the business world. They especially emphasize new opportunities in industry. They answer questions and invite class discussion. Each company involved provides 4 "living witnesses"- young, personable people, who can easily relate to the students.

Co. Personnel Involved: Five people—4 witnesses and 1 steering committee member—are involved in school visits during working hours and training sessions on their own time.

Measure of Success: Success is difficult to assess. The Springfield School Department and the principals and teachers of the schools visited all spoke highly of the program and have asked for its continuance.

"EARN-LEARN" PROGRAM

XEROX CORP.
Stamford, Conn. 06904

Business: Diversified Office Machines
Sales: 1,719
CEO: C. Peter McColough   Employees: 38,339

Contact: H. Daniel Altmere, Program Mgr.
Address: Xerox Corp., Xerox Square
    Rochester, N.Y. 14603
Telephone: (716) 546-4500
Program Reaches: high school students from the Webster
    area, Henrietta and Xerox Square
When Started: July, 1968
Budget: n/a

Program Outline:

An earn-learn program for more than 200 inner city high school students is underway at the Xerox Corporation. The project allows the student to spend about 25% of the 40-hour week in off-the-job discussion and instruction. The program began with these objectives: to allow needy students the opportunity to earn money (each makes $1.80/hour); to introduce them to their first work experience in industry, (their ages are from 16 up, and most have never held a real job); to allow time for counseling and discussions which, Xerox officials hope, will motivate them to continue their education at least through high school and hopefully through college.

About 100 students are at work in the Webster plant, another 20 in Henrietta and about 90 at Xerox Square downtown. They are working in what are described as "non-hazardous" jobs, such as clerks, secretaries, maintenance and draftsmen. About 2/3 of those hired are Negroes. Three-fourths of the total number hired are males. The students spend 2 hours each Monday through Thursday afternoon in group (about 20 in each) activities. Each Friday afternoon, all the groups get together for lectures and discussions. Those students who work in the Webster and Henrietta plants are picked up by Xerox buses at their high schools and taken to work each day. Reading material, with particular emphasis on Black history and consumer education, is available for the students. In recent discussion groups, they have also been discussing the Xerox sponsored CBS-TV news series "Of Black America." If the students do well, Xerox will offer them a job—but not directly out of the program. They must return and at least finish high school. The company hopes to be able to offer summer jobs for those who go on to college, as a major part of the follow-through effort.

Co. Personnel Involved: n/a

Measure of Success: n/a

FIREFIGHTERS INVOLVING TEENAGERS (F.I.T)

XEROX CORP.
Stamford, Conn. 06904

Business: Diversified Office Equipment
Sales: 1,719
CEO: C. Peter McColough   Employees: 38,339

Contact: Arthur J. Zuckerman
Address: Xerox Corp., Xerox Square
    Rochester, N.Y. 14603
Telephone: (716) 546-4500
Program Reaches: n/a
When Started: 1968
Budget: n/a

Program Outline:

Thirty-three teenagers are helping firefighters dispel some of the inner city animosity that exists in Rochester in the summer. They are diplomats, students working in F.I.T., and they are fighting the prejudice and misunderstanding believed to be behind many acts of vandalism, arson and false alarms.

As diplomats, the 16 year old high school students from Rochester's inner city are trying to bridge the communications gap between the firefighters and their communities. As students, they are learning the magnitude of the responsibilities resting on firefighters. As workers, they are doing everything a firefighter does except put out fires.

Some of these tasks include:
    1. Two Puerto Rican youths are spending the summer as interpreters and instructors at the dispatch center. They translate messages coming in on the emergency switchboard and teach the staff key Spanish words or phrases.
    2. Four other youths are tackling the false alarm problem. They follow up each false alarm, walking through the neighborhood, distributing posters and explaining the hazards of false alarms to residents.
    3. Another group of teenagers accompanies the battalion chiefs whenever they respond to an alarm. The teenagers perform non-hazardous tasks at the scene, acting as personal aides to the battalion chiefs.
    4. The rest of the F.I.T. group is employed in a variety of tasks from clerical work to inspecting and repairing equipment.

Co. Personnel Involved: The program is carried out through a grant from Xerox Corporation in cooperation with the Rochester Fire Department and is administered by Rochester Job, Inc.

Measure of Success: n/a

BLACK DIMENSIONS IN CONTEMPORARY AMERICAN ART

CARNATION CO.
5054 Wilshire Boulevard
Los Angeles, Cal. 90053

Business: Food Processing   Sales: 1,148mm
CEO: H. Everett Olson   Employees: 18,100

Contact: J. Edward Atkinson
Address: same as above
Telephone: (213) 931-1911
Program Reaches: impossible to estimate
When Started: 1970
Budget: $25,000

Program Outline:

The purpose of the program is to give an unprecedented exposure to the genius of talented black artists. "Black Dimensions in Contemporary American Art" is a four-color art book that exhibits the works of fifty contemporary black artists. A ten-minute film based on the book completes the offering. The collection reflects a vast untapped wealth of talent. The paintings are galvanized by feelings that mirror the diversity of the artist's individual fabric, background and technique.

Co. Personnel Involved: Two people do routine acitvity and one has complete responsibility.

Measure of Success: Carnation underwrote production and bought 20,000 copies for free distribution to schools, libraries, museums, galleries, etc. New American Library, the publisher, has sold 15,000 copies. This comprises the first printing. The film has been shown on 32 educational television stations and the book has been reviewed on local television in 8 major cities. The book and film are in the permanent collection at the Smithsonian Library and the book alone is in all American Embassies.

BUSINESS IN THE ARTS

DILLINGHAM CORP.
P.O. Box 3468
Honolulu, Hi. 96801

Business: Construction—Property Development; Maritime Services; Resources (mining, quarrying, rock products)
Sales: 553mm
CEO: H. C. Cornuelle   Employees: 14,000

Contact: W. H. Stryker, Dir., P.R.
Address: same as above
Telephone: (808) 946-0771
Program Reaches: 1000s; residents of community
When Started: early 1960s
Budget: n/a

Program Outline:

In their effort to support fine and performing arts in the community, Dillingham makes financial contributions to numerous art organizations. Also, through facilities at Dillingham's Ala Moana Shopping Center, the company provides exhibit areas and meeting rooms for shows and programs.

Co. Personnel Involved: top management and community relations staff members (12 persons, approximately)—endorsement of programs, some planning, assistance in actual program

Measure of Success: response of the patrons of arts, high attendance at company-sponsored art programs, national recognition by ESQUIRE's "Business in the Arts" program for 1971

COLEMAN BLUMFIELD IN CONCERT

FORD MOTOR COMPANY FUND
The American Road
Dearborn, Mich. 48121

Business: Automotive Manufacturing
Sales: 15,000mm
CEO: Lee A. Iacocca   Employees: 431,000

Contact: R. C. Kooi
Address: same as above
Telephone: (313) 322-8711
Program Reaches: over 500,000 young people in over
    500 high schools and colleges
When Started: 1969
Budget: n/a

Program Outline:

The purpose of the program is to arouse an increased
appreciation of classical music among young people.

Coleman Blumfield, a distinguished young concert
pianist, conducts a series of free classical piano recitals at
regular assemblies in high schools and colleges of major
cities. In addition, Mr. Blumfield is available to discuss
cultural programs with school officials and community
leaders.

Co. Personnel Involved: 1000s of members of Ford
Corporate and Dealer Community Relations Committees
who make local arrangements

Measure of Success: standing ovations from audiences,
excellent reactions from school and community leaders,
and extensive press coverage

CORPORATE ART COLLECTION

GEORGIA-PACIFIC CORP.
900 S.W. 5th Avenue
Portland, Ore. 97204

Business: Forest Products of All Kinds
Sales: 1,400mm
CEO: William H. Hunt   Employees: 37,000

Contact: R. O. Lee, V.P.
Address: same as above
Telephone: (503) 222-5561
Program Reaches: 1000s of people
When Started: 1969
Budget: $50-75,000

Program Outline:

The purpose of this program is to support living artists,
particularly in the Northwest, and to stimulate other
industries to give similar support, while at the same time
exposing employees and the public to outstanding work
of contemporary artists. The company has purchased
over 600 original works of art (paintings, prints, tap-
estries, ceramics, sculpture, etc.) from artists in the
Northwest and put these works on exhibit in the new
Georgia-Pacific headquarters building in Portland. All art
in the building is original. Over 100 artists have benefited
and additional work is purchased each year and put on
display. This has been the largest collection assembled by
a private company in the Northwest. It has actually been
responsible for uncovering some great hidden talent and
making a number of "unknowns" successful. Georgia-
Pacific reviewed almost 5,000 objects in compiling the
collection and expects to continue the acquisition program for an indefinite period.

Co. Personnel Involved: two—R. O. Lee and M. C.
Carpenter; both deeply involved as jury and purchasers

Measure of Success: A number of the artists (of great
talent, but no opportunity) are now well established and
highly successful. This program won an award in the
ESQUIRE magazine judgement of corporate involvement
and support of the arts. Program has also given employees
and the public great enjoyment and intellectual stimulation and has resulted in a wave of buying and support
for the artists selected.

COMMISSIONING OF COMPOSER, SAMUEL BARBER

GIRARD BANK
One Girard Plaza
Philadelphia, Pa. 19101

Business: Banking   Sales: not applicable
Assets: 2,801.9mm   Deposits: 2,325.7mm
CEO: William B. Eagleson, Jr.   Employees: 3,032

Contact: Anne L. Sceia
Address: same as above
Telephone: (215) 585-3103
Program Reaches: hard to say—could ultimately reach people throughout the world as orchestras perform the work
When Started: 1969
Budget: n/a

Program Outline:

The purpose of this program is to contribute to socially oriented and cultural aspects of the community and the nation. Girard hopes that this first musical commissioning by a private company will encourage other businesses to participate in supporting the arts.

Co. Personnel Involved: Two people were completely involved on the policy side; 2 people were completely involved in the details; 3 people from the Bank's P.R. agency provided additional back-up as needed.

Measure of Success: favorable response from media in terms of content analysis of clippings; favorable response from the Philadelphia Orchestra; letters from the Bank's customers and the general public

BFG SUPPORT OF THE ARTS

B.F. GOODRICH CO.
500 S. Main Street
Akron, Ohio 44318

Business: Manufacturing Rubber Products
Sales: 1,237mm
CEO: H. B. Warner   Employees: 47,900
Contact: Gary J. Rine
Address: P. R. Dept., same as above
Telephone: (216) 379-3411
Program Reaches: n/a
When Started: 1969
Budget: n/a

Program Outline:

The program assists art institutions and organizations and encourages an all-around better appreciation for and patronage of the arts.

In 1969, BFG provided the first complete business sponsorship of an exhibition in the 50-year history of Akron Art Institute. The sponsorship included the providing of awards and the printing of all promotional materials. Through its support of the arts program, BFG makes financial contributions to and gives advice and assistance in the every-day operation of selected art institutions in communities where the company has manufacturing operations. The assistance includes such things as helping the institutions with their fiscal records and policies and with the printing of a number of promotional pieces.

Co. Personnel Involved: Several people from different areas of the company are involved, and to varying degrees.

Measure of Success: BFG won an ESQUIRE-BCA "Business in the Arts" award in 1970 for its leadership in the field.

GOODYEAR MUSICAL THEATRE

GOODYEAR TIRE & RUBBER CO.
1144 East Market Street
Akron, Ohio 44316

Business: Manufacturing Tires and Rubber Products
Sales: 3,602mm
CEO: Victor Holt, Jr.   Employees: 136,800

Contact: Homer Allen, Pres., Goodyear Theatre
Address: same as above
Telephone: (216) 794-2121
Program Reaches: more than 10,000 theatre-goers annually, plus those involved in production
When Started: December, 1958
Budget: In 1971, the company provided use of the theatre at an approximated cost of $12,000. Materials and other costs exceeded $6,500. Not reflected in annual costs is more than $500,000 spent over the past 6 years for improvements and modifications to the theatre itself.

Program Outline:

The Goodyear Musical Theatre presents local productions of successful Broadway musical plays twice a year. Members of the musical theatre group select the plays, build scenery, create costumes and handle production from start to finish under the supervision of the theatre director. Goodyear provides free of charge to the group, the Goodyear Theatre, a modern 1,400-seat facility located near the corporate headquarters. Materials for scenery, props and other uses by the theatre group are provided primarily by the company. Goodyear's corporate public relations department assigns staff members to develop a planned program of news stories for external release and use in company internal publications.

Co. Personnel Involved: Homer Allen, president of the theatre group, is a Goodyear employee. Most of the active participants are also company employees and spend a major part of their free time on theatre projects.

Measure of Success: Goodyear Musical Theatre officers say that the group could not exist without the degree of support it receives from the company. Company support, they say, has assisted in formation of a cohesive theatre group that has drawn performers and other theatre personnel back again and again. Musical theatre performances are almost invariably sold out. Area critics have given productions largely favorable ratings. Some Goodyear Musical Theatre performers have become professional actors in touring companies and Broadway casts.

5TH NATIONAL STUDENT FILM FESTIVAL (1970)

JOSEPH SCHLITZ BREWING CO.
235 W. Galena Street
Milwaukee, Wis. 53201

Business: Brewing Beer   Sales: 669mm
CEO: Robert H. Uihlein, Jr.   Employees: 5,800

Contact: Ben Barkin
Address: Barkin, Herman and Assoc.
  735 N. Water Street, Milwaukee, Wis. 53202
Telephone: (414) 271-7434
Program Reaches: 347 entries
When Started: 1970
Budget: Prize money: $22,500; Fellowships: $60,000

Program Outline:

The purpose of this program is to offer recognition and the funds necessary to help student film makers continue their work. Because film has become an important communications medium, Schlitz cooperated with the Motion Picture Association and the American Film Institute to encourage student film makers. Cash prizes of $2,500 each to 5 grand prize winners were presented as well as 20 awards of $500 each. In addition, Schlitz sponsored 2 fellowships valued at $30,000 each to enable 2 of the Festival participants to study film for 2 years at the American Film Institute's Center for Advanced Film Studies in Beverly Hills, California.

Co. Personnel Involved: three—1 about half time during the period and 2 others in an advisory capacity

Measure of Success: Schlitz won a 4th award in the ESQUIRE "Business in the Arts" competition.

MILWAUKEE FESTIVAL OF THE ARTS

JOSEPH SCHLITZ BREWING CO.
235 W. Galena Street
Milwaukee, Wis. 53201

Business: Brewing Beer   Sales: 669mm
CEO: Robert A. Uihlein, Jr.   Employees: 5,800

Contact: Ben Barkin
Address: Barkin, Herman and Assoc.
   735 N. Water Street, Milwaukee, Wis. 53202
Telephone: (414) 271-7434
Program Reaches: 1971 Festival attracted 128,000 visitors
When Started: 1963
Budget: n/a

Program Outline:

In its effort to spotlight and sell regional art and make the community aware of its cultural facilities, as well as to help the artists themselves, this 2-day event is held each year on the lakeside slope under the Memorial Art Center. Each year a different theme is featured and, in addition to the displays of the artists, usually personally manned, there is entertainment. The 1971 Festival included internally-known jazz performers; the Milwaukee Pick-a-Pack Players, representing children's plays; a "film orgy" of old movie clips and TV commercials; and demonstrations by potters and other craftsmen.

Co. Personnel Involved: 4

Measure of Success: The 1971 Festival sold around $75,000 worth of art by 175 artists. Schlitz won another ESQUIRE "Business in the Arts" award for its sponsorship of the Festival of the Arts.

NEW YORK PHILHARMONIC CONCERTS IN 12 NEW YORK PARKS

JOSEPH SCHLITZ BREWING CO.
235 W. Galena Street
Milwaukee, Wis. 53201

Business: Brewing Beer   Sales: 669mm
CEO: Robert A. Uihlein, Jr.   Employees: 5,800

Contact: Ben Barkin
Address: Barkin, Herman and Assoc.
   735 N. Water Street, Milwaukee, Wis. 53202
Telephone: (414) 271-7434
Program Reaches: approx. 500,000 each season
When Started: 1965
Budget: n/a

Program Outline:

The purpose of this program is to make the music of the New York Philharmonic available to more people than the 8,000 series ticket holders.

In 1963, Schlitz brought Leonard Bernstein and the New York Philharmonic to Milwaukee for a free concert. Thirty thousand were in attendence—the largest audience this orchestra had ever played to at that time. Learning this, Schlitz decided to make it possible for New Yorkers to hear the orchestra as well. The series covers 6 boroughs of New York.

Co. Personnel Involved: President Robert A. Uihlein, Jr. and the public relations counsel associates

Measure of Success: The audience for the series is said to be 100,000—greater than the entire 8-month subscription series. Schlitz has received national publicity annually and this concert series won for Schlitz the first of its 4 "Business in the Arts" awards from ESQUIRE magazine.

OLD MILWAUKEE DAYS

JOSEPH SCHLITZ BREWING CO.
235 W. Galena Street
Milwaukee, Wis. 53201

Business: Brewing Beer   Sales: 669mm
CEO: Robert A. Uihlein, Jr.   Employees: 5,800

Contact: Ben Barkin
Address: Barkin, Herman and Assoc.
  735 N. Water Street, Milwaukee, Wis. 53202

Telephone: (414) 271-7434
Program Reaches: 500,000 annually plus those who see
  TV shows and movies
When Started: 1963
Budget: about $500,000

Program Outline:

Schlitz was approached by the director of the Circus World Museum at Barabook, Wisconsin, C.P. ("Chappie") Fox, a noted circus historian, to sponsor an old-time circus parade on the Fourth of July as an appropriate patriotic civic affair. Today it is an annual 5-day celebration, opening with the arrival of a train bringing 65 antique circus wagons and is climaxed by the parade which includes more than 30 bands, dozens of clowns, patriotic tableaux, exotic animals and mounted cowboys and Indians.

The 1972 edition will feature a 40-horse hitch pulling a big bandwagon. Free circus acts, fireworks and concerts fill the 5 days. The parade also features a "Yesterday on Wheels" section of antique cars and bicycles. A new feature is added to the parade each year.

Co. Personnel Involved: most of the staff of Barkin, Herman and Associates

Measure of Success: More than 500,000 spectators line the streets of Milwaukee.

SCHLITZ SALUTE TO JAZZ

JOSEPH SCHLITZ BREWING CO.
235 W. Galena Street
Milwaukee, Wis. 53201

Business: Brewing Beer   Sales: 669mm
CEO: Robert A. Uihlein, Jr.   Employees: 5,800

Contact: Ben Barkin
Address: Barkin, Herman and Assoc.
  735 N. Water Street, Milwaukee, Wis. 53202
Telephone: (414) 271-7434
Program Reaches: undetermined
When Started: 1967 Newport Jazz Festival
Budget: n/a

Program Outline:

In order to help jazz musicians and performers as well as audiences who might not otherwise be exposed to this medium, a summer-long program was presented in 1967. The program included sponsorship of a History of Jazz concert on the opening night of the 1967 Newport Jazz Festival, major jazz events in 3 states, and a benefit jazz concert which was a key element in the 1967 Watts (Los Angeles) Summer Festival, as well as a free public jazz concert as part of the annual "Old Milwaukee Days" celebration. Plus, in 1970, a special New Orleans Tribute to Louis Armstrong was held.

Co. Personnel Involved: 2

Measure of Success: favorable publicity in every city where the events were sponsored, plus general recognition for Schlitz's encouragement of this music form, also was the cause of Schlitz's receiving a 4th award from ESQUIRE Magazine in its "Business in the Arts" competition.

SPONSORSHIP OF DEAN DIXON TOUR
(BLACK SYMPHONY CONDUCTOR)

JOSEPH SCHLITZ BREWING CO.
235 W. Galena Street
Milwaukee, Wis. 53201

Business: Brewing Beer Sales: 669mm
CEO: Robert A. Uihlein, Jr. Employees: 5,800

Contact: Ben Barkin
Address: Barkin, Herman and Assoc.
  735 N. Water Street, Milwaukee, Wis. 53202
Telephone: (414) 271-7434
Program Reaches: audiences of 7 orchestras
When Started: 1971
Budget: n/a

Program Outline:

The purpose of this program was to give the United States the opportunity to enjoy the talent of Dean Dixon, the leading Black symphony orchestra conductor, who has been in self-exile in Europe for 21 years.

Schlitz paid the conductor's fee for Dixon's appearances to (1) insure his appearances and (2) contribute to the usually strained budget of each orchestra.

Dixon, a graduate of the Julliard School and Columbia University, made his debut at New York's Town Hall in 1937. He was the first Negro to conduct major U.S. orchestras. However, he found "a Negro didn't have a chance as a symphony conductor in the U.S." so he went to Europe where he was permanent conductor of the Goetburg Symphony in Sweden for 7 years, and then music director of the Hessicher Rundfunk in Frankfort, Germany. He also led orchestras in other European cities and Sydney, Australia.

Under Schlitz sponsorship, Dixon conducted the New York Philharmonic; the Kansas City, Mo. Symphony; the Minnesota Symphony, Minneapolis; the Milwaukee, Detroit, Chicago and San Francisco Symphonies and the National Symphony in Washington, D.C.

Co. Personnel Involved: n/a

Measure of Success: Dixon received enthusiastic critical acclaim in every city.

BOROUGH ARTS AWARDS

STANDARD OIL CO. OF NEW JERSEY
1251 Avenue of the Americas
New York, N.Y. 10020

Business: Petroleum Sales: 21,000mm
CEO: Milo M. Brisco Employees: 145,000

Contact: Robert E. Kingsley
Address: same as above
Telephone: (212) 974-3078
Program Reaches: estimated 500,000
When Started: May, 1971
Budget: $60,000

Program Outline:

A Community Arts Program was launched by Jersey Standard to provide meaningful support to neighborhood arts groups throughout New York City, with funds channeled by the Arts Councils in the five boroughs. As a consequence, groups involved in the production and preparation of youth theatre, ballet, music, dance, opera, and the plastic arts received needed help to carry out special programs. Many events took place over the summer months and especially benefited disadvantaged communities. This initiative was coordinated through the Arts and Business Cooperative Council of the New York Board of Trade, which aims to encourage business support of the arts at the grassroots level. The awards were announced at a special event held at Lincoln Center, called "Sixty Minutes With the Arts: A Business Happening."

Co. Personnel Involved: personal involvement by six company employees and members of management

Measure of Success: Success may be measured by the number of groups assisted, the vast audiences reached through individual programs, and the interest expressed by other members of the business community.

other kinds of involvement

BIBLIOGRAPHY: CORPORATE RESPONSIBILITY FOR SOCIAL PROBLEMS

BANK OF AMERICA
P. O. Box 37000
San Francisco, Cal. 94137

Business: Banking   Sales: not applicable
CEO: A. W. Clausen   Employees: 31,700

Contact: Nadene Mathews
Address: same as above
Telephone: (415) 622-2595
Program Reaches: n/a
When Started: mid-1971
Budget: n/a

Program Outline:

In order to provide a research and reference source regarding corporate commitment in social problem areas such as education, housing, minorities, ecology, etc., Bank of America publishes a bibliography of publications available on these subjects. Special emphasis is placed on publications dealing with costs and expenditures and the development of meaningful and effective social budgets. The Bank hopes to publish a second report by the end of the summer, 1972.

Highlights of the bibliography are reprinted in the *Biblio-View* section of "Profiles of Involvement."

Co. Personnel Involved: n/a

Measure of Success: Excellent cooperation from organizations contacted in providing materials and in suggestions for additional information.

STUDENT RELATIONS PROGRAM

BANK OF AMERICA
P.O. Box 37000
San Francisco, Cal. 94137

Business: Banking   Sales: not applicable
CEO: A. W. Clausen   Employees: 31,700

Contact: Theodore Hoffman, Student Affairs Officer
Address: same as above
Telephone: (415) 622-6938
Program Reaches: over 400,000 students
When Started: mid-1970
Budget: n/a

Program Outline:

The purpose of the program is to bridge the communications gap between the Bank and collegians. Twenty-two college students work as part time employees in branches serving their community and there are 7 full-time student relations officers. They are involved with student groups, faculty, administrators, and local residents in trying to pinpoint and solve social problems. Their efforts range from helping to establish Free Clinics to counseling students about their financial problems and helping them solve their housing problems. In addition, the Bank has developed special checking accounts, overdraft protection, Bank Americard and savings accounts for students.

Co. Personnel Involved: about 30

Measure of Success: Objectively, the wide acceptance of specialized services. Subjectively, the value of establishing Free Clinics, opening channels of communication, etc.

BEECHCRAFT PROGRAM ON AMERICANISM

BEECH AIRCRAFT CORP.
9709 E. Central
Wichita, Kan. 67201

Business: Manufacturing Corporate
and Private Aircraft
Sales: 150mm
CEO: Frank E. Hedrick   Employees: 4,974

Contact: W. G. Robinson
Address: same as above
Telephone: (316) 685-6211, ext. 3366
Program Reaches: millions of people
When Started: February, 1970
Budget: n/a

Program Outline:

The purpose of the program is to highlight the need for involvement in the maintenance and enhancement of loyalty to and love of our country and our flag, recognition of and respect for the basic religious support of our great nation, and the benefits of and the critical need to maintain the American free enterprise system.

This is being done through:

1. The development of and carrying in national magazines brief highlights of selected facets of the American way of life.

2. The mailing of American flag decals and of American flags of several sizes to thousands of people for display purposes ranging from office doors through mailing pieces, desk sets and outdoor flag poles.

3. Presentation of information and encouragement to congressmen and senators at both the national and state level to use their offices to preserve and promote the great many things that are right about the American way of life.

Co. Personnel Involved: a considerable number ranging downward from the Chairman of the Board and the President of Beech Aircraft Corporation

Measure of Success: responses from a great many people expressing approval of and encouragement that the program be continued

INDUSTRIAL COUNSELING SERVICE (I.C.S.)

BLUE BELL, INC.
335 Church Court
Greensboro, N.C. 27420

Business: Apparel   Sales: 293.9mm
CEO: Rodger S. LeMatty   Employees: 1,700

Contact: Nelson Hodgkins, Dir.
Address: Suite 1414, Wachovia Bldg.
Greensboro, N.C. 27420
Telephone: (919) 273-1566
Program Reaches: n/a
When Started: 1965
Budget: n/a

Program Outline:

The service, now supported by 17 industries which employ more than 21,000 people, provides a program of professional counseling to troubled employees and their families in the areas of alcoholism, drug abuse, marital and emotional difficulties. All appointments are kept in the strictest of confidence and patients know there will be absolutely no feedback to their employers. If the resources of I.C.S. are exhausted, referral is made to the appropriate social, mental or physical health service with which I.C.S. has contact. Visits are terminated by mutual consent and emphasis is placed on helping the patient solve his own problems, not having I.C.S. solve them for him.

Co. Personnel Involved: n/a

Measure of Success: n/a

"BEING A COP IS MORE THAN JUST A GIG"

CAMPBELL-EWALD CO.
3044 W. Grand Boulevard
Detroit, Mich. 48202

Business: Advertising Agency   Sales: 116mm
CEO: Hugh M. Readhead   Employees: 575

Contact: Fenton A. Ludtke, V.P. and Asst. to Pres.
Address: same as above
Telephone: (313) 872-6200
Program Reaches: 700,000
When Started: October 5, 1971
Budget: $47,000

Program Outline:

The purpose of the program is to create an advertising campaign that would effectively communicate to young Black men that they are needed and wanted by the City of Detroit to become police officers.

Cognizant of the need for a more representative police force, Campbell-Ewald Company developed an advertising campaign which brings forward the feelings of a Black Police officer relative to this need. It attempts to state why some young Black men become police officers and the rewards gained from the challenge of being a Black cop.

The theme of the program embraces the idiosyncracies of being a cop, i.e., its more than just going to work or having a job—hence, "Being a Cop Is More Than Just a Gig."

Co. Personnel Involved: 6 plus management

Measure of Success: the increased number of Black applicants during the campaign period

---

VOTER REGISTRATION

CITIZENS AND SOUTHERN NATIONAL BANK
99 Annex
Atlanta, Ga. 30399

Business: Banking   Sales: not applicable
Total Assets: 2,065,374,460
CEO: Mills B. Lane, Jr.   Employees: 3,550

Contact: William J. VanLandingham
Address: same as above
Telephone: (464) 588-2774
Program Reaches: residents of Fulton County who are not registered
When Started: 1971
Budget: approx. $600 spent including advertisements

Program Outline:

The purpose of the program is to encourage and facilitate voter registration. The Voter Registration Program now in effect allows 41 of the branch offices of the Bank to act as voter registration sites. Working with the county registrar's office, federal approval was obtained from the Justice Department to allow employees in each branch to be trained as deputy registrars. County registration officials handled all training of Bank personnel.

Co. Personnel Involved: Approximately 100 employees have been trained and qualified as deputy registrars.

Measure of Success: In less than 3 months, over 1,000 new voters have been registered.

ONE STOP COMMUNITY DAY CARE CENTER

THE CHASE MANHATTAN BANK
1 Chase Manhattan Plaza
New York, N.Y. 10015

Business: Banking   Sales: not applicable
Total Assets: 25,000mm
CEO: Herbert Patterson   Employees: 18,900

Contact: Rev. Charles Lott
Address: 20 Sutter Avenue, Brooklyn, N.Y.
Telephone: (212) 773-3041
Program Reaches: 100 children and their mothers
When Started: Fall, 1970
Budget: $335,000 loan

Program Outline:

This 2-pronged, community-based program, designed to help female heads of households without business training find a way out of welfare, was developed to provide the women with both skills to support their families and a stimulating and secure environment for their children during working hours. The 2-story day care center building, purchased last year and renovated from the frame was financed by the Chase Manhattan Bank. Five teachers and 10 assistant teachers have developed a curriculum for the children. Pre-schoolers spend the entire day there and elementary school youngsters are cared for between 3 and 6 P.M.

Just a block away is the One Stop Community Center School where mothers of the Day Care Center children are learning Data Processing skills. The training equipment (key punchers, progress cards for the computers, accounting machines, electric typewriters, sorters and verifiers) was furnished by IBM. The Day Care Center is free to those mothers in the training program and once on the job, they will pay a fee based on a sliding earnings scale.

Co. Personnel Involved: Four, with 2 sharing the primary responsibility

Measure of Success: Since the learning center opened in the fall of 1970, more than 425 people have received training and have earned more than $220,000 in jobs utilizing the skills acquired at the school.

URBAN AFFAIRS SUMMER INTERN PROGRAM

THE CHASE MANHATTAN BANK
1 Chase Manhattan Plaza
New York, N.Y. 10015

Business: Banking   Sales: not applicable
Total Assets: 25,000mm
CEO: Herbert Patterson   Employees: 18,900

Contact: John E. Burke
Address: same as above
Telephone: (212) 552-2222
Program Reaches: n/a
When Started: 1969
Budget: n/a

Program Outline:

This particular program provided a means for undergraduates to channel their concern directly into urban problem solving. Paid by the Bank, they work full time with Public Service Projects such as Harlem Teams for Self Help, The Foundation for Research and Education in Sickle Cell Anemia, the Puerto Rican Legal Defense Fund, the China Town Health Clinic, and Consumer Action Bedford-Stuyvesant. The program establishes a 3-way dialogue among business, community agencies and students. It attempts to provide the students with worthwhile summer employment experience by enabling them to observe business techniques and at the same time involve them directly with urban problems and their solutions.

Most of the 12 interns applied for the program through their school placement service. Wherever possible, all were placed in jobs relating to their particular area of interest, often with agencies of their own choosing.

Co. Personnel Involved: One person from the Urban Affairs staff usually oversees the program with assistance from several others. In addition, interns meet with officers from many areas of the Bank's activities, including senior management, at an orientation and weekly conferences throughout the summer.

Measure of Success: The vast majority of participating interns and agencies have expressed satisfaction with the program's value to them. Each intern's assignment is shaped, if appropriate, so that some concrete results of a summer's work are left behind. Rather than providing general assistance to the agencies' regular work, most interns have special projects designed for full completion by the fall.

**NORTHSIDE CHILD DEVELOPMENT
CENTER, INC.**

CONTROL DATA CORP.
8100 34th Avenue S.
P.O. Box 0
Minneapolis, Minn. 55440

Business: Manufacturing Digital Computing Systems and
   Electronic Components
Sales: 571mm
CEO: William C. Norris   Employees: 37,163

Contact: Norma Anderson, Dir.
Address: 1162 N. 5th Street
   Minneapolis, Minn. 55401
Telephone: (612) 341-2715
Program Reaches: 120 children (3 months-12 years)
When Started: early in 1970
Budget: $277,000

Program Outline:

The purpose of this program is to establish a child care center for pre-school children. The decision to establish this facility was related directly to employee turnover and absenteeism problems encountered during the first year and a half of operating the Northside plant. The facility was designed to provide child care services for female heads-of-families allowing them time to seek and retain meaningful employment.

To reduce operating costs of the Center and to make more openings available in a community which has a severe shortage of day care facilities, Control Data spearheaded the establishment of a consortium of local business firms who have joined in sharing the services and the expenses of operating the center. The center will be run by a separate non-profit corporation as a demonstration project in industry-related child care assisted by Federal Title IV-A matching funds.

Co. Personnel Involved: dozens of parent-employees, some of whom are on the Board of Directors; 3 management people also on the Board of Directors

Measure of Success: n/a

VOCATIONAL GUIDANCE INSTITUTE

DEERE & CO.
John Deere Road
Moline, Ill. 61265

Business: Manufacturing Farm, Industrial and Consumer
   Products Equipment
Sales: 1,188.1mm
CEO: Elwood F. Curtis   Employees: 41,700

Contact: Dr. John Axelson
Address: Northern Illinois U.
   DeKalb, Ill. 60115
Telephone: (815) 753-0414
Program Reaches: 40/year
When Started: 1967
Budget: $3,500

Program Outline:

The purpose of the program is to give the local school counselors, administrators and teachers information on the problems of the disadvantaged with particular emphasis concerning minorities.

The project director is responsible for developing a curriculum and hiring personnel to serve as instructors. Graduates of this program were given 2 graduate credit hours for completion of the course. Participants of this program were exposed to problems of the disadvantaged by personal experience by instructors. Textbook assignments were from current literature dealing with the problems of disadvantaged. Tours were arranged to the disadvantaged and ghetto neighborhoods and visitations were made to local manufacturing units.

Co. Personnel Involved: One member of the Quad City Merit Employment Council was an institute participant. Charles W. Toney, Manager, Minority Relations, attended.
Measure of Success: Hard to determine. Company has had communications from individual educators that the institute has been helpful, but has not had the funds to have a professional follow-up conducted.

PUBLIC SECTOR MANAGEMENT ASSISTANCE

FIRST NATIONAL CITY BANK
399 Park Avenue
New York, N.Y. 10022

Business: Banking
CEO: William I. Spencer

Sales: not applicable
Employees: 31,700

Contact: William G. Herbster, S.V.P.
Address: same as above
Telephone: (212) 559-4211
Program Reaches: indeterminate
When Started: 1970
Budget: management time

Program Outline:

The purpose of the program is to make the technical expertise of the Bank available, in selected cases, to governmental agencies on a public service basis.

The Bank has traditionally encouraged its top officers to participate in advisory capacities to federal, state and local government. Presently, the Chairman serves on the President's Commission on Productivity, and other senior officers serve on other commissions at the various levels of government. Moreover, during the past 2 years, at the request of the Human Resources Administration of New York City, the Bank has designed computer programs to cost out and evaluate the City's job training activities, as well as a totally new welfare payment system which will be tested on a pilot basis in 1972.

Co. Personnel Involved: 1 officer full time and approx. 10 part time

Measure of Success: too early to tell

URBAN AFFAIRS COMMITTEE

FIRST PENNSYLVANIA BANKING & TRUST CO.
555 City Line Avenue
Bala Cynwyd, Pa. 19004

Business: Banking
Deposits: Dec. 31, 1971—2,900mm
CEO: John R. Bunting

Sales: not applicable

Employees: 4,323

Contact: Bertram W. Zumeta, Chairman
Address: 15th and Chestnut Sts.
    Packard Bldg., Philadelphia, Pa.
Telephone: (215) 786-8522
Program Reaches: all employees, plus community at large
When Started: late 1970
Budget: The committee can appropriate funds for various projects. Recently, for example, it set aside $4 million for mortgage lending to low-income groups.

Program Outline:

The committee is responsible for the development, overall direction and monitoring of programs designed to meet the Bank's goal of responsibly serving the community.

Made up of members of executive management and the heads of several key departments, the committee oversees the Bank's involvement in the entire urban affairs arena— from the purchasing of supplies from minority businessmen to the inclusion of Black publications in the advertising program.

The committee's goal is to speed advantageous trends and to halt or reverse trends which will not profit the general public. Special areas of concern are personnel practices, community relations, lending policies and individual employee involvement.

Co. Personnel Involved: The committee directly involves approx. 12 members of top management. To a lesser degree, the committee's activities involve all the Bank's employees.

Measure of Success: Committee requires semi-annual reports on numbers and position levels of minority employees by departments. Similar reports are required to measure departmental loan performance, both consumer and commercial.

ACTIVITY CENTER TRANSPORTATION (ACT) SYSTEM

FORD MOTOR CO.
The American Road
Dearborn, Mich. 48121

Business: Automobile Manufacturing
Sales: 15,000mm
CEO: Lee A. Iacocca   Employees: 431,000

Contact: Foster L. Weldon
Address: 23400 Michigan Avenue, Dearborn, Mich. 48124
Telephone: (313) 337-5220
Program Reaches: metropolitan-wide
When Started: December, 1970
Budget: $3 million to date

Program Outline:

The purpose of the program is to reduce the activity center (e.g. central business district, airport, shopping center, etc.) congestion through the use of an automated electrically propelled people-movement system which would circulate people within activity centers and connect with peripheral parking areas and other activity centers.

The function of the program is to: (1) investigate the causes of urban congestion as manifested within and around major centers of employment, entertainment, commerce, education and transportation; (2) determine technical requirements for implementing a secondary transportation system which would automatically move people along elevated guideways from their automobiles and mass transit stations into the activity center proper at high efficiency and low cost; (3) based on these requirements, design, fabricate, and demonstrate such a system to the general public and appropriate government agencies; (4) through analysis and liaison with public and private groups determine the impact of this system on land-use planning and architectural development.

Co. Personnel Involved: 50 in analytical, engineering, and fabrication efforts

Measure of Success: Cost-benefit, i.e. providing the highest level of transportation service and the least cost. Environmental, i.e. installing such systems to minimize urban intrusion and increase aesthetic appeal of the general surroundings. Institutional, i.e. through the demonstration of the system encourage its acceptance by planners, public officials, and private developers so that a potential solution to urban congestion can be implemented.

PUBLIC RECREATION FACILITIES

GEORGIA-PACIFIC CORP.
900 S.W. 5th Avenue
Portland, Ore. 97204

Business: Forest Products   Sales: 1,440mm
CEO: William H. Hunt   Employees: 37,000

Contact: R. O. Lee
Address: same as above
Telephone: (503) 222-5561
Program Reaches: general public
When Started: 1962
Budget: not formalized

Program Outline:

The program purpose is to provide quality recreational facilities on company timberlands for the enjoyment of the general public. It also provides educational areas in nature study.

In most Georgia-Pacific timberlands throughout the United States excellent public recreation facilities have been established in areas of unusual scenic beauty. Many of these areas or sites are equipped with good water, restroom facilities, stores, etc. In some locations local flora has been identified in "nature" trails. Maps are often provided for sportsmen. In certain instances where specific faunal habitat is fragile, reserves have been created to protect the animals and for study by serious students.

Co. Personnel Involved: several 100

Measure of Success: Reception has been excellent, as witnessed by the number of people using the facilities. Vandalism by a few uncaring members of the public has added to the cost of maintaining areas but most people derive great enjoyment and knowledge from the areas.

"ASTROVIEW MAP" AND "GREATER PHILADELPHIA FOR YOUR BUSINESS FUTURE"

GIRARD BANK
One Girard Plaza
Philadelphia, Pa. 19101

Business: Banking
Assets: 2,801.9mm
CEO: William B. Eagleson, Jr.

Sales: not applicable
Deposits: 2,325.7mm
Employees: 3,032

Contact: Anne L. Sceia
Address: same as above
Telephone: (215) 585-3103
Program Reaches: estimated 30,000 "Astroview Maps" printed and distributed; 12,000 "Greater Philadelphia" printed and distributed
When Started: 1970
Budget: n/a

Program Outline:

The purpose of this program is to encourage more companies to locate and/or expand operations in the Greater Philadelphia area.

The "Astroview Map" and "Greater Philadelphia for Your Business Future" are 2 efforts directed toward stimulating more economic development in the Greater Philadelphia area. The 2 publications are contributed by Girard to help the public and private agencies in this work.

The publications provide businesses interested in the Delaware Valley with information on Philadelphia's accessways for industry and commerce, living areas, room for growth and development and a useful listing and description of 41 agencies and organizations which can supply helpful answers concerning the establishment of operations in the Delaware Valley.

Co. Personnel Involved: One senior vice president and 1 vice president are completely involved on the policy side; 1 assistant vice president and 1 public relations officer are completely involved in details.

Measure of Success: requests from businesses outside the Philadelphia area for the publications, requests from the agencies themselves, press coverage.

JAMES MICHENER'S "THE QUALITY OF LIFE" BARBARA WARD'S "AN URBAN PLANET?" PAUL NADLER'S "PAUL NADLER WRITES ABOUT BANKING"

THE GIRARD CO.
N.W. Corner of Bala and City Line Avenues
Philadelphia, Pa. 19004

Business: Holding Company
Assets: 2,802.9mm
CEO: William B. Eagleson, Jr.

Sales: not applicable
Deposits: 2,323.7mm
Employees: 3,032

Contact: Anne L. Sceia
Address: Girard Bank, One Girard Plaza
    Philadelphia, Pa. 19101
Telephone: (215) 585-3103
Program Reaches: impossible to estimate—25,000 copies of each were printed
When Started: 1969
Budget: n/a

Program Outline:

The purpose of this program is to stimulate public interest and concern for the major issues and problems of our times.

Each annual report essay dealt with a topic of concern not only to the community, but also to Pennsylvania and the nation. The essays presented possible solutions to such problems as race relations, understanding youth, preservation of the environment and urbanism.

Co. Personnel Involved: Four people at the Bank were completely involved and back-up was provided by the Bank's public relations agency.

Measure of Success: Favorable commentary appeared in the press throughout the nation and the world. Thousands of letters of praise for the reports and requests for copies have been received. The letters have come from all over the world and from every walk of life—from the White House to the neighborhood improvement group. Letters from individuals and organizations supplied evidence of the program's resultfulness by indicating how the volumes were being incorporated into various action programs aimed at the problem areas discussed. Mr. Michener's book was published for sale to the general public in both hardback and paperback versions.

AMISTAD HOUSE

THE HARTFORD INSURANCE GROUP
Hartford Plaza
Hartford, Conn. 06115

Business: Diversified Insurance
Sales: 1,000mm
CEO: Harry V. Williams   Employees: 14,000

Contact: Robert B. Keane, Dir. P.R.
Address: P.R. and Adv. Dept., same as above
Telephone: (203) 547-4954
Program Reaches: 24 poverty area residents
When Started: June, 1970
Budget: $150,000

Program Outline:

A company executive of the Hartford Insurance Group was loaned to lay the groundwork for a group home for girls, the first of its kind in Connecticut, and infant day-care center. He was released for 6 months, retaining full pay and company benefits, to assist St. Michael's Parish in converting the parish rectory into the group home. A private, non-profit agency has been incorporated under the name of Amistad House. This facility will house 12 girls with family adjustment problems who are in need of a positive living environment. Also, a portion of the 22-room building will be used as an infant day-care center. The company continues to provide ongoing assistance to Amistad House.

Co. Personnel Involved: 1 staff member full time for 6 months continuing staff assistance, including legal, stenographic, etc.

Measure of Success: Building has been leased from Archdiocese, renovations have begun, executive director and staff have been hired, and funding is complete for the 1st year. The home was fully functioning by mid-April.

EMPLOYEE CONSULTATION CENTER

THE J.L. HUDSON CO.
1206 Woodward
Detroit, Mich. 48226

Business: Retail   Sales: 356mm
CEO: Joseph L. Hudson, Jr.   Employees: 12,000

Contact: George Greer, ACSW, Dir.
Address: same as above
Telephone: (313) 223-5100, ext. 2684
Program Reaches: approx. 1,000/year
When Started: 1944
Budget: n/a

Program Outline:

The purpose of the program is to assist employees, retirees, and ex-employees and their families with improving the quality of their lives.

The program assists persons in resolving personal, family, medical and financial problems which interfere with their effectiveness and well-being. Employees consult with management relative to individual and group relationship problems. The program acts as a repository of information and makes referrals to appropriate outside resources when indicated. It is also responsible for disbursement of Hudson-Webber Foundation funds to employees, retirees and ex-employees in need.

Co. Personnel Involved: 3 social workers and 3 secretaries full time

Measure of Success: (1) constant rate of increase in number of new client referrals; (2) feed-back from clients, supervisors and community; (3) decreased anxiety in clients served

KAISER BAUXITE'S COMMUNITY PROGRAMS

KAISER ALUMINUM & CHEMICAL CORP. (KACC)
Kaiser Center
300 Lakeside Drive
Oakland, Cal. 94604

Business: Aluminum, Chemicals, Specialty Metals
    and Refractories Products, and
    Diversified Operations
Sales: 881mm
CEO: Thomas J. Ready, Jr.   Employees: 26,000

Contact: R. L. Spees, Corp. Dir. of Pub. Affairs
Address: same as above
Telephone: (415) 271-3967
Program Reaches: over 1,000
When Started: 1953
Budget: unable to accurately estimate

Program Outline:

Kaiser Bauxite, a subsidiary of KACC, in mining bauxite on the North Coast of Jamaica, has pursued and is continuing a comprehensive community involvement program so that the people of the area, mostly small land farmers, can understand the mining operation and the company behind it.

As part of this effort the company is involved in a land resettlement/rehabilitation program. The company provides a choice of suitable farm land to those farmers who are displaced by the mining activity. In addition, many are provided new homes and support facilities usually better than their original homes. Farmers are also offered planting and crop education by the company, which also often donates equipment to neighboring farm communities. After a parcel is mined, the company fully restores the property to its original state, complete with plantings and topsoil.

Co. Personnel Involved: Company involvement in the whole community involvement program includes: 5 management personnel; liaison and support from the parent company in Oakland is supplied by 4 senior management personnel. This does not include the 150 Kaiser Bauxite salaried people working directly and indirectly with the various Jamaican communities.

Measure of Success: 90% of the supervisory personnel employed by the company are Jamaicans indicating acceptance by the local people of the company presence.

INSIGHT

KENNECOTT COPPER CORP.
UTAH COPPER DIVISION
10 E. South Temple
P.O. Box 11299
Salt Lake City, Utah 84111

Business: Copper Producing   Sales: 1,133
CEO: Frank R. Milliken   Employees: 30,500

Contact: Employee Relations Director
Address: same as above
Telephone: (801) 322-1533, ext. 2251
Program Reaches: over 100 new people/month
When Started: July 1, 1970
Budget: 1971 costs slightly over $30,000

Program Outline:

The purpose of the program is to provide employees (8,000) and employee dependents (24,000) with professional counseling, utilizing community resources to help them solve their problems.

A Kennecott psychiatric social worker, 2 graduate students from the University of Utah School of Social Studies, and a secretary carry out the program. Employees and their dependents receive help and professional counseling for referral purposes by dialing INSIGHT on the telephone. The service is available 7 days a week 24 hours a day. Employees and dependents voluntarily solicit help for problems such as alcoholism, drug abuse, familial, marital, legal, financial, etc. problems.

Co. Personnel Involved: Two thousand, three hundred employees and dependents have been placed in rehabilitation programs involving the kind of program enumerated above.

Measure of Success: Assuming there are 640 alcoholics (8% of the work force), penetration is 42%. Ninety-seven employees have voluntarily solicited help for drug abuse problems in 20 months. Over 2,400 people—almost equally divided between employees and dependents, have utilized the services of INSIGHT. There have been dramatic reductions in absenteeism, hospital-medical and surgical costs and sickness and accident costs. Return on investment is many times the cost.

NATIONAL AFFAIRS COMMITTEE

MARCOR (MONTGOMERY WARD & CO.)
P.O. Box 8339
Chicago, Ill. 60680

Business: General Merchandising   3,500mm
Sales: 3,500mm
CEO: Leo H. Schoenhofen   Employees: 126,000

Contact: Charles Higgines
Address: same as above
Telephone: (312) 467-2618
Program Reaches: potentially all employees
When Started: 1970
Budget: none—funds allocated as need arises

Program Outline:

The purpose of the program is to advise top management
of the company of directions it should take in the areas
of national issues such as: ecology, discrimination, public
welfare, law and order, urban affairs, etc.

Top management, becoming increasingly aware of the
changing role of the corporation in today's society,
decided one of the best ways of keeping abreast of the
times was to solicit on some structured basis, the opinion
of its own young management employees who would
eventually assure sales of leadership within the corporation. This committee, whose members are both male
and female and members of minority groups, makes
recommendations to management, initiates programs it
deems appropriate and generally keeps management informed of its own feelings on various issues.

Co. Personnel Involved: 30 committee members involved
on a part time basis

Measure of Success: Following are activities resulting
from recommendations of the Committee:
   1. expanded tutoring program
   2. structured minority employment program
   3. investigation of solid waste disposal problem in
company

CRADLE OF BLACK PEARLS DAY CARE CENTER, INC.

MARINE MIDLAND BANK
237 Main Street
Buffalo, N.Y. 14203

Business: Banking   Sales: not applicable
CEO: John L. Hettrick   Employees: 2,250

Contact: Rachel Roberts
Address: 1416 Michigan Avenue
   Buffalo, N.Y.
Telephone: (716) 883-3350
Program Reaches: city children from ages 3-6; 65
   children accomodated
When Started: 1969
Budget: n/a

Program Outline:

The purpose of this facility is to provide day care for
inner city children of the Buffalo area. As the first center
of its kind in the city, the Cradle of Black Pearls Day
Care Center employs the most advanced teaching techniques. Recently the center received a grant to install a
unique toy room designed to provide innovative learning
for preschoolers attending the center. The center was
constructed through the joint efforts of the Black
Business Development Corporation and Marine Midland
Bank—Western's Community Development Corporation.

Co. Personnel Involved: 1, in bookkeeping

Measure of Success: Recently, with the help of Marine
Midland Bank, the center was able to purchase a "Tot-
lot" equipment set.

MDC EMPLOYEE ASSISTANCE PROGRAM

MCDONNELL DOUGLAS CORP.
P.O. Box 516
St. Louis, Mo. 63166

Business: Aerospace   Sales: 2,088mm
CEO: Sanford N. McDonnell   Employees: 92,552

Contact: T. H. Allison
Address: same as above
Telephone: (314) 232-7438
Program Reaches: 250,000-300,000
When Started: 1970
Budget: $90,000/year

Program Outline:

The project purpose is to retain valued employees. McDonnell Douglas helps employees with personal problems which affect their job performance. These problems include, but are not limited to, problem drinking, drug use, poor interpersonal relationships, or a personal crisis in the employee's life. Guidance and counseling is provided to help the employee overcome his problems and restore him to full job effectiveness. To accomplish this, it is necessary to (1) identify an employee with personal problems at the earliest possible stage, (2) motivate him to seek help, and (3) direct him towards the best assistance available.

Co. Personnel Involved: 5 full time employees and 4 part time

Measure of Success: 60-70% recovery rate

THE CENTRAL OHIO TRANSIT AUTHORITY (COTA)

NATIONWIDE INSURANCE CO.
246 N. High Street
Columbus, Ohio 43215

Business: Insurance and Financial Services
Sales: n/a
CEO: Dean W. Jeffers   Employees: n/a

Contact: J. Keith Armstrong, Sec.
Address: 40 W. Broad Street
   Columbus, Ohio 43215
Program Reaches: 800,000
When Started: 1965
Budget: election campaign budget is $65,000

Program Outline:

The purpose of the program is to achieve public ownership of a privately-owned mass transit company.

The program's function is to persuade the voters of the region to approve a 1-mill property tax levy to finance the local share (2/3 of the funding will be federal) of the costs of the acquisition and the cost of expanding and improving the present system.

The program aims to provide a sound, responsive bus transit system as a basis for the future creation of a fully-developed rapid transit system.

Co. Personnel Involved: John E. Fisher, President of the Nationwide Insurance Company, is a member of the COTA Board of Trustees and is Chairman of the Acquisition Committee. William G. Moore is Director of Media Relations and a member of the campaign staff. Donald Cotner, Director of Graphics, is an Advisory Committee member.

Measure of Success: Property tax levy was voted down.

NORTHERN SYSTEMS CO.

NORTHERN NATURAL GAS CO.
2223 Dodge Street
Omaha, Neb. 68103

Business: Natural Gas Transmission
Sales: 516mm
CEO: W. A. Strauss   Employees: 7,871

Contact: Welcome T. Bryant, V.P. and
  Gen. Mgr.
Address: 4701 Lydell Drive
  Cheverly, Md. 20785
Telephone: (301) 322-4705
Program Reaches: n/a
When Started: 1965
Budget: n/a

Program Outline:

Northern Systems Company was formed as a wholly-owned subsidiary of the Northern Natural Gas Company. This company became involved in operating a Men's Job Corps Center in Lincoln, Nebraska. During the past 7 years, Northern Systems Company has also operated job training programs for the disadvantaged in Detroit, Houston, St. Louis, Washington, D.C., and Venice, California.

At the present time, Northern Systems Company is involved in a wide scope of programs for the indigent and disadvantaged:

1. Job skill training, job development and job placement in training programs for the District of Columbia and the State of Nebraska Departments of Correction

2. Job skill training at Maryland State Juvenile School
3. Job related education, orientation and counseling for numerous Jobs '70 programs
4. Consultant services in job counseling, social skills and job related education in a halfway house for the D.C. Department of Correction
5. Providing technical expertise and software in the area of social skills for numerous programs
6. Implementing job skill training programs, including staff training, in "Turn Key" operation for numerous institutions
7. Providing job skill training, software for various organizations including the Federal Bureau of Prisons

Co. Personnel Involved: n/a

Measure of Success: In a preconstruction trades training program for juvenile boys which provided training in construction trades to 24 juvenile boys in conjunction with Maryland Department of Juvenile Services, of the first 10 boys who graduated from the program there was 100% success in that all returned to school and none are presently in trouble.

In a Lorton, Virginia program of construction trades training for legal offenders for the first year of operation 58 multiple offenders were taken into the program, 54 graduated, all of those 54 were placed, and 43 were still employed after one year.

These are 2 specific examples of the success of the programs iniated and operated by the Northern Systems Company.

For further reference see pages 300 and 301.

DEFENDERS ASSOCIATION OF PHILADELPHIA

THE PENN MUTUAL LIFE INSURANCE CO.
Independence Square
Philadelphia, Pa. 19105

Business: Life and Health Insurance
Sales: 354mm
CEO: Frank K. Tarbox   Employees: 1,860

Contact: William Brooks
Address: same as above
Telephone: (215) 925-7300
Program Reaches: Spanish-speaking people in Philadelphia
When Started: January, 1971
Budget: n/a

Program Outline:

The purpose of the program is to make legal aid available to Spanish-speaking residents of Philadelphia.

A Penn Mutual attorney, who is one of Philadelphia's few Spanish-speaking lawyers is working 2 days a week for the Defenders Association of Philadelphia. In January, Penn Mutual granted Silvio S. Sanabria permission to perform the community service on company time. Sanabria spends Tuesdays and Thursdays helping primarily Spanish-speaking persons who request legal assistance from the Association. A United Fund agency, the Association was established to provide legal defense for persons unable to afford lawyers.

The Spanish-speaking population of Philadelphia exceeds 60,000 people. Some of these have difficulties with the law and are in need of the Association's services. Many of these clients who do not speak English very well do not trust or understand the attorneys because of language difficulties.

Co. Personnel Involved: n/a

Measure of Success: After a year Penn Mutual has phased out the program although company has indicated its willingness to participate in the program again.

VOTER REGISTRATION

PENN MUTUAL LIFE INSURANCE CO.
Independence Square
Philadelphia, Pa. 19105

Business: Life Insurance   Sales: 354mm
CEO: Frank K. Tarbox   Employees: 1,860

Contact: William Dikeman
Address: same as above
Telephone: (215) 925-7300
Program Reaches: n/a
When Started: 1971
Budget: n/a

Program Outline:

The purpose of this program was to provide a convenient location and encouragement for citizens of Philadelphia to register to vote.

A voter registration facility, designed for employees of Penn Mutual and any other interested Philadelphian, was set up on September 10, 1971 in the main lobby of Penn Mutual's building. The deadline for registration was September 13, and the registrars were on duty from 11 A.M. to 5 P.M. The individuals registering were encouraged to ask questions on anything pertaining to the mechanics of the coming election.

Co. Personnel Involved: n/a

Measure of Success: Many of the voters who registered at the company facility were new voters between ages 18 and 21. Two hundred twelve Philadelphia voters registered at the lobby facility, 170 from the company staff and 42 from outside the company. The percentage of Philadelphia residents working at Penn Mutual that registered there was 18%.

GREEN COUNTRY, INC.

PHILLIPS PETROLEUM CO.
Bartlesville, Okla. 74004

Business: Petroleum and Petrochemicals
Sales: 2,400mm
CEO: John M. Houchin   Employees: 32,200

Contact: Charles E. Cummings
Address: 4 D4 Phillips Building, same as above
Telephone: (918) 661-4553
Program Reaches: 500,000
When Started: 1965
Budget: n/a

Program Outline:

Phillips is applying its corporate and human resources toward solving some of the problems in its rural backyard. The result is a privately sponsored economic improvement program for a 21-county area known as Green Country. Phillips provided an employee to serve full time as executive vice president of Green Country, Inc. The company continues to provide manpower and other corporate resources wherever appropriate.

A primary goal of the project is the realization of Eastern Oklahoma's vast recreation potential. It offers an abundance of clear streams, large lakes, rugged hills, and rolling grasslands. The organizers of Green Country, Inc. recognized that the area's natural recreation assets, as well as its nationally known museums and historical attractions, could furnish the necessary stimulants for travel- and recreation-based businesses. These businesses, in turn, could provide more jobs and improved living standards for residents. Some Green Country, Inc. sponsored activities have included youth and cultural programs and workshops on local law enforcement, regional medical needs, and agricultural finance problems. Each year thousands of individuals through youth and civic groups take part in the Green Country Environmental Improvement Program, an anti-litter and community clean-up campaign.

Co. Personnel Involved: C. E. Cummings, Ex.V.P.; W. E. Irwin, Agricultural Committee; W. C. Davie, County Director, Washington County; Ken Childes, Environmental Program

Measure of Success: Recreation-oriented businesses such as a boat manufacturing plant have done much to boost the economics of small towns in the region. The project has helped double the number of visitors attracted to the Green Country region with the result that motels, lodges, marinas, restaurants, and other enterprises have experienced substantial increases in business. It is estimated that tourism brought an additional 10 million to Green Country businesses in 1971 alone.

JANE PHILLIPS SORORITY

PHILLIPS PETROLEUM CO.
Bartlesville, Okla. 74003

Business: Petroleum and Petrochemicals
Sales: 2,400mm
CEO: John M. Houchin   Employees: 32,200

Contact: Mary Crump
Address: Phillips Petroleum Co., 7th fl.
   100 Park Avenue Bldg.
   Oklahoma City, Okla. 73102
Telephone: (405) 239-2611
Program Reaches: n/a
When Started: 1938
Budget: n/a

Program Outline:

Founded in 1938, the Jane Phillips Sorority has grown to include nearly 1,100 women employees of Phillips Petroleum Company. The organization is named for the wife of Frank Phillips, the company's founder. Although the sorority serves a social function for members, great emphasis is directed toward improving life for under-privileged, disadvantaged, or handicapped children and adults.

The swimming pool at Girlstown, U.S.A., in White Face, Texas, is one of several major gifts the sorority has made through a national fund supported by its 19 chapters in 13 states. This fund also provided major gifts to a Bartlesville hospital and children's hospitals in Omaha and Denver. On a local level, JPS chapters conduct a variety of charitable activities for the benefit of their communities. Members throughout the sorority periodically visit and provide financial aid or contributions of equipment to children's homes, hospitals, schools for retarded children, and geriatrics and convalescent homes. All chapters furnish food and gifts to needy families or orphans during the Christmas holidays. To provide encouragement to the sorority's program of community improvement, leading executives within Phillips Petroleum have repeatedly emphasized the importance of the JPS people-to-people activities, and have asked supervisors throughout the company to support sorority members in their efforts.

Co. Personnel Involved: varies with different projects

Measure of Success: n/a

ORGANIZATIONAL DEVELOPMENT

SAGA ADMINISTRATIVE DIVISION
One Saga Lane
Menlo Park, Cal. 94025

Business: Food Service Industry
Sales: 167mm
CEO: William F. Scandling   Employees: 25,000

Contact: William J. Crockett
Address: same as above
Telephone: (415) 854-5150
Program Reaches: all employees of Saga—25,000
When Started: 1968
Budget: in excess of $200,000/year

Program Outline:

The Organizational Development program of Saga was undertaken to make the psychological climate of the corporation a non-polluting environment for the people who work there, thus reducing the levels of social pollution that exist in the society as a whole.

Saga designed and implemented the O. D. program to cope with the feeling that many employees had of being lost in a big, impersonal company. Through the implementation of off-site meetings that were held between boss and subordinate teams at all levels of the company, the program attempted to set up effective lines of communication between employer and employee to make them operate as a team, with an awareness of one another as human beings. This program was not designed as a T-Group, but rather an exercise in management attitudes towards productivity and communication with employees.

Co. Personnel Involved: The entire company was involved in the O.D. program for 4 years.

Measure of Success: Saga had Drossler Research Corporation conduct an intensive study on the results of 4 years of O.D. Saga managers' attitudes toward the program were very positive. They considered it a highly productive exercise which strengthened their management techniques, and business and personal relationships. Most of them would like to see the program intensified with additional follow-up information.

INDUSTRY AWARENESS PROGRAM

SCOTT PAPER CO.
Scott Plaza
Philadelphia, Pa. 19113

Business: Manufacturing Sanitary Paper Products
Sales: 756mm
CEO: Charles D. Dickey, Jr.   Employees: 21,700

Contact: Morris L. Smith
Address: same as above
Telephone: (215) 724-2000, ext. 2556
Program Reaches: approx. 800-1,000 students
When Started: 1969
Budget: presently unbudgeted

Program Outline:

The purpose of the program is to assist the educational institutions in making students, parents and teachers aware of employment opportunities available in industry and the preparation necessary to meet these needs presently and in the future. The program is aimed at helping lower- and middle-income students of a city or cities where plants are located and where Blacks make up a high percentage of the population.

Students at the junior high level were exposed to persons of varying occupations (semi-skilled, skilled, scientific, professional and business oriented people) from the business and industrial community throughout the school year. A feedback of information from the students to program organizers played a vital role in presentation format guidelines for individuals participating. Program format was developed jointly by school district guidance counselors, students, and industry coordinating personnel. A general subject matter briefing (business and industrial community) was presented during the early part of the school year. The sessions which followed were smaller ratio student-to-industry personnel (30:1) with specific areas being covered for greater time periods.

The plan is to expose the program to students from kindergarten to 12th grade eventually with more assistance.

Co. Personnel Involved: varies from 50 to 100 depending on the program phase

Measure of Success: After programs, information feedback was obtained from students with the use of a questionnaire in addition to the individual student-initiated contact with industry personnel seeking greater information and expression of gratitude for the exposure.

CORO FOUNDATION

SYNTEX CORP.
Stanford Industrial Park
Palo Alto, Cal. 94304

Business: Pharmaceuticals, Veterinary and Health Care Products
Sales: 100mm
CEO: George Rosenkranz   Employees: n/a

Contact: Frank Koch, Dir. of Corp. P.R.
Address: same as above
Telephone: (415) 855-6111
Program Reaches: approx. 1000
When Started: 1942
Budget: n/a

Program Outline:

Coro is an independent, non-profit, non-partisan organization to which Syntex provides continuing financial support. The purpose of this organization is to encourage and prepare young men and women for responsible roles in public life. Its programs include internships in public affairs; degree programs in urban educational administration and urban teaching, as well as laboratory courses in public affairs in collaboration with Stanford University; school public affairs projects and citizen education.

Co. Personnel Involved: n/a

Measure of Success: regular reports submitted to the company

For further information see page 583.

"STAMP OUT CRIME"

THE SOUTHLAND CORP.
(7-ELEVEN FOOD STORES)
7839 University Avenue
P.O. Box 698
La Mesa, Cal. 92041

Business: Convenience Markets   Sales: 952mm
CEO: Herbert Hartfelder   Employees: 19,500

Contact: Dick Dole or Gene DeFalco
Address: same as above
Telephone: (714) 465-2101
Program Reaches: affects over 400 7-Eleven stores in
  Southern California
When Started: 1970
Budget: $10-20,000/year

Program Outline:

In order to reduce crime in 7-Eleven Food Stores, the company wanted to develop a further awareness and understanding of the person or persons who were committing crimes in 7-Eleven stores with the objective to save lives and money (both cash and capital equipment).

Representatives from the company met with Bob McKinney, Director of Project J.O.V.E. (Job, Occupation, Vocation, Education), an agency of the E.O.C., whose primary objective is rehabilitation of ex-convicts. It was the company's conclusion that no one could help reduce crime better than an ex-convict. The idea, in essence, was to ask the robber why he robbed 7-Eleven stores and what could be done to deter future robberies. A panel was formed of 4 ex-cons and meetings were held in all areas of the Division inviting local police officers, politicians and other businessmen besides 7-Eleven franchise operators to ask questions.

As a result of these seminars, a brochure entitled, "Planning for Protection" was printed and distributed to 7-Eleven stores showing ways of preventing crime in a small business and how to handle it when it happened.

Co. Personnel Involved: Approximately 50—all direct line operational people responsible for the management of 400 stores. There were, however, 2 primarily involved in organizing the project with operation J.O.V.E.

Measure of Success: Through this program company has reason to believe that it not only has saved lives, but the average number of robberies and dollar loss has been substantially reduced. Losses were down 26% in 1971 as compared with 1970 (and 1970 was down as compared to 1969).

COMMUNITY INVOLVEMENT SURVEY

UNITED BANK OF DENVER
1740 Broadway
Denver, Colo. 80217

Business: Banking   Sales: not applicable
CEO: John D. Hershner   Employees: 966

Contact: Bill Funk
Address: same as above
Telephone: (313) 244-8811
Program Reaches: 300 management-level employees
When Started: 1969
Budget: no budget; costs are in overhead and employee
  time

Program Outline:

The purpose of this program (annual, with follow-up) is to provide a survey of Bank personnel's community involvement for use primarily as a management tool and secondarily to assist employees in their knowledge of community opportunities available to them.

Public Affairs Department representatives met with each division officer. At that time a list of individuals in their division who are to be surveyed was made up. Up to 15 people in each division are to be designated for personal interviews; all the others are sent a questionnaire. With the people who are interviewed, a longer range and more detailed strategy is worked out. The survey indicates the depth of present involvement and possible future activities in community or civic affairs. Participants are supplied with information pertaining to their particular interests, i.e. which organizations are most effective in a particular area, how to join, and who in the Bank is already involved in that area.

Co. Personnel Involved: The administration of the Community Involvement Survey and follow-up work involved the Public Affairs Department.

Measure of Success: A report, featuring the results of the follow-up work completed on each individual, including the changes, if any, in the total community and civic involvement of each individual surveyed, coverage of Bank needs and results in the community, are to be furnished to each Division officer within 6 months.

BLACK OPINION LEADERS FORUM

UNITED VIRGINIA BANK AND
UNITED VIRGINIA BANKSHARES, INC.
900 E. Main Street
Richmond, Va. 23219

Business: Banking   Sales: not applicable
CEO: Kenneth A. Randall   Employees: 2,954

Contact: Thomas R. Jarman, Jr.
Address: United Virginia Bank
   P. O. Box 6E
   Richmond, Va. 23214
Telephone: (703) 771-5516
Program Reaches: n/a
When Started: 1966
Budget: n/a

Program Outline:

In an effort to convince the Black Community in Richmond that United Virginia Bank wants their business and that the Bank wants to be of financial assistance to them, the Bank engaged a Black public relations firm located in Richmond and began to discuss ways, means and approaches of communicating their message. Through this contact, the Bank worked in conjunction with the Metropolitan Business League and, in 1967, presented a forum directed toward the small businessman at one of the League's monthly meetings. Later, a "Black Opinion Leaders Forum" was organized including dinner and reception and a panel program with speakers addressing themselves to professionals, women and small businessmen.

Co. Personnel Involved: Two members of the public affairs staff were integrally involved; 6 Black employees and 3 banking officers, to a lesser degree.

Measure of Success: In the first effort, for practical purposes, little or no business materialized as a result of the Bank's efforts. However, replies received to a questionnaire which followed the second, were, on the whole complementary.

PERSONNEL LOANING PROGRAM

WESTERN MASSACHUSETTS ELECTRIC CO.
174 Brush Hill Avenue
West Springfield, Mass. 01089

Business: Public Utility   Sales: 66.9mm
CEO: Robert E. Barrett, Jr. Employees: 987

Contact: Mack W. Jacobs
Address: same as above
Telephone: (413) 785-5871, ext. 298
Program Reaches: difficult to answer
When Started: 1967
Budget: salaries and misc. expenses

Program Outline:

The purpose of the program is to aid and improve the functions of area, urban-oriented organizations by loaning them the expertise of key personnel for periods of 6 months to 1 year.

One man was loaned to the Springfield, Mass. Chapter of the Urban League for 1 year. He was Acting Director during his last 6 months. One (Adm. Asst.) was loaned to the Micah Corporation, a limited divident housing rehabilitation group for 1 year. One man was loaned to the Pittsfield, Mass. Urban Coalition group for 8 months, helping the group from its beginning to become a viable organization. One man was loaned to the "Riverview Housing Project," a Springfield Mass. Housing Authority, low-income, high-rise complex with multitudes of social, ethnic and recreational problems. His task was to initiate an ongoing recreational program for the youths. His stay was 6 months. One man was loaned to the Northern Educational Service, a non-profit tutorial organization for 1 year. This organization utilizes area college students for one-on-one tutoring, maintaining 5 outlets in the Springfield area.

Company feels that this program helps build stronger organizations, which in turn helps the individuals serviced by these limited dividend and non-profit groups. It helps the individual loaned to extend himself and grow and it helps the company to become involved and make friends and contacts through the loaned person.

Co. Personnel Involved: 5 (described above)

Measure of Success: All the organizations are healthy and ongoing at this date. The employees loaned still maintain an involvement after returning from their leave.

SOCIAL SERVICE LEAVE PROGRAM

XEROX CORP.
Xerox International Headquarters
Stamford, Conn. 06904

Business: Diversified Office Machines
Sales: 1,719mm
CEO: C. Peter McColough   Employees: 38,339

Contact: Thomas C. Abbot
Address: same as above
Telephone: (203) 329-8711
          or
Contact: Alfred R. Zipser
Address: 280 Park Avenue
   New York, N.Y. 10017
Telephone: (212) 972-1600
Program Reaches: 1971
Budget: n/a

Program Outline:

The purpose of this program is to enable Xerox employees who are involved in the problems of society on a part time basis to delve into a problem full time. Also, they get a chance to do this during the prime of their working careers and won't have to wait until they retire.

Under the Social Service Leave Program a Xerox employee can get a leave of absence for up to a year—at full pay, with full benefits—to go out and make their contribution to a better society. The employees keep union seniority, provided they return to Xerox as soon as the leave is over. They get the same job back and if for any reason the old job is not available, the employee is guaranteed an "equal" job: one that offers the same pay, responsibility, status, and opportunity for advancement. There are just a few limits to the kind of social service an employee can propose:

(1) It must be a program or activity sponsored or conducted by an existing, functioning, legitimate organization of some kind;

(2) The employee must have written acceptance from the organization of participation he proposes;

(3) What the employee does must be legal;

(4) No partisan politics for any candidate or party, no profit-making sponsoring organizations, no personal schooling is allowed;

(5) The employee pays his own way to and from wherever his mission takes him.

The only other requirement is that the applicants must have completed 3 years of employment with Xerox when they apply.

Co. Personnel Involved: 7 members of the Evaluation Committee who review and decide those who will be granted leave (they serve for 2 years)

Measure of Success: Twenty-one Xerox employees have been chosen from nearly 200 applicants, to participate in the experimental Social Service Leave Program. These 18 men and 3 women granted leaves come from many different Xerox departments and represent a wide range of occupations from factory employee to corporate executive. The youngest is 26 and the oldest, 60.

An Unusual Corporate Profile

Human Resources Network contacted International Basic Economy Corporation with an invitation to participate in *Profiles of Involvement*. Due to the unusual nature of this corporation's policies of social involvement it required a somewhat different write-up. This was compiled by Human Resources Network.

INTERNATIONAL BASIC ECONOMY CORPORATION

1271 Avenue of the Americas
New York, N.Y. 10020

Business: Diversified electronic-electric equipment; Food,
    Chemical Process, Poultry, General Contractor
Sales: 300mm
CEO: Rodman Rockefeller   Employees: 11,800

Contact: Harvey Schwartz
Address: same as above
Telephone: (212) 247-3000
Company Reaches: n/a
When Started: 1947
Budget: not applicable

Corporate Outline:

Savants of the growing literature and public interest in corporate social responsibility have been seeking a shining example of corporate involvement which might be used as a model for other companies and industries. To our knowledge, the International Basic Economy Corporation is the only publicly-held firm which has as its basic philosophy the dual goals of operating at a profit and operating responsibly to satisfy basic human needs reliably and at low-cost. Thus IBEC has chosen as its "market" the provision of human basics—food and shelter—in certain developing areas.

IBEC was founded as a result of the Rockefeller's family interest in the development of Latin America. Nelson Rockefeller (now Governor of New York) served as "Coordinator of Commercial and Cultural Relations between the American Republics" during World War II and it was partially as a result of this experience that he sought to form a vehicle to undertake both extensive and intensive development projects starting in Latin America. In 1947, International Basic Economy Corporation was chartered as a "profit" enterprise, but this excerpt from the preamble of its charter carefully delineates its socially responsible role:

We, the undersigned, desiring in association with others to promote the economic development of various parts of the world, to increase the production and availability of goods, things, and services, useful to the lives or livelihood of their peoples, and thus to better their standards of living, and believing that these aims can be furthered through a corporation dedicated to their fulfillment and employing scientific and modern methods and techniques, do hereby make, sign, acknowledge and file this certificate to form a stock corporation . . . .

A detailed history of the early IBEC years in Brazil and Venezuela is contained in Wayne Broehl's book *The International Basic Economy Corporation* (National Planning Association, Washington: 1968; xxvi + 312 pp.). However, a brief survey of the current IBEC picture is in order here.

SCOPE OF OPERATIONS

IBEC's multitudinous subsidiaries and joint ventures were recently reorganized into five operating groups:

. Food
. Housing
. Distribution
. Industrial
. Financial Services

All activities in the Food group are aimed at increasing the quality and yield of basic edible commodities in various host nations. IBEC produces poultry breeding stock in the U.S. and abroad which is distributed to poultry farmers in 24 countries. A seed production company in Brazil is responsible for developing blight-resistant corn seed and better cultivation methods in Brazil. Other activities include milk processing in Venezuela, and tuna processing in Puerto Rico. In 1971, the Food Group had total revenues of $26,000,000, a loss of $1.4 million, and 1300 employees.

The Housing Group has concentrated its efforts on low- to medium-cost housing—predominantly prefabricated—in the U.S., Mexico, Peru, Puerto Rico, and Brazil. A new industrialized housing component plant has recently been completed in Puerto Rico. In 1971, the Housing Group had 900 employees, $36,000,000 in sales, and a $3.1 million profit.

The Distribution Group is a leader in operating cash-and-carry supermarkets in various Latin American countries. It is the largest integrated food distributor on that continent. Recent moves in South America and Southern Europe with joint venture partners are the construction of a network of wholesale food and non-food product distribution centers. In 1971, the Distribution Group had net sales of $120,500,000, net profits of $4.1 million and operated with 3800 employees.

The Industrial Group consists of three large subsidiaries based in the United States. Originally, IBEC sought to support its nascent development activities abroad with profits from these operations which produced equipment aimed at American industrial markets. Increasingly, however, one subsidiary has been concentrating on the production of capital machinery suitable for use in productive sectors of developing nations. Thus, increased value-added can be retained in the country of origin. In 1971, profits were down to $2.6 million due to a plant move and a slow U.S. economy. Sales approximated $61 million. This group has 2500 employees.

The Financial Services Group has been an instrumental factor in the development of indigenous capital markets in Brazil, Spain, and Thailand. Unlike other foreign-based mutual funds, these funds invest exclusively in the equities available in the country in which they operate. A joint venture in the insurance brokerage field has recently been added. In 1971, these financial management operations had revenues of $6.4 million, profits of $1.7 million, and 900 employees.

A more detailed description of IBEC's variegated operations is included in Appendix I.

METHOD OF OPERATION

IBEC's activities are conducted through subsidiaries which report to the parent firm's headquarters in New York. A large number of these subsidiaries are majority-owned by IBEC, with local management and joint venture partners controlling minority interests. Thus, specialized expertise (as in the case of the insurance brokerage operation) and middle management commitment are brought to bear in the individual subsidiary operations through joint ownership.

IBEC operations have a dual reporting structure. Each activity group has its own executives and a small headquarters staff. Each country has a central IBEC office to guide the operations in local legal, political, and currency details. A central planning group based in New York is responsible for overall corporate planning in addition to new venture analysis. Another responsibility of this group is to assist individual projects with their own long-range planning.

A new resource has been integrated into the IBEC structure. During 1971, International Basic Economy

acquired Development and Resources Corporation, an economic planning "think tank" headed by David E. Lilienthal, former head of the Atomic Energy Commission. D & R undertakes research and planning projects in the economic and regional development of client nations. D & R's systems approach has been applied to identify, develop, plan, and integrate projects in the economic, social, and environmental spheres of various under-developed areas. Long-term, the availability of this expertise to current and projected IBEC projects should augment both the profitability and favorable social impact of the IBEC concept.

PERFORMANCE

The goal of the original IBEC concept formulated in 1947 was to profitably introduce new techniques to solve specific economic problems affecting basic human needs in developing areas. Thus IBEC's performance must be measured along two seemingly conflicting continua: 1) growth and profitability of IBEC itself and 2) favorable social impact in host nations or areas.

The first criterion is an area of easy measurement. Despite the problems involved in converting assets and currencies into dollars for comparative purposes, accountants are willing to certify IBEC's financial performance based on traditional and consistently applied financial principles. This problem is no different for IBEC than it is for any other multi-national firm. The following chart displays IBEC's last ten years of fiscal performance. The 1971 year, a poor one in terms of profits, broke the trend and has been set out from the analysis of compound growth due to the fact that a series of extraordinary events converged on the company. A plant move of one industrial company, the tuna-mercury scare, a corn blight in Brazil, and abnormally low prices in poultry stock are thought to have caused this financial setback.

On the one end of the IBEC "balancing act" - namely profitable growth - IBEC seems to have performed well. But what of the social end? Is there a readily available balance sheet of IBEC's contributions in host countries? The answer, of course, is that there is none. The Company has recently set up an internal social audit committee to produce such an analysis. A statement in the 1971 annual report (page 22) speaks of this commitment:

> More and more, business is being called upon to play a role as an innovator that generates beneficial social change. Under these circumstances, it must find ways of expressing its worth that go beyond traditional accounting methods. Along with a financial audit, there needs to be a social audit that quantifies the social impact of a corporation's activity. Admittedly this is unknown territory. But we intend to

IBEC
10-Year Record

	1962	1970	Total % Change	9 Year Compound Growth Rate	1971
Net Sales & Revenues (thousands)	$98,553	$281,997	+186%	12.4%	$300,459
Net Income Before Extraordinary Items (thousands)	$ 1,035	$ 6,035	+483%	21.6%	$ 2,626
Non-Extraordinary Net Income Per Share	$0.26	$1.45	+458%	21.0%	$0.63

venture into it and will, in the months ahead, undertake to create this kind of yardstick...Why do we feel it is so important to fashion such a tool? It is important because it will provide us with a means of communicating the degree of our contribution toward improving the environment by identifying our objectives with societal priorities, then we gain new strength through a public recognition that our corporate activities have meaning and substance beyond the results of a financial statement. In addition, this new communication will help us gain a feel for our markets, how they are changing, and how we can best serve them. All of these efforts presuppose a solid and adequate profit and are intended to safeguard that profit in the future.

An inkling of IBEC's social record is contained in Appendix I. A far more detailed analysis appears in the Broehl book. The failures as well as the successes are discussed. At one point Broehl concludes: (pp. 287-8)

> The founders of IBEC recognized 20 years ago both the developmental nature of these ventures and the business potential for them . . . .Today's widely recognized successes in IBEC's key activities and the increasing number of similarly successful efforts by other profit-oriented Companies, attest to the strength of the vision itself.

IBEC has recognized that an enterprise which specializes in economic and social development must be well-capitalized, diversified (both as to industries and geopolitically) so that profitable operations may support high-risk ones, and must be willing to commit itself to a much longer "time line" before the achievements or failures of a new venture can be measured. But perhaps the broad-minded attitude and hard-gained expertise of management is the most important factor in IBEC's apparent success. It is heartening to note that similar attitudes and experiences are being utilized in other companies to extend the purpose of "The Corporation" to more than just the profit goal.

IBEC BIBLIOGRAPHY

1. Wayne Broehl, Jr.: *The International Basic Economy Corporation* (National Planning Association, Washington, D.C.: 1968) $3.00 Paper Back.

2. IBEC Annual Report to Shareholders, Available from:
   International Basic Economy Corporation
   1271 Avenue of the Americas
   New York, New York 10020

Appendix I: Breakdown of major IBEC operations by group

FOOD GROUP

Operation	Country of Operation	Function	Measure of Success
Sementes Agroceres, SA.	Brazil	Hybrid seed production.	Now the fourth-largest seed company in the world (and one of the most dramatic IBEC success stories) this operation has greatly increased crop yields in Brazil by teaching farmers how to use hybrid seed (corn) and modern cultivation methods. Experimentation with sorghum, pasture grasses, and legumes currently underway.
INLACA	Venezuela	Milk and Fruit juice production	Availability of fresh milk and juices throughout most of the country.
IBEC FOODS	Puerto Rico	Canned tuna processing	n/a
IBEC El Salvador	El Salvador	Processes soluble coffee for farming cooperative.	n/a
Arbor Acres Farm, Inc.	USA and 24 other countries	Supplies breeding poultry stock to local farming industry.	Responsible for availability of high quality, low cost protein in many countries.

HOUSING GROUP

Operation	Country of Operation	Function	Measure of Success
IBEC Housing International, Inc.	Puebla, Mexico	Housing Project	2500 single-family, low-income housing units are under construction. Financing arranged by Mexican govt.
	Spartanburg, S.C. USA	Housing Project	170 home project of low-income housing available to black families on $200 downpayment.
	Tidewater, Va. USA	Housing Project	200 homes in planning stage.
	Oklahoma, USA and Great Smokey Mtn. Area of North Carolina	"Mutual Help" Housing Projects	Low-cost housing projects in which American Indians help build their own home. 290 homes have already been completed.
	San Juan, P.R. USA	Large scale housing developments	IBEC has already built over 15,000 low- to moderate-cost houses in developments near San Juan. 2500 houses are in the planning stage.
	San Jose dos Campos, Brazil	Housing Project	4200 house development in the planning stage.
RELBEC, Inc. joint venture	Puerto Rico, USA	Manufactured concrete housing components	Plant recently finished. Capable of producing 1500 low-cost housing units/year. Backlogged for two years' production.

DISTRIBUTION GROUP

Operation	Country of Operation	Function	Measure of Success
CADA	Venezuela	Supermarket chain	39 stores currently in operation. Provides reliable market for indigenous agricultural production in addition to allowing greater consumer choice of quality food items at lower cost.
MINIMAX	Argentina	Supermarket chain	15 stores and one bakery in operation.
TODOS	Peru	Supermarket chain	7 stores and one bakery in operation in 1971.
Supermarket joint venture	El Salvador	Supermarket chain	
MAKRO joint venture	Brazil, Spain, Latin America Southern Europe	Wholesale cash-and-carry distribution centers	In development stage. Intended to provide reliable distribution of food and non-food items to small retailers. Provision and stimulation of wholesale infrastructure.

INDUSTRIAL GROUP

Operation	Country of Operation	Function	Measure of Success
Anderson IBEC	USA	Manufacturing production and pollution control equipment	
Bellows-Valvair	USA	Hydraulic control equipment	Industrial Group is said to provide reliable earnings base to support developmental operations abroad.
J.L. Thompson Rivet Corporation	USA	Cold-formed parts including fasteners	

FINANCIAL SERVICES GROUP

Operation	Country of Operation	Function	Measure of Success
Hispanibec joint venture	Spain	Manages Fondo Crecinco-the largest mutual fund in Spain	Now the largest fund in Spain, Crecinco has over 30,000 shareholders and invests primarily in Spanish securities. Has favorably affected the formation of modern capital markets in Spain.
Copernicus	Spain	Real estate, insurance brokerage, and portfolio management	Formed in 1971—too early to assess.
Banco de Investimento do Brasil (minority position)	Brazil	Non-commercial banking, operation of mutual funds, underwriting, brokerage	Funds which IBEC founded starting in 1957 have been merged into this Brazilian-controlled investment banking firm which has over $400 million in assets. IBEC's funds, which now control over $200 million in assets are thought to have contributed greatly to formation of capital in Brazil.
Thai Fund	Thailand	Mutual fund in Thailand	Very small fund has been hampered by sluggish and illiquid capital markets in Thailand.
Rolibec joint venture		Insurance brokerage in 23 countries	Insurance programs include local employee benefit policies—a first in many countries.
IBEC Thailand, Inc.	Thailand	Manufactures and exports silk and cotton design fabrics	Rapidly growing exports to U.S., Canada, and U.K.